The AMERICAN
HERITAGE
Book of GREAT
HISTORIC
PLACES

The
AMERICAN HERITAGE
Book of
HISTORIC

GREAT PLACES

By the Editors of AMERICAN HERITAGE, *The Magazine of History*

Narrative by RICHARD M. KETCHUM

Introduction by BRUCE CATTON

Published by AMERICAN HERITAGE PUBLISHING CO., INC.
in cooperation with SIMON AND SCHUSTER, INC., New York

AMERICAN HERITAGE
The Magazine of History

PUBLISHER
James Parton

EDITORIAL DIRECTOR
Joseph J. Thorndike, Jr.

EDITOR
Bruce Catton

MANAGING EDITOR
Oliver Jensen

Staff for this Book

EDITOR
Richard M. Ketchum

EDITORIAL ASSISTANTS
Helen Augur
Caroline Backlund
Robert Cowley
Margaret Di Crocco
Hilde Heun
Jean Leich
Joan Wharton

SPECIAL ADVISER
Francis S. Ronalds

ART DIRECTOR
Irwin Glusker

ART ASSISTANT
Trudy Glucksberg

ORIGINAL MAPS
Harold Faye

Printed in the United States of America

Library of Congress Catalogue Card Number:
57-11274

Second edition, © 1965

Table of Contents

Introduction

By BRUCE CATTON

The American people are various, and they have been all across the American landscape. Here they built a town, there they built a bridge, and in the next place they climbed a mountain—Jamestown, Concord Bridge, South Pass—and if they fought a battle on this spot, on the next one they endured less dramatic hardships and hammered the rough edges off an enduring dream. They founded villages which never came to much, and they also worked out a way of life which may embody the chief hope of a despairing world; and the names and places of all of this lie strewn all over the continent, from one shining ocean to the other. Trying to make a living, Americans made history, and the country is full of ghosts which come out of racial memories that go to the very heart of the best we have ever tried to be. Take it all in all, America is full of milestones on the road from yesterday to tomorrow.

This book is an attempt to set forth what some of those milestones are; to say what they look like today, how they got there, and what the men and women who put them there thought they were chiefly up to. There is nothing in all the world quite like this, because here history is still new. Europe and Asia were old and slightly faded when the American continent was nameless and nearly empty. Renaissance, Reformation and Counter Reformation, Da Vinci and Martin Luther and Ignatius Loyola—all of these had had their day before any man of European descent had seen the Shenandoah River or laid out a farm in the Mohawk Valley or tried to take a wagon over the sand hills of Nebraska.

Yet if it is new it is very rich. This is our land; here men and women lived and died, consciously serving a dream, moved by that thing which is unique to America—the faith that every tree that was felled and every sod of earth that was turned was somehow helping to bring a better world into existence. Here was the calculated break with the past, here was the point where people determined that what would come after them would go along a different line than anything that had gone before; here was the infinite future burning like a dim flame on the edge of limitless wilderness. Here, in short, was America, coming up out of Virginia swamps and New England rocks and the endless burning plains of an arid West, built after a pattern that would remodel the lives of half the world. In all history there has been no story like this.

The places themselves are there to see today, and we hope that this book will be, in some sense, a guide book and a point of departure—a line of marks on an enormous chart, steering people to those sites where American history took on the haunting gleam of everlasting significance. Yet a word of caution is perhaps in order.

You can, if you have the leisure, go to all of the places which are touched on in this book; but what you will see when you get there depends in the last analysis on what you take with you. When you go, you are not making an excursion into the present; you are going back into the past, and the lights and shadows that give the landscape of the past its true depth do not exist unless you yourself are ready to see them. A willingness to forget the present and to be drawn into the spell of the past is part of your necessary equipment.

For here, spread out from one ocean to another, is the American past, speaking to you out of the things men and women made, the things they dared to do, the things they suffered and died for—or lived for, half forgot about, and then finally clung to—reflected in earth and wood and stone. These places are as silent as the voices of the people who once gave them life. They will speak only to the visitor who is ready to listen; but if he permits them to speak, they do have the gift of tongues.

It is not possible, of course, to catalog in any one book all of the "historic places" in America. What we have tried to do here is to show, in pictures and in text, the most rewarding places, the most significant ones, to tell the stories that lie behind them and, wherever possible, to delineate the shape of the dream that caused them to be shaped and moulded in the first place. Visiting these places, the American may gain a slightly better idea of why they became important; perhaps he will feel a little closer kinship with the people who were there in the first place; perhaps, out of it all, he will get a deeper understanding of what it is to be an American.

This land, to repeat, is very rich—not merely in material goods, but in history, in legends and great stories, and in the intangibles left by forgotten people who put their mark upon the development of a great nation. The land has changed, to be sure, since the first settlers went into it. "Every valley," said Isaiah, "shall be exalted, and every mountain and hill shall be made low; and the crooked places shall be made straight, and the rough places plain." This work has been going on ever since the early 1600's, and the end of it is not yet; but in this book we have tried to catch the spirit of it and to set forth some of the visible reminders of the unending American task. From these towns and hills and fields our own past speaks to us; looking back down the road Americans have traveled, we illogically but surely get a glimpse of the future. The past was built on courage and faith and endurance, and by and large it was good. The future, if it is built in the same way, will be good also.

New England

Fishermen's patron, Gloucester

New England's First Settlements

It is nearly impossible to reach back through the centuries of time and touch any tangible evidence of those first voyages of exploration, or the first abortive efforts at colonizing the New England coast. It is a little like dragging the bottom of a pond, trying to find something which has disappeared in the depths. Not until we reach Plymouth do we strike something hard, and real.

In a way, it is a little unfair that Plymouth should be the place usually associated with the first settlement of New England. For in 1622, when the Pilgrims were desperately in need of food, Edward Winslow journeyed to Maine, hoping to find supplies. There, among fishermen who had been on the Maine coast for more than a century—men from Devonshire, Holland, the Basque country, and Brittany—he received "entertainment and good respect with a willingness to supply all wants." These oddly assorted folk, bound together in isolated settlements by a kind of camaraderie of the sea and a common need, "did what they could freely [for Winslow], wishing their store had been such as they might in greater measure have expressed their own love. . . ."

Nor was this the first time Maine had come to the aid of Plymouth. In March, 1621, when forty-four members of the original *Mayflower* company had perished, an Indian named Samoset appeared, startling them with the words "Much welcome, Englishmen." Samoset had learned English from fishermen off Monhegan Island, and his offer of friendship must have

Fishermen had inhabited the rock-bound New England coast for more than a century when the Pilgrims landed at Plymouth. Symbolic of their tradition is Gloucester's Our Lady of Good Voyage (above), cradling a fishing schooner in her arm.

been one of the few pleasant moments the Pilgrims had since they set sail from Holland.

Their name was not "Pilgrim" but Separatist; there is doubt that they did, in fact, land on "Plymouth Rock"; their monuments are few, and their hour in history lasted but twenty years at most. Yet despite these contradictions, the Pilgrims established themselves forever in American history.

The 102 passengers on the *Mayflower*—35 from Leyden, and the rest "a very mixed lot" from Southampton—sighted land on November 9, 1620. Although they had set sail for the James River, winter was approaching so rapidly that they made the momentous decision to disregard the terms of their patent and settle illegally in New England. Before going ashore at Provincetown, where they landed first, they drew up and signed the now-famous Mayflower Compact. Signed by all able-bodied male adults, including four servants, this set up a government in which sovereignty rested in the entire male community. Completely democratic, with no class or wealth distinctions, the government was morally responsible for promoting "ye generall good of ye Colonie."

Soon after the Cape Cod landing a group of men set out to look for a more hospitable place to settle and decided on Plymouth Harbor. There, on Christmas Day, 1620, they started building their first "common house." It was completed on January 9, only to have a serious fire break out at six o'clock on the morning of January 14. The thatched roof was destroyed completely, and although an icy downpour continued throughout that day, they made no effort to repair it. The reason—it was the Sabbath.

Their piety cost them dear in the resulting epidemic of pneumonia and influenza. By the time Samoset ap-

CONTINUED ON PAGE 14

Plymouth Rock

CONTINUED FROM PAGE 13

peared on the scene, few were left to greet their first New England spring. A monument on the steep slope of Cole's Hill is all that marks the first burying ground, where survivors of the terrible winter leveled the earth over the remains of their companions, "lest the Indians should know how many were the graves."

Not long after Samoset's visit, Chief Massasoit and sixty warriors—who might so easily have annihilated the tiny band of enfeebled settlers—offered them hospitality. And soon afterward an Indian named Squanto, who had been carried off to England as a prize by earlier voyagers, and there learned the language, taught the Pilgrims how to plant Indian corn, which they harvested in the fall of 1621.

For nearly three years the Pilgrims fought off starvation. In November of 1621 the ship *Fortune* arrived, leaving behind her thirty-five new colonists, but no supplies. In 1623 the same story was repeated, this time by the ship *Anne*. But in spite of the fact that they lacked supplies, it is ironic that the Pilgrims should have come so near to failure. The land was reasonably fertile, the harbors full of fish, and the woods abounded in berries and game. The fact was that the Pilgrims had brought with them no horses, cows, plows, or carts. They were equipped with only one kind of hook and net, which were too large for small fish. While they had both powder and guns, they knew little about their use and were slow to learn.

In Plymouth, as in Jamestown, the experiment in communism failed. Bound to work for their backers, the Merchant Adventurers, for seven years, there was little incentive for the individual Pilgrim whose profits went to the parent company. It was not until 1623, when the policy of giving land to families was instituted, making them responsible for their own sustenance and allowing them to keep a profit, that a marked increase in labor was noted.

Poor, honest, and unworldly, the Pilgrims wanted only to live their own lives in their own particular way. Unlike most colonists, they did not seek to expand their territory. But from the rock at Plymouth there emanated ripples of great importance for the history of America. From his stay in Plymouth at a time when the Mayflower Compact was fresh in men's minds, Roger Williams undoubtedly derived ideas on popular government, which he passed on to Thomas Hooker of Hartford. And when the first Puritans at Salem were ravaged by disease, they sought medical assistance from Samuel Fuller of the *Mayflower*. A zealous Separatist, Fuller took with him to Salem ideas on spiritual as well as medical matters and deserves some of the credit for launching Congregationalism in the Massachusetts Bay Colony.

The visitor's first contact with Plymouth Rock is apt to be a disappointing one. He will find it smaller than he imagined, with a crack running through it, and the date 1620 carved into its side. The bars around it, the overshadowing monument, and the possible doubt that this is actually where the Pilgrims came ashore, take something away from its reality.

But reality there is—the reality that they *did* land, and *stayed*. Like the Pilgrims, the rock remained—symbol of those who proved that the colonization of New England was possible, if only one had faith and endurance.

Plymouth was named on John Smith's 1614 map of New England.

Below, Elder Brewster gives a Thanksgiving blessing at the feast celebrating the Pilgrims' first American harvest. At right is Plymouth's Burial Hill, the site of a Pilgrim fort. Later Governor Bradford and other settlers were buried here.

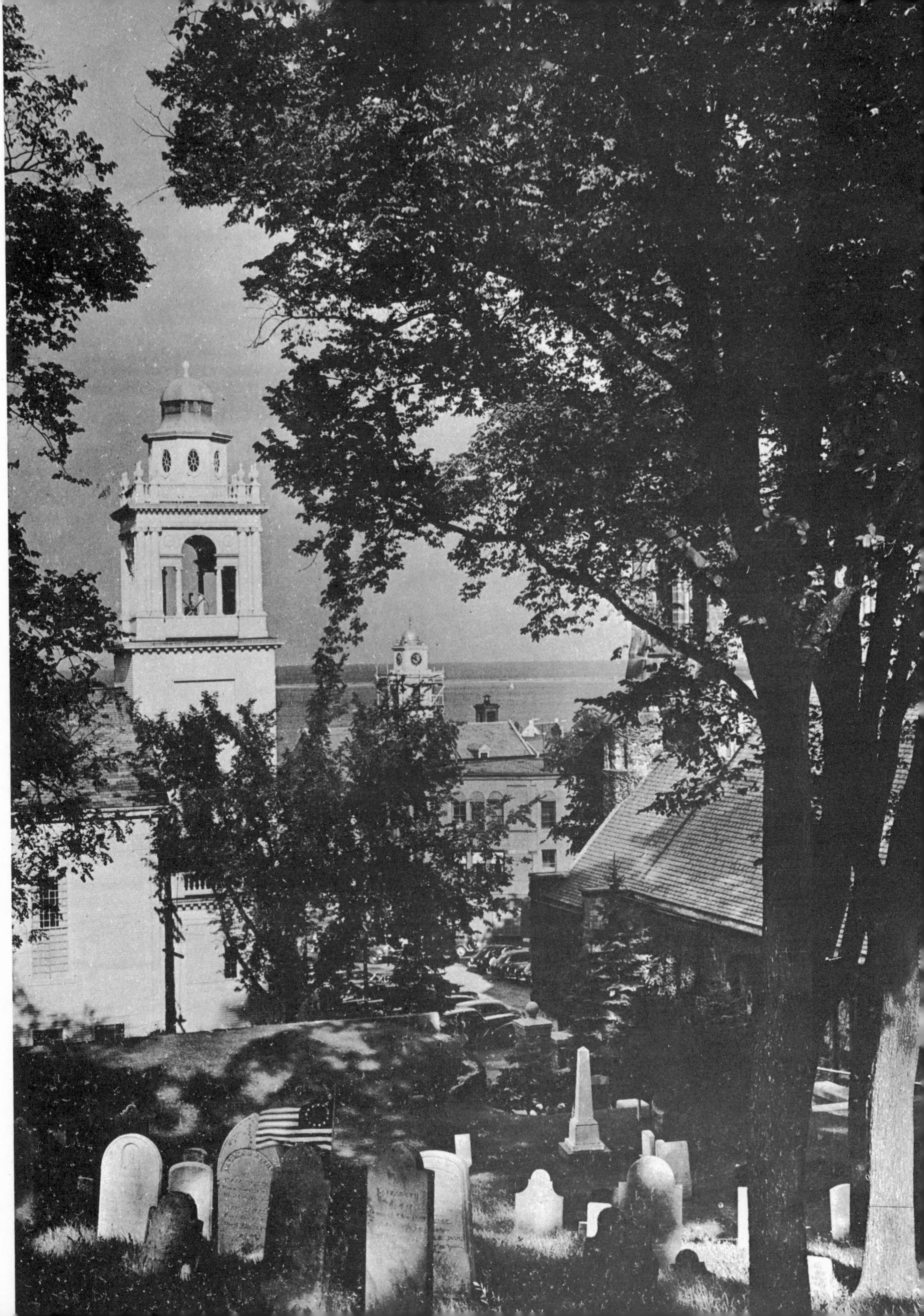

ELIOT ELISOFON, *Life*

Ann Pollard, a Puritan lady

Topsfield's medieval-style Parson Capen House was built in 1683.

Land of the Puritans

There are few surviving landmarks of those first grim years when famine and death watched the Pilgrims with pale, expectant eyes. Not until survival was relatively certain did they, or the Puritans who followed them, have time to construct anything comfortable or permanent.

The story of these first New Englanders has been told—in their own words as well as others'. But the real feeling of the place which remains, after three centuries, the legendary home of the American conscience may still be found in the austere landmarks they built so well.

Starting with the reconstructed Pioneers' Village in Salem, it is possible to trace the outward growth of seventeenth-century New England in almost any direction. The first shelters (and they could scarcely have been more than that) were the bark-covered wigwams, dugouts with sod roofs, and thatched-roof cottages which have been reconstructed in Salem. There, close by a replica of John Winthrop's *Arbella,* are the dwellings, crude furnishings, and utensils first used in Salem in 1630.

CONTINUED ON PAGE 18

Enormous kitchen fireplaces, surrounded by all kinds of utensils, were the natural center of seventeenth-century family life. The one shown here is in the Browne House in Watertown, Massachusetts.

16

Corner pendant on the Capen House

Front hallway of the Capen House

CONTINUED FROM PAGE 16

Massachusetts was backed by a well-organized, powerful corporation and, unlike most other colonies, it was a success almost from the beginning. Among the sixteen thousand settlers who had arrived in Massachusetts by 1640 were a number of skilled craftsmen. The homes they began building were patterned after the familiar—the medieval wooden manor houses of "home," with their steep roofs and leaded casement windows. But as time and the frontier played their parts, this style began to change into something better suited to severe winters, Indian raids, and different kinds of building materials. The basic pattern remained, however, and today when we pass the dark, brooding Richard Jackson House in Portsmouth, the Parson Capen House in Topsfield, or Salem's House of Seven Gables, their angular simplicity is a visible reminder of that New England conscience that permeated northeastern America during the seventeenth century.

This was the conscience which, at the height of its intensity, allowed a few fanatics to feed the flames of

On Salem's grim Gallows Hill, nineteen people were hanged for witchcraft and thrown into a common burial pit. Of some two hundred arrested in one year, many died in jail.

In this painting of the George Jacobs witchcraft trial, girls writhe in "convulsions" supposedly brought on by the presence of a witch. On such evidence Jacobs was hanged.

witchcraft and press Giles Corey to a slow death between heavy weights for supposed transgressions; it was the conscience that sent an ailing Roger Williams into a January snowstorm, banished forever from the Bay Colony for challenging Puritan orthodoxy. It was the conscience that caused a New York merchant visiting Boston in 1750 to observe: ". . . they are very Strict Observers of the Sabath day and in Service times no Persons are allow'd the Streets but Doctors if you are found upon the Streets and the Constables meet you they Compell you to go either to Curch or Meeton as you Chuse. . . ."

Bound up in their determination that man's spiritual and communal lives were inseparable, it was natural for the Puritan elders to insist on a ruling elite of those who could interpret the true path for the followers. There could be no tolerance. In fact, one Puritan divine stated in a sermon: "'Tis Satan's policy, to plead for an indefinite and boundless toleration." (So the dangerous Quakers, with their talk of an Inner Light, were driven out.) And as for democracy, John Winthrop pronounced it "the meanest and worst of all forms of government."

But the stream of immigration flowed on, bringing shipbuilders, merchants, indentured servants, artisans, shopkeepers—among them men and women who refused to commit their lives and souls to the rule of God's elect. The first pockets of settlement filled up, and the overflow trickled out into the wilderness beyond.

Unlike the lone trapper or hunter of a later West, the Puritans moved in groups, settling whole communities at a time. Across the Massachusetts hills, into New Hampshire, Maine, and the verdant Connecticut Valley they went, possessed of an insatiable land hunger which endured as long as land was to be had for the going. Their communities grew older and prospered, and gradually they began to reject the rule of theologians. They turned away from government by the representatives of God, toward those values which came to be called life, liberty, and the pursuit of happiness.

Yet even when challenged by those two impelling forces—the frontier and commerce—the Puritan conscience had a vitality which sustained and perpetuated it. In Northampton, Massachusetts, in 1734, it emerged in Jonathan Edwards' sermons on "Justification by

Gossips were silenced by a metal "brank" which fitted over the head.

Faith," when he called for a return to the worship of God in the Puritan tradition. In Edwards' wake, George Whitefield and James Davenport fed the fires of the "Great Awakening," as it was called, arousing a religious revival surpassed only by the Fundamentalists of the "Bible Belt." And when the Reverend Charles Chauncy of Boston denounced the Great Awakening, saying that respectability, sobriety, and reason were the roads to salvation, he gave voice to another side of the Puritan character.

Both sides of this argument, both outcroppings of the New England conscience, affected America's growth. One was the root of the later frontier's evangelism, the other the backbone of New England's literary greatness.

Although the end was in sight for many years, it was the Revolution that finally broke the power of the Puritan dynasty. During and after the war, special privileges of all kinds came under attack, and people turned naturally to religions which were based on men's equality, rather than one dominated by a few specially selected individuals.

DAVID E. SCHERMAN

Salem's fascinating House of Seven Gables, built in 1668, was probably the inspiration for Hawthorne's famous romance.

The Frary House is the only survivor of the 1704 raid.

Deerfield: The Frontier

In the chill hour before dawn on February 29, 1704, Deerfield's town sentry shivered and dozed, completely unaware of nearly 350 stealthy figures crossing the fields outside the village. There was no warning for anyone that morning—only an awful awakening to sudden, terrible death. In some houses the frenzied, howling Indians, led by Frenchmen, burst in on sleeping families and clubbed and stabbed them in their beds. Elsewhere they waited for the flames to drive them out. When it was over, more than half of Deerfield's settlers had been killed or taken prisoner. Those who were captured began the long march to Canada. If they fell behind they were slaughtered, like three-year-old Marah Carter, and Parson John Williams' wife, just risen from childbed.

Since 1669, when the first families moved there,

Deerfield had been a focus of Indian attack. Six years after it was settled, sixty-four Deerfield men were massacred on the banks of Bloody Brook, and the community settled back into the wilderness.

The visitor who happens on Deerfield will find it almost as it was in the early years of the eighteenth century. The Frary House was all that survived intact the terrible raid of 1704; but it is still there, as is Bloody Brook Tavern (moved from its old site).

With all its beauty, there is a feeling of loneliness about Deerfield when you come upon it. Quiet and peaceful, it is a place where one can still look out across the fertile valley of the Connecticut and see what it was that brought men here, and at the same time sense what it was like to live in the "white man's farthest outpost in the wilderness."

In this old etching of the 1704 massacre, Indians break into a Deerfield home to slaughter a family in their beds.

The Ashley House (right), once a Tory meeting place, is one of many beautiful old homes on Deerfield's main street.

Days of Maritime Glory

Considering the wealth that fishing brought to New England, it is no wonder that a "Sacred Cod" occupies a place of honor in Boston's State House. This carving is a masterpiece of wood sculpture.

Down by the lobstermen's shanties in old fishing ports like Boothbay Harbor, Maine, one can still see the grounded hulls of high-masted schooners, relics of a glorious maritime past.

Just outside the tiny village of Damariscotta, Maine, there is a heap of shells over six feet high, the accumulation of centuries of Indian clambakes. No one knows for sure how long the mound has been there, except that it was begun by Indians who came to the coast every summer to fish, at least a thousand years ago. The imagination must leap the conventions of history as well as centuries of time to connect a Damariscotta shell heap with Salem's McIntire houses, yet each records New England's age-old debt to the sea.

Generations of mariners have testified to the ocean's bounty—in the "Sacred Cod," that marvelous and deceptively simple carving that hangs in Boston's State House; in the exquisite scrimshaw work of the Nantucket Whaling Museum; in a statue of a Hawaiian war god and ship models in Salem's Peabody Museum; in the frieze of blubber spades and harpoons on a Sag Harbor church. What the sea took away is remembered, too—in *Moby Dick*, Melville's haunting portrayal of whaling and the struggle between good and evil; in the Gloucester statue to those who have gone down off the Grand Banks; in the log of the *Essex*, whose tortured pages record the horror of a voyage when men were forced to turn cannibals; or in a Kingston graveyard epitaph for Simeon Washburn—"drowned July 6, 1805, aged thirty-four years."

A stony soil made sailors of men who had intended to be planters, and hardly a New England village did not, in some way, feel the sea's influence. In the great days of sail a Boston merchant could make up, from within half a mile of State Street, a cargo of all essential ingredients of civilized life. Oil for lamps; pepper, tea, and coffee for housewives; tin to be made into wares for Yankee peddlers—all were possible because of the Atlantic and the enterprising men who took advantage of it.

Hardly changed since the days of the sailing ship, Boston Light is the oldest in New England. This austere white tower is located on a remote island at the mouth of Boston Harbor.

23

The riches of the Indies filled the warehouses lining Salem's busy Crowninshield Wharf when George Ropes painted this scene

Salem: Great Yankee Seaport

In Hong Kong there is still a place called "Ice House Street" where great cargoes of ice, cut from Walden, Saugus, and other New England ponds and transported fourteen thousand miles in double-sheathed vessels, were unloaded in the middle of the last century. And during World War II, when the United States Navy was planning the invasion of the Marshall and Gilbert Islands, the source it turned to for information on those islands was Salem's Peabody Museum.

These two isolated instances are among hundreds that survive the glorious days of New England's maritime supremacy. Of all the places to visit, none is better than Salem in which to recapture the adventure and prosperity of the Far East and India trade. It was there that Elias Hasket Derby, America's first millionaire, and men like Joseph Peabody, Jacob and George Crowninshield, and Ichabod Nichols lined the long wharves with ships and goods such as America had never seen.

By the time of the Revolution, the mercantile tradi-

Abraham Whipple once captured ten British merchantmen on ten successive nights. He was one of the Yankee shipmasters who made a profit from privateering in the Revolution.

A mere sampling of the Peabody Museum's superb collection includes figureheads, ship models, Bowditch's quadrant and spyglass, masks, and a carved Hawaiian war god.

n 1805. From the countinghouse at the far left, a watcher with a spyglass scans the horizon for incoming East Indiamen.

tion was firmly established, and privateering and the opening of non-English markets gave it further impetus. The scope of privateering was such that it engaged the energies of 90,000 men—more than the total number of Continentals and militia in any year except 1776. Salem alone had fifty-nine vessels in 1781, carrying four thousand men. Stirring as John Paul Jones' victory over the *Serapis* was, New England's sons were lured to sea more often by exploits like those of Captain Abraham Whipple. On one occasion Whipple disguised the identity of his ship *Providence* and joined a large convoy of British merchantmen bound from the West Indies to England. On each of ten successive nights he boarded and captured a vessel from the convoy, put a prize crew aboard, and sent it off to Boston. Eight of the ships reached that port, and their cargoes brought more than a million dollars.

When peace came it was not surprising that men began to talk of the China trade, or that realistic merchants were among the staunchest advocates of a strong central government which would protect our shipping.

The town whose motto was "To the farthest port of the rich East" was a place of wealth and cosmopolitan taste, the focal point of Samuel McIntire's architectural genius, the home port of America's great navigator Nathaniel Bowditch, and the site of an old granite museum which houses one of the most remarkable collections in existence. Founded in 1799 as the East India Marine Society, a collection point for members' sea journals and the curious articles they picked up on voyages all over the globe, Salem's Peabody Museum contains the fascinating memories of that time when men first sailed out to "trye all ports." It re-creates an era when a merchant walked down Essex Street followed by his Chinese boy in bright silks, ate a dinner served by a turbaned East Indian, or, like Jacob Crowninshield, brought back from Africa the first elephant seen in the United States. There is nothing like it anywhere, for there was never, in America, a place quite like Salem.

ARNOLD NEWMAN, REPRINTED FROM *Holiday*

One of these scrimshaw whale's tooth engravings portrays the clipper ship *Cosmos;* in the other an elegant hunter idles with his lady and dog.

The Golden Age of Whaling

Martha's Vineyard, New Bedford, New London, Fairhaven, Sag Harbor—these and thirty other ports along the eastern seaboard were engaged in whaling. But the first great period began in a place the Indians called "the faraway land"—Nantucket. Indians in flimsy canoes once sought out large whales off the island, killing them with stone or bone-pointed harpoons, and towing them ashore by hand. The victims were for them what the buffalo was for the Plains Indian—a wholly useful source of food, lighting, medicine, and building material. Then in 1712 a Nantucketer named Christopher Hussey, by mistake or good fortune, harpooned the most fearsome monster of them all, and from that moment on, the men of Nantucket were pulled into what Melville called "the charmed churned circle of the hunted sperm whale."

Along the difficult cobbled streets of Nantucket are beautiful houses reflecting the good fortunes of the era when nearly the entire male population followed the sea. By 1768 the town had a fleet of eighty whaling ships, and Nantucket men ranged from the Davis Straits in the Arctic to the distant South Sea islands. A great fire in 1846, along with the Gold Rush, were real blows to Nantucket's pre-eminence, and New Bedford, with its deep-water harbor and railroad connections, surged ahead. By 1863 the ledger account of Nantucket ships recorded simply: "No ship fitted this year Whaling from here."

Left semi-deserted after the decline of its chief industry, Nantucket fortunately retained the charm and character of its early years. Lining the elm-shaded Main Street are Federal-style and Greek Revival mansions, among them the brick houses known as the "Three Brothers," built in 1837 by Joseph Starbuck for his three sons. Near the wharf stands a faded red brick building—once a sperm-candle factory and warehouse, now a whaling museum crammed with the implements and by-products of those unbelievable four- and five-year voyages when the hardiest of men searched for the great sperm whale.

These houses on Nantucket's Main Street, known as the "Three Brothers," were built by whaling master Joseph Starbuck for his sons. Such mansions might almost have risen from the sea, for sea-derived wealth made them possible.

Below, an 1830's painting from the Peabody Museum shows some operations of whaling. At left, a strip of blubber is being peeled from a dead whale. On the ship at right, those not engaged in the chase are boiling down blubber into oil.

Mystic Re-creates the Past

In a great burst of genius that was the end of its maritime glory, New England produced the clipper ship. Those that Donald McKay and other builders made had names like music, and their speed and strange, mysterious beauty were legendary from the moment they were launched. Their captains made America, for a time, the greatest and most efficient maritime power in the world; and the ships, while they lasted, were a symbol of all that was best in the passing tradition of sail. None of the lovely clippers survive, but there is, in the little town of Mystic, Connecticut, a wonderfully tangible record of an age when sailing ships were New England's pride and joy. At the wharf a visitor can board the *Charles W. Morgan,* the only remaining whaler of its kind; see the square-rigger *Joseph Conrad* and the coasting schooner *Australia.*

This little Connecticut town never attained the eminence of Salem or New Bedford, but it is the only place where one can still see what New England's sailing ports looked like. In addition to the ships, there are, on old Seaport Street bordering the harbor, a countinghouse built in 1833, an apothecary shop, sail loft, ropewalk, a figurehead carver's shop, and the Stillman Building, which houses a fine museum of nautical relics.

Along the harbor's edge in Mystic, Connecticut, Old Seaport Street is an accurate re-creation of a New England port of the early 1800's. Projecting into the foreground is the prow of the *Charles W. Morgan,* last whaling ship of its kind. The *Lightning,* shown at left, was one of the fastest clipper ships. These vessels were originally designed to cut sailing time to the Orient. Adorning ship prows, carved wooden figures like those at right were supposed to give a ship long life and good fortune.

28

SAMUEL CHAMBERLAIN

FROM LEFT: CAPE ANN HISTORICAL ASSOCIATION, PEABODY MUSEUM OF SALEM, MARINE HISTORICAL ASSOCIATION OF MYSTIC

Bulfinch's experiments with unified residential blocks inspired the row of bow-front houses on Boston's Louisburg Square. Above is Samuel McIntire's portrait.

Architectural Heritage

The heritage of maritime New England is the heritage of men who still took pains with their work—of architects, shipbuilders, carpenters, and masons who had a near-religious feeling for their craft. At a time when every day brought a ship to port, men felt the greatness of what was going on. Why else would the owners and masters of Salem have commissioned the best artists, like Antoine Roux of Marseilles, to paint the portraits of their ships? In the same spirit they engaged men like Samuel McIntire—New England's skilled architect and woodcarver—to design homes like the Peirce-Nichols House, or the Pingree House, which made Salem one of America's great architectural sights.

One of the remarkable things about Salem, in fact, is that it is one of those New England towns where you can literally see the development of architecture from one period into the next. Here, as in Portsmouth, Providence, Boston, and other places, there is an uninterrupted flow of architectural preservation from Puritan medieval style, through various Colonial forms, into the Georgian influence and the more elaborate mansions like those designed by Charles Bulfinch and Samuel McIntire.

Generally speaking, the early New England dwelling was a four-room house, with two rooms upstairs and two on the ground floor, grouped about a huge central chimney of stone or brick. Facing south to take advantage of the sun, most of them had a narrow entrance hall and a stairway hugging the chimney. The floors of the upper rooms were supported by a huge, hand-hewn "summer" beam, which was supported in turn by the chimney and outside wall.

In that age, as in any other, it took money to build great houses; and while money was a long time coming on the seventeenth-century frontier, it became available—in large quantities—to those who controlled the means of trade in the young nation's burgeoning seaports.

William Bentley of Salem described Samuel McIntire, who was to become that town's presiding architectural genius: "He was descended of a family of carpenters who had no claims on public favor and was educated at a branch of that business. By attention he soon gained a superiority to all of his occupation & the present Court House, the North & South Meeting Houses, and indeed all the improvements for nearly thirty years past have been done under his eye. In sculpture he had no rival in New England. . . ."

In 1782 McIntire built the Peirce-Nichols House, a masterpiece which is often considered the finest three-story wooden house in New England. As in so

CONTINUED ON PAGE 32

Bulfinch probably designed Gore Place in Waltham. The oval rooms of this villa (above) were a luxurious departure from the traditional austerity of New England architecture.

Samuel McIntire built the Peirce-Nichols House in Salem in 1782. Square, simple, and framed by classic pilasters, this building is one of the finest examples of the Federal style.

PHOTOGRAPHS SAMUEL CHAMBERLAIN

This elegant Salem gatepost is a copy of McIntire's work.

CONTINUED FROM PAGE 30

many others of his design, the crowning feature of this house was the magnificent wood carving with which he decorated it. Along Salem's Chestnut Street even the houses built after McIntire's death in 1811 reflect his influence. Most of them are square, hip-roofed buildings of white clapboard or brick laid in flawless Flemish bond. Front doors are framed in fanlight and sidelights, shaded by elliptical or oblong porches whose roofs are supported by slender columns. A Palladian window opens into a formal garden in the rear. Most of the interiors are simply arranged, usually four rooms to a floor, and embellished with the carving so typical of McIntire's work.

At the same time McIntire was transforming Salem for posterity, Charles Bulfinch was achieving eminence as a New England architect. One of the finest examples of his work is the house built in 1795 for Harrison Gray Otis, now the headquarters of the Society for the Preservation of New England Antiquities, in Boston. Another great house, thought to be a Bulfinch design, is Gore Place in Waltham—one of the most splendid private residences ever constructed in New England.

Portsmouth, Newport, and Providence, at this time, were among the many coastal cities enjoying the fruits of maritime prosperity, and the beautifully constructed homes which have endured until the present time testify eloquently to the manner in which those first merchant princes lived. One of the finest examples is the Wentworth-Gardner House in Portsmouth, formerly owned by the Metropolitan Museum of Art of New York—a house with a superb doorway and proportions which make it one of the finest Georgian structures in America.

About the time Bulfinch was creating his houses on Boston's Beacon Hill, the outlying provinces were also beginning to think in terms of more elaborate structures. Into this situation stepped a gentleman

named Asher Benjamin, a clever carpenter from Greenfield, Massachusetts, who probably had more direct influence on New England architecture *in toto* than any other individual. Benjamin, in 1797, had the happy idea of writing and publishing a book, called *The Country Builder's Assistant*. Although it was not the first book on architecture printed in the United States, it was the first genuinely American treatment of the subject, and carpenters throughout the countryside began to pattern their construction work on Benjamin's plans. Asher Benjamin was astute enough to recognize a state of affairs which Benjamin Franklin had described some years earlier, when he wrote that Americans were not so miserable as the poor of Europe, but "there are also very few that in Europe would be called rich; it is rather a happy mediocrity that prevails. There are few great proprietors of the soil, and few tenants; most people cultivate their own lands, or follow some handicraft or merchandise; very few [are] rich enough to live idly upon their rents and incomes, or to pay the high prices given in Europe for painting, statues, architecture, and the other works of art, that are more curious than useful."

Benjamin produced his book with this market in mind, and craftsmen all over the northeastern states went to work with the plans he made available to them. The First Congregational Church in Bennington, Vermont, one of the loveliest of all New England churches, was built by the carpenter Lavius Fillmore, and resembles closely one of the plans in *The Country Builder's Assistant*. To their credit, local builders extemporized on Benjamin's basic drawings, but the total result is a definite pattern which helps give New England its unique flavor.

The graceful pediment scrolls of this doorway from Portsmouth's Wentworth-Gardner House (left) are crested with a gilded pineapple, traditional symbol of hospitality. Shown below is a detail of a decorative wheat-sheaf motif, molded by McIntire on a mantel in Salem's Pingree House.

JOHNSON, *Ladies' Home Journal*

Like other New England seaport towns, Portsmouth owes its fine mansions to the bounty of the sea. Here on Middle Street are three of the high, square, hip-roofed houses built by the rich shipbuilders and sea captains of the eighteenth century.

Paul Revere's engraving of the Boston Massacre was potent propaganda. Five men died, not seven, and Custom House had no "Butcher's Hall" sign. The rioters in front of Old State (center) were far from docile, as drawn here.

The BLOODY MASSACRE perpetrated in King——Street BOSTON on March 5th 1770 by a party of the 29th REGT

Engrav'd Printed & Sold by PAUL REVERE BOSTON

Unhappy Boston! see thy Sons deplore,
Thy hallow'd Walks besmear'd with guiltless Gore:
While faithless P—n and his savage Bands,
With murd'rous Rancour stretch their bloody Hands,
Like fierce Barbarians grinning o'er their Prey,
Approve the Carnage, and enjoy the Day.

If scalding drops from Rage from Anguish Wrung,
If speechless Sorrows lab'ring for a Tongue,
Or if a weeping World can ought appease
The plaintive Ghosts of Victims such as these:
The Patriot's copious Tears for each are shed,
A glorious Tribute which embalms the Dead.

But know, Fate summons to that awful Goal,
Where JUSTICE strips the Murd'rer of his Soul:
Should venal C—ts the scandal of the Land,
Snatch the relentless Villain from her Hand,
Keen Execrations on this Plate inscrib'd,
Shall reach a JUDGE who never can be brib'd.

The unhappy Sufferers were Messrs SAML GRAY, SAML MAVERICK, JAMS CALDWELL, CRISPUS ATTUCKS & PATK CARR
Killed. Six wounded; two of them (CHRISTR MONK & JOHN CLARK) Mortally

Boston's Old State House today

DAVID E. SCHERMAN

The Cradle of the Revolution

At the head of State Street in Boston there is an old brick building that looks small now, compared to the newer ones which surround and shadow it. But if there is a single place to which one can point and say "This is where it began," few are more deserving than Old State House.

In February of 1761 the great square room on the second floor was jammed with lawyers and merchants, waiting anxiously, even desperately, for the outcome of a hearing. This was the same room, with nine long windows, deep fireplace, and glistening chandelier, where Sir William Pepperrell had planned the expedition against Louisbourg in 1745. Sixteen years later it was crowded with men determined to test the legality of something called "writs of assistance."

Two attorneys pleaded the colonists' case—Oxenbridge Thacher and James Otis. In the audience, intent on every word, were men who would begin a revolution, and others who would resist it as long as they could. When the time came for Otis to speak, he arose like a "flame of fire" to attack with "a torrent of impetuous eloquence the terrible menacing monster" of oppression. For five hours he talked, passionately denying that Parliament possessed unlimited authority over the colonies. He told the court and his listeners that the colonists possessed certain fundamental rights which no parliament could take away, one of which was the right to have their homes and property secure against search or seizure.

James Otis lost his plea, but few men who heard him forgot what he said. Fifty years later John Adams, who had heard him speak, wrote: "Here this day, in the old Council Chamber, the child Independence was born."

On Monday, March 5, 1770, snow fell on the lion and unicorn atop Old State, and the cobbled street outside was covered with ice. About eight o'clock that evening a barber's boy whistled at Captain Goldfinch, a British officer, and called him names. A sentry chased the boy, and hit him with the butt of his musket. Soon, in front of Murray's barracks in Water Street, a crowd collected. Before long they were scuffling with the "bloody backs," throwing snowballs and ice at them. Someone rang the fire bell in Brick Church at the north end of town, and at once the streets were alive with running people. In Dock Square, outside Faneuil Hall, a figure described as a "tall large man in a red cloak and white wig" harangued the gathering crowd.

A little after nine o'clock another crowd began to taunt the sentinel at the Custom House. As they came closer, he dodged for his life, until Captain Preston appeared with eight other British soldiers. "Lobsters!" "Bloody backs!" the crowd jeered, "You dare not fire!" And the square in front of State was filled with flying ice, chunks of wood, snowballs, oyster shells. One redcoat, struck by a missile, lost his footing and dropped his gun. At this the other eight fired their muskets into the crowd, killing three men instantly, and mortally wounding two others.

CONTINUED ON PAGE 38

CONTINUED FROM PAGE 37

To the tattoo of drums, additional soldiers appeared, while the winter night echoed with the cry: "To arms! Town-born, turn out!" From the balcony of Old State, Governor Hutchinson appealed to the seething, angry crowd, but not until the British commander agreed to jail Captain Preston and his men did the mob subside. By three o'clock next morning the crowd had dispersed, except for a citizens' guard who patrolled the streets for the rest of the night.

After the "Boston Massacre," one man did more than any other to keep alive the flame of liberty between 1770 and 1773. Samuel Adams was his name. A town man, bred to city politics, Sam Adams lived in a shabby house on Purchase Street and knew practically everyone in Boston. Willing to serve the town in any capacity, he deemed no job too small for him. He never had any money, failed at all his business ventures, and was surely the worst—and most popular —tax collector Boston ever had. In his shabby brown jacket with the buttons missing, he sat on the wharf with workmen, talked in the taverns with lawyers, spoke at endless meetings in Faneuil Hall and Old South Meeting House, wrote letters to the *Independent Advertiser* and Boston *Gazette* under names like Puri-

tan, Populus, Determinatus, or Bostonian, and in 1772 organized the Committee of Correspondence which became the network of resistance and independence.

Because of Sam Adams the colony boycotted English goods. "The female spinners kept on spinning six days of the week," one Tory wrote, "and on the seventh the Parsons took their turns and spun out their prayers and sermons to the long thread of politics." And in 1773 when cargoes of the East India Company's tea arrived in Boston, Sam Adams was behind the mass meeting in Old South Meeting House, to demand that it be sent back to England. For days negotiations went on with the royal governor. Finally, when the patience of the crowd was at an end, Sam Adams rose in the church and said, "This meeting can do nothing more to save the country."

As if at a signal the meeting broke up, and a band of men disguised as Indians swept down to the docks, boarded the tea ships, and dumped £18,000 worth of property into Boston Harbor.

Parliament reacted to this outrage by passing four new measures to punish the city. The most serious was an order to close Boston port, and General Thomas Gage, who had served under Amherst and Braddock,

In various ways these four Harvard graduates typified the revolutionary movement in Boston. At upper left is merchant John Hancock, the richest New Englander on the patriot side. Next to him is Samuel Adams, a gregarious rabble-rouser who kept the rebellion alive, and probably organized the Boston Tea Party. At bottom left is Joseph Warren, the group's leading intellectual spirit, a doctor who deserted his practice for politics, eventually dying in the fight at Bunker Hill. The man on his right is James Otis, brilliant lawyer and leader who was lost to the movement when his mind failed.

was sent to enforce it. Through Gage, George III offered a pardon to every American patriot under arms—"excepting John Hancock and Samuel Adams"—but with its port closed, Boston was virtually in a state of siege. With most of the population out of work, the city would certainly have starved, if other colonies had not sent food and supplies. Yet in this city of unemployed Gage found no workmen to build his barracks.

Occupied by British troops, denied the lifeblood of trade, faced with privation, Boston was like a boiler whose pressure rises until all men know it will burst but cannot say when. Gage was uneasily aware that the New England colonies had been organizing their militia and collecting military supplies all through the winter of 1774-75. Early that spring he decided to send between six hundred and eight hundred men to Concord to capture the stores there. Although he kept his plans a secret, the Bostonians missed little that was going on, and guessed his intentions. Dr. Joseph Warren, Sam Adams' close friend and symbol of the intellectual revolutionary in New England, sent instructions to Paul Revere. The forty-year-old silversmith, engraver, and general craftsman had already been a courier for the patriots, carrying messages to Sons of Liberty as far away as New York and Philadelphia. At ten o'clock on the night of April 18, 1775, he had the sexton of Old North Church hang two lanterns in the tower to warn Charlestown patriots that the British were coming that way. Leaving his house in North Square, Revere rowed around the stern of the British man-of-war *Somerset* and landed at Charlestown. There he borrowed a horse and galloped off for Lexington to warn Sam Adams and John Hancock that the British were planning to arrest them. Although he was ambushed by a British patrol, he managed to escape, and crossed the Mystic River twice to warn citizens along his route. When Revere rode up to Lexington Green at midnight, it was quiet, and he headed for the Hancock-Clarke House where Hancock and Adams were staying. Minutemen guarding the house asked him not to disturb Mr. Hancock but Revere, furious, shouted, "Noise! You'll have noise enough before long! The regulars are out!"

His mission complete, Revere relaxed by the fire until twelve thirty, when Billy Dawes, the Boston cordwainer who had ridden to Lexington with the same message over the land route, arrived and the two decided to go on to Concord. As they left Lexington

CONTINUED ON PAGE 40

Revere portrayed the 1768 landing of British troops on Boston's Long Wharf. The second church from the right is Old North.

Setting off from his house (top left, facing page) in Boston's North Square, Paul Revere rowed to Charlestown, and took horse for Lexington to warn Sam Adams and John Hancock that the redcoats planned to seize them. En route, he crossed the Mystic River (extreme right) twice, warning patriots along the way, and arrived in Lexington about midnight. There, minutemen were assembled at the Buckman Tavern (bottom right). Billy Dawes joined Revere in Lexington, and on the way to Concord they met Samuel Prescott. The three were ambushed by a British patrol near the Hartwell Farm (top right), but Prescott managed to escape and carry the alarm to Concord. The painting of Revere below is by Copley.

CONTINUED FROM PAGE 39

they met Dr. Samuel Prescott, on his way back to Concord after a date with a Lexington girl. But as they neared the Hartwell farm, they were ambushed by a British patrol. Billy Dawes raced for a nearby farmhouse with two regulars in hot pursuit, and then fell off his horse. Although Revere was captured, the British freed him after taking his horse. Fortunately, Prescott sneaked around the Hartwell farm and rode on to warn the men at Concord.

Meanwhile, Revere walked back to the Hancock-Clarke House, helped Hancock and Adams get away, then went to Buckman Tavern to get Hancock's trunk. The sun was rising as he came out of the tavern, and he saw the redcoats under Lieutenant Colonel Smith and Major Pitcairn march onto the green and stop before John Parker's seventy minutemen. As he watched, the first historic shot was fired; but Revere, not realizing the significance of the moment, picked up Hancock's trunk and walked away.

Revere's alarm had assembled Captain John Parker and his company of minutemen, and at 4:30 A.M. Thaddeus Bowman galloped up to Buckman Tavern with word that the British were approaching. As the old belfry on the hill tolled the alarm, about seventy men ran out of the tavern and formed two lines along the road. When they saw the size of the British force, some of Parker's men suggested they withdraw. He silenced them, saying, "Stand your ground! Don't fire unless fired upon! But if they mean to have a war let it begin here!" A few minutemen drifted away as the British appeared, and Parker himself finally saw the hopelessness of the situation. He gave the order to disband. Who fired the first shot on that cold morning was something men would deny or claim for years, for

TEXT CONTINUED ON PAGE 45

The first stop on Revere's famous ride was Boston's Old North Church. He had the sexton hang lanterns in the tower to warn Charlestown patriots in case the British held him up.

BATTLE GROUND

NORTH BRIDGE

BULLET HOLE HOUSE

Concord River

HARTWELL FARM

PRESCOTT

CONCORD

REVERE AND DAWES
STOPPED BY THE BRITISH

HANCOCK-CLARKE
HOUSE

BUCKMAN TAVERN

BATTLE GREEN

BELFRY

LEXINGTON

RUSSELL HOUSE

REVERE

Mystic River

BRITISH RETREAT

BRITISH ADVANCE

BUNKER HILL

CHARLESTOWN

"OLD NORTH"

BOSTON

BOSTON HARBOR

Charles River

DORCHESTER HEIGHTS

DAWES

PICTURES FROM TOP LEFT, CLOCKWISE: JOAN WHITNEY, BLACK STAR; KOSTI RUOHOMAA,
Life (2); SAMUEL CHAMBERLAIN; MUSEUM OF FINE ARTS, BOSTON, COURTESY *Time*

Lexington Green was quiet and deserted when Paul Revere arrived at midnight. This photograph, taken at that time of night, gives an idea of what he saw as he sped on his way to the Hancock-Clarke

These pistols belonged to Major Pitcairn, who led the British at Lexington. Minutemen found the guns in the saddlebags of Pitcairn's horse after he lost his mount in the retreat to Boston.

House. Four and a half hours later, news of the redcoats' approach created a scene of frantic activity. At the Green, seventy minutemen formed two uneven lines, while those lacking guns looked on.

This boulder on Lexington Green marks the place where John Parker and his minutemen waited for the British regulars. Parker escaped injury but his cousin was among the first killed.

Amos Doolittle's engraving above shows the British regulars firing on the minutemen at Lexington Green. Scattering in confusion, the Americans had eight dead, ten wounded.

While orderly redcoats march into Concord to destroy an arms cache, two British officers survey the terrain from a hilltop cemetery. Major Pitcairn is shown leaning on a stick.

it was an act no one dared, at the same time knowing it must come. Suddenly the shot rang out, and the war began that was at once rebellion and civil war and social revolution, and a spark that would lift the hopes of men all over the world and make them say "It could be us, as well."

The first British volley cut down Captain Parker's cousin Jonas and seventeen other Americans, and as the minutemen broke up in confusion the redcoats cheered and marched off to Concord. By the time the redcoats arrived there, refreshed themselves at Wright's Tavern, and set fire to the courthouse, three or four hundred minutemen from neighboring towns had collected on a hill outside town. When they saw the smoke, a small company marched toward Concord and met the British at the "rude bridge." In two or three minutes the fight was over. The British regrouped and at noon set out for Boston.

At Meriam's Corner, just outside Concord, militiamen who had arrived too late for the battle at the bridge skirmished with the British again, and the real fighting began. Hidden behind houses, trees, and walls all the way to Boston, the Americans sniped at the harried, weary redcoats. At the Jason Russell House in Menotomy (now Arlington) a pitched battle took place, and at Cambridge there was a mile and a half of continuous fighting, through Somerville and Prospect Hill. Finally the British crossed the little isthmus connecting Charlestown with the mainland and were safe at last. In twenty hours they had marched thirty-five

TEXT CONTINUED ON PAGE 46

A modern replica over the Concord River replaces the wooden bridge where a small band of minutemen met the British rear guard in a brief skirmish. One minuteman related how "We wair all orded to Load and had stricked order not to fire . . . firs, then to fire as fast as we could." First to shoot, the redcoats were quickly driven back.

SAMUEL CHAMBERLAIN

By the time the retreating British reached Meriam's Corner, on the outskirts of Concord, the whole countryside bristled with militiamen. This marker shows where they fell upon the redcoats with a fury that made one survivor comment: "They seemed to drop from the skies." For eighteen miles the British met steady rebel sniping.

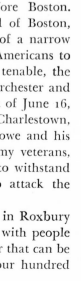

The Bunker Hill Monument actually stands near the site of the redoubt on Breed's Hill which saw the heaviest fighting. Bunker Hill lay to the north; and though the battle was named for it, almost no action took place there.

In John Trumbull's painting, Joseph Warren expires on the ground as the British carry the Breed's Hill redoubt. At far left Israel Putnam calls for a retreat; while at right center a dying Major Pitcairn falls in the arms of his son.

With its commanding view of Boston, the Dillaway House in Roxbury was an important patriot headquarters during the siege. From its rear windows, spectators witnessed the distant Battle of Bunker Hill.

TEXT CONTINUED FROM PAGE 45

miles, fought continuously for half the distance, and lost 73 killed, 174 wounded, and 26 missing. Before the battle Earl Percy, who had reinforced the British at Lexington, called the Americans "cowards" and "timid creatures." Afterward he wrote, "I never believed, I confess, that they wd have attacked the King's troops, or have had the perseverance I found in them yesterday."

At ten o'clock on the morning of April 19, postrider Israel Bissel mounted his horse at Watertown and rode night and day through Connecticut, to New York, down through New Jersey, and to Philadelphia, carrying the "momentous intelligence" of Lexington and Concord to "all Friends of AMERICAN Liberty." By June, 15,000 men under Artemas Ward and Joseph Warren of Massachusetts, John Stark of New Hampshire, Nathanael Greene of Rhode Island, and Israel Putnam of Connecticut encamped before Boston.

The British were in complete control of Boston, but since that city was then at the tip of a narrow peninsula, it was relatively easy for the Americans to bottle them up. To make their position tenable, the British would have to command both Dorchester and Charlestown peninsulas, but on the night of June 16, Breed's Hill and Bunker Hill, back of Charlestown, were secretly fortified by the patriots. Howe and his generals, confident of their fleet and army veterans, and contemptuous of the rebels' ability to withstand any kind of frontal assault, decided to attack the Charlestown position.

Early on June 17, the Dillaway House in Roxbury and rooftops all over town were covered with people watching "one of the greatest scenes of war that can be conceived." Below Breed's Hill twenty-four hundred

scarlet-clad troops, gun barrels and bayonets flashing in the sun, disembarked from barges and began to advance in line up the hill while the great guns of the British fleet belched forth fire and smoke. Behind a fence on the beach and in a redoubt on the hill the Americans waited until they "could see the whites of their eyes" before firing their murderous volleys. If only Ward's and Putnam's fresh troops had supported the indomitable Colonel Prescott in the redoubt, the tide might have turned; but they did not, and the Americans finally had to retreat when their ammunition gave out. But the British victory, if it could be called that, was achieved at terrible cost. Of twenty-four hundred men, nearly half were shot, including every man on Howe's staff, while the Americans lost less than five hundred. The effect of the battle was indicated in a letter Gage wrote, saying, "The conquest of this country is not easy."

On July 2, an "amiable, generous, and brave" Virginian named George Washington arrived in Cambridge and took over the Wadsworth House as his first headquarters. Seven weeks earlier, Ethan Allen and Benedict Arnold had captured Fort Ticonderoga, and that winter Washington put their spoils to good use. He sent Henry Knox to drag the fort's heavy guns all the way from Lake Champlain to Boston by sledge and oxen, and these weapons, coupled with the occupation of Dorchester Heights, forced Howe to evacuate the city. By March 20, American troops were in full possession of Boston, and that summer Washington moved to the Vassall House (now the Craigie House) which he used as headquarters for nearly a year. With the exception of minor engagements, the war that began in New England left, never to return.

Isaac Hull, by Stuart

In the year 1812 few would argue that the British Navy was not the finest in the world. Time and again the King's vessels had been up against numerical odds and had come through victorious, and the British public could survey with warm satisfaction the names Cape St. Vincent, the Nile, Trafalgar, and a host of others. It was with considerable assurance that a London journalist cast his contemptuous eye toward America and its "few fir-built frigates, manned by a handful of bastards and outlaws."

Isaac Hull was a modest man, but he was also a very brave and patriotic one, and he had no such fixed notions about the British fleet. He was in command of the frigate *Constitution*, a ship so heavily timbered as to deserve the nickname "Old Ironsides," yet with lines so clean she could outsail nearly anything afloat,

Old Ironsides

Thrice rescued from the scrap heap, and by now the most famous American ship, the *Constitution* (right) rests at anchor in the Charlestown Navy Yard

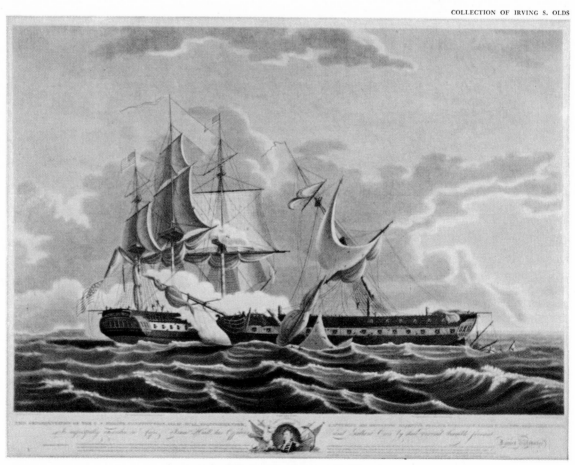

A French lithograph depicts Hull's victory.
The *Constitution*'s broadsides have unmasted
the *Guerrière* and set the frigate's decks on fire.

and officered and manned by the best her country had. So when Captain Hull and the *Constitution* ran down the *Guerrière* on August 19, 1812, and knocked her helpless in half an hour of slam-bang broadsides, the Captain took it as a matter of course. But the American public (not to mention the British) did not, for this was the first ray of hope in an unpopular war which had been disastrous from the beginning. Only the victories of the *Constitution*—and later the *Wasp*, *Hornet*, and *United States*—kept the nation's hopes alive, and if the people sometimes overlooked this fact, they never completely forgot it.

By 1830 the *Constitution* was obsolete, and the Navy recommended junking her. When a young student named Oliver Wendell Holmes heard this, he sent his protest to the Boston *Daily Advertiser*:

Nail to the mast her holy flag,
Set every threadbare sail,
And give her to the god of storms,
The lightning and the gale!

Reprinted in newspapers throughout the country, the poem aroused public sympathy to save Old Ironsides. Seventy years later, again in danger of destruction, she was rescued by the Society of the Daughters of 1812. And in 1927, when the secretary of the navy appealed for funds to save her once more, a steady flood of pennies, nickels, and dimes flowed in from all over the United States, much of it from school children, and the *Constitution* was preserved. No one who sees her today in Charlestown Navy Yard in Boston will forget —or fail to be grateful.

From left to right in the view of Shelburne are the Horseshoe Barn, East Shelburne House, Shaker Shed, Cavendish Homestead, Gray Barn, White Stagecoach Inn, Red Barn, and the Old Covered Bridge.

Shelburne Museum

Nothing of momentous importance took place in Shelburne, Vermont, but there is near this little town in the Green Mountains one of the great collections of early Americana. In sharp contrast to the elegance of Winterthur and Williamsburg, Shelburne Museum contains the simple folk art of rural America.

Just beyond the old covered bridge which leads to the grounds is the 1840 meetinghouse, a simple, dignified stone structure. Dirt roads lined with fruit trees,

ELIOT ELISOFON, *Life*

lilacs, elms, and maples connect the other buildings, which represent a cross section of New England architecture. There is a stagecoach inn built in 1783, with ten fireplaces and a second-floor ballroom, which contains the museum's weather vanes, figureheads, and trade signs. An early Shaker building houses woodworking tools, household and kitchen utensils, a 150-year-old cobbler's shop, and a harness maker's equipment. The horseshoe-shaped barn contains the Webb family collection of carriages, sleighs, wagons, and fire fighting equipment. Added to the rare assortment of everyday objects of colonial life are some fine pieces of primitive American sculpture—circus figures and copper centaurs, mermaids and lightning rods. On top of a hill overlooking the grounds, Colchester Lighthouse once again surveys the S. S. *Ticonderoga*, last of the coal-burning side-wheel steamers, and a fine example of the craft that once dominated our inland waters.

51

Sturbridge: Eighteenth-Century Community

This wooden Indian surveys Old Sturbridge's village green from a lookout on the front porch of Grant's General Store.

There are few places in the country where one can see so well what life was like in the eighteenth and early nineteenth centuries as in Old Sturbridge Village. Built alongside the gentle Quinebaug River in south central Massachusetts, Sturbridge was the creation of two industrialists named Wells, who devoted years to collecting and restoring more than thirty buildings in the community, and furnishing them with the authentic implements and appurtenances of the period. It was not their purpose to re-create an actual town, but to reconstruct a typical, functioning community where one can see what life was like then.

There is a traditional village green, a meeting-house, school, country store, sawmill and gristmill, a blacksmith shop, and houses ranging in style from a simple one-room cottage to an imposing Georgian mansion. Most of these buildings house collections of early New England crafts and tools, and Old Sturbridge Village is a working community where cabinet-maker, miller, potter, weaver, and coppersmith carry on trades as their forbears did.

A convincing background for the skill, ingenuity, and thrift of New England's preindustrial days, Old Sturbridge Village is a place of unusual educational interest, where the eighteenth century and the remarkable contributions of its inhabitants are handsomely preserved for posterity.

Corn meal and buckwheat flour are still ground at the Wight Gristmill (left), powered by a huge undershot water wheel.

The interior of the Hitchcock Boot Shop is fitted out with the tools which cobblers used in the late eighteenth century.

53

Provisions for the Peddlers

For a time sea and river sufficed as the high roads of colonial commerce but, because of the perverse way men had of moving constantly toward the western sky, the day came when a better means of supplying the families of the interior had to be devised. The Yankee peddler was the answer.

Loaded down with more dead weight than most of us would care to lift—much less carry—these men slogged through torrential rains, blistering heat, ankle-deep mud, and were bitten by dogs, snakes, and every known kind of insect in their appointed rounds. For nearly two hundred years these "damn Yankees from Connecticut" and other parts of New England plied their trade, visiting every house and settlement in the remote, lonely interior. What they did required little knowledge or capital, and for most of them it spelled opportunity.

They supplied housewives with tinware, pins, gingham, and bits of ribbon; husbands with nails, jack-knives, and tools; children with candy sticks, jew's-harps, and trinkets. In return they received the honey, coonskins, beaver pelts, and hand-carved furniture that were the farm families' sole currency. Several million people depended on these shrewd, inquisitive men to bring them the articles they needed (and some they didn't know they needed), and as fast as the Yankee peddler sold his wares the mills of the Northeast worked to replace them.

Early in our history New Englanders began to take advantage of the rocky hills and tumbling streams God had given them, it seemed, instead of topsoil. By 1650 there was, at Saugus, Massachusetts, an ironworks which was the wonder of its day. It had a rolling and slitting mill that compared with the best in Europe, from which came iron to be made into nails, guns, cooking utensils, chains, hardware, and farm implements for the burgeoning frontier. Out of home and mill came rope, candles, earthenware, leather goods, glass, paper, and a host of other products in increasing numbers.

There are still many places where New England's industrial beginnings can be seen. At Saugus, for example, the entire ironworks has been reconstructed into a working museum where visitors may inspect the ingenious mechanisms devised by their forebears. Just up the hill from the ironworks is the old iron-master's house—a dark seventeenth-century remnant of the Elizabethan style which is one of the finest surviving examples of this type of dwelling, and one of the earliest frame houses in America.

On Nantucket a windmill continues to produce corn meal, as it has since 1746. Near the village of Wickford, Rhode Island, with its concentration of eighteenth-century houses, is the old snuff mill operated by Gilbert Stuart's father. Farther north, in a town the Indians called Pawtucket, or "the place by the waterfall," Samuel Slater built a textile mill in 1793 which still stands. When President Madison decided to enhance the prestige of American cloth, he gave it his approval by wearing a suit of Pawtucket woolen at his inauguration.

At Simsbury, Connecticut, John Higley minted the first copper coins in the colonies, stamping them with the charming inscription: "I am good Copper—Value me as You Will." No such happy thoughts ever graced the bowels of Newgate Prison, in nearby East Granby, where the ore was mined. Here, seventy feet below the grim ruins, are caverns where circles were worn in the rock floor by the pacing feet of chained prisoners—Tories, thieves, and debtors forced to work in iron collars, handcuffs, and leg irons.

In an elm-shaded glen in New London, Connecticut, there is a low, gambrel-roofed gristmill established in 1650. Although the overshot wheel is a replica of the first one, the beams, gears, and grinders of the original mill remain.

The old stone mill in Newport has been the subject of controversy for years. Often attributed to Norsemen, it is more probably the ruin of a windmill built by Benedict Arnold's great-grandfather, the first governor of Rhode Island. The mill owes its preservation to Judah Touro, a son of the first regular rabbi of Jeshuat Israel Congregation in Newport, who lived and made a fortune in New Orleans and served with Andrew Jackson in the War of 1812. When he died he left $500,000 to churches and other institutions of many faiths, and gave the city of Newport $10,000 to buy and improve the grounds around the old mill.

In the painting above, a Yankee peddler has descended from his wagon to extol the virtues of a coffee grinder to a matronly assemblage. The Eastham windmill pictured at right is still in operation. Once a common sight along the Massachusetts coast, windmills were used for the grinding of corn. Shown below is the restored Saugus Ironworks. From left to right are the wharf and warehouse, the blast furnace, the forge, and the rolling and slitting mill. Partly hidden among the trees is the ironmaster's house, built in the seventeenth century.

Emerson's grandfather watched the battle at North Bridge from his study in the Old Manse. Scarcely changed since 1769, it was the home of Emerson, and later of Nathaniel Hawthorne, who wrote *Mosses from an Old Manse* here.

New England's Literary Heritage

The flowering of what we often call "literary New England" was the impact of the poet on the Puritan spirit. What these writers had to say can be understood much more readily if it is measured against the surroundings that colored their work.

It is all very well to visit the Craigie House in Cambridge and think that this was where Henry Wadsworth Longfellow lived when he taught at Harvard. But if we remember that the Craigie House had been there since 1759, in the heart of those origins the poet so wanted to make into a national tradition for his countrymen, his poems come to life a little bit more.

Maybe Thoreau would be better understood if he were read on the banks of Walden Pond, where he stated the belief that man need not be hampered by civilization's material things. And to visit the quiet old village of Concord is to understand better how Emerson, back from his travels to think, to walk, and to observe life, found that "The purpose of life seems to be to acquaint every man with himself." Parts of Concord are unchanged since the time when he found in them a philosophy of individualism that seemed to set men free and provide them with a new energy.

If you walk along Highland Avenue in Salem as the sun goes down, Gallows Hill stands out in stark relief as it did for Nathaniel Hawthorne, one hundred years ago. And in the House of the Seven Gables and Witch House there are still memories of the grim Puritan past which both fascinated and repelled him.

There is Seamen's Bethel, in New Bedford, where Herman Melville sat and heard sermons which he united with his knowledge of the sea and the whale hunt to produce what has been called "the perfect and final result of the Puritan's desperate three-century-long struggle with the problem of evil."

One of the many other places with long memories is the serene brick house in Amherst that harbored Emily Dickinson from the world and its confusions and allowed her to discover something of the human soul. And in Portsmouth, New Hampshire, and South Berwick, Maine, you can see the beautiful homes of Thomas Bailey Aldrich and Sarah Orne Jewett, which were scenes of their delightful New England stories.

Morning mists rise from Walden Pond where Thoreau came to escape a way of life which made men "tools of their tools."

56

Henry David Thoreau   Ralph Waldo Emerson   Nathaniel Hawthorne

Roger Williams

Conformist and

In nearly all the old towns of New England, facing the village green or common, are the towering white spires of Congregational churches which are lineal descendants of the early Puritan meeting-houses. Of all these, perhaps only one really dates back to Puritan times—the Old Ship Church in Hingham, Massachusetts, built in 1681, and now a Unitarian church. Plain to the point of severity, it is a fine example of its makers' deliberate indifference to aesthetics which resulted so often in dignity and simple beauty.

The beginning of religious liberty in the United States was largely the story of those folk who fled the intolerance of the Massachusetts Bay Colony. Roger Williams left Salem for Rhode Island, determined to "hold forth a lively experiment that a most flourishing civil state may stand and best be maintained with full liberty in religious concernments." For years the Baptists who found refuge there had no church, meeting under a tree or in a member's house; but finally, in 1775, they erected in Providence the First Baptist Meetinghouse "for the publick worship of Almighty God." And although Baptists in those days frowned on frivolities, they nevertheless hung a bell in their place of worship which bore the inscription:

For freedom of conscience the town was first planted,
Persuasion not force, was used by the people:
This church is the eldest and has not recanted,
Enjoying and granting bell, temple and steeple.

In Newport, the Central Baptist Church has withstood time's ravages since 1733, and the Newport Historical Society has preserved the lovely interior

With its classic portico and high, graceful steeple, the Congregational Church in Litchfield, Connecticut, displays the best qualities of New England church architecture.

George Whitefield

Thomas Hiscox

Jonathan Edwards

Cotton Mather

Nonconformist

of the Seventh Day Baptist Church, oldest of that denomination in the country. Newport is also the site of the Touro Synagogue—oldest synagogue building in America—built by descendants of Sephardic Jews who arrived in 1658.

Perhaps if Massachusetts Bay Colony had been governed by a William Penn instead of a Cotton Mather, those terrible months of the witchcraft craze would never have occurred. (Penn's answer to a charge that a Pennsylvania woman went riding on a broomstick was to state caustically that Pennsylvania had no law against riding on broomsticks.) But such was not the case, and Penn's New England brethren suffered much at Puritan hands. Despised, often whipped, mutilated, or hanged (if they succeeded in gaining entrance to the colony), the Quakers had already survived some years of persecution by the time Penn established his "Peaceable Kingdom" in 1681. One landmark of their survival still stands on the Great Road, near Saylesville, Rhode Island. An ell of this plain wooden meetinghouse, built from hand-hewn timbers mortised together with pegs, dates back to 1703.

One of the most interesting of the lesser religious denominations that flourished in New England was known as "The United Society of Believers in Christ's Second Appearing"—or the Shakers. Their celibacy and a belief in separation from the world led to their gradual decline; but near Canterbury, New Hampshire, one may still see, clustered about a white meetinghouse built in 1782, the sparsely furnished frame houses of those who protested against the adornments of a vain world.

Newport's Touro Synagogue, dedicated in 1763, is the oldest in America. Corinthian columns, chandeliers, and wainscoted seats adorn its red, white, and blue interior.

FROM LEFT: MUSEUM OF FINE ARTS, BOSTON;
BROWN BROTHERS; CULVER SERVICE; BROWN BROTHER·

John Quincy Adams   Brooks Adams   John Adams   Henry Adams   Charles Francis Adams

The Adamses of Quincy

One day in 1945, Henry Adams was taking a friend through the Adams house in Quincy, Massachusetts. When they reached the study, he pointed to an old chair and remarked, "There is the chair in which John Adams was stricken." He paused for a moment, then turned to his friend. "Do you know how I know?" His guest shook his head. Adams turned the chair over and showed him a piece of paper tacked to the bottom. There, in a fine script, were these words: "Father was seated in this chair when he was stricken July 4, 1826. [signed] John Quincy Adams."

The big comfortable house in Quincy which so many generations of Adamses knew as the "Old House" is not particularly distinguished architecturally. In terms of history, however, it is one of the great American homes. It was purchased in 1787 by John Adams, the ambitious young lawyer, who, with his cousin Sam, was referred to contemptuously by Governor Shirley as "this brace of Adamses." John believed in the law, and demonstrated it by defending the British troops who fired on the Americans in the Boston Massacre. He believed in freedom, and helped make it by signing the Declaration of Independence. He was largely responsible for Washington's appointment as commander in chief when the Revolution broke out. He served abroad from 1778 to 1788, became first envoy to the Court of St. James, Vice President under Washington, and, in 1797, the second President. And in one of those strange and wonderful coincidences of history, he and Thomas Jefferson died on July 4, 1826—the fiftieth anniversary of that Declaration of Independence they both signed and did so much to preserve.

On a hill not far from this house John's wife, Abigail, held the hand of their little boy, John Quincy Adams, and listened to the British guns firing on Breed's Hill. That boy was the sixth President of the United States when his father died, and in 1831 he was elected to the House of Representatives—something achieved by no other President. There he remained for literally the rest of his life. In 1848 he collapsed at his desk and died two days later.

The next owner of the house was John Quincy's son, Charles Francis Adams, who became Lincoln's minister to Britain during the Civil War. Upon his death the mansion passed to his sons, among them Henry, Charles Francis II, and Brooks, the famous writers and historians. Through the years in which this one family made and lived American history, they brought to the "Old House" its fascinating relics—portraits of George and Martha Washington which John Adams paid Edward Savage $46.67 to paint (the receipt is still on the back of the canvas); a cradle that rocked two United States Presidents; and the great collection of books in the library (facing page). Under the lid of John's desk, used when the house was the summer White House, is an index to his personal filing system, with headings such as "From Secretary of War and Navy," "Drafts of Speeches," and "Letters from General Washington."

ROBERT W. KELLEY, *Life*

Four generations of famous Adamses made the "Old House" in Quincy their summer home.

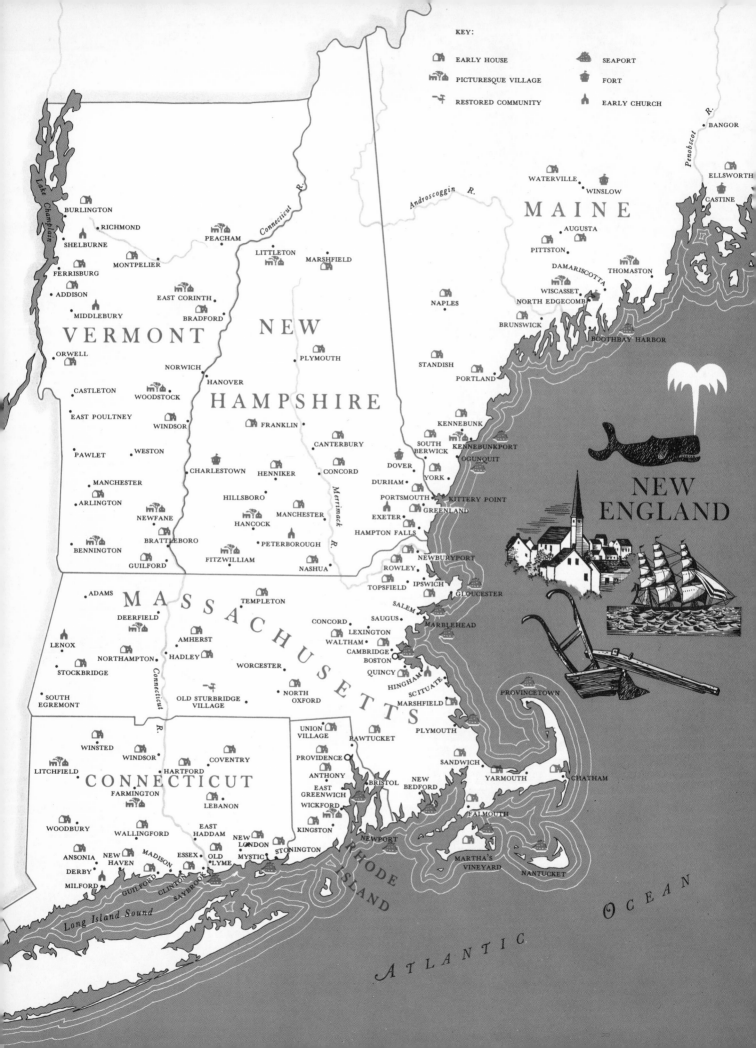

A note about the listings: To supplement the text, a list of interesting places follows each geographic section of the book. Obviously it would be impossible to catalog all the historically important sites in the United States or to pass judgment on their relative significance. These lists have been compiled from information furnished or checked by authorities in each region. But it is not possible to ensure that the condition of sites listed here will remain unchanged as time passes. So far as can be determined, these locations are open to the public unless otherwise noted; but the reader should check with the local authorities for admission prices, dates and hours for visiting, street addresses, and detailed information.

CONNECTICUT

ANSONIA
Richard Mansfield House (1747) Example of a Connecticut salt-box.

BRANFORD
Branford Electric Trolley Museum Operates over thirty ancient horse, cable, and electric trolleys on its mile of track.

CLINTON
Stanton House (1789) Has exhibits of early country store, period furnishings and décor.

COVENTRY
Nathan Hale Homestead (1776) A fine old farmhouse, furnished in the period.

EAST LYME
Thomas Lee House (1660) An important 17th-century house, with projecting window frames, hewn steps, and exhibits of china and kitchen utensils.

EAST HADDAM
Nathan Hale School Where Hale taught 1773-74.

ESSEX
This Connecticut River town is preserved almost intact from the past. The furnishings of the *Pratt House* (c. 1725) and the steamboat print collection of the *Griswold Inn* (1776) are notable.

FARMINGTON
A beautiful old town, with well preserved 17th- and 18th-century architecture. *The Stanley-Whitman House* (c. 1660) is one of finest surviving frame houses. Most houses privately owned, including four *Cowles dwellings* and the *Judd Homestead.*

GREENWICH
Putnam Cottage (c. 1731) Originally Knapp's Tavern where General Putnam was supposedly staying in 1779 when surprised by British.

GROTON
Fort Griswold (1781) Earthworks of fort stormed by British under Benedict Arnold.

GUILFORD
Hyland House (1690) Where America's first town clock was built.
Henry Whitfield House (1639) Very rare 17th-century stone house with massive chimney. Probably Connecticut's oldest dwelling.

HARTFORD
Old State House (1796) Designed by Bulfinch, this fine early Federal building is in striking contrast to a neighboring skyscraper. Has a famous unsupported spiral staircase and some period furniture.
Mark Twain House A rambling Victorian residence where the author lived, 1874-94.

LEBANON
Revolutionary War Office (1775-83) Small building used by Governor Trumbull.
Jonathan Trumbull House (1740)

LITCHFIELD
Another lovely town, full of fine buildings. *Ethan Allen Birthplace,* a small gambrel-roofed house, is reputedly town's oldest. Other good examples are the privately-owned *Benjamin Tallmadge House* (1775), *Tapping Reeve House* (1773) beside the first American law school, and the magnificent *Congregational Church* (*see* p. 58).

MADISON
Nathaniel Allis House (1739)

MILFORD
Eels-Stowe House (1669) Used as a hospital during the Revolutionary War.
First Congregational Church One of the loveliest churches in Connecticut.

MYSTIC
A town known chiefly for its *Marine Museum* and reconstructed seaport with old shops, sail loft, and rope walks (*see* p. 28).

SAMUEL CHAMBERLAIN

Henry Whitfield House, Guilford

The famous whaler *Charles W. Morgan* and the windjammer *Joseph Conrad* are moored alongside the wharf. Nearby is the fine *Stillman Whaling Museum.*

NEW HAVEN
Bowditch House (c. 1815) Where Eli Whitney died. Has frequent art exhibitions.
Connecticut Hall (1752) Oldest building at Yale, where Nathan Hale roomed.
New Haven Colony Historical Society Has a model of Whitney's original cotton gin.
Pardee-Morris House (c. 1680) Burned by British, 1779, and rebuilt same year. Has early American furnishings, herb garden.

NEW LONDON
Nathan Hale School (1774) Building where patriot taught stands in "Yᵉ Antientest Burying Ground," laid out in 1653.
Hempstead House (1678) House used as Underground Railway station. Shows development of Colonial architecture.
Old Town Mill Established by John Winthrop, Jr., in 1650, rebuilt in 1742.
Shaw Mansion (1756) Impressive stone house with 19th-century porches. Home of New London County Historical Society.

NORWICH
The *Grave of Uncas,* Captain John Mason's Mohegan ally in the Pequot War, is in a small enclosure off the Chelsea Parade. Lincoln spoke at *Breed Hall* before the Civil War.

OLD LYME
A good many houses in this peaceful village contain treasures from its seafaring days. Two of the noteworthy buildings are the *Congregational Church,* a fine copy of the original (1816); and the *Moses Noyes House* (1712), altered in 1750 and 1816, showing the changing pattern of colonial architecture. The *Griswold House* (1798) has an elaborately carved doorway.

SAYBROOK
William Tully House (1750) Fine doorway.

STONINGTON
Denison House (Pequotsepos Manor, 1717) Restored and furnished. By appointment.
Stonecrop Farm (1750) Delightful house furnished with heirlooms. By appointment.
Old Stone Lighthouse This octagonal tower contains figurehead of the *Great Republic,* largest sailing vessel of her era.
Peleg Brown House (1798)

STRATFORD

Judson House (1723) Typical New England home with fine interiors, slave quarters, overhanging gables and notable 12-foot chimney.

WALLINGFORD

Wallingford Historical Society (1770) Gambrel-roofed residence with antiques and documents.

Nehemiah Royce House (1672) Exhibit of 17th-century furniture, pewter, costumes, china. Open summers.

WETHERSFIELD

Williams House (1680) Best example of transition from end-chimney, one-room house to central-chimney style, with addition of second room. Very fine restoration, completely furnished. Private.

Webb House (1752) A real showplace. Scene of Washington-Rochambeau conference, 1781. Beautifully furnished and maintained.

WINDSOR

Ellsworth Homestead (1740) Fine late-Colonial home of Oliver Ellsworth. Well furnished in period.

Walter Fyler House (1640) Headquarters of the Windsor Historical Society.

WINSTED

Solomon Rockwell House (1813) A graceful structure with unusual porticos. Museum of the Winsted Historical Society.

WOODBURY

Glebe House (17th-18th century) Scene of organization of Episcopal Church in the United States, 1783.

MAINE

AUGUSTA

Blaine Mansion (1830-36) Home of 1884 presidential nominee, now Governor's Mansion.

Fort Western (1754) Restored garrison

Jacataqua Oak Named for French-Indian princess courted here by Benedict Arnold, 1775.

State House (1832) Much-restored Bulfinch building.

BOOTHBAY HARBOR

Grounded old schooners are reminders of the great days of sail (*see p. 23*).

BRUNSWICK

Bowdoin College Founded 1794; noted alumni include Hawthorne, Longfellow, Admiral Peary. *Walker Art Gallery* on campus has important colonial portraits. *Harriet Beecher Stowe House* (1804) Where *Uncle Tom's Cabin* was written.

BUXTON

Quillcote (1805) Home of Kate Douglas Wiggin.

CASTINE

Blake House (1797) Original furnishings. *Fort George* (1779) British earthworks on height once stormed by Massachusetts forces.

COLUMBIA FALLS

Ruggles House (c. 1820) Famed for porch and window detail, interior woodwork.

ELLSWORTH

Black House (1802) One of the best early Federal houses, with excellent museum.

GORHAM

Baxter Museum (c. 1798)

KENNEBUNK

Arnold's Trail Benedict Arnold's 1775 route to Quebec is well marked.

Wedding Cake House Extraordinary gingerbread construction.

KENNEBUNKPORT

Once a fairly important seaport. Many old houses still have the captain's walks. The *Booth Tarkington House* contains a good maritime collection.

KITTERY POINT

Lady Pepperrell House (1760) Elaborate Georgian home built by Sir William's widow.

William Pepperrell House (1682) One of best surviving 17th-century houses in New

SAMUEL CHAMBERLAIN

Wedding Cake House, Kennebunk

England. Built by father of the victor of Louisbourg.

MACHIAS

Burnham Tavern (1770) Revolutionary inn.

NAPLES

The Manor (1799)

NORTH EDGECOMB

Fort Edgecomb (1808-9) Octagonal stronghold with earthwork remains.

Marie Antoinette House (1774) Intended as a refuge for the French Queen; contains some of her belongings.

PITTSTON

Colburn House (1765) Owned by descendants of the man who built bateaux for Arnold's famous march on Quebec. Private.

PORTLAND

Wadsworth-Longfellow House (c. 1785) An excellent early Federal town house.

L. D. M. Sweat Mansion (1800) Has a striking entrance; contains fine works of art.

Tate House (1755) Built for George Tate, mast agent for British Navy, when Portland was center of supply for masts and spars.

SMALL POINT

Sewall family collection of ships' mastheads, bowsprits, figureheads. Private.

SOUTH BERWICK

Hamilton House (c. 1770) Fine mansion in superb riverside-garden setting. Scene of Sarah Orne Jewett's *The Tory Lover*.

Sarah Orne Jewett Home (1774) Birthplace and residence of the regional novelist. Fine interiors furnished with her possessions.

SOUTH WINDHAM

Parson Smith Homestead (1764) Sturdy farmhouse on site of Old Province Fort.

STANDISH

Daniel Marrett House (1789) A typical homestead of the period and region.

THOMASTON

Montpelier A replica of the original structure owned by General Henry Knox, containing personal effects, furniture, Stuart portrait.

WATERVILLE

Redington Museum (1814) Built by veteran of Valley Forge. Old furniture, Indian relics.

WISCASSET

A gracious seaport of distinctive charm, filled with former homes of merchants and sea captains. The *Clapp House* is one of the most picturesque old cottages.

Lee-Payson-Smith House (early 19th century) House of great architectural distinction, with captain's walk, semi-elliptical porch. Private.

Lincoln County Courthouse (1824) Typical Georgian building still in use. Private.

Nickels-Sortwell House (1807-12) One of New England's noblest three-story mansions.

Tucker Mansion (1807-8) Supposedly copy of Scottish manor. Rare elliptical staircase.

Abiel Wood House (1811-24) Distinguished mansion with excellent proportions.

WINSLOW

Fort Halifax (1754) New England's only surviving colonial military blockhouse.

YORK

McIntire Garrison House (c. 1645) Probably the best example of loophole timber building with second-story overhang. Private.

YORK VILLAGE

Jefferds' Tavern (1750) Restored and furnished as it was in Revolutionary times.

Old Gaol (1653) Supposedly the oldest public building in New England. Dungeons still intact. Summer museum.

MASSACHUSETTS

ADAMS
Susan B. Anthony Birthplace (c. 1815)

AMESBURY
Macy-Colby House (1650) Frontier-type home.
Whittier Home (c. 1830) House where most of the author's poems were written.

AMHERST
Emily Dickinson Home (c. 1813) House with important literary associations. Private.
Nehemiah Strong House (1744) Gambrel-roofed house of hand-hewn timbers, old hardware.

ANDOVER
Phillips Academy dominates the many stately homes in this serene town. The *Deacon Amos Blanchard House* (1819) is a fine one.

ARLINGTON
Jason Russell House (c. 1680) Still has bullet holes from battle of April 19, 1775, when Russell and eleven minutemen died here.

ASSINIPPI
Jacobs Farmhouse (1726) Has a fine collection of early fire apparatus in barns.

BARNSTABLE
Crocker Tavern (1754) Stopping place for generations of Cape Cod travelers.

BEVERLY
John Balch House (c. 1638) One wing of house was an early Puritan dwelling.
Cabot House (1781) Home Lafayette visited in 1824 has documents, ships' logs.
Hale House (1697) Built by ancestors of Nathan and Edward Everett Hale.

BOSTON
The city has so many places of historic interest it would be impossible to enumerate them all. Among those of more than usual interest are the *Boston Latin School, Faneuil Hall* (see pp. 37-47), *Old State House* (see p. 37), and the *Athenaeum. King's Chapel, Old South Meetinghouse* (see pp. 37-47), and *Old North Church* (see p. 40) are among the many fine churches which should be included in a tour; and

down at the water's edge the frigate *Constitution* will reward any visitor (see pp. 48-49). The *Massachusetts Historical Society,* oldest in the country, is rich in important historic manuscripts, and the *Museum of Fine Arts* has a fine collection of naval prints and three rooms designed and executed by Samuel McIntire. Few cities possess a finer collection of architecture than the houses in the *Beacon Hill* and *Louisburg Square* sections (see pp. 30-33). One of the most interesting houses to visit is the *Harrison Gray Otis House* (1795) (see p. 32), designed by Bulfinch. Headquarters of the Society for the Preservation of New England Antiquities, it has a fine museum and preserves the patrician setting of post-Revolutionary Boston with complete authenticity. The original portion of the *State House* (1795) is considered Bulfinch's masterpiece. Facing the building is St. Gaudens' fine monument to Robert Gould Shaw, who raised the first company of Negro troops in the Civil War. *Paul Revere's House* (1670) is the oldest in the city (see p. 41), and in nearby Dorchester the *James Blake House* (1648) is an earlier, well-restored example of the steep-roofed Elizabethan dwelling. The *Dillaway House* (1714) and the *Bunker Hill Monument* (on Breed's Hill) recall the siege of Boston during the Revolution (see p. 46).

BOURNE
Aptuxcet Trading Post Reproduction of the place where colonists bartered with Indians.

BOXFORD
Holyoke-French House (1760) Home of descendant of man for whom Mount Holyoke was named.

BROOKLINE
Edward Devotion House (1750) Now surrounded by a modern school. Original furniture, books.

CAMBRIDGE
Brattle House (c. 1727)
Christ Church (1761) Has beautiful interior.
Cooper-Frost-Austin House (c. 1657) Oldest house in Cambridge, with notable fireplace.
Craigie-Longfellow House (1759) Handsome residence which Washington used as headquarters, 1775-76; later Henry W. Longfellow's house.
Harvard Yard The original center of the college retains much of its charm. *Massachusetts Hall* (1720) is Harvard's oldest building; other characteristic structures are the almost identical *Hollis* (1763) and *Stoughton Halls, Holworthy Hall* (1812), and the beautiful *University Hall* (1815), designed by Bulfinch. Tiny *Holden Chapel* (1744) is one of the purest examples of Georgian Colonial architecture.

CHATHAM
Atwood House (1752) One of the best

houses in this old Cape Cod town.

CHELSEA
Bellingham-Cary House (1659) Contains a secret passage and colonial stairway.

COHASSET
Wilson House (1810)

CONCORD
One of Massachusetts' most historic towns, with a great many surviving buildings of unusual interest. Among the fine houses are the *Louisa May Alcott House,* where *Little Women* was written; the *Emerson House;* and the *Old Manse,* all with important literary associations (see pp. 56-57). The *Concord Antiquarian Society Building* houses some fine period rooms, with good Emerson and Thoreau collections, and is one of New England's best exhibits. The "rude bridge," French's statue of the minuteman, *Monument Green, Wright Tavern* (1747), and *Sleepy Hollow Cemetery* will interest anyone retracing the path of the town's important battle (see pp. 44-45). Also in Concord is Amos Bronson Alcott's picturesque *School of Philosophy* and the first normal school in New England, and just south of the village is Thoreau's *Walden Pond* (see p. 57).

CUMMINGTON
William Cullen Bryant Homestead (1800) Boyhood home, where poet wrote "Thanatopsis."

DANVERS
Rebecca Nurse House (1678) Home of the aged woman executed in the witchcraft hysteria.
Jeremiah Page House (1754) Patriot's home.
James Putnam House (1780) Birthplace of famous lawyer and staunch loyalist.

DANVERSPORT
Samuel Fowler House (1810) Beautifully preserved brick house with original wallpapers.

DEDHAM
Fairbanks House (1636) Reputedly the oldest frame house in the United States.

Massachusetts Hall, Cambridge

Old Ship Church, Hingham

SAMUEL CHAMBERLAIN

Door from Old Indian House, Deerfield

DEERFIELD

One of the loveliest of all New England villages where, with the exception of the *Academy,* almost nothing has changed for more than 200 years. Most of the houses along the ancient, tree-lined street are privately owned, but enough of them are open to make a visit to Deerfield a most rewarding one (*see* pp. 20-21).

DUXBURY

John and Priscilla Alden House (1653) Said to be the only house extant actually occupied by *Mayflower* Pilgrims.

GLOUCESTER

James Babson Cooperage Shop (1658) One of New England's earliest stone buildings.
Cape Ann Historical House Contains an exhibition of ship models and charts.
Gloucester Fisherman A bronze memorial to fishermen lost at sea.
Sargent-Murray-Gilman-Hough House (1768) Winthrop Sargent's wedding present to his daughter Judith.

GREAT BARRINGTON

William Cullen Bryant House (1759) Two-and-a-half-story house where the poet was married.

HADLEY

Old Hadley Farm Museum (1782) Large remodeled barn with collection of farm implements.
Porter-Phelps-Huntington House (1752) Has a fascinating collection of family papers and household articles from every generation which has lived in the house.

HANOVER

"Drummer" Samuel Stetson House (1694)

HARVARD

Prospect Hill A group of interesting buildings has been assembled on this commanding site, including *Fruitlands* (c. 1717), where Bronson Alcott tried to create a "New Eden," an early *Shaker House* (1781), and a fine *American Indian Museum.*

HAVERHILL

Buttonwoods (1814) Named for nearby trees, planted 1739. Once home of Salton-

stall family. Contains several collections.
John Ward House (1645) A fine preservation of the town's earliest frame house.
John Greenleaf Whittier Birthplace (1688)

HINGHAM

Old Garrison House (c. 1635) Used as a fort against Indians by early colonists.
Old Ordinary (c. 1650) Good example of an early tavern. Houses Hingham Historical Society collection of old furniture.
Old Ship Church (1681) The only surviving Puritan church. Construction shows influence of ship carpenters who built it.

IPSWICH

Emerson-Howard House (c. 1648) A charming building with narrow hewn overhang.
Hart House (1640) Fine period rooms, one of which was chosen by Metropolitan Museum as excellent example of 17th-century work.
Whipple House (1640) Another excellent example of Puritan architecture. Overhanging gable end, massive chimney, fine furnishings.

KINGSTON

Major John Bradford House (1674) Furnished in style of an authentic Pilgrim home.

LANESVILLE

A fishing village with a striking view of the coast.

LENOX

Church on the Hill (1805) A lovely sight in this handsome old town.

LEXINGTON

The town where the Revolution's first shots were fired has many reminders of the event (*see* pp. 40-44). Among them are the *Buckman Tavern,* where minutemen met; *Hancock-Clarke House* (1698), where Samuel Adams and John Hancock were sleeping when Paul Revere arrived (house now contains a fine collection of Revolutionary relics); *Munroe Tavern* (1695), Earl Percy's headquarters; *Lexington Green;* the statue of Captain John Parker; and the monument to the minutemen.

LINCOLN

Hartwell Farm (1636) Near here Revere, Prescott, and Dawes were caught by British. Prescott escaped, rode to warn Concord (*see* p. 41).

LOWELL

James McNeill Whistler Birthplace (1824)

MANCHESTER

Trask House (c. 1830) Contains model of *Constitution* made by one of its sailors.

MARBLEHEAD

This old seaport has a wealth of fine houses, among them the *King Hooper Mansion* (1728) built by a great merchant prince (private); *Jeremiah Lee Mansion* (1768), a beautiful Georgian home with magnificent staircase; *St. Michael's Church* (1714) and *Old North Church* (1824); the *Old Town House* (1727); and the *Old Brig* (1720), where a famous fortuneteller lived in the shadow of *Old Burial Hill.* Other sites worth seeing are *Fort Sewall* (1742), the *Old*

Tavern built in 1680, and the private home once owned by Revolutionary hero General John Glover.

MARSHFIELD

Winslow House (1699) Fine early house.

MARTHA'S VINEYARD

This triangular island off Cape Cod was first permanently settled in 1642, although Leif Ericson may have visited it hundreds of years earlier. Among the charming old homes which were here in the whaling days is the *Thomas Cooke House* (1776). Others are the *Norton House* (1752) in Oak Bluffs, and the *Captain George Claghorne House* near Peaked Hill, home of the designer of "Old Ironsides." During the Revolution British men-of-war took refuge in *Tisbury Harbor* (Vineyard Haven), and the town was raided by Major General Grey in 1778. Vineyard Haven's *Historical Building* contains relics of the early settlers.

MEDFORD

Andrew Hall (1703)
Royall House (1638) Earliest part was built by Governor John Winthrop.
Peter Tufts House (1678) Said to be the oldest brick building in New England.

SAMUEL CHAMBERLAIN

Hancock-Clarke House, Lexington

NANTUCKET

Memories of the great whaling days linger on in Nantucket's quiet old streets (*see* pp. 26-27). The *Jethro Coffin House* (1686) is the island's oldest. On its chimney is an ornament to discourage witches from entering. The *Starbuck Houses* on Main Street, built for three brothers of the family, are among the many fine ones along that avenue. The town is full of homes built by shipmasters and whalers, and it has probably the finest *Whaling Museum* in the country. The *Old Mill* is a conspicuous landmark. The *Maria Mitchell Memorial House* (1790) is well worth seeing as the home of America's first woman astronomer, and *Rotch's Warehouse* and *Sankaty Light* are additional points of interest.

NEW BEDFORD

Another great whaling port. New Bedford's

industrialization has removed much of the atmosphere Nantucket still possesses, but the town has many spots which will reward the visitor. Some of these are **Seaman's Bethel Church,** dedicated in 1832 to the port's mariners and immortalized in *Moby Dick;* the **Bourne Office Building** and the famous **Bourne Whaling Museum;** as well as the **Whaleman's Statue.**

NEWBURY
Tristram Coffin House (1651) A well-preserved example of 17th-century New England.

Short House (c. 1732) Mellow brick-ended wood house with notable doorway and fine interior paneling and furnishing.

Swett-Ilsley House (c. 1670) Where Newbury's first newspaper was printed.

NEWBURYPORT
The harbor once filled with ocean-going vessels is now clogged with sand, but the town has some excellent examples of early New England architecture. The stately houses on **High Street** are some of the best samples of Federal style, and among the places which should be seen are the **Pettingell-Fowler House** (1792); the **Jackson-Dexter House** (private), built in 1771, once the residence of "Lord" Timothy Dexter, who sold warming pans to natives of the West Indies; **Old South Church** (1756), where George Whitefield preached; the **Sumner House;** and the **Cushing House.**

NORTH ADAMS
Fort Massachusetts (1745) A restoration of a stronghold important in Indian wars.

NORTHAMPTON
Isaac Damon House (1812) Built by one of region's outstanding architects; contains a number of Jenny Lind mementos.

Cornet Joseph Parson House (1658) Interesting exhibits of housewares, costumes.

Sessions House (1700) Secret staircase said to have been used by General Burgoyne.

Wiggins Country Store This is a faithful picture of a rural Yankee general store.

NORTH ANDOVER
Historical Society Cottage (1796) Gives an accurate picture of modest 1800 homestead.

NORTH OXFORD
Clara Barton Birthplace (1804)

PITTSFIELD
Arrowhead Herman Melville spent most of his later life here.

PLYMOUTH
The site of the Pilgrims' colony is rich with historic buildings and collections. On **Cole's Hill** is the Pilgrim burial ground overlooking the early settlement. The **Howland House** (1667) is one of the finest old residences, but there are many others, including the **William Crowe House;** the **William Harlow House** (1677), built of timbers from the original fort; and the **Kendall Holmes House** (1666), all unusually interesting. Some of the earliest Pilgrim structures have been reproduced at **Plimoth Plantation,** and the **Mayflower Society House** (1754), built by the great-grandson of Governor Winslow, is worth

visiting. The **Antiquarian House** (1809) is characteristic of a prosperous family dwelling in the early 19th century. No visit to Plymouth would be complete, of course, without seeing historic **Plymouth Rock** and the statue of Massasoit, the Pilgrims' friend (*see* pp. 12-15).

PROVINCETOWN
There are several monuments in this picturesque Cape Cod town marking the site of the Pilgrims' first landing in America.

QUINCY
Probably no family in the United States participated more in this country's history than the Adamses, and Quincy is fortunate in having their priceless heirlooms. The birthplaces of John and John Quincy

Pioneers' Village, Salem

Adams are both here, but one of the nation's greatest treasures is the **Old House,** built in 1731, purchased by John Adams, and used continuously by the family until it was presented to the government a few years ago. The rooms, furnishings, and the magnificent library are exactly as they were when the family lived here (*see* pp. 60-61). The **Quincy Homestead,** begun about 1636 and remodeled in 1706, was the birthplace of Dorothy Quincy, John Hancock's wife.

READING
Parker Tavern (1694) A fine salt-box.

ROCKPORT
Old Castle (1715) A comfortable early dwelling in this famed artists' colony.

ROWLEY
This early town has many fine houses, among them the **Chaplin-Clark-Williams House** (1671), open on request; the **Platts-Bradstreet House** (c. 1677); and the **Burnham Inn** (1640), many of whose rooms are in the Metropolitan Museum of Art.

SALEM
No seaport in New England has more associations with the great sailing days than Salem (*see* pp. 24-25), and the town is also important as one of the earliest settlements (*see* pp. 16-19). The **Pioneers' Village** is a reconstruction of the wilderness settlement,

and nearby is a full-scale model of the ship **Arbella.** One of the best Puritan houses is the **Hathaway House** (1682), one of a group near the **House of Seven Gables** (c. 1688). The latter is probably the house Hawthorne immortalized, and has an exceptionally interesting collection of fine furnishings as well as the famous secret staircase (*see* p. 19). The **Witch House** (c. 1662) was the home of a witchcraft judge, and the little **John Ward House** in the garden of the Essex Institute contains an early cent shop. **Gallows Hill** is still a grim reminder of the witchcraft days (*see* p. 18). The **Retire Beckett House,** built in 1655, is another in the House of Seven Gables group. **Chestnut Street** is one of the most beautiful avenues in America, and Samuel McIntire's genius is represented elsewhere in the **Peirce-Nichols House** (1782), with McIntire carvings (*see* p. 31); the **Pingree House** (1804), McIntire's finest brick house; and the **Ropes Mansion** (1719) with its exquisitely carved fence. Inside and out, these and many other Salem houses reflect the opulence of the town's wealthy maritime princes. **Salem Maritime National Historic Site** includes the **Custom House** (1819); the **Derby Mansion** (1761); and **Derby Wharf** (1762). Other sites are the **East India House** (1706); the **Essex Institute**'s fine library and museum; and the **Peabody Museum,** which has the finest maritime collection in the country (*see* pp. 24-25).

SANDWICH
This old town was the site of the early glassmaking industry, and the museum has a notable collection of beautiful objects. **Hoxie House** (1637) is oldest on the Cape.

SAUGUS
This reconstruction of the early ironmaking industry is a fine educational exhibit. In addition to the ironworks themselves, the **Ironmaster's House** (1640) is one of the outstanding examples of period architecture, and the nearby **"Scotch" Boardman House** (1651) is equally good (*see* pp. 54-55).

Mission House, Stockbridge

SCITUATE
Cudworth House (1723) A typical gambrel-roofed homestead with shingled sides.

SOUTH EGREMONT
Old Egremont Tavern (1730) Still an inn.

STOCKBRIDGE
Mission House (1739) A well-restored structure in this lovely old community.

OLD STURBRIDGE VILLAGE
One of the finest restorations, which recreates a complete village typical of the region. Implements and furnishings are all authentic, and a visit to the community is an extremely worthwhile experience (*see* pp. 52-53).

TOPSFIELD
Parson Capen House (1683) Certainly one of the finest examples of a Puritan dwelling, with high pitched roof, small panes, weathered siding, and fine interior furnishings (*see* pp. 16-17).

TEMPLETON
Narragansett Historical Building (c. 1810) Serene old house, once a village store.

TOWNSEND HARBOR
Spaulding Gristmill (c. 1840) The old machinery is still in working order.

WALTHAM
Gore Place (1802-4) Considered one of the truly great houses in America, and surely one of the most impressive (*see* p. 31).
Lyman House (1793) Built from plans by Samuel McIntire.

WATERTOWN
Abraham Browne, Jr., House (c. 1690) Another fine Puritan home, with unique windows (*see* pp. 16-17).

WENHAM
Claflin-Richards House (1664)

WEST SPRINGFIELD
Josiah Day House (1754) One of the extremely rare brick salt-box houses.

New England Colonial Village Buildings dating from 1750 give this restoration a genuine atmosphere of an early community.

WINTHROP
Deane Winthrop House (1637) An early salt-box.

WOBURN
Count Rumford House (1714) Birthplace of Benjamin Thompson, scientist and inventor, who became a count of the Holy Roman Empire.

WORCESTER
Salisbury House (c. 1835) One of the best Classical Revival houses in New England.

YARMOUTHPORT
Thatcher House (c. 1680) Contains fine paneling of later period than the house.
Winslow-Crocker House (c. 1780) Has fine woodwork and outstanding furniture. Open by appointment.

NEW HAMPSHIRE

CANTERBURY
Shaker Village, nearby, is a group of white frame structures dominated by the *Meetinghouse* (1792). A brick building displays products made by members of the religious community (*see* p. 59).

CONCORD
Boston & Maine Railroad Station Has one of the old Concord coaches on display.
New Hampshire Historical Society Holds a rare collection of N.H. records and manuscripts, furniture, china, glassware, and paintings. Sculpture on the building is by Daniel Chester French.
State House The front part of this neoclassic building was completed in 1819.

CORNISH
St. Gaudens Memorial (1800) Originally a country tavern, later the sculptor's studio. Contains many examples of his work.

DOVER
Dame Garrison (1675) Built as a protection against Indian raids in this vicinity. Preserved as part of *Woodman Institute*.
Guppy House (1690) A two-story salt-box, notable for construction. Not open.

DURHAM
General John Sullivan House (c. 1750) A handsome Colonial house in fine condition.

EXETER
Cincinnati Hall (1721) This house was used as the state treasury during the Revolution.
Congregational Church (1798) Has unique façade.
Gilman-Clifford House (1658) A garrison house in the Indian wars.

FITZWILLIAM
This pretty little village has a well-kept common, a graceful old church, and a number of fine houses representative of the period.

FRANKLIN
Daniel Webster Birthplace Reproduction of small frame house where the great orator was born.

GREENLAND
Weeks House (c. 1670) One of New England's oldest brick houses.

HAMPTON
General Jonathan Moulton House Some rooms from this house have been removed to the Metropolitan Museum of Art, but much remains.

HAMPTON FALLS
Governor Meshech Weare House (1748) Home of an important Revolutionary figure.

HANCOCK
Historical Building (c. 1800) For many years a tavern on the Hancock-Milford Turnpike; has good historical collection.

SAMUEL CHAMBERLAIN

Town Hall, Fitzwilliam

HANOVER
Dartmouth Hall A facsimile of original structure built at the college in 1791.

HENNIKER
Ocean-Born Mary House (c. 1760) Named for child born at sea while pirates were boarding ship. The pirate captain gave her a piece of silk later made into her wedding gown. The house is full of atmosphere.

HILLSBORO
Franklin Pierce Homestead (1804) Boyhood home of the former president is a fine country house of the period. Some original wallpaper and stenciling.

LITTLETON
Another lovely town well worth seeing.

MANCHESTER
Stark House (c. 1760) Home of hero of the Battle of Bennington.

NASHUA
Colonial House (1803) Fine example of late Georgian Colonial style. Not open.
Marsh Tavern (1804) Stagecoach stop on Boston Post Road. Not open.

NEW BOSTON
Wason Memorial Library Has Molly Stark Gun, brass cannon brought to America by Montcalm, captured by Wolfe at Quebec, used by Burgoyne, captured by Stark, retaken by British in War of 1812, finally recaptured by Americans at the Battle of Lake George.

NEW CASTLE
Fort Constitution Originally Fort William and Mary, renamed after raid by Sullivan and Langdon in one of the first armed acts of the Revolution, December, 1774.

NEW IPSWICH
Barrett House (1800) Country mansion with period furniture.

Peirce Mansion, Portsmouth

ORFORD

A beautiful little town with many handsome period houses. Samuel Morey, a resident of Orford, ran a steamboat on the Connecticut River some years before Fulton's experiment on the Hudson.

PETERBOROUGH

Bleakhouse (1792) Owned by Society for Preservation of New England Antiquities; open only to members.
Goyette Museum of Americana Depicts early New England street with typical shops, authentic antiques, vehicles, other items.
MacDowell Colony Famous refuge for creative workers, founded by Edward MacDowell, the composer, and carried on for many years by his widow.
Unitarian Church (1824) One of purest examples of a New England church; by Bulfinch.

PLYMOUTH

Museum of Original U.S. Patent Models Displays American inventions patented 1793-1890.

PORTSMOUTH

One of the handsomest towns on the Atlantic coast, this old seaport boasts some of New England's finest architectural specimens (*see* pp. 34-35). Some of the best are: *Jackson House* (c. 1664), said to be the oldest house in the city and one of the very best examples of a Puritan home; *Folsom-Salter House* (1808), where President Monroe and Samuel F. B. Morse boarded in 1817; *John Paul Jones House* (1758), where the naval hero awaited completion of his ships *Ranger* and *America; Governor John Langdon Memorial* (1784), one of the best early Federal houses; the private *Langley-Boardman House* (c. 1805); imposing brick *Larkin-Rice House* (1815), built by auctioneer of captured British ships; *Jeremiah Mason Mansion* (c. 1809), a well-preserved house with original wallpaper; the lovely old *Moffatt-Ladd House* (1763) overlooking the waterfront; *Peirce Mansion* (1799), designed by Bulfinch but, unfortunately, much altered; the *Portsmouth Athenaeum* (1803), which has valuable collections of documents, portraits, and ship models, besides its fine library; the *Portsmouth Public Library* (1809), built from Bulfinch designs; *Rundlet-May House* (1806), with unusual coach house; *Pheadris-Warner House* (1716), usually considered the finest brick town house of its period; *Jacob Wendell House* (1789), one of the best-preserved houses in the U.S.; the privately owned *Wentworth-Gardner House* (*see* pp. 32-33) one of America's best examples of Georgian architecture. *Sheafe's Warehouse* on the waterfront is where Jones fitted out the *Ranger. St. John's Church* (1807) contains a bell captured at Louisbourg and recast by Paul Revere. The *Thomas Bailey Aldrich House* (1790) was the scene of *The Story of a Bad Boy.* About two miles from the center of town is the *Governor Benning Wentworth House* (begun in 1695), which is being restored (private). Off the beaten track is the *Governor Levi Woodbury House* (1809), whose original builder, Captain Samuel Ham, hanged himself after the housewarming.

SHARON

Laws House (c. 1800) White cottage with second-story overhang; part of the *Sharon Arts Center.*

RHODE ISLAND

ANTHONY

General Nathanael Greene Homestead (1770) Built by the Revolutionary hero.

BRISTOL

This quiet old town was once the fourth busiest seaport in America. Many of its old houses are exceptionally fine.

CRANSTON

Thomas Fenner House (1677)

EAST GREENWICH

Kent County Courthouse (1750) One of the few colonial governmental structures still in use. Kept in excellent condition.

EAST PROVIDENCE

Philip Walker House (1679) Private.

JAMESTOWN

Old Windmill (1787)

JOHNSTON

Clemence-Irons House (c.1680)

KINGSTON

This quiet town, with elm-lined main street, is almost untouched by commercialism and has a large number of fine old buildings, such as the *Congregational Church* (1820); *Old Kingston Courthouse,* where the General Assembly met in 1776; *Kingston Inn* (c. 1757), with its interesting old taproom; the *Post Office,* built before 1759; and many fine houses, nearly all of them privately owned.

LINCOLN

The *Eleazer Arnold House* (c. 1687) in Lincoln is a fine surviving example of the R.I. "stone-ender." Along the *Great Road,* which runs from Providence to Worcester, are many historic sites. One building known as the *Butterfly Factory* (1811) derives its name from a configuration in the stone. It has been made into a private dwelling with the "butterfly" in the chimney. The *Friends Meetinghouse* (1703) is the oldest of any denomination in Rhode Island still open for worship. The ax and adz marks are visible on its ancient timbers. *Hearthside* (1825) is a fine example of period architecture, as are the *Eleazer Whipple* (1676) and *Valentine Whitman* houses (both private). *Moffitt's Mill* (c. 1812) is one of the early water-power mills of the state.

LITTLE COMPTON

In dramatic open country on a wide tip of land jutting into the Atlantic, the town has the *Tomb of Elizabeth Alden Pabodie,* thought to be the first white woman born in New England, and the *Amasa Gray House* (c. 1684), a picturesque, rambling home in nearly original condition (private). *Adamsville,* a sleepy inland village, and *Sakonnet Point* are also within the township limits.

MIDDLETOWN

Whitehall (1729) Quaint hip-roofed house built by the noted Irish philosopher Dean Berkeley. Beautifully restored, it contains fine period furniture and interesting relics.

NEWPORT

The town, founded in 1639, has several distinctly different sections, each of interest

Amasa Gray House, Little Compton

to visitors. The first is the old portion of the city down by the wharves, its narrow, crooked streets little changed from the Newport of 200 years ago. Many sympathetic restorations add to the city's appeal. The *Wanton-Lyman-Hazard House* (late 1600's), a fine Jacobean type, is the oldest in Newport, and there are a number of early churches—among them the first American *Friends Meetinghouse* (1700), *Central Baptist Church* (1733), and *Old Trinity Church* (1726), which resembles Boston's Old North. It retains the first church bell to ring in New England, and the unique wineglass pulpit crowns the interior of one of America's most beautiful churches. *Touro Synagogue* (1763), home of Congregation Jeshuat Israel, which was founded in 1658, is the oldest synagogue in the U.S., and the *Seventh Day Baptist Church* is the oldest of its denomination in the world (*see* pp. 58-59). The *John Mawdsley House* (c. 1680) is an excellent example of Georgian Colonial. Other historic houses are the *Hunter House* (1748), with its unusual paneling; the *Prescott House,* a gambrel-roofed home of fine proportions occupied by a British general in 1777 (not open); *Vernon House,* Rochambeau's headquarters (open by appointment); and *Old Colony House* (1739), one of the finest Colonial brick structures in the country, which was one of the state capitols before 1900. The *Whitehorse Tavern,* built in part before 1673, is being restored. The most curious landmark is *Old Stone Mill* in Touro Park, a circular tower which was the center of controversy for years. Thought by some to have been built by Norsemen, it is now generally accepted as the ruin of a windmill constructed by Benedict Arnold, governor of the colony in the late 17th century and great-grandfather of the Revolutionary traitor. The showplace of resort Newport is *The Breakers,* the huge three-million-dollar "cottage" built by Cornelius Vanderbilt. Other examples of the period are the *Marble Palace,* home of Frederick Prince, and *Crossways* (both private).

Old Stone Mill, Newport

NORTH KINGSTOWN

South County Museum An ancient barn; houses thousands of old tools.

Gilbert Stuart's Birthplace (1755) The water wheel and machinery of the family snuff mill have been restored.

NORTH SMITHFIELD

Practically none of the group of homes known as *Union Village* are open to the public, unfortunately, but the charm of their setting makes a visit here a pleasurable experience.

PAWTUCKET

Daggett House (c. 1685) Set in pleasant surroundings in Slater Park, the house contains exhibits of furniture and glassware.

Old Slater Mill (1793) The first successful cotton mill in the U.S. Restored.

PROVIDENCE

Appropriately, the *First Baptist Meetinghouse* (1775)—founded by Roger Williams and mother church of its denomination—still stands in this early sanctuary of religious freedom (*see* pp. 58-59). Other interesting churches are the *Round Top Church* (1808); *St. John's Cathedral* (1810); and the *First Unitarian Church* (1816). Among the many fine buildings in the city are the *John Brown House* (1786), home of

the R.I. Historical Society, which John Quincy Adams described as "the most magnificent and elegant private mansion that I have seen on this continent"; the *Carrington House* (1812), another fine example of a wealthy merchant's house; and the *Joseph Brown House* (1774); and the *Market House* (1773) which Brown designed. The *Esek Hopkins House* (1756) was the home of the first commander in chief of the American Navy. His brother Stephen was a signer of the Declaration, and his house, built in 1747, also remains. The *Old State House* is where Rhode Island signed its own declaration of independence on May 4, 1776, and *University Hall* (1770) on the Brown campus has many Revolutionary associations. The *John Carter Brown Library* houses a fine collection of early Americana. The *Betsy Williams Cottage* (1773) was the home of a descendant of Rhode Island's founder. Other interesting buildings are the *Shakespeare's Head* (1772), with its garden; the *Seril Dodge House* (c. 1789); the *Truman Beckwith House* (1826); and the *Providence Athenaeum* (1836), which is associated with the romance of Edgar Allan Poe and Sarah Helen Whitman. The *Providence Arcade* (1828), built as a shopping center, is the only surviving structure of its kind. Some noteworthy private homes are the *Joseph Nightingale House* (1791), a fine Federal mansion; the *George Benson House* (1796); the imposing *Thomas L. Halsey House* (1801); and the *Thomas P. Ives House* (1806).

SAUNDERSTOWN

Edward P. Casey House (1725)

WICKFORD

Near Wickford are a number of historic sites, including *Smith's Castle,* believed to be the location of Roger Williams' trading post. The *Daniel Updike* (1794) and *Immanuel Case* (1786) houses, and the *Cottrell House* (1745), built by John Updike (all private), are good examples of 18th-century homes. *St. Paul's Episcopal Church* (1707) is exceptionally fine.

VERMONT

ADDISON

Barnes House An inn for a century; now a treasure house of historical relics, antique furniture, weapons, and Indian artifacts.

Strong Mansion (1796) A fine brick house built by a veteran of the Revolution.

ARLINGTON

Brick Farmhouse (1779) Probably the oldest brick home in Vermont continuously occupied.

BENNINGTON

Stately Vermont homes at their best may be seen in the section called *Old Bennington,* near the *Battle Monument.* A few miles from here, in New York State, is the site of the battle which the stone shaft and a statue of Seth Warner commemorate.

Among the many fine private houses is the *General Robinson Homestead* (1795); and the simple *Old First Congregational Church* (1806) is as lovely as any in New England. The *Historical Museum* contains documents, military relics, and household articles of Vermont pioneers.

BRADFORD

Low Mansion (c. 1796) A classic 26-room house with Doric portico. Private.

BRANDON

Stephen A. Douglas Cottage Birthplace of the "Little Giant," Lincoln's adversary.

BRATTLEBORO

Naulahka (1892) This Indian-style bungalow was built by Rudyard Kipling for his bride; he wrote the *Jungle Books* here.

BROWNINGTON

Old Stone House (1836) Contains antiques, costumes, tools, and documents.

BURLINGTON

Ethan Allen Park Site of the farm where Allen spent his last years.

Fleming Museum of the University of Vermont Has much valuable historical material; the collection of Indian relics is outstanding.

Grassemount (1804) Considered the best Georgian-style house in Vermont; now a dormitory of the University.

Greenmount Cemetery Graves of Ethan Allen and other Revolutionary soldiers.

CALAIS

Kent Tavern (1833) Built by the grandfather of Atwater Kent. Now a museum, owned by the Vermont Historical Society.

CASTLETON
Federated Church (1833) Greek and Gothic styles combine in this meetinghouse. Has a magnificent pulpit.
Langdon-Cole House (1833) A charming oddity, with bay windows from ground to roof. Private; open by appointment.

EAST CORINTH
Certainly one of Vermont's most-photographed villages, perhaps because it looks the part.

EAST DORSET
Site of first marble quarry in the state.

EAST MONTPELIER CENTER
Meetinghouse (1823) The only meetinghouse left in Vermont in its original condition.

EAST POULTNEY
Eagle Tavern (c. 1790) A distinguished building where Ethan Allen was a frequent guest and Horace Greeley later boarded. The columns were originally cut as masts for the British Navy.

FAIRFIELD
Chester A. Arthur House A reproduction of the former President's birthplace.

FERRISBURG
Rokeby (c. 1784) Home of poet Rowland E. Robinson; once an Underground Railway station.

GRAND ISLE
Jedediah Hyde Log Cabin (1783) A log cabin of rot-resistant white cedar still perfectly sound, built by a Revolutionary engineer.

GUILFORD
Benjamin Carpenter House (c. 1722) Has unusual Palladian windows. Private.

HUBBARDTON
The site of the only Revolutionary battle fought on Vermont soil, in which Seth Warner and his Green Mountain Boys delivered the first setback to General Burgoyne's campaign. A museum is under construction.

MANCHESTER
This town, which has one of the handsomest streets in the state, was for many years the summer home of Robert Todd

SAMUEL CHAMBERLAIN

Old First Congregational Church, Bennington

Lincoln. He pursued his hobby of astronomy at an observatory which he built at his residence, *Hildene* (private).

MIDDLEBURY
Battell House (1814) One of Vermont's best large houses.
Congregational Church (1809) Similar to Bennington's church, but with a more elaborate steeple.
Sheldon Museum Devoted to early Vermont life. Period furnishings.

MONTPELIER
Admiral George Dewey House Birthplace of the Manila Bay hero. Private.
Museum and Library of the Vermont Historical Society Has a rich collection of historical relics, including the Stephen Daye press, oldest printing press north of Mexico.

MORRISVILLE
Noyes House (c. 1820) A museum of local history.

NEWFANE
Windham County Courthouse (c. 1825) A noble Greek-style building.

NORWICH
Olcott-Johnson House (1773) Has some of the finest paneling in this region. Private.

ORWELL
Willcox-Cutts House (1843) Greek Revival, with fine staircase and ceiling. Private.

PAWLET
Sargent-Leach House (1800) A handsome house in a village which was once more prosperous. Private.

PEACHAM
A once-influential village, now a pleasant, secluded place of old homes and orchards (*see* pp. 10-11).

PLYMOUTH
Calvin Coolidge Homestead Here, at 2:47 A.M., August 3, 1923, Coolidge was sworn in as President by his father, a notary public.

RICHMOND
Round Church (1812) Actually a 16-sided building with octagonal cupola. Vermont's first union church, built by five sects.

ROCKINGHAM
Meetinghouse (c. 1787) A well-proportioned, austere house of worship.

SHAFTSBURY CENTER
Governor Galusha House (1804) A sophisticated dwelling, built for a Revolutionary hero and probably designed by Fillmore. Private; open on request.
Munro-Hawkins House (c. 1820) A surprisingly aristocratic farmhouse.

SHELBURNE
Shelburne Museum A unique outdoor museum of Americana, housed in authentically restored buildings, including the *Dutton House* (1782), a Vermont version of the salt-box, superbly furnished (*see* pp. 50-51); and the steamer *Ticonderoga*.

SOUTH HERO
Ebenezer Allen Tavern Site The farmhouse now on the site is thought to incorporate part of the original tavern. It was

SAMUEL CHAMBERLAIN

Colchester Lighthouse, Shelburne Museum

after a convivial night here with his cousin Ebenezer that Ethan Allen died, in 1789.

STRATTON
Daniel Webster Memorial Acre Beautiful mountain site where, in 1840, Webster addressed a crowd of 15,000 New Englanders.

SUDBURY
Vail House (1826) This farm has been in the same family since 1763. Has interesting interior with family collection. Private.

VERGENNES
In the square is a monument to Commodore Thomas Macdonough, who established a shipyard at Vergennes during the War of 1812, to strengthen the defenses of Lake Champlain. The fleet built here defeated the British in the Battle of Plattsburgh, September 11, 1814, one of the most decisive actions of the war. The *General Samuel Strong House* (1793), now an antique shop, is notable for fine proportions.

WALLINGFORD
This peaceful town is typical of many attractive New England villages. The *Old Stone Shop*, where Lyman Batcheller established his first pitchfork factory in the 1830's, is a picturesque building, now an antique shop.

WETHERSFIELD
Warren-Maxwell House Dignified whitewashed brick house; notable ell. Private.

WESTON
The *Farrar-Mansur House* (1797) built as an inn and now maintained as a house museum, is next door to *Vermont Guild of Old Time Crafts and Industries.* The town has a typical old-time *Country Store.*

WEYBRIDGE
U.S. Morgan Horse Farm Operated by the Department of Agriculture to perpetuate the famous breed of horses originated in Vermont in the 1790's.

WINDSOR
Old Constitution House (c. 1768) Tavern where Vermont's constitution was written, 1777. Now a museum.
South Meetinghouse (1798)

WOODSTOCK
Dana House (1807) This is a fine period house in one of Vermont's most attractive old towns. Contains a museum.

OVERLEAF: KOSTI RUOHOMAA, BLACK STAR

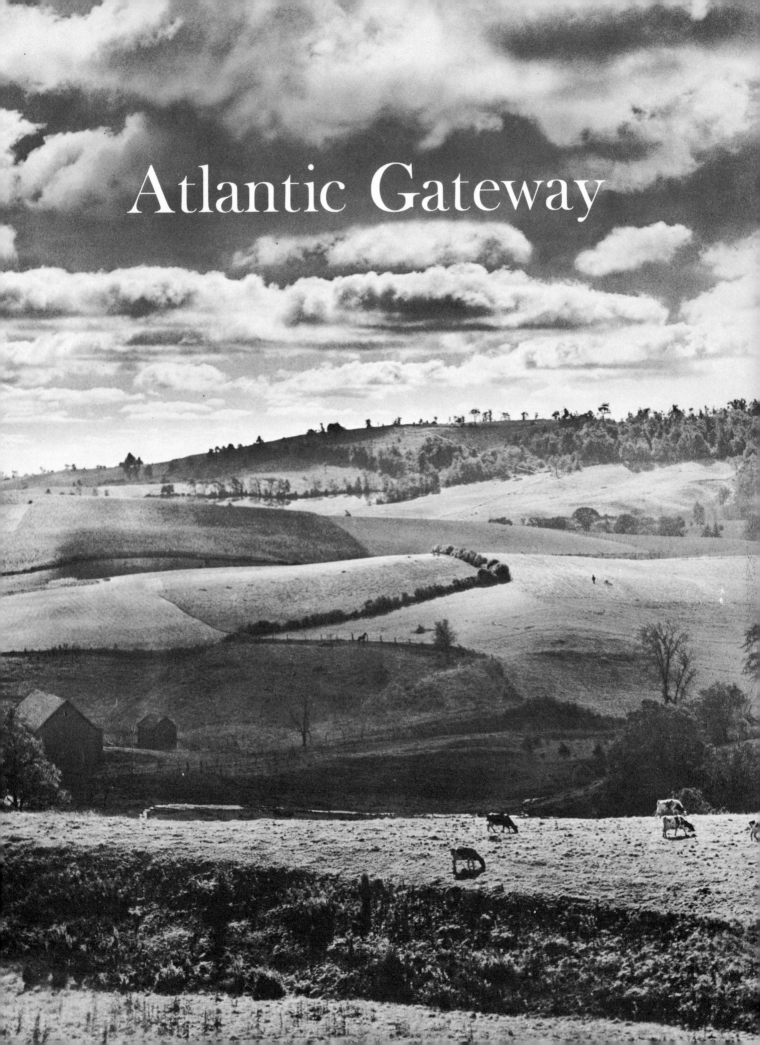

Atlantic Gateway

Peter Stuyvesant

The Hudson River Valley

From the east bank, Ichabod Crane paused to look out over the great river. As he watched, "The sun gradually wheeled his broad disk down into the west. The wide bosom of the Tappan Zee lay motionless and glassy, excepting that here and there a gentle undulation waved and prolonged the blue shadow of the distant mountain. . . . A slanting ray lingered on the woody crests of the precipices that overhung some parts of the river, giving greater depth to the dark-gray and purple of their rocky sides. A sloop was loitering in the distance, dropping slowly down with the tide, her sail hanging uselessly against the mast; and as the reflection of the sky gleamed along the still water, it seemed as if the vessel was suspended in the air."

This was the way Washington Irving remembered the Hudson in 1819. So unchanged is the picture that he could have been describing the "mighty deep-mouthed river" seen by Giovanni da Verrazano in 1524, Henry Hudson and the crew of the *Half Moon* in 1609, or the visitor today. On a rocky peak in the Adirondacks which the Indians called "the cloud splitter" lies Lake Tear-of-the-Clouds, from whose waters a little brook begins. Joined by others, the deepening stream flows southward for over 300 miles, past Storm King, Bear Mountain, and the awesome cliffs of the Palisades, past the great piers of Manhattan Island, and then channels a deep undersea canyon that extends into the vast Atlantic more than 135 miles beyond Ambrose Lightship and nearly a mile and a half below the surface of the ocean.

In the little towns along its banks once stood the whitewashed or yellow brick houses, overhung with trees, where broad-hatted burghers sat with their *vrouws* to smoke an evening pipe. And from Hell Gate to Albany, every cove and crag of the river had its legend. At Hell Gate, a man known as the Pirate's Spook, whom Peter Stuyvesant had killed with a silver bullet, appeared in stormy weather in his little boat. The ghost of Rambout Van Dam, a resident of Spuyten Duyvil who was cursed forever for defying the Sabbath, rowed with muffled oars back and forth across the Tappan Zee. Men heard the eerie chant of a ship's crew at midnight when the moon was up near Point-no-Point, and captains of all real Dutch ships used to lower their peaks when they approached Thunder Mountain, in deference to the goblin in a sugar-loaf hat who was keeper of the mountains.

All these legends persisted when Washington Irving made his first trip up the Hudson in 1800, and as he grew up around Tarrytown and Sleepy Hollow he absorbed the magic of the old Dutch life, as well as the knowledge of those people on whom his charming distortions were based. Katrina Van Tassel of "The Legend of Sleepy Hollow," for example, was actually the belle of the Van Alen family, whose portrait hangs in their old house near Kinderhook. And Ichabod Crane was modeled after a cruel schoolmaster who taught where the present Crane School now stands, near Rensselaer.

The place that mirrors both the legends of Irving and the patroon system that determined the character of the Hudson Valley for more than two centuries is Philipse Castle, in Tarrytown. In 1683 Frederick Philipse built this establishment in the center of his 25,000-acre manor, and the visitor who crosses the little wooden footbridge over the milldam once pic-

OWEN, BLACK STAR

Iroquois Indians paddled out to meet Henry Hudson's *Half Moon* as it sailed up the river named for the explorer.

The restored gristmill and the stone milldam of Philipse Castle look almost
like the original ones which Currier & Ives pictured a hundred years ago.

tured by Currier and Ives can see the house that was home, office, and fortress for the Lord of the Manor. The stone walls of the house are two feet thick, with gun ports in the cellar walls to protect the manor against river pirates. A ramp which was used to take cattle indoors to safety during raids leads to the cellar, which has a dairy, a storeroom for a year's supply of food, and a slave kitchen with an enormous fireplace. Also in the house are the Lord of the Manor's office, and a secret passage which enabled Philipse to eavesdrop on his indentured servants. Furnished in the Dutch tradition—which was to buy what the owner liked and to use it in the most comfortable fashion— the Castle has the earliest tablecloth in America; what is thought to be the first painting of New Amsterdam; a lovely, blue-curtained cabinet bed; and a rare collection of candelabra and candlesticks.

Not far from Philipse Castle are the slave house and the smoke house. The old mill, built by the first Lord as part of his industrial settlement, looks out over the wharf where Philipse's ships once landed their cargoes. Tenant farmers brought their grain to the mill, paid their rents, then made their purchases at the trading post. Down the road from the mill is the Sleepy Hollow Church, built by Philipse, where everyone for

miles around worshiped. It was "the sequestered situation of this church" that made it seem to Irving "a favorite haunt of troubled spirits. . . . To look upon its grass-grown yard, where the sunbeams seem to sleep so quietly, one would think that there at least the dead might rest in peace." TEXT CONTINUED ON PAGE 76

PHILIPSE CASTLE RESTORATION

The Philipse Castle dining room is unmistakably Dutch, with
pewter, delft, and a brass chandelier brought from Holland.

75

John Quidor painted the terrified Ichabod Crane and his horse "Old Gunpowder" fleeing from the Headless Horseman through Sleepy Hollow woods.

TEXT CONTINUED FROM PAGE 75

It was "the very witching time of night" when Ichabod Crane passed the spot where Major André was seized, and neared the "deep black part of the stream, not far from the church, [where] was formerly thrown a wooden bridge; the road that led to it, and the bridge itself, were thickly shaded by overhanging trees, which cast a gloom about it even in the daytime, but occasioned a fearful darkness at night." Today, there is a bridge near the place where Ichabod saw the Headless Horseman, and it is a fittingly short walk to the place where Washington Irving is buried, near the ghosts of the river he loved so well.

There are, of course, other survivals of the Dutch. Fort Crailo in Rensselaer is an old brick building built about 1705 and used as a fortress against the Indians. It was here that Dr. Richard Shuckburgh is supposed to have written the words of "Yankee Doodle," while seated on the curb of an old well in the garden. One entire street in Hurley is practically a museum of these early eighteenth-century houses, and Fishkill, one of the most attractive villages along the Hudson, has the Hendrick Kip House and a Dutch Reformed Church built about 1784. Nearly all the old Hudson Valley towns have one or more examples of the Dutch heritage. Two houses which conjure up an image of the patroon system are Van Cortlandt Manor at Croton-on-Hudson and the Van Rensselaer Manor House at Claverack. Another is Albany's Schuyler Mansion, the scene of Alexander Hamilton's marriage, and "Gentleman Johnny" Burgoyne's con-finement after Saratoga. There are more modest buildings, too—homes of simpler folk which preserve the medieval flavor of their prototypes in Holland. The typical house was a two-story-and-loft building, usually made of Holland bricks, with an entrance stoop and stepped gable which faced the street. Washington Irving's elaborate Sunnyside at Tarrytown, which he described as "full of nooks and corners as an old cocked hat," is actually constructed around the ruins of a simple farmhouse built about 1690. Other good examples are the William Stoutenburgh House in East Park, with its low-pitched gable roof, and the Jan Pieterse Mabie House at Rotterdam Junction, one of the Mohawk Valley's earliest Dutch dwellings.

On Staten Island is the Voorlezer's House, believed to be the nation's oldest elementary school building. A *voorlezer* was a layman hired to teach children and conduct limited religious services, and he lived as well as worked in this house. At Broadway and 204th Street in New York City is the Dyckman House, built in 1783, which is now a museum. Another old Dutch house is the Senate House at Kingston, built in 1676 by Colonel Wessel Ten Broeck and partially burned by the British in 1777.

Although the Dutch tradition has been fastened to the Hudson Valley, this is unfair to the far more

TEXT CONTINUED ON PAGE 78

Washington Irving is buried in the old Sleepy Hollow graveyard which Ichabod Crane passed on his legendary ride.

76

The first successful steam packet on the Hudson was Fulton's *Clermont,* shown here on its maiden voyage in 1807.

TEXT CONTINUED FROM PAGE 77

numerous and influential groups from other nations who followed them. The British fleet which claimed New Netherland in 1664 for James, Duke of York, was the advance agent of thousands of English who eventually dominated the area. The Billopp House on Staten Island and Fraunces Tavern in lower Manhattan, where Washington said farewell to his officers in 1783, are two fine examples of the pre-Revolutionary period. British enthusiasm for the valley kindled the desire of families from all over Europe to settle there, and in 1710 a thousand people poured into New York in one week, and eighteen languages were spoken in the city.

In 1677 a small group of French Protestant refugees had settled in New Paltz, and there are still six fieldstone houses from this Huguenot village grouped along a ridge overlooking the Wallkill River. But in most cases, immigrants who came into the valley found no means of obtaining land from the manor

The sidewheeler *Mary Powell* was the most elaborate of all the "floating palaces" once so numerous on the Hudson.

The variety of architecture along the Hudson is remarkable. At top are two colonial buildings, the Hasbrouck House (left) from the New Paltz Huguenot settlement and the Livingston family manor, Clermont. A pair of curiosities are shown below. Octagonal houses like the one at left were a fad a century ago; Bannerman's Castle, however, is unique, no doubt inspired by the river's Rhine-like setting. At bottom are two homes with a Gothic flavor: Martin Van Buren's Lindenwald (left) and Washington Irving's villa, Sunnyside.

lords whose vast holdings lined the banks of the river. The British had perpetuated the Dutch patroon system by granting huge estates to families like the Livingstons and Schuylers, and at the end of the Revolution, when tenant farmers expected to take over confiscated Tory property like the Philipse lands, they found that patriot manor lords had already snapped them up. Largely for this reason, the valley was never heavily populated between New York and Albany.

Although whaling was once a big and profitable business for Hudson River ports, with Hudson the principal center, this industry was largely the property of Sag Harbor, on Long Island. Salt breezes still blow past the picturesque houses built by whalers 150 years ago, and the town is full of reminders of a time when life centered around the Long Wharf and one of the largest whaling fleets in the country dropped sail there.

The whaling industry never recovered from the Panic of 1857, but new activity took its place on the Hudson. In 1807 Robert Fulton had steamed upstream in the *Clermont,* and his wife's powerful relative, Chancellor Livingston, soon controlled a monopoly on the building and operating of all boats propelled by "force of fire or steam." Fulton's "folly" was christened in honor of the house which still stands near Germantown. Built in 1729-30 by Robert Livingston, it was rebuilt by his son's widow after the British burned it in 1777, and it was here that Fulton married the great-granddaughter of the original owner.

Two monuments to the era of opulence are the Vanderbilt Mansion at Hyde Park and the Ogden Mills Mansion at Staatsburg, both built in the 1890's. The fifty-room Vanderbilt palace, with its elaborate carving and tapestried walls, is surrounded with magnificent old trees and shaded drives which command a majestic view of the great river. During the twentieth century, most of the great manorial estates along the Hudson beween New York and Albany were gradually turned over to institutions. Although the tenant farmers who dreamed of owning land along its banks never fulfilled their dream, today thousands of people live on the river in monasteries, schools, colleges, and in homes for the aged and orphanages which have taken over the great manors.

William Penn's Plantation

William Penn was no industrialist, and if he could return today to discover that his next-door neighbor was a gigantic steel mill he would undoubtedly find this product of man's ingenuity a remarkable thing to behold. But whether he would find it surprising is open to question. The view of U.S. Steel's Fairless Works from the lawn at the reconstructed Pennsbury Manor is not an aesthetic one, but it is, somehow, a tangible reminder of the faith William Penn had in his fellow man. Because of him, men found in Pennsylvania a climate of freedom—an atmosphere which extended into many fields of endeavor—so that Henry Adams, describing the United States of 1800, could judge Pennsylvania the "only true democratic community." It was the "ideal American State, easy, tolerant, and contented," Adams thought, and "had New England, New York, and Virginia been swept out of existence in 1800, democracy could have better spared them all than have lost Pennsylvania." A good deal of the credit belongs to William Penn.

When Penn and 100 followers set sail for the New World in September, 1682, George Fox had a *bon voyage* message for them: "My friends that are gone, and are going over to plant, and make outward plantations in America, keep your own plantations in your hearts, with the spirit and power of God, that your own vines and lilies be not hurt." The formal gardens, orchards, and vineyards at Penn's "beloved manor," along with the main house and its outbuildings, reflect the calm, quiet mood which the great Quaker brought to seventeenth-century America. He purchased his lands from the Indians, for 350 fathoms of white wampum, a score each of blankets, guns, coats, shirts, and stockings, 40 axes, 40 pairs of scissors, 200 knives, and a handful of fishhooks; but Penn was not content with mere commercial settlement. In the spirit of Fox's wish, he confirmed the sale in a treaty of "purchase and amity," meeting the Indians at Shackamaxon in what is now Philadelphia and signing a compact which Voltaire called "the only treaty never sworn to, and never broken." The belt of wampum said to have been presented to Penn by Chief Tammany still exists in the Historical Society of Pennsylvania.

Another Quaker held in high esteem by the Indians was James Logan, who came with Penn on his second trip to America, to serve as his secretary. For half a century Logan represented the proprietary interests in Pennsylvania, carrying on the founder's policy of fair play with the Indians. In 1730 he completed construction of a country house at Germantown which is a fine example of the early Georgian style. A stately dwelling, three stories high, it combined Quaker plainness and taste with elegance, and its overall feeling of simplicity is characteristic of the scholarly, eminent man who built it.

Stenton and Pennsbury Manor are, of course, far more elaborate than the first dwellings built along the Delaware River. The Swedes had settled there in 1638, and were joined not long afterward by a new party headed by Johan Björnsson Printz, a man weighing 400 pounds who was immediately, and understandably, christened "Big Tub" by the Indians. Nothing but the foundation remains of the Printzhof, the old Swedish capitol at Tinicum Island (Essington), but nearby, on Darby Creek, there are still a few examples of that remarkable, durable Swedish contribution to the American frontier—the log cabin. Descendants of the first Tinicum Island settlers also built, in 1700, the red brick church known as Gloria Dei. In those days it was quite a way to the "clever town built by Quakers," but the church is now within the city limits of Philadelphia.

One of the most fascinating remnants of the Penn era was built in 1690 by Hans Millan, in Germantown. The original part of the long, ivy-covered stucco house stood beside what is said to have been an Indian trail, and a later house, erected across the way, was eventually joined to it. The Wyck House, as it is called, has never been sold, but has passed from one relative to another, preserved much as it was, with neither gas nor electricity in the house.

A survivor of the short-lived Swedish colony on the Delaware, this Tinicum Island log cabin was built about 1650. It is probably the oldest structure of its kind in the United States.

LAURENCE LOWRY, REPRINTED FROM *Holiday*

Benjamin West's idealized painting above depicts William Penn's meeting with the Indian chiefs under the elm at Shackamaxon. At left center, Penn points to the charter parchment, while a blanket is held up for the approval of the sachem Tammany, the white-robed Indian standing at right. The photograph at left shows Pennsbury Manor, the reconstructed home of William Penn near Morrisville. The estate faces the Delaware River, on which Penn commuted to Philadelphia by barge in the days before the Main Line. The gravel pits of U.S. Steel's Fairless Works are in the background.

81

THE FOREST AND THE FORTS

CANADA

St. Lawrence River

FORT FRONTENAC

CROWN POINT
(FORT ST. FREDERICK)

FORT TICONDEROGA

Lake Champlain

Lake George

Hudson R.

FORT WILLIAM HENRY

FORT ONTARIO
(OSWEGO)

LAKE ONTARIO

FORT GEORGE FORT ANNE

FORT STANWIX (ROME)

FORT KLOCK STONE ARABIA

Oswego R.

Oneida Lake

Mohawk R. JOHNSTOWN

FORT NIAGARA
(YOUNGSTOWN)

FORT HERKIMER FORT JOHNSON

FORT HENDRICK FORT FREY

FORT ERIE

CHERRY VALLEY FORT PLAIN

SCHENECTADY

LAKE ERIE

SCHOHARIE ALBANY

NEW YORK

Susquehanna River

FORT PRESQUE ISLE
(ERIE)

KINGSTON

FORT LE BOEUF
(WATERFORD)

French Creek

Hudson River

Allegheny R.

WYOMING FORT PITTSTON

FORT VENANGO
(FRANKLIN)

FORTY FORT WILKES-BARRE

PENNSYLVANIA

FORT JENKINS (BERWICK)

Delaware River

FORT AUGUSTA
(SUNBURY)

BETHLEHEM

Ohio R. PITTSBURGH

NEW YORK

FORT McKEE

Juniata River

NEW

FORT PITT
(DUQUESNE)

BUSHY RUN
BATTLEFIELD

FORT HARRIS
(HARRISBURG)

Susquehanna R.

FORT LIGONIER FORT SHIRLEY

BRADDOCK'S
ROAD

TRENTON

CARLISLE

FORBES' ROAD

JERSEY

WHEELING

FORT LOUDON

LANCASTER

PHILADELPHIA

Youghiogheny R.

FORT BEDFORD
(RAYSTOWN)

FORT CHAMBERS

YORK

FORT NECESSITY

Monongahela R.

FORT FREDERICK

FORT CUMBERLAND

BALTIMORE

DELAWARE

WEST VIRGINIA

Potomac River

MARYLAND

ATLANTIC OCEAN

KEY:

■ EXISTING EARLY FORT

□ SITE OF EARLY FORT

The first white men edging westward from the settlements along the central coast found a forest that was simply beyond their imagination. Not in the memory of living men had there been anything quite like it. Nearly twenty centuries had elapsed since the Germanic peoples huddled together in settlements in the great woods, and Europeans had forgotten what a primeval forest was like. The deep impression it made is evident from the way men spoke of it. In their march through the wilderness, General Edward Braddock's men camped near a fearsome place known as the "Shades of Death." And there are stories of men walking through the giant sycamores, walnuts, and towering stands of pine and hardwood for days on end without catching a glimpse of the sun. In Pennsylvania's Cook State Forest Park, where some of the great virgin timber remains, one can get an idea of what it was like.

Fort Niagara

The reconstructed stockade, Fort Necessity

What was there had been there, virtually undisturbed since the last glacier retreated—majestic rivers, the "Endless Mountains," valleys where not even the red man had set foot, deer, buffalo, wolves, and elk, and lonely peaks where the panther screamed. Only the millions of birds who rose above the ancient leaf-banked forest could see its total immensity—the unbroken dark green mass that stretched from the Atlantic to the sea of grass far to the west.

But gradually into this hunting ground of the Shawnees, Delawares, and Mingoes the white man threaded his way, bringing with him those changers of nature, the ax and the plow. Along the tumbling blue ranges of the Alleghenies, isolated little forts and blockhouses sprang up in a protective arc, stretching southwesterly across central Pennsylvania to shield it from the Iroquois. At the Juniata River the line of outposts turned south, following the Conococheague. Beyond this, in 1758, there was only Fort Bedford at Raystown—pointing like an arrow at the heart of the Indian hunting grounds and New France. One hundred miles to the west lay Fort Duquesne, built by the French at the point of a "Y" where the Allegheny and Monongahela meet to form the Ohio.

Fort Klock

In 1758 General John Forbes hacked a road across the mountains, captured Duquesne without firing a shot, and named the place "Pittsbourgh." To anyone visiting the tiny Fort Pitt blockhouse today, it seems inconceivable that its possession affected seriously the destinies of two great empires, yet Forbes' victory was one of the most significant of the French and Indian War.

Behind the four-foot walls and oak doors of the château at Fort Niagara, during the Revolution, the halls were hung with American scalps, for which the English paid the Indians eight dollars apiece. The old earthworks remain at Fort Ontario, a star-shaped redoubt built in 1759, and Fort Necessity has been carefully reconstructed. To the north, along the great corridor of the Mohawk, is the stone mansion named Fort Johnson and, twelve miles away, Johnson Hall with its protecting blockhouse. The Mohawk Valley has other forts—most of them built for peaceful purposes, but used as blockhouses out of necessity—like the farmhouse called Fort Klock, the Dutch Reformed churches at Schoharie and Stone Arabia, and Fort Herkimer church. Eastward, along the famous north-south route of war parties, are the ruins of Fort George. Only a few stones mark the site of Fort St. Frederic, Fort Crown Point has the ruins of two original barracks, and Fort William Henry is restored. At the point where Lake George empties into Champlain, 100 feet above the water, is the stone guardian which has seen more American history than any such place in the country—Fort Ticonderoga.

Ruins of Fort Frederick near Clearspring, Md.

Fort Pitt blockhouse, Pittsburgh

Fort Frey, Palatine Bridge, N.Y.

ILLUSTRATIONS (FROM TOP): OLD FORT NIAGARA; FORT NECESSITY NATIONAL BATTLEFIELD SITE; KOSTI RUOHOMAA, BLACK STAR; A. AUBREY BODINE; PA. DEPT. OF HIGHWAYS; KOSTI RUOHOMAA, BLACK STAR.

Two Roads West

In the middle of the eighteenth century not many men understood that the wardrums that beat along the Mohawk and the Allegheny were pounding out an overture to a struggle which would determine the fate of America, the destiny of France, and the fortunes of England. In the little houses and cabins which were windows in the frontier wilderness men thought of survival, not the fate of empires. But there were those in Paris and London who recognized the importance of the Ohio Valley. The French began building a string of forts such as Presque Isle, Le Boeuf, and Duquesne at the junction of the Monongahela and Allegheny Rivers, and what began as an argument between the French and British over fur-trade rights became a war whose outcome was control of a continent.

In November, 1753, Virginia's Governor Dinwiddie sent George Washington, then 21 years old and a major in the militia, to the commander at Fort Le Boeuf, "to know his Reasons for this unjustifiable Step in invading our Lands." When Washington returned with news that it was the "absolute design" of the French to "take possession of the Ohio," he was sent back again—this time with a few troops—and surprised a French force at Jumonville Glen near a swampy vale called Great Meadows. Nothing but a little plaque marks the grave of the French commander below the rocks at Jumonville Glen where, as Horace Wal-

pole realized, "The volley fired by a young Virginian in the backwoods of America set the world on fire."

There is a fine reconstruction of the "small, palisado'd fort" which Washington built soon afterwards in the Great Meadows and called Fort Necessity because it was quite literally that. This round stockade stands on the site of his only surrender, which took place six weeks after the fight at Jumonville Glen. News of loss of the fort decided the English on a plan of attack against Forts Duquesne, Niagara, Crown Point, and Beausejour, and command of the most important expedition—against Fort Duquesne—was given to Major General Edward Braddock. With over 1,500 men, a unit of artillery, 500 baggage horses, and 150 Pennsylvania wagons, Braddock inched his way across the "Endless Mountains," as the pioneers called the Alleghenies, and crossed the Monongahela at what is now the town of Braddock. The cumbersome train had just started into the woods on the other side of the river when a bloodcurdling war whoop sounded and shots rang out from behind the trees. In the slaughter that followed, few British ever saw their French and Indian attackers. Of 86 English officers, 63 were casualties, including Braddock, whom Washington buried near Fort Necessity. To prevent Indians from desecrating the grave, he had wagons and foot soldiers march over it as the columns began their long retreat. In 1824 workmen repairing Braddock Road came upon a human skeleton, near which they found buttons and insignia of a high-ranking British officer.

The road Braddock followed, traces of which are still visible in the woods not far from Fort Necessity, was blazed originally for the Ohio Company by Nemacolin, a Delaware Indian, and Thomas Cresap, the frontiersman. Extending from Wills Creek (Cumberland, Maryland) to the Monongahela River, it was known variously as Nemacolin's Path, Gist's Trail, Washington's Road, and Braddock Road. Not until 1817, when the Old National Pike replaced it, was the crooked old route abandoned.

Braddock's defeat left the whole frontier unprotected, from Pennsylvania to North Carolina, and death in a painted face swept out of the forest. Settlers were shot, children scalped alive, women and girls tomahawked or burned or dragged away to slavery. Finally, at a moment when Lord Chesterfield was crying "we are undone both at home and abroad," the right man for the hour became head of the govern-

PETER STACKPOLE, *Life*

En route to Fort Le Boeuf, Washington followed this Indian trail through the Pennsylvania wilderness late in 1753.

In Alonzo Chappel's painting (right) a mortally wounded Braddock is transported from the scene of his disaster.

ment in England. Under William Pitt, Quebec and then Montreal fell to the British, and as part of the same campaign Brigadier General John Forbes and 5,000 men headed for Fort Duquesne in the autumn of 1758. Before Forbes' main force arrived the French withdrew, burning the fort behind them. The scope of Forbes' undertaking can be seen by the traveler who takes U.S. Route 30 from Bedford to Pittsburgh, following virtually the same route that was hacked through the "immense uninhabited Wilderness, overgrown everywhere with trees and underbrush so that no where can anyone see twenty yards." This road, and the taking of Fort Duquesne (rebuilt and renamed Fort Pitt) opened the West for English settlement.

But not until the end of 1763 could any settlement breathe easily. Pontiac had united the western tribes for a final desperate stand against English territorial advances. He besieged Detroit and Fort Pitt, and within a single month captured Forts Sandusky, Saint Joseph, Miami, Ouiatenon, Michilimackinac, Le Boeuf, Venango, Carlisle, Bedford, and Presque Isle, butchering most of their occupants. The climax came at a little knoll called Edge Hill, about twenty-six miles east of Pittsburgh near the present Greensburg.

Colonel Henry Bouquet, sent to relieve the three-month siege of Fort Pitt, reached the hill near Bushy Run on August 5, 1763, when he was attacked by a "shouting and yelping" horde of Delawares, Shawnees, Mingoes, and Wyandots, led by Chief Guyasuta. After a raging, two-day battle, when victory seemed hopeless, Bouquet sprang a trap which routed the Indians. Pontiac's uprising was broken at Bushy Run, and for the first time the Alleghenies were relatively safe.

In November, 1763, the English commander at Detroit received an unusual message:

My Brother . . . all our young people have buried their casse-têtes [war clubs]. I think you will forget the bad things which have taken place for some time past. Likewise I shall forget what you may have done to me, in order to think of nothing but good . . . I am sending this resolution to you in order that you may see it. If you are as kind as I you will make me a reply. I wish you a good day.

Pontiac

In 1766, at Oswego, Pontiac agreed to final peace.

Sir William Johnson

The Mohawk Corridor

Of the men who lived in the Mohawk Valley 200 years ago, few are more fascinating from the standpoint of personality or their imprint on the region's history than the young man of 23 who arrived from Ireland in 1738 to manage his uncle's lands. In those days the 150-mile course of the Mohawk from Rome to Cohoes was marked with the paths of the powerful "People of the Long House." In one of those strange incidents of history which pop up again and again to alter the course of events, many of these people—the Six Nations of the Iroquois—had been alienated from the French in 1609 by Samuel de Champlain, who first used firearms against them.

The young man from Ireland was quick to take advantage of this inheritance. He made friends with the Indians, treated them with respect and kindness. He became a student of their language, customs, and habits. And they seemed to be impressed as much by his flowery language as by his fair trading and political adroitness. When the German girl who was his wife died, he bestowed his favors upon Molly Brant, sister of the Mohawk chief Joseph Brant. The "brown Lady Johnson," as she was called, not only gave him eight children but presided over his household with dignity while he went about such business as building churches in the valley, sponsoring the translation and printing of an Indian prayer book, acting as Britain's Superintendent of Indian Affairs, conducting scientific experiments, and serving as an eminently successful general.

This was William Johnson, dubbed Warraghiyagey or "Chief Big Business" by the Indians and Sir William by His Majesty George II. One of the wealthiest men in the colonies, his influence with the Iroquois was such that he singlehandedly kept them on the side of the Crown during the French and Indian War.

One of the three homes built by Sir William in the valley is the gray stone, two-story building which became known as Fort Johnson after a palisade was built around it during the wars. The hip-roofed house, with paneling and hardware imported from London, was completed in 1749, and was the scene of many important Indian councils, with as many as a thousand Iroquois camped around it at one time.

Twelve miles away in Johnstown, partly hidden by trees, is the more luxurious home Johnson built in his later years. A stately Georgian Colonial frame house with wainscoted halls and rooms, it was situated on a royal grant of 80,000 acres. The house was flanked by two stone blockhouses, one of which still stands, just to the rear of the house.

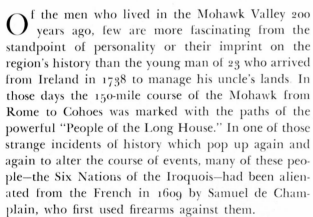

Indians of the powerful Six Nations once gathered for councils at Johnson Hall, Sir William's large fortified house near Johnstown. At one such meeting in 1774 Johnson died after an impassioned harangue to the visiting Mohawks. As the photograph above indicates, only one of the blockhouses survives.

On a wooded bluff overlooking Nowadaga Creek is Indian Castle Church, site of the upper "castle" of the Mohawk Bear Clan between 1700 and 1775, and the place where Sir William Johnson built Fort Hendrick. It was here that Johnson met Molly Brant and had the simple clapboard church built for his Indian friends. After Johnson's death Molly returned to the castle, where she was to play an important part in the area's worst Revolutionary battle.

Even more than the French and Indian conflict, the Revolution turned the Mohawk Valley into a dark, bloody ground, torn by the fiercest kind of fighting between Tory, patriot, and Indian. Sir William's Tory son John, Joseph Brant, and Walter Butler led Indian attacks against such places as Stone Arabia, Wyoming Valley, and Cherry Valley, where 48 defenders were killed and more than 60 carried off as prisoners. But the major battle occurred at Oriskany.

As part of the three-pronged British attack designed to cut the colonies in half, Barry St. Leger was leading about 800 British regulars and 1,000 Iroquois east from Oswego to rendezvous at Albany with Burgoyne and Howe. Burgoyne was advancing south from Canada, and the plan called for Howe to march north from New York City to join them. Against St. Leger,

Nicholas Herkimer took off with 800 patriot militia of the valley to relieve the small garrison at Fort Stanwix. Hearing of this movement, Molly Brant sent a warning from the castle to her brother Joseph, and the British and Indians ambushed the Americans in a marshy ravine at Oriskany. In a bloody hand-to-hand battle which lasted six hours, Herkimer was mortally wounded and his men were severely mauled, but the action was halted by the threat of reinforcements under Benedict Arnold. This, with the loss of his Indian allies, forced St. Leger to return to Canada, and dealt a severe blow to Burgoyne's campaign.

Today a stone shaft overlooking the Mohawk marks the site of Oriskany battlefield, and you can see, between two low hills, the ravine where the ambush occurred. Near Little Falls is the interesting Herkimer home, where the hero of Oriskany is buried.

After the violence of revolution and Indian wars passed, the old valley became even more of a historic corridor with the digging of the Erie Canal, begun in 1817. The thick forests have vanished from the graceful, gently rising hills, and many changes have taken place; but somehow the fertile valley—with its battlegrounds, Indian castle sites, colonial houses, and towpaths—has never lost its air of history.

Rows of long-silent cannon protrude from the stonework battlements of restored Fort Ticonderoga.

Ticonderoga's British commander was trouserless when Ethan Allen surprised him in the fort's barracks.

Revolutionary Battlegrounds

It is easy to forget nowadays how important water transportation was in colonial times, but the classic reminder of how control of the water lanes could mean control of a continent is Fort Ticonderoga.

Between French and British, and later British and American settlements, the vast wilderness was penetrable only by means of narrow Indian trails, which meant that no army of the time could cross it readily. Strategists were quick to realize that the happy juxtaposition of Lake Champlain, Lake George, and the Hudson River provided a military highway. To the French, the route spelled conquest of the English settlements; to the British in Canada it offered a means of splitting the rebellious colonies in two. But the plan which seemed so easy was never once successful.

Between 1689, when the first invasion was launched, and 1814, when the last was attempted, every southward attack failed. Men under the easy spell of maps never seemed to realize that the route itself was behind their failures. Any advance up Lake Champlain had to be by the lake alone. And the lake precluded the use of skillful maneuvering or flank attacks, left little chance for surprise, and demanded a head-on collision between attacker and defender. No matter what any commander might wish, the focal point for that collision was almost inevitably the height of land between Lake George and Lake Champlain, commanded by Fort Ticonderoga.

This aerial view shows Fort Ticonderoga's strategic location between Lake George (background) and Lake Champlain.

The Iroquois' enmity for the French which William Johnson found so useful dated back to 1609, when Champlain met a band of Indians and defeated them near the fort's site. But not until 1755 did the architects of New France begin building the star-shaped stone building which they called Fort Carillon. For the next sixty years the great walls watched history being made along the Champlain shore. Here, in 1758, Montcalm and a relative handful of troops defeated 15,000 British and Colonials led by a fat, ineffectual man called "Aunt Nabby-Cromby"—General James Abercromby. A year later, with the French cause losing ground, Montcalm departed, leaving the near-empty fort to Jeffery Amherst, who rebuilt it and called it Ticonderoga. By the time of the Revolution the bastion had begun to disintegrate. Resembling a backwoods village more than a fort, it was manned by only fifty men, some women and children.

Before dawn on May 10, 1775, a flamboyant Ethan Allen and an ambitious Benedict Arnold crowded 83 men into two boats over on the eastern shore of the lake and landed half a mile below the fort. It was still dark, and the men huddled together against squalls of wind and rain. By the time they landed it was too late for the boats to bring over the rest of the group, so they advanced to the main entrance in the south wall, which at that time was almost in ruins. Overrunning the guard, they rushed inside, where Allen met an officer wearing a coat and waistcoat—his trousers in his hand. "Come out of there, you damned old rat!" shouted Ethan, who demanded the surrender of the

CONTINUED ON PAGE 90

CONTINUED FROM PAGE 89

fort (he wrote later) "in the name of the Great Jehovah and the Continental Congress." Although Allen was reputedly on poor terms with both parties, the British acquiesced, and by December of that year Henry Knox had dragged the fort's guns over the mountains for the siege of Boston.

In 1777 Gentleman Johnny Burgoyne's plan for conquering the rebels was approved in London, and he headed south to join St. Leger and Howe at Albany. The force which caused the Americans to abandon Ticonderoga must have presented quite a sight coming up the lake. There were Indians in war paint, the massed scarlet of British regulars, dark blue German uniforms, the green of the jägers, and the dragoons' light blue. Sunlight glinted on row after row of polished musket barrels, bayonets, shining brass, and regimental facings, and caught the cadenced flashing of thousands of wet paddles and oars.

Truly a conquering army, but after taking Ticonderoga Burgoyne's troops encountered one obstacle after another—not the least of which were their preposterous uniforms, which made wilderness marches nearly impossible. General Philip Schuyler put a thousand axmen to work destroying bridges, felling trees, and burning crops along the British route, and in three weeks Burgoyne was able to advance only 23 miles. A foraging expedition under Colonel Baum met disaster at Walloomsac, New York, near Bennington, where John Stark's militia and Seth Warner's Green Mountain Boys turned out in force. A pretty young girl named Jane McCrea was scalped by Burgoyne's Indians, inflaming the countryside with anger and sending hundreds of volunteers into the American forces. St. Leger was turned back after Oriskany, and finally Burgoyne received the crushing news that Howe was not coming to join him after all.

When Burgoyne arrived at Stillwater, south of Saratoga and about halfway between Fort Edward and Albany, there were 9,000 men—500 of them Daniel Morgan's riflemen—waiting for him. After an initial engagement, Burgoyne waited for reinforcements which never came, while the American ranks swelled to outnumber him two to one. Finally, on October 7, Burgoyne chose to advance.

Although Gates was technically in command of the Americans at Saratoga, it was the personal daring and leadership of Benedict Arnold, galloping onto the field to lead the attack, and of Daniel Morgan, rallying men again and again with his turkey call, which made possible the British defeat. In addition to its strategic significance, Saratoga was also the site of the war's most important single rifle shot. Arnold, who realized the importance of British General Fraser's personal leadership, assigned Tim Murphy, one of Morgan's Pennsylvania riflemen and an old Indian fighter, to dispose of him. And dispose of him Tim did, from a range of 300 yards—a shot which began the demoralization of the British troops, contributing to the long rifles' reputation as ". . . the most fatal widow and orphan makers in the world."

Finally, compelled to retreat to Saratoga, and completely surrounded, Burgoyne and his staff rode out to meet General Gates. "The fortune of war," he said, "has made me your prisoner." To this Gates replied, "I shall ever be ready to testify that it has not been through any fault of Your Excellency," and invited the party to dine with him. Because the victory at Saratoga led to the alliance with France, contemporaries recognized it as the turning point of the Revolution: "Rebellion which a twelvemonth ago was a contemptible pygmy, is now in appearance become a giant."

Following Burgoyne's defeat, Ticonderoga was occupied once more by Americans, but never again did it have much strategic importance. Finally abandoned, it fell into ruins until its restoration was undertaken in 1909. Because of the work done there, no fort of the Revolutionary period offers the visitor more rewards. The great brooding walls survey the magnificent sweep of Lake Champlain, and inside the original stone barracks are a wealth of uniforms, maps, guns, and other objects dating back to the days when the fort was a key to the continent.

Nearly two centuries afterward, the Revolution is so remote, so far distant as to dim the awareness of what really took place. A schoolchild learns that George Washington crossed the Delaware one snowy Christmas night and surprised some Hessians; and that sometime later he and his men had a terrible time at a place called Valley Forge. And because it was so long ago and because there is so little time to learn about it and so little space in the books for a real description of what happened, neither Washington nor the men who stuck it out with him ever quite come alive.

There were times when the flame of independence came so close to flickering out that it is a wonder we ever got it at all. Among the men who realized it at the time was a thin, bright-eyed Quaker who had elected to serve in Washington's army without pay. His name was Tom Paine, and he sat with the rem-

DAVID E. SCHERMAN, REPRINTED FROM *Holiday*

Benedict Arnold was shot in the leg at Saratoga. This monument honors the only truly American part of him.

Crossing the Hudson with five thousand men, Cornwallis scaled the Jersey Palisades to rout the Americans at Fort Lee, and split Washington's army in two. Viewing the maneuver, Thomas Davies of the British artillery painted this watercolor.

nants of Continental forces in New Jersey one night in November of 1776, hunched over a drum, on which there was a piece of paper. He was a man who could write what he felt in a way that everybody could understand. General Charles Lee called him a "man with genius in his eye," and John Adams, who hated him, nevertheless admitted that he was "the first factor in bringing about the Revolution." Paine's pamphlet *Common Sense* had made a revolution out of rebellion and clarified the issues for which it was to be fought, which led Benjamin Franklin to observe that others could rule and many could fight, but "only Paine can write for us."

This is what he began to write, in the *Crisis*, that November night in 1776: "These are the times that try men's souls: The summer soldier and the sunshine patriot will, in this crisis, shrink from the service of his country; but he that stands it Now, deserves the love and thanks of man and woman. Tyranny, like hell, is not easily conquered; yet we have this consolation with us, that the harder the conflict, the more glorious the triumph."

Between July and December there had been nothing but disaster. At the time the Declaration of Independence was proclaimed in Philadelphia, General Howe was landing 32,000 trained, disciplined professional soldiers at Staten Island. He took 20,000 of them to Long Island and overran the Americans. Only Washington's planning, the skill of two amphibious regiments from Marblehead and Salem, and some God-given nasty weather saved the army from complete annihilation. In quick succession, Howe routed the colonials again at Kip's Bay—better known today as 34th Street and the East River, just down the street from the East Side Airlines Terminal—pushed them back through Harlem to White Plains, then captured Forts Lee and Washington on the Hudson in one of the great disasters of the war. Forced to retreat across the Jerseys, the broken remnants of the American army were in truly desperate straits and even Washington admitted, "If this fails, I think the game will be pretty well up."

At the time Tom Paine was writing the *Crisis*, Washington had less than 6,000 barefoot, exhausted men who had known nothing but defeat. Worse yet, this rabble had only two weeks more of life, for so

CONTINUED ON PAGE 92

91

CONTINUED FROM PAGE 91

many enlistments were due to expire December 31 that there would be no more than 1,400 of them left to face the greatest expeditionary force Great Britain had ever sent out from its shores. In this hopeless situation Washington came up with a plan born of "necessity, dire necessity," which he disclosed to his officers in the Merrick House on the west bank of the Delaware on Christmas Eve. It meant risking his entire army in one awful gamble, for once across the river, his retreat was cut off.

As dark fell on Christmas night the crossing began about nine miles above Trenton, at a place known as McKonkey's Ferry. At the old tavern which still stands on the Pennsylvania side, one of Washington's officers stopped long enough to make an entry in his diary: "Christmas, 6 P.M. . . . It is fearfully cold and raw and a snow-storm setting in. The wind is northeast and beats in the faces of the men. It will be a terrible night for the soldiers who have no shoes. Some of them have tied old rags around their feet, but I have not heard a man complain." It was one of the most daring movements in military history. On a bitter, pitch-dark night, in the middle of a driving blizzard, Washington's "flock of animated scarecrows" were ferried over the ice-choked river by Glover's intrepid Marbleheaders—the same men who rescued the defeated troops at Long Island—to surprise three regiments of professional soldiers.

It very nearly failed to come off. The crossing had been so difficult that the Americans were four hours behind Washington's schedule, and it was almost eight in the morning when they reached Trenton. Fortunately, the Hessians had celebrated Christmas in hearty fashion, and most of them were still in the barracks because their commander had failed to heed a warning message the night before. In the "great, informal battle royal" which followed the attack, both sides had to rely on artillery and bayonets since their muskets were too wet to fire, and in less than an hour it was over—a remarkable victory which would have satisfied a lesser man than Washington. Although his men's enlistments were due to run out in four days, and Howe was on the march, Washington took his prisoners to Pennsylvania and, in another fateful gamble, returned once more to the Jersey side.

Near Trenton, where Cornwallis confronted him on January 2, Washington again maneuvered brilliantly. Leaving a rear guard to keep his fires going, he marched around Cornwallis' left under cover of darkness, and surprised Mawhood just outside Princeton. Overpowered at first, the panicked Americans were rallied by Washington, who rode into the hottest fire within thirty paces of the British, and Mawhood's men finally fled down the road to Trenton. In Princeton,

the Continentals forced the surrender of nearly 200 British in Nassau Hall, and the battle was over.

By this time, only a few days after they made the extraordinary crossing of the Delaware and took Trenton, the ragged Americans had been under arms for forty continuous hours in the dead of winter, with no time out for meals or any kind of rest. They had marched sixteen miles over terrible roads in total darkness, and then fought a battle. Realizing there was nothing left in them, Washington headed for winter quarters in the wooded, hilly section of Morristown.

These not inconsiderable victories had an effect totally beyond their military significance. They heartened the people of the colonies with hope of ultimate success, encouraged enlistments, and strengthened enormously Washington's reputation at home and abroad. As Christopher Ward says in *The War of the Revolution,* this feat "had been accomplished by an army of fewer than five thousand ragged, shoeless, ill fed, poorly equipped, often defeated amateur soldiers, mostly militia, operating against twice that number of veteran professionals, abundantly supplied with all martial equipment, and within a space of eleven days in the depth of winter."

For a fleeting moment, the crisis was past; but there would be many others in the six long years before the war ended. During that time, although they lost one battle after another, the Americans would demonstrate again and again the courage they had shown in this terrible December of 1776. Washington would learn only too well how many sunshine patriots there were, but somehow there was always a core of belief that never gave way. It was this weapon that Tom Paine knew so well, and it was this that the enemy lacked. The great idea that men were willing to die for was what made them, finally, unconquerable.

There are places in the Middle Atlantic region where the visitor is rewarded with a glimpse of surroundings little changed since the days when Continentals battled redcoats for their possession. One of them is the little town of Chadds Ford, with a population of about two hundred, which was the center of the Battle of the Brandywine in September, 1777. The creek that once ran deep enough to require a ferry is now a mere trickle, but the octagonal schoolhouse which changed hands eleven times in 45 minutes during the fierce engagement is little changed. In an incongruous way, this was a battle with religious associations. It took place within sight of the Birmingham Meetinghouse and the Kennett Meetinghouse; and the paper used in American cartridges came from the German "Brethren" at Ephrata, who placed the printed sheets of an edition of Fox's *Book of Martyrs* at the service of their country a few days before the fight.

CONTINUED ON PAGE 95

After an evening full of Christmas spirits and carousing, most of the Hessian force was still asleep in Trenton's Old Barracks when Washington made his surprise attack.

From here Washington's ragged army was ferried across the ice-choked Delaware River. Once on the Jersey bank, they had to march nine miles before attacking Trenton.

Artist Edward Hicks painted this primitive version of Washington's Delaware crossing about 1834. He made two copies, one for each end of a covered bridge erected at the site. Without romanticizing the scene, he conveyed successfully the cold darkness and desperate drama of that bitter Christmas night of 1776. The determined Washington led his men across the river, while downstream two less resolute American commanders, deciding he would never make it, ordered their troops to turn back.

At Valley Forge, Washington's men were housed in crude log huts, like the snow-covered restoration at left.

The Ford Mansion was Washington's Morristown headquarters. At right, Baron von Steuben drills troops at Valley Forge.

CONTINUED FROM PAGE 92

Philadelphia and civilization have encroached on Germantown, but the Chew Mansion (or Cliveden) is still a little island of Revolutionary times right in the center of town. The handsome stone house is almost exactly as it was when it became the focus of the battle in October, 1777. In this home the British barricaded themselves and poured a continuous, deadly fire into the attacking Americans, and the marks of that fight are still visible on the exterior. In the same vicinity are Germantown Academy and the long, white Wyck house, both used as hospitals after the battle.

Near Freehold, New Jersey, the Old Tennent Church looks out across the three-mile stretch of Monmouth Battlefield and the graves of the men who fell near it so many years ago. Close by are Freehold Courthouse, St. Peter's Episcopal Church, and the Hankinson Mansion, all occupied by British or Americans at the time of the battle which brought fame and the name Molly Pitcher to Mrs. John Hays, and disgrace to General Charles Lee, who permitted the retreat.

It is fitting, however, that the real spirit of the Revolution survives best at two places which were not battlefields at all. The story of that war was one of survival and incredible courage, and at Morristown and Valley Forge these two qualities still hang on the cold winter air like thin notes from a Revolutionary bugle. Every summer thousands of Americans visit the old encampments, but anyone who goes there when the icy wind is out of the north will feel the image of gaunt, suffering men who endured untold agony for the sake of an ideal. What happened at Morristown and Valley Forge is no less poignant because of the conditions that made it—it is simply more incredible. A good deal of what the army went through was caused by the lack of manufacturing in the colonies—

woolens, for example, were almost unobtainable, regardless of price. But what was far worse, soldiers underwent privations because the country at large failed to support either the war or the pitiful little army that was waging it.

At Morristown, the Continental soldiers were "absolutely perishing for want of clothes." Sometimes two or three days without food, the men huddled in log huts and tents, where they "were actually covered . . . and buried like sheep under the snow." The first winter a smallpox epidemic ran through the camp; three years later the snow piled up twelve feet deep. On the old camp site the small redoubt and the log huts have been reconstructed, the parade ground on which the troops marched "over Frost and Snow, many without a Shoe, Stocking, or Blanket" is there, and so is the dignified old Ford Mansion, where the anguished Washington had his headquarters.

Similar monuments exist in the peaceful park at Valley Forge, the scene of horrible suffering during the winter of 1777-78. In addition to soldiers' huts, silent cannons, and the Grand Parade Grounds where von Steuben somehow made an army out of the "Ragged, Lousy, Naked" regiments, there are the houses where Washington, Knox, Lafayette, and Stirling stayed.

But the meaning of Valley Forge and Morristown is not in the buildings. It is to be found in the heart-stricken words of George Washington, writing: "To see men without clothes to cover their nakedness, without blankets to lie on, without shoes, for want of which their marches might be traced by the blood from their feet, and almost as often without provisions as with them . . . is proof of patience and obedience which in my opinion can scarce be paralleled."

95

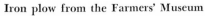

Iron plow from the Farmers' Museum

K. PAZOVSKI, *Farm Quarterly*

Cooperstown

COURTESY *Time*

Cooperstown's cigar store Indian once stood in front of a Kansas City shop. On the facing page is a typical 1820 kitchen, in the Lippitt Farm at the Village Crossroads. The shops and houses at right are also at Cooperstown's Village Crossroads, where the visitor may see a re-created New York village of pre-Civil War days.

When the visitor arrives at the shore of Otsego Lake, the headwaters of the Susquehanna River, he is in the heart of Leatherstocking country. The round top of Council Rock, where the Indians once came to "make their treaties and bury their hatchets," is visible above the still surface of the lake, and the ghosts of Natty Bumppo and Chingachgook are not far away. This is the land where James Fenimore Cooper spent much of his childhood and most of his later years, absorbing the lore of Indian and pioneer and transforming them into the stories that have thrilled generations of American youth.

It is also a place where one may see a fascinating group of buildings housing some very diverse but authentic bits of Americana. There are the Farmers' Museum and the Village Crossroads, re-creating the life of an average settler on the early frontier. The museum's collection of tools and implements for home, farm, and shop, and its demonstrations of ancient crafts are as fine as anything to be seen. The Crossroads is actually a re-creation of a little New York settlement of the period 1800 to 1850, and it includes schoolhouse, country store, blacksmith shop, lawyer's office, tavern, and farmhouse among the many old buildings moved here from their former locations.

Fenimore House contains what is probably the most comprehensive collection of American folk art in existence, most of it nineteenth-century, with hundreds of objects from toys and trinkets to large figureheads on display. The museum's collection of wood carving is particularly impressive, as is the remarkable series of life masks done by Browere about 1825 —among them five of the first eight Presidents of the United States.

And few baseball fans need to be told that the National Baseball Hall of Fame and Museum is here at Cooperstown, where Abner Doubleday laid out what is claimed to be the first baseball diamond and played the game which grew out of One Old Cat, a favorite in colonial times.

NEW YORK STATE HISTORICAL ASSOCIATION

The unusual arcade through the center of New Castle's Old Town Hall originally led to the stalls of the town market.

The stuccoed tower and high, shingled steeple of Immanuel Episcopal Church rise above New Castle's elm-shaded Green.

Built in 1801, the elegant George Read House recalls a time when New Castle was an important Delaware River port.

New Castle and Winterthur

There is an air of tranquillity in the tree-lined streets of Delaware towns like Odessa or Smyrna or Dover which seems to say that nothing very momentous ever happened there. Each of these old-fashioned villages has its roots along the water front that brought it trade, and few communities in the country have changed so little in the past two hundred years. Walking up past New Castle's Packet Alley from the Delaware River, the visitor sees the cupolas of the town hall and the Georgian Colonial courthouse amid the great elms lining the broad open streets. Behind them is the Green laid out by Peter Stuyvesant, and close by are Immanuel Episcopal and Old Presbyterian—two ancient churches. The long, two-story brick building at the corner is the old Academy, planned in 1772 as a "public seminary of learning" and completed in 1811. Near the Green are two streets of houses built between 1675 and 1830 by landowners, merchants, and lawyers. Beautifully preserved, these homes are out-standing examples of a pure, simple architecture that dominated those years when New Castle was capital, court town, seaport, and market town. Architecturally, one of the finest is the George Read House, built in 1801 in late Georgian style. Superbly furnished, it is the high-water mark of the town's prosperity.

Demonstrating the close link between decorative arts and history, the Henry Francis du Pont Winter-thur Museum near Wilmington is a great collection of Americana which has been brought together from other places. Formerly Mr. du Pont's home, the museum contains about a hundred rooms, either restored or in their original state, which are superb examples of American architecture, furniture, metalwork, textiles, ceramics, and paintings from the period beginning about 1640 and ending two hundred years later.

A tribute to those skillful craftsmen who were employed by the young nation's merchants, clergy, and shipowners, the museum houses a fine collection of paintings by artists like Copley, Stuart, and Benjamin West; the silverwork of Paul Revere and some of the earlier Boston mintmasters; and a notable group of Duncan Phyfe furniture.

This graceful staircase was brought to Winterthur from the Montmorenci mansion in Warrenton, North Carolina.

Like other Winterthur rooms, the Walnut Room is a composite of different periods and places. The woodwork came from Belle Isle plantation in Virginia, and the trestle-foot folding bed is a mid-eighteenth-century New England piece.

Low Bridge

To an English visitor it appeared that "Old America seems to be breaking up and moving westward." By 1830 Ohio had more inhabitants than Massachusetts and Connecticut combined, and a hundred hamlets were growing into towns and cities, because of something called "Clinton's ditch." Also because of it, New York City changed almost overnight from a market town on the Hudson into the nation's leading port.

DeWitt Clinton was not the first American to think of a canal—George Washington planned what is still one of the country's most picturesque waterways, the lovely Chesapeake and Ohio Canal that runs along the north bank of the Potomac; William Penn dreamed of joining the Susquehanna with the Schuylkill and Delaware Rivers; and practical old Ben Franklin endorsed heartily this "quiet and always manageable" form of travel. But from the moment it was completed in 1825, the Erie Canal was one of those supremely happy combinations of the right thing at precisely the right time. For eight years and for 363 miles, laborers had dug with pickax and shovel, swearing, singing, brawling, and, it was said, drinking taverns into existence at the rate of one per mile of canal until they connected Albany with Buffalo. Almost at once, freight rates between Albany and the lake dropped from $100 to $9 a ton; emigrants by the thousands surged westward on packet boats; village outposts like Detroit and Cleveland became growing cities; and a vast communication system connected New York with the new western lands, the Mississippi, and New Orleans.

The old painting on this page makes canal travel look idyllic, but there was scant comfort aboard the boats. Fanny Kemble thought them preferable to a coach journey over abominable roads, but like everyone else she complained bitterly about the "bridges over the canal, which are so very low, that one is obliged to prostrate oneself on the deck of the boat, to avoid being scraped off it; and this humiliation occurs, upon an average, once every quarter of an hour."

Passengers might complain about the accommodations, but no one traveling the Erie failed to be impressed by the ingenuity which made it possible. The days have gone when fifty or sixty boats were lined up at a lock, waiting to go through, but even today the

vestiges of the canal in Lockport are quite a thing to see. In the center of town there are five of the original locks used to raise or lower the canal level sixty feet. And just west of the village of Amsterdam is Schoharie Creek Aqueduct, another remarkable monument to its builders. To carry the canal high above the river, thirteen great piers held up a wooden trunk containing the 41½-by-7-foot water section of the canal, and fourteen graceful 40-foot arches supported the towpath and braced the piers. Parts of the Erie have become the modern Barge Canal, but an observing eye will still locate some of the well-trodden towpaths, half-hidden by underbrush, that mark the old route.

The Erie, of course, was far from unique—the whole Middle Atlantic region seemed to go canal-crazy early in the nineteenth century. Evidences of many of these waterways still survive, like the Schuylkill, from Philadelphia to Pottsville; the Delaware and Hudson; the Lehigh, from Mauch Chunk to Easton; the Morris, a real engineering wonder from Jersey City to Phillipsburg; and most scenic of them all, the Chesapeake and Ohio. But for sheer inventiveness, none surpassed the Pennsylvania Canal, parts of which still wind peacefully through Pennsylvania farmlands.

Opened in 1834, the Pennsylvania was a combination of 118 miles of railroad and 283 miles of waterway. Starting from Philadelphia, passengers traveled ten hours by train to Columbia on the Susquehanna. There they transferred to a packet boat which was hauled 172 miles up the Susquehanna and Juniata rivers to Hollidaysburg, passing through 108 locks on the way. At Hollidaysburg the really spectacular part of the trip began. To cross the 2,500-foot crest of the Alleghenies, the boats were loaded onto flatcars and pulled—first by horses, later by steam engines—over a series of five levels and inclined planes up the mountain and then down the other side. At its most mechanized stage, this operation involved 33 power changes, and added to these hazards was the psychological one, described by Charles Dickens in 1842: "Occasionally the rails were laid upon the extreme verge of a giddy precipice; and looking from the carriage window, the traveler gazes sheer down, without a stone or scrap of fence between, into the mountain depths below. . . ." Many a passenger must have welcomed the sight of Johnstown, where he resumed the trip to Pittsburgh by canal.

Like many another, the Pennsylvania was a little too costly and a little too late. With the coming of the railroads, most canals fell into disuse and passed slowly from the American scene.

Westward-bound emigrants and their worldly goods crowded the roofs of Erie Canal barges like the one in this scene.

Mule-drawn tourist barges still navigate the C. & O. Canal.

An old drawing shows portage railway flatcars at the summit of the Alleghenies. Below, a crumbling arch remains of the canal aqueduct crossing the Mohawk at Little Falls.

Armchair table   Printer's memorabilia   Benjamin Franklin   Fireplace stove   Electrical machine

Ben Franklin's Philadelphia

When Benjamin Franklin walked up High Street in Philadelphia on a Sunday morning in October of 1723, he entered a busy city of some 10,000 people. William Penn in 1681 had instructed the city's builders to "Let every house be pitched in the middle of its plat . . . that so there may be ground on each side for gardens or orchards, or fields, that it may be a green countrie towne, that will never be burnt, and always be wholesome." But forty years later the population had increased, plots had been subdivided, and the narrow streets resembled picturesque Elfreth's Alley, which is the only one to survive nearly intact.

By packet from New York and the north, by horseback over rough trails from the south, by ship from Europe, new arrivals came to Philadelphia, making it the most important city in the colonies. There was no place in the New World like it: young men were studying French, light music was played in fashionable drawing rooms, and people thronged to fishing parties on the Schuylkill, and to dances. Just then, few of these activities were available to the young printer's apprentice; but not long after his arrival Benjamin Franklin began to exert on the city and on the whole country a profound intellectual influence.

So astoundingly diversified were Franklin's interests that it is almost impossible to list them. More than ever today, in an age of specialists, it is hard to imagine how he had time and energy to pursue his ever-widening range of activities. He invented bifocals and the lightning rod and the Franklin stove. He introduced Philadelphia palates to Scotch cabbage, their first kohlrabi, and Chinese rhubarb. He gave the city paved streets and street lamps—the first in America. In 1751 he persuaded Philadelphia's city fathers to replace the volunteer night watch with paid constables, although a uniformed police force was not created for a hundred years. He organized the country's first fire department in 1736, and twelve years later the first insurance company—the "Hand-in-Hand," so called from its seal. He started the Library Company of Philadelphia in 1731; known as "Mr. Franklin's Library," it was the first circulating library in America. In 1751 he established the Pennsylvania Hospital and the Academy for the Education of Youth, which eventually became the University of Pennsylvania. One of his most important contributions was the formation, in 1727, of an informal club known as the Junto. From this small group the American Philosophical Society was formed in 1743—an organization which lists as members twelve Presidents, fifteen signers of the Declaration of Independence, and eighteen signers of the Constitution—whose collection of scientific books and papers, rare manuscripts, paintings, and other historical treasures is priceless today.

Meanwhile, Franklin prospered as publisher of the Pennsylvania *Gazette* and of his annual *Poor Richard's Almanack*. While he hoped to devote his time to the study of scientific matters, from 1754 until the end of his life he was drawn constantly into public affairs, in the service of his country. As a diplomat he knew Europe better than any other American, America better than any European. In diplomacy as in all his affairs, he was a man who perceived a need and sought its solution. When he died at the age of 84, people all over the world lamented the passing of the greatest American of his time. Perhaps the tribute he would have enjoyed most is the fact that his contributions to Philadelphia and to the nation he loved are as healthy and active today as they were in his own time.

Elfreth's Alley has changed so little in two centuries that Benjamin Franklin might recognize it if he were alive today.

Independence Hall

JEROME K. ANDERSEN, REPRINTED FROM *Holiday*, © 1955 BY THE CURTIS PUBLISHING CO.

For those Americans who want to recapture the spirit of their nation's beginnings, few places offer them more of it than the serene brick building on Chestnut Street, between Fifth and Sixth, in Philadelphia.

The small legislative Assembly which looked after the Province of Pennsylvania's affairs had no formal meeting place for many years; instead, it met in private houses, rented by the year. By 1729 the members decided the province needed something more permanent, and they agreed on a site on the outskirts of town. The uneven land was covered with whortleberry bushes, and across the street there was a fine peach orchard. Work on the new State House, supervised by carpenter Edmund Woolley, went slowly, and not until 1748 did the president and Council meet in the big room on the second floor. The doorkeeper and his family lived in the west wing, and now and again Indian delegations were lodged or entertained there.

In 1753 the bell tower was completed and the State House bell (which is, of course, the Liberty Bell) was hung. Ordered from London, it was a "bell of about two thousand pounds weight," and the Council stipulated that it should have cast around its crown the words from Leviticus: "Proclaim liberty throughout all the land unto all the inhabitants thereof." To everyone's disappointment the brand-new bell was cracked "by a stroke of the clapper without any other viollence as it was hung up to try the sound"; but two workmen named Pass and Stow recast it successfully, and up the steeple it went, early in 1753.

From that time on, the State House became the center of almost all Philadelphia's important happenings. The officers who survived Braddock's disaster in 1755 gave a memorable ball there after their return to civilization; settlers from the frontier came to plead with the Quaker-controlled Assembly for protection against Indian raids; and Germans from the "back settlements" sixty miles from Philadelphia drove a big Conestoga wagon up to the steps and unloaded the corpses of their scalped neighbors for the Assembly to see. It was the scene of mourning over passage of the Stamp Act, the scene of rejoicing over its repeal, the scene of town meetings to protest the tax on tea. Citizens filled the square at the news of Lexington and Concord, and a few weeks later John Hancock called the Second Continental Congress to order in the State House.

Independence was in the air during those months, and on June 7, 1776, Richard Henry Lee, delegate from Virginia, arose in the State House to propose "Certain resolutions respecting independency." It was

At night the square around Independence Hall is lighted by 56 gas lamps, one for each signer of the Declaration.

104

John Trumbull's painting shows the committeemen who wrote the Declaration presenting it to chairman John Hancock (seated). From left to right are Adams, Sherman, Livingston, Jefferson, and Franklin.

just a question of time now, and excitement rose with each passing day. A committee composed of Thomas Jefferson, John Adams, Benjamin Franklin, Roger Sherman, and Robert Livingston was appointed to "prepare a declaration to the effect of the . . . resolution," and on July 1 debate began. On July 2, Congress declared "these United Colonies . . . Free and Independent States," and gathered the next morning in the State House to hear the draft of the final and complete charter of freedom. As author Jefferson agonized, delegates edited his words and ideas, cut out passages of his text, and wrangled until evening; but on the morning of July 4 the Declaration of Independence was approved and signed by John Hancock and Secretary Charles Thompson.

For nine months during the Revolution, the British occupied Philadelphia, and they used the State House as a barracks and as a hospital after the battle of Germantown. When Congress finally was able to return, in June of 1778, New Hampshire delegate Josiah Bartlett reported that the building was in "a most filthy and sordid situation," with "the inside torn much to pieces." Three years later, the glorious news from Yorktown was announced at the State House, and in 1787 delegates began drifting into town for a convention which was supposed to draft a constitution.

For four months in the sweltering heat of a Philadelphia summer the debate went on, and when the Constitution was finally signed, Benjamin Franklin pointed to the chair which the visitor may still see there—the one with a gilded half-sun painted on the back—and said: "I have often and often in the course of Session, and the vicissitudes of my hopes and fears as to its issue, looked at that [sun] behind the President without being able to tell whether it was rising or setting: But now at length I have the happiness to know that it is a rising and not a setting Sun."

For a good many years after the Union came into being, the State House was neglected. Although Philadelphia was the temporary capital from 1790 until 1800, both House and Senate met in the building now known as Congress Hall, which witnessed Washington's second inauguration, his last message to Congress, and the inauguration of John Adams. As a matter of fact, the State House was almost torn down in 1816, but the city of Philadelphia fortunately bought the building and the square where it stands for $70,000. Even then, no one paid much attention to it until an aged Lafayette made a visit there in 1824. Then, suddenly, the public woke up to the fact that a great many important things had happened in the old brick structure. About this time, someone attached the name "Independence Hall" to it, and generations of Americans began paying their respects to the place that has heard more of the great voices of America than any other spot in the land.

105

WAYNE ANDREWS

Mount Pleasant, Benedict Arnold's house

WAYNE ANDREWS

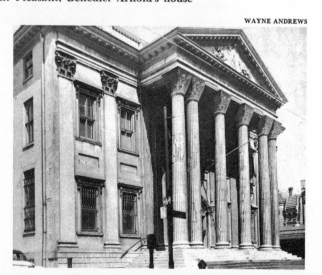

The First Bank of the United States

Philadelphia's

At the time of the Revolution, Philadelphia was the second-largest English-speaking city in the world and, if we may believe the Duc de La Rochefoucauld, "one of the most beautiful." It was also, in the score of years before 1800, the gay, bustling center of America's cultural, political, intellectual, and economic life; a city which could point with pride to the remarkable Dr. Franklin and many other men of uncommon ability. There were the painting Peales; the naturalists John and William Bartram; Charles Brockden Brown; Philip Freneau, the "Poet of the Revolution"; David Rittenhouse; Dr. Benjamin Rush; Joseph Priestley; and fascinating French emigrés like the Duc de Talleyrand, La Rochefoucauld, and Chateaubriand.

The setting for eighteenth-century Philadelphia's social life may be seen today in Fairmount Park, where some of the city's historic houses have been moved to form a "Colonial Chain." There is a little two-story building known as the Letitia Street House, a rare specimen of an early urban dwelling, built about 1715, and furnished in Queen Anne style. The Georgian Colonial mansion Cedar Grove was built in 1721; Strawberry Mansion in 1798; Woodford in 1742; and all are furnished appropriately. Probably the masterpiece of this group is Mount Pleasant Mansion, a yellowish-gray stucco house which was begun in 1761 by a Scottish sea captain, and sold later to General Benedict Arnold and his beautiful wife, Peggy Ship-

Peter Cooper's 1720 view of Philadelphia is the oldest extant.

Colonial Chain

pen. Bartram's Gardens, begun in 1731 by the naturalist, are among America's most important botanical exhibits, and inside the grounds is the stone house built by John Bartram in 1731.

Some other notable Philadelphia houses are the Samuel Powel House, home of the city's last pre-Revolution and first post-Revolution mayor; the red brick Wistar, or Shippen House; and the distinguished Morris House, built in 1786, which is set in its original garden. There is the lovely brick Christ Church where Washington, Robert Morris, Franklin, and so many other notables of the Revolution worshiped; and St. Peter's Episcopal Church is another fine example of colonial architecture. Carpenter's Hall, begun in 1770, was where the First Continental Congress assembled, and the First Bank of the United States is a tangible symbol of Alexander Hamilton's efforts to stabilize national finances. The American Philosophical Society and its priceless collections occupy the "neat, sufficient building" erected in 1787; and the cornerstone of the Pennsylvania Hospital—the first in America—reminds one that it was built in "MDCCLV, George the second happily reigning." Anyone interested in personal contact with American history will go also to Germantown, to see the Germantown Academy and the Historical Society, the Chew Mansion which was the focal point of the 1777 battle, the Perot-Morris House, and the handsome Upsala.

Christ Church, where patriots worshiped

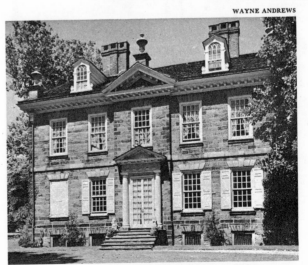

Cliveden, center of the Germantown fight

A few of the structures shown in this 1854 print of the du Pont Brandywine Works still stand. The mills were built with an open wall facing the river, to direct explosions away from town. Hopewell iron furnace, below, once consumed the equivalent of an acre of woodland every 24 hours. Among the pieces of early American glass at right are a creamer, bowl, and flask probably made by Stiegel.

Friends

Iron, Glass, and Powder Kegs

Years before men combined Lake Superior ore with Allegheny coking coal by means of the Great Lakes and created the heartland of heavy industry between Pittsburgh and Duluth, iron manufacturing had taken root along the eastern seaboard. The first attempt was made at Falling Creek, Virginia, in 1619, but this community was wiped out by unsympathetic Indians three years later. Saugus, Massachusetts, was the earliest successful works, and the industry soon spread down into Pennsylvania, New Jersey, and Maryland.

Most of the old forges and furnaces have all but disappeared into the landscape, but Hopewell Furnace in Pennsylvania survived long enough to make it worth reconstructing for future generations to see. Built in 1770 by Mark Bird near the site of his father's earlier forge, Hopewell prospered for nearly seventy years. Then coke-fired hot blast ovens began to replace the charcoal-burning furnaces, and in 1883 Hopewell was "blow'd out" for the last time.

Because Hopewell Village, isolated in the hills back of the Schuylkill River, became a ghost town, it remains today much as it was when the blast roared and flames lit up the sky for miles around. At the brink of a natural embankment is the stone furnace from which molten metal spilled into molds of scorched sand called sows and pigs. Across the road are the best-preserved buildings—the office and store, and the big house where Mark Bird and later ironmasters lived—and down the road, past the blacksmith shop, are four stone houses once inhabited by workmen.

Another man whose meteoric career began as an ironmaster was Henry William Stiegel. By 1764, when he built the first of the glass works which brought him lasting fame, his income from the iron industry enabled him to live in a style which earned him the title "Baron." Others, notably the South Jersey manufacturers, had preceded him in the making of fine glass, but to Stiegel belongs the distinction of producing superb lead glass—the first of its kind in America. Clear, amethyst, blue, and green, sometimes engraved or enameled, Stiegel glass possesses a beauty scarcely rivaled by other U.S. manufacturers.

With his debut as a glassmaker, the Baron had founded a little town called Manheim, in the rolling farmlands of Pennsylvania, and in 1770 he owned the entire community. His mansion, which still stands on Manheim's town square, was famed for miles around, and he donated the ground for Manheim's Lutheran church, in exchange for an annual rent of one red rose which the trustees still pay his heirs. But as colonial taxes rose higher and higher, Stiegel's customers dwindled, and after several years of splendor he was thrown into debtor's prison. After his release and until his death, he eked out a wretched living teaching in the church his fortune had built.

If industry was coming to the young country, nowhere was it more noticeable at the end of the eighteenth century than along the busy banks of the Brandywine. Ten years after the Revolution the Duc de La Rochefoucauld said Brandywine Creek turned nearly sixty mills in its course of seven or eight miles through Delaware. Actually, he underestimated the case. The Delaware *Gazette* in 1793 reported fifty mills grinding corn and wheat alone, and listed more than thirty of other types. Four of these were paper mills, which were largely responsible for the Duc's astonishment at another American phenomenon. "All these people busy themselves much with politics," he observed, "and from the landlord down to the house maid they all read two newspapers a day."

For the next fifty years, nearly every sort of mill product in America was made along the Brandywine, and just as its flour mills set the price of wheat for the country, the price of gunpowder came to be fixed by a concern which began life under the unwieldy name of Du Pont de Nemours, Père, Fils et Compagnie. Eleuthère Irénée du Pont made a personal survey of the competition, discovered that explosions and British manufacturers had put most American powder mills out of business, and bought a 95-acre tract along the river as the site of his operations. On a bluff above the winding stream he built a stone and stucco mansion which is still a du Pont home, and close at hand, the original office building, now used as a guest house. Below the residence there are still a few vine-covered walls, all that remain of the first mills which operated for more than a century. The curious construction of these buildings was intentional. Two sides and the rear wall were made of stone, and an open wall faced the river. Irénée du Pont knew enough about powder manufacturing to understand its hazards fully. If a nail got under the rollers, or if a bearing overheated, there was a flash and roar that rattled windows for miles around, and the insides of the mill were strewn all over the landscape. By placing an open wall toward the river, he directed the explosion that way, rather than toward the little community which lay behind the mills.

Dawn's Early Light

*O say can you see ~~the ship~~ by the dawn's early light
what so proudly we hail'd at the twilight's last gleaming,
whose broad stripes & bright stars through the perilous fight
O'er the ramparts we watch'd were so gallantly streaming?
And the rocket's red glare, the bomb bursting in air
Gave proof through the night that our flag was still there,
O say does that star spangled banner yet wave
O'er the land of the free & the home of the brave?*

Francis Scott Key wrote "The Star-Spangled Banner" as a poem, on the back of a letter.

At 5:46 on the morning of September 13, 1814, the British fleet opened fire on Fort McHenry. Already 5,000 of Wellington's veterans had been ashore for 36 hours, striking toward Baltimore from the east in a combined land-sea attack. The navy was to reduce Fort McHenry by a massive bombardment, after which the British could take Baltimore as easily as they had taken Washington three weeks earlier.

For the rest of that day and all through the night, mortar shells and rockets poured down on the brick and sod fort. Inside the works, Colonel George Armistead had about a thousand men—and not one gun with enough range to reach the English fleet.

The War of 1812, which had begun with the eager cry "On to Canada!" had reached a critical stage. Abortive American attempts to invade their northern neighbor had died on the vine or been thrown back decisively. In the summer of 1814, the chief U.S. source of support—Napoleon—was exiled to Elba, and America's defenses were so pitiful that for five days in August 4,000 British regulars marched up the Patuxent River without firing a shot. In response to an urgent summons for 95,000 militia, less than 7,000 showed up at Bladensburg. Although they outnumbered the redcoats nearly two to one, most of the Americans panicked and ran when they had suffered 66 casualties, and the British pushed on to Washington that night, arriving in time for some of the officers to eat a White House dinner prepared for President and Mrs. Madison. During the days that followed, they diverted themselves by burning most of Washington's public buildings, including the Capitol and the White House, then proceeded leisurely back to their ships for the strike against Baltimore. En route, they stopped in Upper Marlboro, Maryland, and took captive "a medical practitioner called Beanes."

His close friend, a young Washington lawyer named Francis Scott Key, obtained permission from a har-

The fifteen-starred flag flying over the ramparts of Fort McHenry is a copy of the one Key saw "by dawn's early light."

assed Madison to obtain Dr. Beanes' release. Key took a packet boat from Baltimore under a flag of truce, and on September 6 met the British fleet preparing to attack the city. Admiral Cochrane agreed to release Beanes, but refused to let the Americans go until the movement against Baltimore had been executed.

From two miles out in the harbor, the anguished Key watched all day as the British shelled the helpless garrison. In the failing light of dusk, he could see nothing of the fort through the smoke and flames, but just as darkness closed around it, he caught sight of the flag. Half wild with anxiety, he paced the deck all night as the relentless bombardment continued. When the first light of dawn streaked the sky, Key strained for a glimpse of the fort. As the darkness lifted, he saw it—the flag still flew. And Francis Scott Key pulled a letter from his pocket and began to write on it some verses filled with the emotions of that night.

For nearly an hour more shells burst and smoke rolled over the fort, but at 7 A.M. on September 14 the attack ceased. Two hours later the fleet began to withdraw down the river, and Admiral Cochrane notified the land forces of his failure to destroy Fort McHenry. On September 15 the infantry re-embarked—some for Halifax, the rest for the West Indies, where the expedition against New Orleans was assembling.

In a hotel that night Key rewrote his verses, and a friend took the stirring words to a local print shop, where they were run off in handbill form. On September 20 the poem was published in the Baltimore *Patriot* under the title of "The Defense of Fort McHenry." One morning a few days later, an actor named Ferdinand Durang and some twenty companions well fortified with juleps sang it for the first time to a tune all of them knew well, a drinking song called "To Anacreon in Heaven."

In the years that followed, Key's song of an unconquerable flag came to be accepted popularly as the national anthem, but not until 1931 did Congress pass a bill recognizing "The Star-Spangled Banner" as the official song of the United States of America.

111

Harpers Ferry, at the junction of the Shenandoah and Potomac rivers (below), still looks much the way it did at the time of John Brown's raid in 1859. In the photograph at left, taken just before the raid, "Old Brown of Osawatamie" is wearing the beard he grew as a disguise. The brick enginehouse where he and his men were cornered by Robert E. Lee's marines stands today on the grounds of Storer College.

The Invasions of the North

The trail of the "middle-aged, middle-sized man, with hair and beard of amber color streaked with gray" began in Connecticut. It led out to Ohio and on to Kansas, where he was called "Old Brown of Osawatamie," north across the border to Canada and, in the summer of 1859, to the sleepy little town of Chambersburg, Pennsylvania. He said he was a prospector named Isaac Smith, so no one considered it strange when large boxes marked "Tools" were delivered to the weathered gray house at 225 King Street. Then he left town as quietly as he had come, taking his boxes with him to a little farm in Maryland, just across the Potomac from the long narrow hump of land known as Harpers Ferry. And on the night of October 16, 1859, while Harpers Ferry slept, the contents of the boxes became carbines, Isaac Smith became John Brown, and he and 22 followers marched over the bridge and seized the federal arsenal.

Robert Harper, 125 years before, had been so thrilled by the wild beauty of the place where the Shenandoah and Potomac rivers meet that he gave two squatters $65 for their cabin, canoe, and corn patch, paid Lord Fairfax sixty guineas for the land, and settled there. He started a ferry service across the Potomac and gradually a little village grew up around it. The water power which eventually led Congress to establish an arsenal there was not always a blessing; the town suffered from floods, and for years men remembered the great Pumpkin Flood of 1753, so called because of the great numbers of pumpkins it washed downstream from the Indian fields.

Thomas Jefferson had seen Harpers Ferry as a place so lovely it was "worth a trip across the Atlantic." John Brown saw it as the natural entrance to the slave country, a stronghold in the southern mountains to which Negroes could flee. But it was not so easy as all that. By afternoon of October 17, companies of militia and bands of angry men from the Virginia hills converged on the town, blocking Brown's escape, and that night ninety marines arrived from Washington, led by Colonel Robert E. Lee and Lieutenant J. E. B. Stuart. Holed up in the square brick enginehouse which stands today on the grounds of Storer College, John Brown was wounded and ten of his men killed before he surrendered. Two of those men were his sons. And for John Brown it was all over but the hanging.

Harpers Ferry was destined to have little peace for the next five years, as the great struggle of which John Brown had been one wild symptom tore at the roots of American society. Just three years after Brown appeared there, the town played its part in the battle which, as much as any other, determined the war's final outcome.

The Army of the Potomac was reeling from the beating it took at the Second Battle of Bull Run, and Robert E. Lee decided to strike again quickly—this time in an invasion of the North. With supreme contempt for the abilities of General George B. McClellan, Lee had divided his army in two, sending part under Stonewall Jackson to take Harpers Ferry, while he and the rest worked their way north. As the fog lifted off the rivers on the morning of September 15, 1862, Jackson's men saw a white flag waving, and knew that Harpers Ferry, with 12,000 Union troops and 13,000 small arms, was theirs. Stonewall himself received the surrender—the "dingiest, worst-dressed and worst-mounted general that a warrior who cared for good looks and style would wish to surrender to"—and as he rode down into Harpers Ferry the boys in blue

CONTINUED ON PAGE 114

A. AUBREY BODINE

Attacking from the hill in the background, Union troops crossed Burnside's Bridge at Antietam after heavy losses.

113

This pensive-looking young private from Georgia posed for his photograph shortly before he was killed at Malvern Hill.

CONTINUED FROM PAGE 113

were so curious to see this legendary figure that they lined the sides of the road, some of them uncovering as he passed them. Jackson returned their salute, and one of the Union lads said what many of them felt, that he didn't look like much, "but if we had him we wouldn't be in the fix we're in." To the unfortunate Federal troops and, indeed, to the victorious Confederates, it looked as if this might be it. Lee's great drive for the defenseless cities of the North was going according to plan. His army, tired as it was, had victory under its belts, and the element of surprise was all his.

All, that is, except for one small hitch. While McClellan and the Army of the Potomac were pursuing Lee, wondering where he was going and what he would do, a corporal in the 27th Indiana and one of his buddies, lounging in a field outside Frederick, found a bulky envelope in the grass. Corporal Mitchell opened it and pulled out a piece of paper wrapped around three cigars. The cigars alone would have satisfied any soldier, but the paper in which they were wrapped was something beyond the wildest dreams of generals. It contained Lee's Special Orders No. 191, which told in detail the whereabouts of every division of Lee's army, and his immediate plans. Probably never in American history was a commanding officer so favored by luck as McClellan was that day in 1862.

With this information, even as cautious a man as he

should have had no trouble finishing off Lee then and there. At this moment, Lee's army was in several different pieces, and McClellan was closer to them than the pieces were to each other. The only thing that was required to crush them separately was immediate action; but of this, George B. McClellan was incapable. Then, as always, he was obsessed with the notion that Lee outnumbered him, and when he decided to attack Lee's rear guard at South Mountain, it was done not quite vigorously or quickly enough. Actually, Lee had only 19,000 dead-tired men of Longstreet's and D. H. Hill's commands. Against him, McClellan had 70,000, and while these were not all combat troops, even if the rest of the Confederates did arrive in time from Harpers Ferry it would still be a two-to-one fight.

Yet Lee, in what was probably the boldest act of his military career, crossed Antietam Creek and turned to fight it out at Sharpsburg. This is as beautiful a spot today as it was then, and the little village that lies among rich farmlands between the creek and the wide-swinging Potomac River has changed hardly at all. Into this quiet, peaceful place the two armies moved that hot September 16, taking their places for the battle that would change American history. But time was beginning to run out for George McClellan and his opportunity. That morning Jackson's men—weary and sore of foot from a seventeen-mile night march from Harpers Ferry—had come up. Although Lee still had barely 25,000 men, McClellan thought he had 100,000—and decided to wait for Franklin's 18,000 troops to arrive.

Not until daybreak of September 17—nearly five days after Lee's lost order had been found—did McClellan launch his attack, and then, instead of making one big push, he did it piecemeal. Just about a mile north of what is now the National Cemetery there stood a Dunker church, a little white building backed by the West Wood on one side, and facing the East Wood across the Hagerstown pike. Between the wood lots was a cornfield, and just south of it a sunken road. Within these few thousand square yards, and within a little less than five hours, the bloodiest fighting of the whole war took place that morning. The battle exploded when Joe Hooker and his troops moved south along the Hagerstown road toward the cornfield, and Hooker remembered that soon "every stalk of corn . . . was cut as closely as could have been done with a knife, and the slain lay in rows precisely as they had stood in their ranks a few moments before." The Confederate line finally broke as the Union soldiers reached the fence at the end of the field, and the boys in blue ran toward the church, victory in sight. Suddenly, without warning, John Bell Hood's division boiled out from behind the church, and the Union charge changed to retreat. Back and forth across the forty-acre cornfield the conflict flamed, a hand-to-hand fight to the finish that ended with the Union troops at the Dunker church, but with Hooker's I Corps completely wrecked.

General Sumner, marching up to seal the victory, ran head-on into reinforcements Lee had sent up just in time, and at the end of fifteen minutes more than 2,000 Union soldiers were dead or wounded. After just four hours, 12,000 men were lying on the ground, killed or hurt, and when McClellan sent a courier to Sumner suggesting he renew the attack, Sumner's horror at the slaughter was so great that he cried out: "Go back, young man, and tell General McClellan I have no command." By this time Lee's battle line was a thin thread, held together by a few bits and pieces of outfits that just refused to give up, but when he got Sumner's message, McClellan decided not to throw Franklin's fresh troops into the attack.

The final stage of the furious battle began when the IX Corps crossed what has been called, ever since, Burnside's Bridge. Although the Antietam is so shallow a man can walk across it in most places, the Union commanders decided to storm the bridge—and storm it they did, at a horrible cost in lives before they got across. Burnside, who had 12,000 men in his command, inexplicably made his attack with only 3,000, but even so the 2,400 tired rebels were being pushed back slowly, just to the brink of Sharpsburg, when suddenly from out of nowhere Confederate General A. P. Hill came storming up at precisely the right time and place and drove back the blue line. Hill had made a terrible seventeen-mile forced march from Harpers Ferry, driving his exhausted men at the point of his sword, and although nearly half his division was left along the roadside, enough arrived to keep the war going for two and a half years more. It was just that close. While Lee had not a man left he could call a reserve, Burnside never used his extra troops, McClellan never sent in the 10,000 fresh men who could have put an end to the Army of Northern Virginia, and the Battle of Antietam was over.

The Union army lost fifteen per cent of its men on that unspeakable battlefield—the Confederates over one-fourth of theirs. Militarily, it was a standoff. What it accomplished, however, was to give Lincoln enough of a victory—a shaky, uncertain one, it is true—but enough for him to issue the Emancipation Proclamation. When Lee's gray columns turned back into Virginia, and when Lincoln announced that he would declare free all the slaves in territory still resisting the Union, it ended the threat of foreign intervention. The war would be fought out at home, to the terrible, bitter end, and the question of the Union and the

The expression of this youthful Northern infantryman seems less carefree than his Napoleonic stance and jaunty attire.

issue of slavery would be decided, right here.

Less than ten months after the Battle of Antietam the long gray lines were on their way north again, and ahead of them a rising tide of fear struck deep into the cities and countryside of Pennsylvania. Broadsides signed by Governor Curtin screamed, "The Enemy is Approaching!!" and local militia companies bustled into frenzied activity. Across the river from Pittsburgh, at the old Allegheny Diamond, a mass meeting was held on the evening of June 13, 1863, and within a few weeks 14,000 men—butchers, clerks, steelworkers, steamboat men and students—were building fortifications around the nervous city. They had good reason to be scared. Lee's lean, brown veterans were superb fighting men, and they were swinging north to an untouched land of milk and honey with the confidence born of having licked their more numerous opponents nearly every time they had met them. They were 70,000 strong, trained in combat, and about as fine an army as ever headed into action.

Within these same ten months the Army of the Potomac had fought the same four great battles—Second Bull Run, Antietam, Fredericksburg, and Chancellorsville—but they had fought each one under a different commander. The veterans were as good as anything Lee could throw against them, but the army was full of untrained regiments, and it had hardly been favored

CONTINUED ON PAGE 116

115

CONTINUED FROM PAGE 115

by topnotch generalship. They were pushing hard now, trying to keep up with Lee and stay between him and Washington, and on June 28 George Gordon Meade was roused from sleep by a War Department official and told that he was in command of the army. Just then that army was engaged in a race—a race to the finish that depended on how its legs held out—and there was no time for Meade to make changes or do anything at all except keep up; which meant that the battle they were heading for would be decided by the men in the ranks.

Up the thin strip of land between the Potomac River and the Chesapeake and Ohio Canal they marched, dead-tired men dropping out of the ranks by the dozens, up the dusty roads past Frederick, winding through the mountains past towns where cheering villagers and pretty girls came out to greet them with handouts of lemonade and pie, apple butter and fresh bread.

Lee's men had ranged from York in the east to Chambersburg in the west, but now they were beginning to concentrate east of the great barrier of South Mountain. Late in the afternoon on the last day of June, 1863, General John Buford and his division of troopers in skin-tight pants and big black boots rode into the town of Gettysburg to have a look around. Gettysburg then, as now, was the center of roads converging from all directions, and Buford figured that Lee could not be far away. The Army of the Potomac was on the march that bright moonlit night, but neither the men in the ranks nor the men who commanded them had any notion that a battle which would decide the destiny of the United States of America would begin on the morrow.

The monuments and statues that line the roads of Gettysburg today were put there toward the end of the last century by men trying to capture something of what happened at this place. They can be trying to the visitor who wants to hurry through, but no one in a hurry is likely to find much of what Gettysburg means. The best way to see the battlefield is to go there armed with some of the facts, and to walk from place to place, stopping every now and again to think about it all. To think, for example, that the battle was fought here by accident (not that it could have been avoided; it was going to happen somewhere), since neither Lee nor Meade had considered Gettysburg as a place to stand and fight.

The Confederates of A. P. Hill's corps were heading into town on that first day of July because they heard there were some shoes there, and as the light began to trickle over the hills into the fields and pastures along the Cashtown road, the dun-colored skirmishers of Harry Heth's division came striding over the western

ridge, muskets at the ready. And when John Buford climbed up into the white bell tower of the Lutheran Theological Seminary on the ridge west of town to survey the situation, he saw them and knew that a fight was in the making—a big one. He had no support at the moment, but he was a man who liked to fight and he decided this was probably as good a place as any to do just that.

The first Federal infantry to come up was the Iron Brigade; and the 1,800 westerners with black slouch hats tilted over their eyes marched up the Emmitsburg road with flags waving and a fife-and-drum corps playing them into their last fight. They were the most famous outfit in the Army of the Potomac, and when the Confederates saw them they knew it wasn't going to be easy. Near the Seminary (and not far from the present Eisenhower farm) these "damned black-hat fellers," as the rebels called them, fought until they were hemmed in on three sides, and had to retreat. Along with the I Corps, they fought their way back through town and finally patched up a line on Cemetery Ridge. By that time, the I Corps had lost all but 2,400 men out of nearly 10,000, and the Iron Brigade lost 1,200 out of 1,800, which put an end to it as a fighting unit. On the night of July 1 there were only 5,000 Union troops occupying the line between Cemetery Ridge and Culp's Hill, and most of them were too worn out to notice a little sign which said that the town would fine anybody five dollars for discharging a firearm within the cemetery grounds.

On the second day boys who had never been in action before made up for it in a hurry. All over the field men traded their lives for the few minutes or hours the Army of the Potomac had to have if the war was not to end right then and there. The 1st Minnesota was one such outfit—262 men went into action and only 47 came out. Confederate James Longstreet smashed through the Peach Orchard at General Dan Sickles' extended line, and men fought and died for pieces of ground called Devil's Den and Little Round Top. Two lads from Gettysburg named Culp and Wentz who had gone south to join the Confederates came back for this battle—Culp to die on the hill where he was born, and Wentz to find himself with his battery in his father's back yard. General officers rode madly off for help, and outfits slated to go into line at one place were commandeered to plug a hole somewhere else. Over everything there was the ear-shattering roar of battle, the piercing screech of the Rebel yell, the unending crackle of small arms, and the screams of the wounded. As the great arc of flame and smoke surrounding the Federal position pulled inward, desperate men fought at close quarters, yelling at the top of their lungs and clubbing each other with anything

CONTINUED ON PAGE 118

116

A Confederate cannon overlooks the town of Gettysburg from Oak Ridge. On the first day of fighting, outnumbered Union troops held out here against fierce assaults until a Rebel victory in the open fields below forced them to withdraw.

Near the Trostle Barn (above), the Union army corps commanded by General Sickles was shattered in the Peach Orchard fight. At left is one of the granite outcroppings of Devil's Den which sheltered Confederate snipers. From this position they picked off Union gunners on Little Round Top.

117

CONTINUED FROM PAGE 116

they could lay their hands on. All through the second uneasy night, men startled by a sound opened fire at it. The night was filled with moans and rending cries of the wounded; behind the lines field hospitals were hideous with blood and parts of bodies.

On the morning of the third day the Federal troops still held their position on the long ridge trailing off Cemetery Hill, and when they looked out across the valley they saw more guns staring at them than they had ever seen before. Until one o'clock in the afternoon the field was ominously silent, and then 130 guns opened in a roll of thunder that carried a storm of exploding hell to the Yankee line. The field around the little white house where Meade had his headquarters was the worst hit of all, and for what seemed like hours the terrible bombardment went on, blasting showers of awful debris into the air. Then, suddenly, the furious cannonade abated, and the signal station

on Little Round Top wigwagged: Here they come.

The soldiers of the Army of the Potomac saw something across the mile-wide valley they would never see again—and never forget as long as they lived. It was a line of battle a mile and a half long—15,000 men shoulder to shoulder, marching forward with flags flying, musket barrels glinting in the sun, heading across that field as if they were on parade. The whole Union line opened on them, artillery blasting great holes in the ranks, but they kept on coming. Confederate General Lewis Armistead, holding his hat high on his sword, led the center right up into the Union line. There was a terrible hand-to-hand fight, every man on his own and the fate of a nation riding on what happened in those next few and dreadful minutes. Finally,

Paul Philippoteaux's epic painting of the battle of Gettysburg depicts the moment when Pickett's charge and the hopes of the South were broken along the stone walls of Cemetery Ridge. At center, Armistead's brigade has just penetrated the Union line

almost as suddenly as it had begun, the fighting sputtered out like a faulty fuse and the Confederates who did not surrender started back toward their own lines. When an officer rode up to tell George Meade that Lee's charge had been broken Meade raised his hand and thanked God.

The next day a wagon train seventeen miles long headed south, bearing what was left of Lee's supplies and his wounded, and along with this nightmare of pain and suffering went the hopes of the Confederacy for winning the war. Between them, the two armies had lost over 50,000 men.

It wasn't long before the governors of the Northern states decided to provide a proper cemetery for the men who fell at Gettysburg, and they planned to dedicate the ground on November 19. They invited Edward Everett, the most illustrious orator of his day, to make the principal speech and, almost as an afterthought, the President of the United States to lend his presence. The night before the ceremony the President worked over a draft of his talk at David Wills' house in Gettysburg, and the next day he was part of the great procession marching out to the battlefield. It was a rare Indian summer day, but by the time the crowd had heard Everett drone on for two hours they were listless and ready to go home.

When his turn came to address the audience, the tall, gaunt man in the black frock coat spoke from two little sheets of paper he held in his hand. He talked for less than three minutes, and after it was all said and done he had the feeling that his remarks were unsuccessful, since few of the 20,000 people seemed to have heard or caught the meaning of his words.

only to be overwhelmed in a desperate crush of hand-to-hand fighting. The clump of rock oaks at right center was the "High-Water Mark" of the Confederate advance, if not of the Confederacy. In this single assault, Lee's army lost five thousand men.

This earthenware dish was fashioned by a Pennsylvania Dutch potter late in the eighteenth century. It was a love gift, the two doves uniting in a single, heart-shaped figure.

As they grow older, these smiling, quaintly dressed Amish boys will not pose for the camera so willingly, for photographs are considered by their religion as graven images.

A long funeral caravan of boxlike Amish buggies heads for the burying ground. With their aversion for new-fangled, "worldly" things, the Amish still hold out against cars.

DISH AND TROUGH: NATIONAL GALLERY OF ART, *Index of American Design*

The barnlike buildings at left, at Ephrata Cloister, housed Johann Conrad Beissel's Seventh Day Baptist monastic community. Above is a dough trough decorated with tulips.

Fast Clocks, Plain Food and "Fraktur"

Of all the people who found William Penn's colony a sanctuary, the "Pennsylvania Dutch" folk with their colorful customs and handiwork fastened themselves most firmly in the popular imagination. Frugal, hard-working, and God-fearing, these are people who still keep their clocks half an hour fast because it is frivolous to be late; who serve "plain food" in gargantuan quantities, loaded with butter; who eat *schwenkfelder* bread on Thanksgiving, *fasnachts* on Shrove Tuesday, and dandelion greens on Maundy Thursday to ward off fevers. They throw water from the baptismal bowl over a rosebush to ensure rosy cheeks for the newly baptized child, and feed ashes from Good Friday's fires to their pigs to keep them in good health.

Not Dutch at all (their ancestors came from Germany, and they referred to themselves as *Deutsche*, thus confusing generations of Anglo-Saxons), neither are they one homogeneous group. Each sect had its disagreements with the others, but one thing they did have in common—knowledge of the great German hymns and a background of the same devotional literature.

The settlements of Menno Simons' followers—the Mennonites—are much in evidence in Lancaster County, where the best-known sect—the Amish—still clings to the Pennsylvania Dutch language and the seventeenth-century culture of Swiss-German ancestors. The bearded, black-robed men and their plainly clothed wives are vigorously opposed to automobiles, telephones, and higher education.

Bethlehem has the finest examples of Moravian culture. Many of the buildings are old log structures, covered since with stucco or clapboard, but colorfully painted to relieve the severity of design.

There were the Dunkers, pacifists and antislavery people, who split up into several groups—among them the followers of Johann Conrad Beissel who founded a community called Ephrata Cloister. There are four main buildings, five cottages, and a few outbuildings still standing, the remains of this Christian communal colony. Beissel had written: "Asia has fallen and its lamp gone out. For Europe the sun hath set at bright midday. America shall see a lily blooming whose perfume shall spread to the heathen." Visiting the buildings, it is understandable that the bloom came off the lily for later generations. In the ascetic life of the cloister, there were two persons to a cell. Each cell was only four floor boards wide, with a small high window. Beds were narrow wooden ledges, too short for comfort, and pillows were wooden blocks eight inches long. Low narrow doors and passageways symbolized the straight and narrow path and required constant stooping, to remind the brothers and sisters to be humble.

The followers of George Rapp, founder of Harmony, were skilled craftsmen who enjoyed considerable prosperity. After selling Harmony, they migrated to Indiana, built up another successful colony, sold it to Robert Owen, and moved to Economy on the banks of the Ohio at Ambridge, to found their third and final home. The seventeen buildings which still stand are an impressive group, including the 35-room Great House of hand-made brick with large, well-furnished, high-ceilinged rooms. There is a three-story music hall with a beautiful Colonial doorway, a five-story granary with hand-timbered first floor, a store, post office, apothecary shop, tailor and shoe shop with a stone-vaulted wine cellar beneath it, a cabinet shop, community kitchen, and the community gardens with their grotto, a building of rough stone boulders and beautiful interior.

The most widely known contribution of the Pennsylvania Dutch, of course, has been the outpouring of their creative fancies: painted chests, decorated barns, colorful household articles, slipware and sgraffito pottery, *fraktur* (illuminated writing elaborated with decorations drawn in color), and *Taufscheine*—those lovely illustrated baptismal certificates. Almost never, in these original pieces of work, was the religion which played such a part in their daily lives forgotten. Flowers stood for Christ, the Flower of Life. Christ was also the rose and the lily. The heart stood for God's heart—the "heart" of man's nature. There were stars ("There shall come a star out of Jacob, and a sceptre shall rise out of Israel"), and the Sun of Righteousness.

Driving through the great farm country of Pennsylvania, seeing the fieldstone houses and barns with steep roofs, decorative signs, and outward-curving eaves, hardware shaped into hearts and lilies and peacocks, and the other evidences of their imaginative skill, it is plain to see that these good folk gave something of their own to the land, without which it would not be quite the same.

SURRATT.
BOOTH.
War Department, Washington, Ap
$100,000 REW
THE MURDER
Of our late beloved President, Abraham
IS STILL AT LAR
$50,000 REWA
FORD'S THEATRE
Friday Evening, April 14th, 1865
BENEFIT!
LAST NIGHT
LAURA KEENE
MR. JOHN DYOTT
MR. HARRY HAWK.
TOM TAYLOR'S CELEBRATED ECCENTRIC COMEDY,
ONE THOUSAND NIGHTS,
OUR AMERICAN
COUSIN
BERLIN

Booth posed for this picture at the height of his acting career.

George Atzerodt went to murder Andrew Johnson; lost his nerve.

Caught with Booth in Virginia, feeble-minded David Herold was sentenced to hang.

John Surratt fled to Europe; he was later tried but not convicted.

Ford's Theatre

O n Tenth Street in downtown Washington there are two old brick buildings which share a tragic memory. In one of these, Ford's Theatre, John Wilkes Booth assassinated Abraham Lincoln on the night of April 14, 1865; and although the theater was closed after Lincoln's death, the building remains as a museum. The mute fragments gathered here tell a nightmarish story of the plot carried out by the men on this page. There is the gun that killed Lincoln; Booth's spurred boot and the flag on which it caught as he jumped from Lincoln's box to the stage, causing him to break his leg; and the strange diary Booth kept during his flight. Across the street is the tailor Petersen's house, where the President was carried, mortally wounded. At the rear of the house is the close, dark room where he lay across a walnut bed which was pitifully small for his great frame. Here, on that rainy April morning, Secretary Stanton said, "Now he belongs to the ages."

Accused of helping Booth escape, stagehand Edward Spangler was imprisoned.

Ex-Confederate Lewis Payne knifed Secretary of State Seward.

Michael O'Laughlin was jailed for his knowledge of the plot.

Among the mementos from Ford's Theatre shown are a Lincoln life mask; Booth's pistol, diary, dagger, hotel key, boot, and compass; Mary Lincoln's opera glass case; and the door to the presidential box with a peephole (lower right) bored by Booth only a few hours before he assassinated Lincoln.

Mrs. Surratt, who was hanged, ran the boarding house where the plotters met.

Capital of the Nation

The Jefferson Memorial in spring

Like a good many decisions which have been reached there since, the one that put the nation's capital on the bank of the Potomac River was the result of a political bargain. Since 1776 the government had been on the run. It had sat in Baltimore, Lancaster, York, Princeton, Annapolis, and Trenton, and when it moved from New York to Philadelphia in 1790, residents of New York predicted gloomily that their city would soon be deserted "and become a wilderness, peopled with wolves, its old inhabitants." The new site, chosen as a sop to the South, was hardly popular in the North. It was quite literally in the middle of nowhere, and most people described the location accurately as a fever-ridden swamp. Beyond Baltimore the road to Washington wandered through forests, and a driver picked the least dangerous-looking track to follow. Coming down from Philadelphia, Abigail Adams' hapless coachman lost his way completely, got off on the Frederick road, and spent more than two hours in the woods without finding so much as a path. Writing of the capital's beginnings, Henry Adams described what it looked like in 1800: ". . . the half-finished White House stood in a naked field overlooking the Potomac, with two awkward Department buildings near it, a single row of brick houses and a few isolated dwellings within sight, and nothing more; until across a swamp, a mile and a half away, the shapeless, unfinished Capitol was seen, two wings without a body, ambitious enough in design to make more grotesque the nature of its surroundings."

It was a long time before the capital began living up to the grandeur imagined for it by its planners. George Washington had appointed the engineer-architect Major Pierre L'Enfant to draw up plans for the city, but aside from L'Enfant and a few others, not many had the vision to see what the federal city might one day become. A number of landowners were persuaded to donate property (some, like the Scotsman David Burnes, on whose land the White House stands, held out for concrete evidence of gratitude), but when they heard the streets were to be as much as

The floodlighted Capitol dome is made of cast-iron shells painted white. It is capped by a bronze statue of Freedom.

160 feet wide they were horror stricken. Later, when a house was torn down because it stood in the path of what was to be New Jersey Avenue, the ambitious planner was fired.

Strange things sometimes happened after the L'Enfant scheme languished. When the Treasury building burned down for the third time, nobody could agree on a site for it. One day while President Andrew Jackson was out walking, someone asked him where he thought it should be. He stopped, drove his sword cane into the ground and replied firmly: "Right here!" And right there is where they put it, thereby interrupting the proposed sweep of Pennsylvania Avenue from the Capitol to the White House.

Fortunately, the L'Enfant plan was reactivated about the turn of the twentieth century, and little by little the city became what it is today—the one place in America that seems to sum up the aspirations of all its citizens. It is, too, the one place where Americans can see the men entrusted with their nation's future working against a background of the nation's past, and this makes it one of the most important and exciting cities in the land.

Yet Washington often gives visitors the impression that it is, underneath, a small town, probably because the people who live here are, after all, very much like those who are drawn to it as tourists. Few of those who come to see the great public buildings, monuments, and statues fail to be captivated as well by a city made more beautiful by trees, the sweeping Potomac, parks and gardens and flowering shrubs and a quiet old canal, long white bridges, the colorful atmosphere of foreign visitors, the openness of streets and broad avenues, and the towering, lovely cathedral on the heights overlooking the city.

Downstream and across the river is Alexandria, upriver is Georgetown—both thriving ports before the capital existed, now in their retirement exuding a kind of warm glow that comes from row after row of handsome old brick houses. On the Mall is the great shaft of the Washington Monument, reaching ever upward to honor the man who led the new nation into being, and due west of it, across the reflecting pool, is the beautiful white temple where Lincoln sits,

CONTINUED ON PAGE 126

CONTINUED FROM PAGE 125

caught forever in marble the way most Americans will always think of him. South, over the quiet surface of the Tidal Basin, the columns of Thomas Jefferson's memorial seem to rise out of the water, serene and shining in the sunlight; and to the north is the oldest public building in Washington, the white mansion where every President since John Adams has lived. Across Memorial Bridge, near the house where Robert E. Lee lived, is a simple and beautiful block of white marble, watched over by men in uniform, where a soldier known only to God sleeps eternally.

There are literally hundreds of places to visit in Washington, each one rewarding in its own way; but to millions of Americans the symbol of their country is the great-domed building at the end of Pennsylvania Avenue—the Capitol of the United States. This home of representative government faces east, away from the city of Washington, because it was L'Enfant's belief that it should look toward the rising sun. Jenkins Hill was chosen as the site for the Capitol in 1791, and two years later George Washington, wearing a Masonic apron embroidered for him by Madame de Lafayette, laid the cornerstone; but not until 1863 did the statue of Freedom finally stand on top of the completed dome. Inside the portico where the Chief Justice of the Supreme Court administers the oath of office to each President is the vast Rotunda canopied by the nine-million-pound dome. There is a cathedral-like atmosphere here that makes the visitor pause for a silent moment to look upward at the circling fresco far above the floor. Toward the House of Representatives is another vaulted chamber, a room lined now with silent statues where once the voices of men like Webster and Calhoun rang out, and beyond it is

the largest legislative forum in the world. In the north wing, across the length of the Capitol, is the Old Senate Chamber where the Louisiana Purchase was ratified, where Henry Clay brought the Missouri Compromise into being, and where men debated the issues of union and states' rights.

Democracy is the handiwork of people—people who make mistakes and people who have their moments of shining triumph—and democracy will offer them something better so long as a single voice is able to contribute to all that has been done before. Each day in the halls of the nation's Capitol the elected representatives of America have an opportunity to add to democracy's continuing tradition; and while the voices sometimes sound discordant and confused, the fact that they are raised at all is the best testimony to the American belief that the efficiency of one-man rule

is not worth the cost of human suffering and the loss of individual dignity which accompany it.

Here in this city is the focal point of democracy in the United States—something Grover Cleveland realized when he became President in 1885. In a speech that described perfectly the meaning of Washington, D.C., he said that any man taking the oath of office "only assumes the solemn obligation which every patriotic citizen—on the farm, in the workshop, in the busy marts of trade, and everywhere—should share with him. The Constitution which prescribes his oath, my countrymen, is yours; the government you have chosen him to administer for a time is yours; the suffrage which executes the will of free men is yours; the laws and the entire scheme of our civil rule, from the town meeting to the state capitols and the national capitol, is yours."

A. AUBREY BODINE

ARNOLD NEWMAN, *Life*

Millions of visitors to the Lincoln Memorial have been moved by Daniel Chester French's magnificent statue of Abraham Lincoln.

Towering above the capital sky line, the shaft of the Washington Monument is a striking 555-foot-high obelisk of white masonry.

In Fraunces Tavern, oldest house in Manhattan, George Washington took leave of his officers in 1783.

This is the New York that Washington knew. Trinity Church is behind the rigging of the ship, the Battery to the right.

New York City:
Then and Now

In this city whose face is altered so constantly, where towering shafts of metal, glass, and concrete seem to rise almost overnight on the ashes of the old, it is a wonder that any historic landmarks remain. Those stubborn enough to survive are dwarfed now by the sheer walls around them, providing a striking contrast between ancient and modern, and reminding the visitor that twentieth-century New York does indeed have a past. At the very bottom of Manhattan Island, where once New Netherland thrived, nothing but street names recall the Dutch settlement bounded by the wall which gave the financial district its name. Fraunces Tavern, where George Washington bid farewell to his officers, dates from a later period but is the oldest house left in Manhattan. St. Paul's Chapel, built in 1764, is the oldest and one of the most beautiful churches in the city; and the Sub-Treasury Building stands on the site of Federal Hall, where Washington was inaugurated as the first President and where government under the Constitution began.

Out in the harbor is the great statue which has symbolized America and liberty to so many millions of people, and overlooking the East River is the modern headquarters of the United Nations, that organization on whose future so much may depend.

nside the United Nations building representatives of eighty
ations work on problems of world affairs. The Secretariat
the skyscraper behind the domed General Assembly.

France presented the Statue of Liberty to the United States
in 1884. Erected in New York Harbor, it has been a symbol of freedom for millions who have come to America.

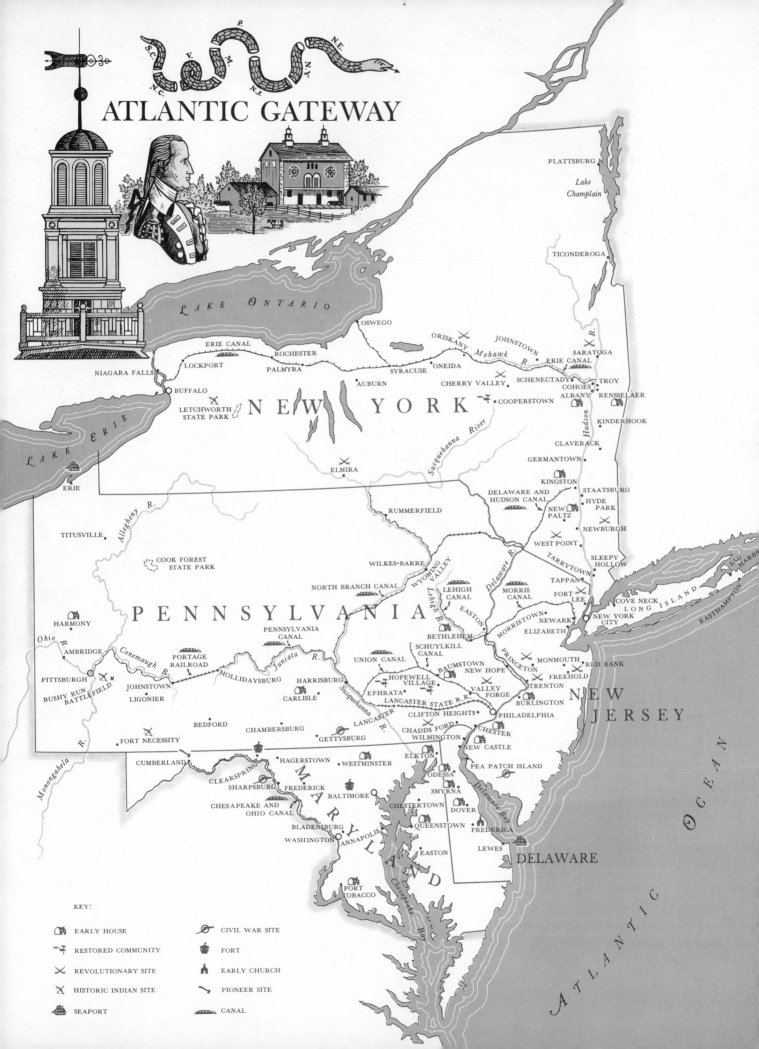

ATLANTIC GATEWAY

S.C. P. V. M. N.E.
N.C. N.J. N.Y.

PLATTSBURG

Lake Champlain

TICONDEROGA

LAKE ONTARIO

OSWEGO

ERIE CANAL
LOCKPORT
ROCHESTER
PALMYRA
SYRACUSE
NIAGARA FALLS
BUFFALO
LETCHWORTH STATE PARK
AUBURN
ORISKANY JOHNSTOWN SARATOGA
Mohawk R. ERIE CANAL
ONEIDA SCHENECTADY TROY
CHERRY VALLEY COHOES
COOPERSTOWN ALBANY RENSSELAER

NEW YORK

LAKE ERIE

ERIE

ELMIRA

Susquehanna River

KINDERHOOK

CLAVERACK

GERMANTOWN

KINGSTON

DELAWARE AND HUDSON CANAL
NEW PALTZ
STAATSBURG
HYDE PARK
NEWBURGH

RUMMERFIELD

TITUSVILLE

COOK FOREST STATE PARK

WILKES-BARRE
Wyoming Valley
NORTH BRANCH CANAL
Lehigh R.
LEHIGH CANAL
EASTON
MORRIS CANAL
WEST POINT
TARRYTOWN
SLEEPY HOLLOW
TAPPAN
FORT LEE

Delaware R.

PENNSYLVANIA

Ohio R.
AMBRIDGE
HARMONY
Conemaugh R.
PORTAGE RAILROAD
PITTSBURGH
BUSHY RUN BATTLEFIELD
JOHNSTOWN
LIGONIER
HOLLIDAYSBURG
Juniata R.
PENNSYLVANIA CANAL
UNION CANAL
HARRISBURG
EPHRATA
CARLISLE
BEDFORD
CHAMBERSBURG
GETTYSBURG
LANCASTER
Susquehanna R.
HOPEWELL VILLAGE
SCHUYLKILL CANAL
BETHLEHEM
BAUMSTOWN
NEW HOPE
VALLEY FORGE
LANCASTER STATE R.R.
CLIFTON HEIGHTS
CHADDS FORD
WILMINGTON
MORRISTOWN
NEWARK
ELIZABETH
PRINCETON
MONMOUTH
FREEHOLD
TRENTON
BURLINGTON
PHILADELPHIA
CHESTER
NEW CASTLE
PEA PATCH ISLAND

NEW YORK CITY
COVE NECK LONG ISLAND
EASTHAMPTON SAG HARBOR

NEW JERSEY

RED BANK

ATLANTIC OCEAN

FORT NECESSITY
CUMBERLAND
CLEARSPRING
SHARPSBURG
HAGERSTOWN
WESTMINSTER
FREDERICK
BALTIMORE
CHESAPEAKE AND OHIO CANAL
BLADENSBURG
WASHINGTON
ANNAPOLIS
EASTON
ELKTON
ODESSA
SMYRNA
DOVER
CHESTERTOWN
QUEENSTOWN
FREDERICA
LEWES

MARYLAND

Delaware Bay

DELAWARE

PORT TOBACCO

Chesapeake Bay

Monongahela R.

Allegheny R.

KEY:

🏠 EARLY HOUSE   ⚓ CIVIL WAR SITE

⚒ RESTORED COMMUNITY   🏛 FORT

✕ REVOLUTIONARY SITE   ⛪ EARLY CHURCH

✗ HISTORIC INDIAN SITE   ⚒ PIONEER SITE

⛵ SEAPORT   ▦ CANAL

DELAWARE

WAYNE ANDREWS

BROAD CREEK
Christ Church (1771) Never altered, this church near Laurel is still in almost perfect condition.

DOVER
County seat since it was laid out by William Penn's order in 1683, and state capital since 1777, Dover is rich in historic interest. The *Old State House* (1787-92) is believed to be the second oldest in active use in the U.S. *Christ Church* (1734) is still in use, and the *Old Presbyterian Church* (1790) now houses some Delaware State Museum exhibits. The *Dickinson Mansion* (1740), home of statesman John Dickinson, is a fine colonial plantation dwelling. Private homes, such as the *Loockerman* (1742) and *Ridgely* (1728) houses, *Woodburn* (c. 1790) and nearby *Aspendale* (1771) are open on Old Dover Days, the first weekend in May.

FREDERICA
Barratt's Chapel The "Cradle of Methodism in America," where the first sacrament was administered by authorized Methodist preachers in 1784.

LEWES
Zwanendael House Modern museum in Dutch Renaissance style, housing colonial relics.

NEWARK
In this town are *Newark Academy* (chartered 1769), and *Old College Hall* (1834) at the University of Delaware. Nearby are the *Old Welch Tract Church* (1746) and *Cooch's Bridge*, where the U.S. flag is reputed to have been raised for the first time in the Revolution. Close by is the *Cooch House* which British General Cornwallis occupied during the advance from Head of Elk to Philadelphia.

NEW CASTLE
This lovely old town (*see* p. 98) is a unique survival of the principal features of a colonial capital and Federal town. Among its landmarks are *Immanuel Church* (1703); *Old Presbyterian Church* (1707); the *Acad-*

Old Drawyers Church, Odessa

emy (begun 1798); the *Dutch House* (late 1600's), probably the oldest dwelling in the state; and the *Amstel House*, built before 1730, where George Washington was once a wedding guest. The *Old Court House* (1730) was the meeting place of the Colonial Assembly until 1776 and the state capitol in 1776-77. Its cupola was the point from which the curved Pennsylvania-Delaware boundary line was drawn in 1750, and in it Delaware's first constitution was adopted. Private houses open on Old New Castle Day, the third Saturday in May, include the *Read House* (1797), the *Kensey Johns House* (1790), and the homes of two Revolutionary patriots—the *Gunning Bedford House*, and the *Van Leuvenigh House* with its beautiful boxwood garden (both c. 1730). The town's lovely paulownia trees, with their purple spring blossoms, are said to have been brought from the Orient by a local sea captain.

ODESSA
Once a busy port, this sleepy village boasts some of the state's finest brick houses, such as the *David Wilson Mansion* (1769), a Georgian structure with splendid paneling. The *Corbit House* (1773) is a handsome private dwelling which is open, with others of interest, on Odessa Day; the *Friends*

Meeting House (1783); and nearby, the beautifully preserved *Old Drawyers Presbyterian Church* (1773) influenced by the Quaker style.

PEA PATCH ISLAND
Fort Delaware (1848) A bleak granite pentagon, used as a prison in the Civil War and for coastal defense until 1945. Now under development as a state park and military museum.

SMYRNA
Another quiet town whose handsome houses are its only witnesses to past wealth and activity. Most of them are still in private hands, such as *Belmont Hall*, begun in 1684 and fortified during the Revolution; the *Cummins House* (late 1700's), where the office of the affluent merchant who built it may still be seen; the *Abraham Pierce House* (c. 1750); and the *Enoch Spruance House*, built before 1791. The latter once housed the only bank between Wilmington and Dover.

WILMINGTON
At The Rocks, in Wilmington, a monument donated by the people of Sweden marks the site of *Fort Christina*, built by the Swedish expedition under Peter Minuit which established the first permanent settlement in Delaware in 1638. Buildings of interest in or near Wilmington include *Old Swede's Church* (begun in 1698), probably the oldest Protestant church still in active use in North America; *Old Town Hall* (1798), now the museum of the Delaware Historical Society; and the *Winterthur Museum* (*see* p. 99). The remains of about twenty early 19th-century Du Pont mills (*see* pp. 108-9) are preserved in the *Hagley Yard*, on the outskirts of the city, where the Eleutherian Mills-Hagley Foundation is developing a museum to illustrate the country's industrial past through reconstructions, models, and exhibits. Outside the Hagley Yard are two War of 1812 textile mills in good repair.

DISTRICT OF COLUMBIA

WASHINGTON
Among the countless important sites in the capital city are the *White House*, the *Capitol*, the memorials to our greatest Presidents (*see* pp. 124-27). Of absorbing interest, too, are various government departments, museums, and other institutions housed, for the most part, in relatively modern buildings. A partial listing follows of other historic structures in Washington:
The Arts Club Erected in 1802-5 on a portion of a tract known as "The Widow's Mite." James Monroe lived here while serving as secretary of state and of war, and for a time while President.

Blair House Opposite the White House, this is the nation's "guest house." Built in 1842 for Dr. Joseph Lovell, first surgeon general of the Army, it was later a residence of the influential Blair family. During the renovation of the White House, President Truman was living here when an attempt was made to assassinate him.
Decatur House The first private house on Lafayette Square was designed by Latrobe for Commodore Stephen Decatur, hero of the Barbary Wars. He lived here little more than a year before he was killed in a duel by Commodore Barron. Other noted residents were Henry Clay and Martin Van Buren. Now owned by the National Trust

for Historic Preservation, it is to be opened to the public. In the former carriage house is the *Truxtun-Decatur Naval Museum* with exhibits of maritime history (open). *Dumbarton House* Built between 1780 and 1795, the house was moved to this site. The interior is one of the finest examples of the Federal style. Headquarters of the Colonial Dames.
Dumbarton Oaks This Georgian mansion and its additions house a museum and center of research in early Christian and Byzantine humanities; owned by Harvard University. Has a notable garden.
Ford's Theatre The National Park Service maintains a museum in the 10th Street

theater where Lincoln was shot in 1865 (*see* pp. 122-23).

Fort Stevens Park One of a whole chain of forts built to defend Washington, this one repulsed a Confederate attack led by Jubal Early in July, 1864.

The Lindens Mid-18th-century Georgian mansion which was moved to its present site at 2401 Kalorama Road, NW, from Danvers, Massachusetts, where it was occupied by Thomas Gage, colonial governor. Private.

Marine Barracks Built on site selected by Jefferson in 1801, seized by British and partially destroyed in 1814. The **Commandant's House** (1805) is the oldest surviving structure. Aaron Burr was confined here while awaiting trial for treason.

John Marshall House (1825) Built by Tench Ringgold, later owned by Charles Carroll of Carrollton. Chief Justice John Marshall boarded here. Private.

The Octagon (1789) Headquarters of the American Institute of Architects. Built by Dr. William Thornton, first architect of the Capitol. Treaty of Ghent was signed here by Madison while house served as tempo-

AMERICAN INSTITUTE OF ARCHITECTS

The Octagon, Washington

rary executive mansion after the White House was burned by the British.

Old Stone House The only pre-Revolutionary house in Georgetown dates from the 1760's. Being restored by National Park Service.

Petersen House Where Lincoln died; now a museum (*see* pp. 122-23).

Pierce Mill Only survivor of eight mills flourishing in Washington in the early 19th century. Its undershot water wheel is still used to grind corn and wheat.

St. John's Church The "church of the Presidents," built in 1815 by Latrobe. The nearby **Parish House** (1836) was once the residence of Lord Ashburton, British minister sent to settle the U.S.-Canadian boundary dispute. Private.

Tudor Place (1790) The architect Thornton built this house for Robert Peter, first mayor of Georgetown. Private.

MARYLAND

ANNAPOLIS

This lovely town, site of the U.S. Naval Academy, has one of the largest groups of distinguished Georgian homes to be found in any American city. Many of them, like other great houses throughout Maryland, are still privately owned, often by descendants of the families for whom they were originally built. Although many of these may be visited only on request, or during the Maryland House and Garden Pilgrimage or tours given by Historic Annapolis, Inc. each year, their exteriors alone are worth seeing. Some of the finest Annapolis houses are: the **Hammond-Harwood House** (1774), designed by William Buckland, and perhaps the best example of Georgian style in America; the **Chase-Lloyd House** (1769), where Francis Scott Key was married; the lovely brick **Brice House** (c. 1745) which is private; the beautifully proportioned **Ridout House** (private); the **Paca House** (1773), home of a signer of the Declaration, now part of the **Carvel Hall Hotel;** the

MD. HOUSE AND GARDEN PILGRIMAGE

Holly Hill, Friendship

Upton Scott Mansion (c. 1765), where F. S. Key spent much of his youth; and **Acton,** private, which was once a plantation home. The **Carroll-Davis House** (1722), birthplace of Charles Carroll, barrister, and one of the oldest houses in the state, has been moved to the campus of St. John's College, which was chartered in 1784. Also on the handsome campus are **McDowell Hall,** reconstruction of a house begun in 1742 by Governor Bladen and known as "Bladen's Folly"; and the ancient **Liberty Tree,** beneath which Revolutionary meetings were held. The austere brick **State House,** begun in 1772, is the oldest capitol building in the U.S. still used as such. Meeting here between December, 1783, and June, 1784, Congress received Washington's resignation as commander in chief and ratified the Peace of Paris. The **Old Treasury** (1735), with heavy batten doors hung on strap hinges, is also on the State House grounds. Other interesting buildings in Annapolis are **Reynold's Tavern** (c. 1735), which houses the Public Library; the **Maryland Inn** (c. 1780), restored and once more used as a hotel; **Ogle Hall** (1739), where Lafayette visited (private); the **Jonas Green House** (c. 1680), home of a noted 18th-century publisher who was the official "Poet, Printer, Punster, Purveyor, and Punch-Maker General" of the famous Tuesday Club (private); the **Peggy Stewart House** (1740), home of the owner of the brig of that name which, with its cargo of tea, he burned in 1774 at the demand of the Annapolis patriots (private); **St. Anne's Church** (1858), undistinguished architecturally, contains interesting relics. The **U.S. Naval Academy,** opened in 1845, has a number of buildings which will reward the visitor. Among them are the chapel, with the tomb of John Paul Jones, and the museum with a magnificent collection of ship

models and naval mementos. Near the city is **St. James Episcopal Church,** locally called Herring Creek Church (1765), which has been skillfully restored, and **Whitehall** (c. 1765), a superb Georgian mansion (private; open on request).

BALTIMORE

In dignified Mt. Vernon Place, in the heart of the city, is a **Washington Monument** begun in 1815, before any other in the country. A local museum is in the base. Baltimore also has the New World's first monument to Columbus, erected in 1792. **Mount Clare** (1754) in Carroll Park, is the only colonial mansion left within the city limits. Now a museum, it was the home of Charles Carroll the barrister. The more famous Carroll of Carrollton, the signer, spent his last years in the **Carroll-Caton House** (1823); not open. Another Carroll mansion is the classic **Homewood** (1801), now part of Johns Hopkins University, whose other buildings have been built in this same style. Edgar Allan Poe began writing short stories while living in the **Poe House** in the 1830's; the **Flag House,** now a museum of the War of 1812, is where Mary Pickersgill made the banner which flew over **Fort McHenry** and inspired Francis Scott Key (*see* pp. 110-11). The fort itself has a collection of old weapons and historic relics. The **Maryland Historical Society** has a fine collection of historic documents and relics; period rooms; silver; costumes; paintings; Key's original manuscript of "The Star Spangled Banner"; and a Chesapeake Maritime Museum. Many historic paintings and objects are in the **Peale Museum** (1813), founded by Rembrandt Peale as the first museum building ever built in the U.S., and now Baltimore's Municipal Museum; and the **Baltimore Museum of Art** contains some beautiful period rooms taken from old Maryland mansions, silver, and outstanding art collections. The unusual *B&O Museum of Transportation* houses a collection of historic railroad material and some wonderful early trains in the original B&O passenger station (1830) and roundhouse (1884). Some of Baltimore's interesting churches are: *Otterbein Church* (1784), a charming Georgian structure; the *Cathedral of the Assumption* (begun in 1806) designed by Latrobe and one of the most notable ecclesiastical buildings of the period; and the *First Unitarian Church* (1818), where William Ellery Channing preached the sermon which outlined the Unitarian faith. In Patterson Park are breastworks known as *Rodgers Bastion,* which were manned by 12,000 volunteers when the British attempted unsuccessfully to attack Baltimore in September, 1814. Northeast on Route 40 is the site of Joppa Town, once seat of Baltimore County. Now only gravestones and the *Rumsey Mansion* (c. 1720) remain.

BEANTOWN
Mudd House After the assassination of Lincoln, John Wilkes Booth's broken leg was set here by Dr. Samuel Mudd. Sen-

Brice House, Annapolis

tenced to life imprisonment in Fort Jefferson, Florida, Mudd was later pardoned for his services in a yellow fever epidemic.

BEL AIR
Tudor Hall (1822) Birthplace of Edwin and John Wilkes Booth; contains family relics.

BROOKEVILLE
Caleb Bentley House President Madison set up a temporary White House here in August, 1814, after the British captured Washington. Private.

CALIFORNIA
St. Richard's Manor (late 1600's) One of the few remaining manor houses with no structural changes. Open on request.

CALVERT
East Nottingham Friends Meetinghouse A detachment of General Smallwood's Continentals housed their wounded here in 1778. Still used as a meetinghouse.

CENTREVILLE
Pratt Mansion To the earlier portion, built in 1710, a Georgian house was added in the late 18th century. Private.
Readbourne One of the finest plantation houses in Maryland. The main house was built about 1731. Private.

CHARLOTTE HALL
Cremona (1819) One of Maryland's later great houses; has an extraordinary hanging stairway. Private.

CHESTERTOWN
This gracious town on the Chester River has many old brick houses, most of them private. Among them are the *Bacchus House* (c. 1780); the *Palmer House,* built with old sailing ship timbers; the former *White Swan Tavern* (c. 1750); and the handsome *Widehall,* built before the Revolution. The President's house at Washington College (founded 1782) is the 18th-century *Ringgold Mansion.* Seven miles from town is *Providence Plantation* (1781), one of the most charming homes in Maryland, with all the original woodwork. It is open by appointment.

CHURCH HILL
St. Luke's Protestant Episcopal Church Built in 1731 at a cost of 140,000 lbs. of tobacco. Near here is *Kennersley* (1704), a beautiful house overlooking Chester River.

CHURCH CREEK
Old Trinity Protestant Episcopal Church Built before 1680. Being restored.

CLEARSPRING
Fort Frederick Typical of the frontier forts of the time, this one was built in 1756 for defense against the French and Indians. The stone walls are 17 feet high (*see* p. 83).

CLINTON
His Lordship's Kindness (1735) One of the finest Georgian mansions in Maryland. Its name supposedly commemorates the Earl of Shrewsbury's land gift to his niece, who married a man without means. Private.

COLLEGE PARK
On the campus of the University of Maryland is the former *Rossburg Inn* (1798), now a Faculty club.

CONOWINGO
Nathan Rigbie House (1732) Where Lafayette put down a threatened mutiny of his troops in 1781.

CRISFIELD
Makepeace A well-preserved house with fine paneling and stairway. One of the finest of its type on the peninsula.

CROWNSVILLE
Belvoir Manor (c. 1690) Private.

CUMBERLAND
In Riverside Park there is a log cabin, traditionally believed to have been used by Washington during the French and Indian Wars. On a hill nearby is the site of *Fort Cumberland,* used by General Braddock as an advance base for his fatal expedition against Fort Duquesne. The town was also the eastern terminus of the National Road.

Hammond-Harwood House, Annapolis

CUMBERSTONE
Tulip Hill (1756) One of Maryland's finest houses. Stands in a grove of ancient tulip poplars on a rise of land. Beautiful entrance hall. Private.

EASTON
The *Third Haven Meeting House* (1682-83) is one of the oldest frame houses of worship in America. William Penn once held meeting under the oaks in the yard. Near Easton is *The Anchorage* (1763), an imposing mansion (open by appointment) once owned by the Rev. John Gordon, famous for operating a race track behind his chapel where he and his congregation bet after services. *Myrtle Grove,* near Easton, is another house of great charm which has been owned by the same family since 1724 (open by appointment). Some unusual private homes in the vicinity are *Troth's Fortune* (late 1600's), almost medieval in appearance; *Boston Cliff* (early 1700's), built of brick weathered to an exquisite color; *Ratcliffe Manor* (1749) on the Tred Avon River; and *Fairview,* with magnificent lawns and boxwood. *Wye House* is a handsome Georgian home with superb heirlooms.

ELLICOTT CITY
Doughoregan Manor (c. 1727), near here, was the manor house of Charles Carroll of Carrollton. Private.

ELKTON
Troops under Washington, Lafayette, and General Howe passed through here in the Revolution. The owner of *The Hermitage* (c. 1735), a Tory, entertained British naval officers in 1777. Washington and Howe stayed at the *Hollingsworth Tavern* (c. 1750) within a few days of each other, in 1777. *Partridge Hill* (1768) is a stone house with fine paneling. About four miles from town is the Mason and Dixon tangent stone, set in 1765, which bears the Baltimore and Penn arms.

FAIRLEE
St. Paul's Church (1713) This church is one of the oldest in Maryland still in continuous use.

FREDERICK
A noteworthy group of Federal style build-

ings surrounds Court House Square. Hessians captured during the Revolution were imprisoned in **Frederick Barracks,** later permitted to "escape" and work for German farmers in the vicinity. The reproduction of the **Barbara Fritchie House** (1780) contains relics and mementos of famous visitors. The **Stephen Steiner House** (c. 1807) is furnished with fine antiques, and the **Roger Brooke Taney House** (1815) is where the Chief Justice lived early in his career. It contains mementos of Taney and Francis Scott Key, his brother-in-law.

FRIENDSHIP

Holly Hill Begun in 1667, this is one of the earliest homes in southern Maryland, and one of the most attractive. It has an unusually fine interior, well restored by the present owners. Open by appointment.

GLENBURNIE

Rising Sun Inn (1753) Restored.

HAGERSTOWN

Hager's Fancy (c. 1740) This remarkably unaltered house was built by Jonathan Hager, founder of the town, over two free-flowing springs. Some unusual artifacts have been discovered here. Open by appointment.

HOLLYWOOD

Sotterley (1730) One of Maryland's finest early 18th-century houses.

IRONSIDES

Durham Church (1732 and rebuilt 1791)

KINGSVILLE

Jerusalem Mills Unusual stone and frame structure begun in 1772. The builder, although a Quaker, manufactured guns for the Continental Army. Mill still operates.

LAUREL

Montpelier A large brick house, late 1700's. Fine Georgian example. Private.

LEONARDTOWN

St. Andrew's Church (1767) A brick structure of unusual interest, it has two square towers and Palladian window. The original chalice and salver are still in use.

Tulip Hill, Cumberstone

Tudor Hall (1750) Now a public library.

LUSBY

Charles Gift (1650) Said to have been the seat of Puritan government in the 1650's. Open by appointment.

MECHANICSVILLE

St. Francis Xavier Church (1767) On the site of a church built over 100 years earlier; well restored.

MILLINGTON

Higman Gristmill (1760)

NEWBURG

Mount Republic (1792) Fine example of Federal architecture with brick walls 18 inches thick. One owner, Franklin Weems, had a copious wine cellar and maintained a pack of 100 fox hounds. Open on request.

OLDTOWN

Cresap's Fort Only ruins remain of the fortified dwelling and trading post built in the 1740's by Colonel Thomas Cresap, one of the leading figures on the western frontier.

OXON HILL

Fort Washington Near the District of Columbia line is one of the country's most interesting old military structures, designed by L'Enfant after the War of 1812. Commands fine view of Potomac; is encircled by a deep dry moat with drawbridge.

PIKESVILLE

Garrison Fort A granite blockhouse said to have been here in 1698. Private.
Old Stone Chapel (1862) Beautifully proportioned Classic Revival structure.

POINT LOOKOUT

Monument to some 3,000 Confederate soldiers who died in a Union prison camp here.

PORT DEPOSIT

Smith's Falls Named by Captain John Smith, who in 1606 ascended the Susquehanna until the falls blocked his passage.

PORT TOBACCO

Habre de Venture (1742) A unique tidewater plantation house of brick and frame construction, it was the home of Thomas Stone, a signer of the Declaration of Independence. Open on request.
Rose Hill (c. 1734) Home of one of Washington's physicians. A house of impressive proportions with fine interior woodwork.

QUEENSTOWN

Wye Plantation (c. 1740) Home of Governor William Paca, a signer of the Declaration. Carefully preserved, with restored elaborate gardens. Private.

REHOBOTH

Rehoboth Church (c. 1705) Oldest house of worship in U.S. used exclusively by Presbyterians; erected by the Rev. Francis Makemie, founder of the sect in America.

SALISBURY

Green Hill Episcopal Church (1733) A brick church which has never been altered.

ST. MARY'S CITY

Site of first settlement by Lord Baltimore's colonists. On the grounds of **Trinity Epis-**

Hampton, Towson

copal Church is a marker where Leonard Calvert and companions came ashore from the *Ark* and the *Dove*. Also here is the site of Maryland's first **State House,** built in 1676. A reproduction has been erected, made of brick from old buildings. **Cross Manor** (1643) is said to be one of the oldest brick buildings in the state. Private.

SANDY HOOK

John Brown House In 1859 John Brown rented this farmhouse under an assumed name and cached arms for the Harpers Ferry attack.

SHARPSBURG

Antietam National Battlefield Site Burnside's Bridge is much the same today as when it was a key to the Confederate right flank, and the town has changed but little. Wounded were brought to Mt. Airy, and **Ferry Hill** (1813) is a sturdy brick house where Lee's wounded son was treated. Other scenes of combat on the battlefield, such as Bloody Lane, are well marked for the visitor's benefit.

SHOWELL

St. Martin's Episcopal Church (1756)

TOWSON

Hampton National Historic Site (1783-90) One of the great Georgian houses of America and a Maryland showplace. Home of the Ridgely family for over 150 years, restored in 1948. One diarist noted that 51 persons sat down to dinner in the great hall and "everyone had plenty of room." Original furnishings, gardens.

UPPER MARLBORO

Marlboro House (c. 1732) Distinguished though neglected Colonial building, once an inn.
St. Barnabas Church (1774) Georgian church of brick laid in Flemish bond.

WESTMINSTER

Old Shellman House, or Historical House (1807) A homelike museum with rooms in Colonial, Federal, and Victorian styles.

WYE MILLS

St. Lukes Church or Wye Chapel (1721) A lovely little church which has been handsomely restored.

NEW JERSEY

ALLAIRE
Restoration of an early 19th-century ironworks is in progress.

BORDENTOWN
Bonaparte Park A remnant of the luxurious estate bought in 1816 by exiled King Joseph of Spain, Napoleon's brother. The *Gardener's Lodge* is the only remaining original building. Private.
Thomas Paine House Home of the famous pamphleteer of the Revolution, 1783-89.

BURLINGTON
James Fenimore Cooper Birthplace
Revel House (1685) Probably the oldest dwelling in town; now a museum.
Captain James Lawrence House Birthplace of the "Don't give up the ship" hero.

CALDWELL
Grover Cleveland Birthplace Furnished with mementos of the President.

CAMDEN
Charles S. Boyer Memorial Hall A handsome house, begun in 1726, which illustrates changing styles in architecture.
Walt Whitman Home and Tomb

ELIZABETH
Boudinot House (Boxwood Hall, c. 1750) Home of the first president of the Continental Congress.
First Presbyterian Church (1786) One of New Jersey's best Georgian churches. Restored.

ENGLISHTOWN
Hulse House Washington's headquarters before the Battle of Monmouth. Private.
Village Inn (1732) Here Major General Charles Lee is supposed to have written the letter which, with his conduct in the Battle of Monmouth, led to his court-martial and dismissal from the Army. Washington drew up the charges against Lee in the dining room of the inn.

FORT LEE
Fort Lee Reconstruction is planned for one of the redoubts of the fort captured by the British in November, 1776, a few days after the fall of Fort Washington across the Hudson. Loss of these forts was a shattering blow to the Americans (*see* p. 91).

FREEHOLD
Not far from Freehold is the battlefield of Monmouth, marked by the *Old Tennent Church* (1751) and its cemetery. General Clinton spent the night before the engagement in the *Hankinson Mansion* (1755), oldest house in town (private). The present courthouse is on the site of one in which Clinton left British wounded after the battle. *St. Peter's Episcopal Church,* occupied by both British and Americans, is one of the oldest churches still in use in the state.

GLOUCESTER POINT PARK
The remains of a British frigate, sunk after the Battle of Red Bank, are on display here.

HACKENSACK
Church on the Green A fine Dutch Colonial church.

HADDONFIELD
Indian King Tavern (1750) A building with many Revolutionary associations.

HANCOCK'S BRIDGE
Hancock House (1734) Scene of a massacre by loyalist troops in March, 1778.

MORRISTOWN
Wooded *Jockey Hollow,* in *Morristown National Historical Park,* looks much as it did when Washington's troops encamped here in the bitter winter of 1779-80. The parade ground has been preserved, and a camp hospital and soldiers' huts have been reconstructed. In town is the *Ford Mansion* (c. 1774) with many of the furnishings used by Washington and his staff (*see* p. 95), and the *Historical Museum* has one of the nation's most valuable collections of Washingtoniana. Alexander Hamilton courted Betsy Schuyler at the *Schuyler-Hamilton House* (c. 1765). At Jockey Hollow, the *Wick House* (c. 1750), is where Major General St. Clair stayed in 1780.

MOUNT HOLLY
John Woolman Memorial (1771) A small brick house on land once owned by the noted Quaker, an early foe of slavery.

NEWARK
First Presbyterian Church (1791) A serene Georgian church with gambrel roof.
Plume House (1706) Oldest dwelling in Newark. Now a rectory; private.

NORTH HACKENSACK
Steuben House (1751) A Dutch Colonial house given to Baron von Steuben in 1783.

PATERSON
Westside Park On display here is the first successful submarine, built in 1881.

PHALANX
The *Old Hotel* is all that remains of the community established here in the 19th century by disciples of Fourier, who called themselves the North American Phalanx.

PREAKNESS
Theunis Dey Mansion (1740) This served twice as Washington's headquarters in 1780.

PRINCETON
Nassau Hall (1756) The first building of Princeton College, and the largest in the colonies at the time of the Revolution. From June to November, 1783, Princeton was the nation's capital, and it was here that Congress had official word of the Peace of Paris, which ended the Revolution.
Morven, now the governor's mansion, was built in 1701. The home of Richard Stockton, a signer of the Declaration, it was used as a headquarters by Cornwallis. It is open to the public on occasion.

RED BANK
Whitall House (before 1776) The Quaker mistress of this house went on spinning while the Battle of Red Bank raged around her in October, 1777.

ROCKY HILL
Berrien Mansion (1730) Washington wrote his farewell address to the Army here.

SHREWSBURY
Christ Episcopal Church (1769) An austere building which contains a copy of the rare Vinegar Bible, printed in 1717.

SOMERS POINT
Somers Mansion (1730) Historical exhibits.

SOMERVILLE
Old Dutch Parsonage (1751)
Wallace House Washington's headquarters in the winter of 1778-79, where he laid plans for the Indian campaign of 1779.

SPRINGFIELD
First Presbyterian Church (c. 1790)
Cannonball House (c. 1740) Survived the Battle of Springfield, June 23, 1780; has unusual paneling. Open by appointment.

TRENTON
Battle Monument There is a small museum in the base of the monument.
Douglass House The retreat to Princeton

N.J. DEPT OF CONSERVATION
AND ECONOMIC DEVELOPMENT

Boxwood Hall, Elizabeth

may have been planned by Washington here. Private.
Old Barracks (c. 1759) The only remaining unit of five barracks erected by the Colonial Assembly during the French and Indian War. British, Hessian, and American soldiers were quartered here during the Revolution (*see* p. 93).
William Trent House (1719) Furnished in accord with the inventory taken in 1726.

WEST ORANGE
Edison National Monument Houses the great inventor's library and laboratory. His home, *Glenmont,* which he called his "thought-bench," is but a short distance from the laboratory, or "work-bench."

WHARTON ESTATE
This huge tract, gradually acquired by Joseph Wharton, founder of America's nickel industry, is now mostly swamps and ghost towns. Restoration is planned for the best-preserved of the estate's 18th-century communities, Batsto, whose *Manor House* (c. 1750) is the only remaining evidence of past wealth. During the Revolution Batsto's ironworks supplied cannon for the American armies.

135

NEW YORK

(Towns in Long Island, N.Y., are listed alphabetically under heading **LONG ISLAND**.)

ALBANY
Ten Broeck Mansion (1798) A fine example of Georgian architecture, built by General Abraham Ten Broeck, who served in the militia during the Revolution.
Schuyler Mansion (1762) "Gentleman Johnny" Burgoyne was an honored prisoner here after his defeat at Saratoga, and in 1780 Alexander Hamilton was married here to General Schuyler's daughter Elizabeth. Furnished with original family pieces.

AUBURN
William H. Seward Mansion (1816) Home of Lincoln's secretary of state. Fine Victorian furnishings.

AURIESVILLE
Shrine of Our Lady of Martyrs A memorial to Jesuit missionaries slain by Indians in the 1600's.

Schuyler Mansion, Albany

AUSABLE CHASM
A galley of the light-draft type used during the Revolution is displayed here.

BATAVIA
Holland Land Office (c. 1815) A Greek Revival structure of historic significance.

BELMONT
Belvedere (c. 1809)

BEMIS HEIGHTS
Remains of the British and American redoubts and a reconstructed blockhouse and powder magazine can be seen in the *Saratoga National Historical Park (see* pp. 88-95). The ***John Neilson House,*** where American staff officers were quartered, is the only contemporary building still on the battlefield.

BRANCHPORT
Friend's Home (c. 1790) House of Jemima Wilkinson, unorthodox Quaker preacher who called herself the "Public Universal Friend."

BREWERTON
Fort Brewerton (1759) Earthworks remain of one of the forts which protected the northern frontier from the French and Indians.

BROWNVILLE
Jacob Brown Mansion (1811) Home of a hero of the War of 1812.

BUFFALO
Milburn House President McKinley died here on September 14, 1901, eight days after he was shot on a visit to the city. Across the river from the city, in Ontario, is restored Fort Erie, scene of some of the fiercest fighting in the War of 1812. The original was demolished by the Americans in 1814.

CANAJOHARIE
Van Alstyne House (c. 1750) Headquarters of Tryon County Committee of Safety in 1774-75.

CANANDAIGUA
Granger Homestead (1815)

CLARKSON
George Selden House Birthplace of the "father of the automobile."

CLAVERACK
Dutch Reformed Church One of the handsomest of its kind in existence.
Old Hudson Courthouse (1786) Alexander Hamilton argued on behalf of freedom of the press here in 1804.

CONSTABLEVILLE
Constable Hall (1819) A fine Georgian house which is one of the most handsomely furnished in northern New York.

COOPERSTOWN
The heart of Leatherstocking country, and location of the ***Farmer's Museum,*** the ***Village Crossroads*** and the ***Fenimore House*** *(see* pp. 96-97).

CROWN POINT RESERVATION
On the reservation are the remains of Fort St. Frederic and Fort Crown Point (1759).

DUANESBURG
Christ Episcopal Church (1793) The oldest unaltered Episcopal church in New York.
Duane Mansion (c. 1816) Georgian Colonial house of unusual proportions. Private.

ELMIRA
Newtown Battlefield Reservation, near Elmira, marks site of the battle by which the Sullivan-Clinton expedition put an end to Tory-Indian resistance in this area (1779).
Mark Twain Study (1874) Most of *Tom Sawyer* was written in this replica of a Mississippi pilot house, now at Elmira College.

ESSEX
The gunboat *Philadelphia,* sunk in Lake Champlain in 1776, is preserved here.

FORT EDWARD
The Great Carrying Place, between the Hudson and Lake Champlain, was fortified during French and Indian War. The grave of Jane McCrea *(see* p. 90) is here, as well as the ***Old Fort House.***

FORT HERKIMER
Dutch Reformed Church The church, begun in 1730, served as a fort during the French and Indian War and the Revolution.

FORT HUNTER
Schoharie Creek Aqueduct (1841)
Queen Anne's Parsonage (1712) A part of a former chapel which the Queen had built for the Mohawk Indians.

FORT JOHNSON
Butler House (1742) Home of the hated Tory Walter Butler.
Fort Johnson (1749) Sir William Johnson's second Mohawk Valley home, much of it constructed of materials brought from England *(see* pp. 86-87).

FORT PLAIN
Indian Castle Church A surviving Mohawk church, built in 1769 and given by Sir William Johnson to his Indian friends *(see* pp. 86-87).
Herkimer Home (1764) Next to Johnson Hall, the most pretentious early dwelling in the Mohawk Valley. Built by General Nicholas Herkimer, the hero of Oriskany *(see* pp. 88-95).
Fort Herkimer Reformed Dutch Church (c. 1730) Part of a stockaded fort during the Revolution.
Paris-Bleeker House Originally the Paris Trading Post, built in 1786. Now a D.A.R. museum, with Indian and colonial relics.

GERMANTOWN
Clermont (1778) The Livingston manor house, with many historic associations. Robert Fulton's steamboat was named for the estate *(see* p. 79).

HARMON
Van Cortlandt Manor House This is one of the Hudson Valley's most historic houses, seat of the 87,000-acre manor established in 1697 by Stephanus Van Cortlandt, first native-born mayor of the city of New York.

HEART ISLAND
Boldt Castle The owner of the Waldorf-Astoria Hotel spent millions on this Rhine-style castle, left unfinished at the death of his wife in 1903.

HURLEY
Van Deusen House A noteworthy pre-Revolutionary stone house. In the town are several 18th-century houses which give the main street the appearance of an early Dutch village.

House of History, Kinderhook

HYDE PARK
Franklin D. Roosevelt National Historic Site The lifelong home of F. D. R., whose grave is in the rose garden. Contains many mementos. In a separate building is the Roosevelt library, maintained by the National Archives.
Vanderbilt Mansion (1898) Great Renaissance-style house designed by Stanford White, now a National Historic Site

ILION
Remington Homestead (1810) Eliphalet Remington made his first rifle and began the manufacture of firearms here.

JOHNSTOWN
Fulton County Courthouse Red brick building erected by Sir William Johnson in 1772.
Fulton County Jail (1772)
Jimmy Burke's Inn (1793) Early tavern.
Johnson Hall (1763) Sir William's last home, a two-story Georgian Colonial house with protective blockhouse nearby. Confiscated by patriots during Revolution (*see* pp. 86-87).

KINDERHOOK
House of History (c. 1810) A lavishly furnished home of the Federal period.
Lindenwald (1797) Martin Van Buren's home; private (*see* p. 79).

KINGSTON
Senate House (1676) In 1777 the New York Senate held its first session in this house, built by a member of the Ten Broeck family which had come to New Netherland with Peter Minuit in 1626. Adjoining museum has a collection of paintings by Aaron Burr's protégé, John Vanderlyn.

LAKE GEORGE
Fort George Ruins of uncompleted fort begun by Lord Jeffery Amherst in 1759.
Fort William Henry A restoration.

LE ROY
Le Roy House (1815)

LETCHWORTH STATE PARK
A Seneca council house and the home of Mary Jemison, the "White Woman of the Genesee," can be seen in the park, which is near Castile.

LOCKPORT
The original set of five double locks built for the Erie Canal remain in the town.

★ ★ ★
LONG ISLAND

BAY SHORE
Sagtikos Manor Headquarters of British General Clinton during the Revolution.

COVE NECK
Sagamore Hill (1884) Theodore Roosevelt's Victorian home, crammed with mementos.

CUTCHOGUE
Old House (1649) One of the oldest residential structures in the country.

EASTHAMPTON
John Howard Payne House (1791) Home of the author of "Home, Sweet Home."

Whaler's Museum, Sag Harbor, L.I.

HUNTINGTON
On Route 110, near Northern State Parkway, L.I., is the *Walt Whitman House.*

LAWRENCE
Rock Hall (1767) Georgian building.

OYSTER BAY
Raynham Hall (c. 1730) Here Benedict Arnold met the British spy, André.

SADDLE ROCK
Saddle Rock Gristmill (1715)

SAG HARBOR
Once a great whaling port, Sag Harbor's claim to be "the most historic village on Long Island" is emphasized by the many fine old buildings still in the town. One of the most noteworthy is the *Old Customs House* (c. 1789). The *Whaling Museum* (1845), an exquisite Greek Revival structure, contains thousands of exhibits, illustrating the great days of whaling, and the *Whalers' Monument* (1856) pays tribute to Sag Harbor men who died at sea.

★ ★ ★

MIDDLEBURG
Congregational Church (c. 1775-90)

MONROE
Old Museum Village of Smith's Clove More than twenty buildings, some of them old structures moved from other rural sites, display household objects of a century ago. The buildings include old log homes, various shops, a fire house, a machinery museum, and an unusual treadmill building which shows how animals once provided power to operate farm machinery.

MOUNT LEBANON
Shaker Settlement A few austere buildings, remnants of the first formal Shaker Society, organized here in 1785.

MOUNT McGREGOR
Grant Cottage U. S. Grant died here of cancer in 1885, just a few days after completing his *Memoirs.*

NEWBURGH
Newburgh was the site of the last cantonment of the Continental Army, 1781-83. There is a historical museum here, as well as the *Hasbrouck House* (1750), Washington's headquarters. The house which was General Knox's headquarters is at Vail's

Gate. A mile from there is Temple Hill, site of encampment of Continental Army while Washington was at Newburgh.

NEW PALTZ
There are six houses dating from the late 17th and early 18th centuries on one street in this village, which was founded by Huguenot refugees (*see* p. 79).

NEW ROCHELLE
The Thomas Paine Cottage (c. 1803) is near the modern *Paine Memorial Building.*

NEW YORK
Although the city of New York is constantly renewing itself, and destroying many of its landmarks in the process, anyone who searches the five boroughs for historic structures can still find some rewarding ones (*see* pp. 128-29). Manhattan's *City Hall* (1812), one of the best examples of post-Colonial architecture, has a fine collection of paintings on American subjects. Federal Hall, scene of Washington's first inauguration, no longer stands; but in the *Sub-Treasury Building* on the site is a museum of Washingtoniana. The *Jumel Mansion* (c. 1765) and *Fraunces Tavern* (1719) are also associated with Washington, as is *St. Paul's Chapel* (1766), the oldest church remaining in Manhattan. Other historic churches are *St. Mark's-in-the-Bouwerie* (1795), *Trinity Church* (1846), where Alexander Hamilton is buried, and *St. Peter's* (1836) mother church of the city's Roman Catholics. Worth a visit are the *Dyckman House* (1783); *Hamilton Grange;* the *Old Merchant's House* (1830); *Cooper Union* (1858),

Jumel Mansion, New York City

historic both as building and as institution; and the *Roosevelt House,* Theodore Roosevelt's birthplace. More recent landmarks are *Grant's Tomb,* the *Statue of Liberty,* and the *United Nations.* Particularly interesting historically are the *Museum of the American Indian* and the *Museum of the City of New York,* the *New-York Historical Society Museum,* and the *Metropolitan Museum of Art* with its fine American Wing. Brooklyn's *Lefferts Homestead* dates from 1777, and the borough claims an abolitionist stronghold in Henry Ward Beecher's *Plymouth Church of the Pilgrims* (1849). The Bronx boasts an example of Colonial architecture on the grand scale in the *Van Cortlandt Mansion* (1748). Other points of interest there are *St. Paul's*

Church (1765); the **Bartow Mansion** (1836); and **Poe Cottage** (1812), where "The Raven" was written. In Queens are the **Bowne House** (1661), an early meeting place of the Friends, and the **King Mansion** (c. 1757); while Staten Island has the **Voorlezer's House** (c. 1696), the **Billopp House** (c. 1688), the **Stillwell-Perine House** (1679), and **Britton Cottage** (c. 1700).

NORTH ELBA
John Brown's Farm Brown came here in 1849 in an abortive scheme to provide farms for Negroes. His grave is here.

OGDENSBURG
Remington Memorial (1809) Houses a collection of Frederic Remington's art.

ONEIDA
Oneida Community Mansion (1860) This was the first large community house of the religious sect known as Perfectionists. A convert devised an improved method of manufacturing silver plate, giving rise to a vast business which continues today, although the society was disbanded in 1881.

View from Battle Monument, West Point

OSWEGO
Fort Ontario (1775) The fort served in all United States wars until 1945. Present structure is of Civil War vintage.

PALATINE BRIDGE
Fort Frey A fortified 18th-century stone dwelling; private (*see* p. 83).

PALMYRA
Joseph Smith Farm In this house, in 1823, Smith claimed to have had a vision of the Angel Moroni, who revealed to him that on nearby Hill Cumorah he would unearth the gold plates of Mormon. The Book of Mormon, the scriptures of the Church of Jesus Christ of Latter-Day Saints, purports to be a translation of these plates.

PLATTSBURG
Kent DeLord House (1797, later remodeled)

PORT CHESTER
Bush Homestead General Israel Putnam's headquarters, 1777-78.

POUGHKEEPSIE
Clinton House (c. 1767)

REDFORD
The town is the site of a famous glass factory, established in 1831.

REMSEN
A replica of Baron Von Steuben's log house is near his grave in **Steuben Memorial Park.**

RENSSELAER
In or near the town are many old houses, among them **Fort Crailo,** a much restored 18th-century building where "Yankee Doodle" is said to have been written. **Beverwyck,** built between 1840 and 1843 as the Van Rensselaer manor house, is now a Franciscan monastery. Near here is the **Van Alen Homestead** (1737).

ROCHESTER
Susan B. Anthony House
Campbell-Whittlesey House (1836) A particularly fine Greek Revival house.
George Eastman Birthplace (c. 1830) and the **Eastman Mansion** (1905), now a museum of photography.

ROTTERDAM JUNCTION
Jan Pieterse Mabie House (1709)

SACKETS HARBOR
Pickering-Beach Historical Museum (1817)

ST. JOHNSVILLE
Fort Klock (1750) Fortified farmhouse; private (*see* p. 83).

SARANAC LAKE
Robert Louis Stevenson Memorial Cottage The author completed *The Master of Ballantrae* while at the sanatorium here in 1887-88.

SARATOGA (see BEMIS HEIGHTS)

SCHENECTADY
The **Abraham Yates House** (1730) is a characteristic Dutch Colonial home. A few miles west of town are some well-preserved remains of the old Erie Canal.

SCHOHARIE
Old Stone Fort (1772) Originally a Dutch Reformed Church, the building was stockaded in 1777 and repulsed the sallies of Johnson and Brant in 1780. Now a museum.

SCHUYLERVILLE
Saratoga Battle Monument is maintained here by New York State.
Schuyler House (1777) Replaced an earlier one burned by the British.

SCOTIA
Glen Sanders House (c. 1712) Not open.

STAATSBURG
Ogden Mills Mansion (1895) A palace-like building designed by Stanford White.

STONE ARABIA
Dutch Reformed Church (1788) One of the finest architectural monuments of the Mohawk Valley.

STONY POINT
The **Stony Point Battlefield Reservation** commemorates the area captured by Anthony Wayne, July 16, 1776. There is a museum.

SYRACUSE
Fort Ste. Marie de Gannentaha A reproduction of a Jesuit mission built in 1656.

Billopp House, Staten Island

TAPPAN
The British spy Major André was executed near here in 1780, after a trial by court-martial in the little Dutch church, since rebuilt as the **Tappan Reformed Church.** In the town are the **76 House** (1755), where he was imprisoned, and the **DeWindt House** (1700), where his death warrant was signed by Washington.

TARRYTOWN
Old Dutch Church (1685) Oldest church on the Hudson.
Philipse Castle (now Philipsburg Manor, Upper Mills, 1683) A fascinating early Dutch manor, beautifully restored (*see* p. 75).
Sunnyside The home of Washington Irving, unique architecturally (*see* p. 79).

TICONDEROGA
Fort Ticonderoga Once the key to the continent, this historic fort has been carefully restored (*see* pp. 88-89).

TROY
Cluett House (1827) A Federal-style home which now houses the Rensselaer County Historical Society.
Samuel Wilson Monument During the War of 1812 Wilson supplied meat to the Army, each piece stamped "US" [United States]. Soldiers maintained that "US" stood for "Uncle Sam," and the name was soon applied to other government property and activities.

WARSAW
Gates House A station on the Underground Railroad.

WATERVLIET
Schuyler House (1666) Once a manorial estate where life was much like that on a southern plantation, the low brick house has been altered considerably. Private.
U.S. Government Arsenal (1813) The arsenal has supplied guns for all United States wars since its establishment.

WESTFIELD
McClurg House (1818) A regional museum.

WEST COXSACKIE
Bronck House (c. 1663) One of the oldest and best-preserved houses in the state. The

stone central wing, in Dutch pioneer style. was built by the son of Jonas Bronck, for whom the Bronx was named.

WEST POINT
Since 1778, when Kosciusko helped plan the fortifications, the American flag has flown over West Point, and in 1779 Washington made it his headquarters for a time. Commanding a long and critical stretch of the Hudson, West Point was chosen as the site of the *United States Military Academy,* which opened on July 4, 1802. The Academy buildings, mostly of a modified Gothic style, rise above the river as though hewn out of the rock on which they stand. Most of them are open to the public. Near the *Battle Monument,* which commemorates the Regular Army men killed in the Civil War, are several links from the 180-ton

chain which was stretched across the Hudson from West Point to Constitution Island to block British ships during the Revolution. The Academy has a fine collection of military relics.

WHITE PLAINS
During the Revolution Washington spent some time in the *Elijah Miller House* here, as well as in the *"Washington Headquarters House"* (1738). *Fort Washington,* captured by the British in 1776, is not far away. Chatterton Hill, actual site of the Battle of White Plains (October 28, 1776) is now a crowded residential area. Between White Plains and Tarrytown is the *Hammond House* (1719), a typical Hudson Valley farmhouse of the time.

YONKERS
Philipse Manor Hall (1682) The brick

wing of the house was added about 1745.

YOUNGSTOWN
The present *Fort Niagara* is the third which the French built on the site; the first was erected by La Salle in 1678. Captured by the British in 1759, the fort changed hands several times, finally becoming United States property in 1815. An impressive restoration of the fort, based on plans in the colonial archives of the French War Department, was completed some years ago, and the buildings now appear much as they did during the French and Indian War (*see* p. 83). The imposing *Castle,* built like a manor house to deceive the Indians, has walls four feet thick. The great oak doors weigh 1500 pounds but are so well balanced that a child can open them.

PENNSYLVANIA

ALTOONA
Allegheny Furnace (1811) Remains of an early ironworks.
Baker Mansion (1846) Fine example of Greek Revival architecture. Now a museum.

AMBRIDGE
Old Economy was the third and final home of the Harmony Society (*see* pp. 120-21). Seventeen of the Society's buildings remain, including the *Great House,* the *Music Hall,* community dwellings, and shops. They are being restored by the state of Pennsylvania.

AUDUBON
Mill Grove Farm (1762) This was the estate of the great bird painter Audubon. House is an Audubon museum.

BAUMSTOWN
Daniel Boone Birthplace Site Boone was born in 1734 in a log cabin which this stone house, built by his father, replaced. Restored.
George Boone House (1773) The home of Daniel's grandfather. Private.
Lincoln Homestead (1733) Built by Abraham Lincoln's great-great-grandfather Mordecai. Private.

BEDFORD
The site of *Fort Bedford,* built in 1757 and already in ruins at the time of the Revolution, is indicated by a marker. Interesting structures in town are the *Espy House* (private), Washington's headquarters during the Whiskey Rebellion; and *Bedford County Courthouse,* a noteworthy early example of the Greek Revival style. *Bedford Springs,* the well-known watering place, is nearby; the medicinal properties of the springs are thought to have been known before the coming of the white man.

BETHLEHEM
Many of Bethlehem's older buildings are associated with the Moravian religious community which was established here in

the 18th century. Among the most interesting remains are the *Gemein Haus* (1741), the oldest structure in town, which housed married members of the group; the *Sisters' House* (1742); the *Old Chapel* (1751); and the *Schnitz House* (1749), a community center whose name refers to the fact that the unmarried men and women might mingle only for the making of *schnitz,* a dried-apple delicacy. The *Widow's House* (1768) is still used as a home for the widows of Moravian ministers, and in the *Central Moravian Church* (1806) the playing of chorales by a trombone choir carries on a tradition begun in 1754. Other historic structures in Bethlehem are the *Bell House* (1745), which housed the first girls' boarding school in the thirteen colonies; and the *Simon Rau Drugstore* (1752), thought to be the first pharmacy in the United States. On the campus of Moravian College is *Colonial Hall* (1758), originally the Brethren's House, which contains some of the finest antique furniture in the area. Bethlehem is believed to have had the first community waterworks in the country; a circular reservoir remains, near a stone structure (private) erected in 1761 to replace the original pumping-house of 1754

BIRDSBORO
William Bird Mansion (1751) A stone house built by the famous ironmaster.

BIRMINGHAM
Brinton House (1704) An authentic restoration of the stone house built by William Brinton, prominent Quaker.

BRYN MAWR
Idlewild Farm (1717)

BUCKINGHAM
General Greene Inn Nathanael Greene's headquarters in 1776. Private.

BUSHY RUN BATTLEFIELD STATE PARK
In the park north of Greensburg is the site of Henry Bouquet's *"Flourbag Fort"* (see

pp. 84-85). There is also a reproduction of a Lenni-Lenape ceremonial house.

CARLISLE
Blaine House (1794) Brick house built by Revolutionary officer who was James G. Blaine's ancestor. Private.
Carlisle Barracks Second oldest army post in U.S., with powder magazine built by Hessians in 1777 still standing.
First Presbyterian Church (c. 1760) A local declaration of independence was adopted here May 23, 1776.
Dickinson College "Old West" is a stone building designed by Benjamin Latrobe in 1804.

CATAWISSA
Friends Meeting (c. 1775) Log building, an early Quaker house of worship.

CHADDS FORD
This village was the scene of the Battle of the Brandywine (*see* pp. 88-95) which began near the *Kennett Meeting House* (1710), and surged around the *Octagonal Schoolhouse* (1753). Markers indicate the

WAYNE ANDREWS

Sisters' House, Bethlehem

spot where Lafayette was wounded, and the site of the Sandy Hollow engagement, bloodiest action of the battle. Other noteworthy structures are the *Birmingham Friends Meeting House* (1763) and the *Chadds Ford Inn* (1737). Near here, at Chester Springs, are Washington's headquarters (restored).

CHESTER

Colonial Courthouse (1724) The oldest civic edifice in Pennsylvania, used until 1919. The town, settled by Swedes and named Upland, was the seat of Pennsylvania government, 1681-83. *Caleb Pusey House* (1683) Believed to be the oldest English-built house in the state.

CLIFTON HEIGHTS

Lower Swedish Cabin (c. 1650) One of the few remaining Swedish colonial log cabins (*see* p. 81).

CORNWALL

Cornwall Banks Oldest iron mine in continuous operation in the New World.
Cornwall Furnace A surviving example of a charcoal-burning iron furnace operated 1742-1883. Cannon were cast here for the American forces in the Revolution.

DOYLESTOWN

The Bucks County Historical Society Museum here contains some 25,000 implements and machines used in America before 1820.

EASTON

Ferry Tavern (1761-65) Private.
Lehigh Canal Has been preserved from Easton to New Hope.
David Martin House (1739) Stone building was home of ferry operator at the Forks of the Delaware. Private.
William Parsons House (1757) Built by founder of Easton.
First Reformed Church (1776) Town's oldest public building.
Nathaniel Vernon House (c. 1750) Log house with clapboard finish. Private.

EPHRATA

Several buildings of the religious com-

Washington's Headquarters, Valley Forge

munity known as *Ephrata Cloister* are still standing and are being restored with great care by the state. The most important are the *Saal,* or House of Prayer (1741), built with wooden pins in place of nails; and the *Sharon,* or Sister House (1743) (*see* pp. 120-21).

ERIE

The Niagara Oliver Hazard Perry's flagship in the Battle of Lake Erie (1813) can be seen in Lakeside Park here. Its remains were raised and repaired in 1913.
Old Custom House (1839) Perhaps the first marble structure west of the Alleghenies. Home of Erie County Historical Society.
Wayne Memorial A reproduction of the blockhouse where "Mad Anthony" died in 1796.

ESSINGTON

Printz Park Site of the capital of the Swedish settlement of 1643, named for the founder, Colonel Johan Printz.
Morton Homestead An early log and stone building; restored.

FORT NECESSITY NATIONAL BATTLEFIELD SITE

Fort Necessity (*see* p. 83) has been reconstructed and *Mount Washington Tavern* (1818) nearby, originally a stagecoach stop, is now a museum with relics of the Braddock expedition. At some distance from the park is Braddock's grave, marked by a monument, and still farther off is *Jumonville Glen,* where rock steps lead down to the grave of the French commander surprised by Washington's men in 1754 (*see* pp. 84-85). Nearby, at New Geneva, is *Friendship Hill* (1789), home of Albert Gallatin, Secretary of the Treasury under Jefferson and Madison. Private.

GETTYSBURG

More than two thousand markers and monuments recall events and personages of the 1863 battle which is commemorated in *Gettysburg National Military Park* (*see* pp. 112-19). Among the many scenes of action are *Little Round Top,* the *High-Water Mark,* and the *Bloody Angle* where Pickett's charge was turned back. Thousands of the men who gave their lives in the battle are buried in the *Soldiers' National Cemetery;* 970 of them were identified. The *Lincoln Address Memorial,* a semicircular monument, has been erected nearby. Within the park is a log farmhouse of Colonial design which was Meade's headquarters until he was driven out by artillery fire. In the town is the *Wills House* in which Lincoln finished work on his address. *Lower Marsh Creek Presbyterian Church* (1790), said to have been used as a hospital by the Confederates, is not far from town. The memory of the great Civil War struggle overshadows Gettysburg, but some interest attaches to the *Dobbin House* (1776), one of the earliest classical schools west of the Susquehanna, now a museum; and to the *Russell Tavern* (private), not far from town, a stopping-place of Washington's at the time of the Whiskey Rebellion.

HARRISBURG

John Harris Mansion (1766) The Georgian Colonial home of the city's founder.
William Maclay Home (1791) Distinctive stone residence of a member of the first U.S. Senate. Private.

HARMONY

Many of the buildings in the town, including the original log cabin, are just as they were when the Harmony Society established its first settlement here in 1805. The residence of the society's founder, "Father" George Rapp, is still in fine condition. The steep-pitched roof of the *Bentle House* (1809) is typical of early Harmonite construction; the famous Angel of Peace lintel over the doorway is ascribed to Rapp's adopted son.

HARTSVILLE

Near Hartsville is the *Moland House* (1763), known as "Headquarters Farm," where Lafayette joined the Continental Army in 1777.

HEIDLERSBURG

Rock Chapel (1773) Oldest Methodist place of worship in this region.

HOPEWELL VILLAGE

Restored iron furnace and forge, near Birdsboro; now a national historic site (*see* pp. 108-9).

LAHASKA

Buckingham Friends Meeting House (1768)

LANCASTER

Wheatland The home of President James Buchanan.
The Pennsylvania Farm Museum, located near Lancaster, has a collection of crafts, farm implements, and utensils said to be one of the best in existence.

LIGONIER

Fort Ligonier A restoration of the fort whose successful defense in Pontiac's War (1763) made possible Henry Bouquet's relief of Fort Pitt.

LITTLESTOWN

Christ Reformed Church One section was erected in 1798.

LUMBERVILLE

Lock 12 of the *Bristol-Easton Canal* is located here. Between the road and the canal stands an inn built in 1745.

MANHEIM

Stiegel Mansion Built by the great glassmaker who founded the town in 1762 (*see* pp. 108-9). Private.

MILLBACH

Muller House (1752) No other dwelling in the state, it is said, is as fully representative of the German Renaissance. The craftsmanship of the interiors, some of which have been removed to the Philadelphia Museum of Fine Arts, is superb.

MORRISVILLE

In Morrisville is a house called *Summerseat* (1773), where Washington stayed in 1776 and which later became the home of Robert Morris. Below, on the Delaware, is *Pennsbury Manor* (*see* pp. 80-81), where the mansion and gardens of William Penn have been restored on forty acres of the estate which he bought from Indians in 1682.

NAZARETH
Another town with a religious background; the *Gray House* (1740) is the oldest Moravian building in the state. Eighteenth-century Moravian paintings are on exhibit in the *George Whitefield House*, which members of the sect built in the mid-1700's for the fiery Methodist preacher from England. *Nazareth Hall* (1754), a Georgian Colonial stone building which is now a children's home, has wide floor planks two centuries old and in the tower a bell cast in Holland in 1752.

NEW HOPE
This attractive town, which boasts many fine old buildings, including an 18th-century inn, was a principal stop on the Bristol-Easton barge canal, opened in 1832. The canal has been restored near New Hope, and visitors can walk on the towpath and ride a mule-drawn barge.

NEW OXFORD
Conewago Chapel Original Jesuit chapel built in 1787; one of oldest in U.S.

NORTHUMBERLAND
Dr. Joseph Priestley Home (1794) The discoverer of oxygen lived here until 1804. Furnished in period style.

PAOLI
There are several interesting structures near Paoli which are privately owned; the *Great Valley Mill*, founded about 1710 and still in operation; the birthplace of Anthony Wayne; and *Valley Brook Farm*, General Howe's headquarters in 1777.

PHILADELPHIA
Philadelphia is another of those cities so rich in historic sites that only a brief and partial listing of them can be attempted (*see pp. 102-7*). Besides *Independence Hall*, the *American Philosophical Society*, and the *Pennsylvania Hospital*, some of the most significant public buildings are *Carpenters' Hall*, begun in 1770; *Congress Hall* (1780); *Old City Hall* (1791); and the *First Bank of the United States* (1798), which was considered Philadelphia's architectural masterpiece when it was erected. There are many historic churches in the city: *Old Swedes' Church* (1700); *Christ Church*, begun in 1727, where Washington, Franklin, and Robert Morris worshiped, and in the churchyard of which Franklin is buried; *St. Peter's Protestant Episcopal Church* (1761); *St. Mary's Roman Catholic Church* (1763), with Commodore Barry's grave; *St. George's Methodist Church* (1769); *First Church of the Brethren* (1770); and the *Arch Street Friends Meeting House* (1804). A number of splendid houses, furnished in the period, are in the "Colonial Chain" in *Fairmount Park:* the masterpiece of the group is *Mount Pleasant Mansion*, begun in 1761, which Benedict Arnold bought for his pretty bride, Peggy Shippen, in 1779; and others are *Cedar Grove Mansion* (1721); the *Letitia Street House*, built before 1715; *Strawberry Mansion* (1798); *Sweetbrier* (1797); and the *Woodford Mansion* (1756). Other distinguished houses in the city are the *Morris House* (1786); the *Samuel Powel House* (c. 1765); the *Wistar* or *Shippen House* (c. 1750); and *Woodlands*, built sometime after 1770, with its collection of exotic trees. The *Betsy Ross House* (c. 1700) is much visited, although some historians not only deny that the first American flag was stitched here, but maintain that Betsy herself never lived in the house. The *Edgar Allan Poe House* (c. 1830) contains manuscripts and first editions. Several beautiful 18th-century rooms are exhibited at the *Museum of Art*. The *Botanical Gardens* established about 1731 by John Bartram are now among the most important in the country; his house is on the grounds. *Stenton* (1728) and the privately owned *Cliveden* (1761) and *Wyck* (1690) are splendid examples of the historic houses to be found in old Germantown. Others are the *Academy*, founded in 1760; the *Dove House*, where Cabinet meetings were held in 1793; the *Perot-Morris House* (1772), George Washington's refuge from the yellow fever epidemic of 1793; and *Upsala* (1801), a private house which is a particularly fine example of the post-Colonial style. The *Mennonite Meeting House* (1770), also in Germantown, retains its original furnishings.

PITTSBURGH
William Croghan House (c. 1835) The finest Greek Revival house in western Pennsylvania.
Fort Pitt Blockhouse Erected in 1764 by Colonel Henry Bouquet, this is the last reminder of frontier Pittsburgh (*see p. 83*).
Point Park, occupying site of old Fort Pitt, will have a museum.
Stephen Collins Foster Memorial Building A modern structure containing a collection of Fosteriana.
Robert Neal House (c. 1787) A well-preserved log house. Private.

POTTSTOWN
Pottsgrove (1752) A simple but noble house built by the Quaker John Potts, a leading ironmaster. Well furnished, and well worth seeing.

RUMMERFIELD
Near Rummerfield is the site of *Azilum*, where refugees from the French Revolution formed a colony which flourished from 1793 to 1804. The distinguished emigrés included Louis Philippe, later King of France, and Talleyrand. The former *Grande Maison* is said to have been the largest log house ever built in the U.S.

SUNBURY
Fort Augusta Built by the British in 1756, the fort was an American stronghold during the Revolution. The magazine and a well are all that remain now, but the *Hunter Mansion* (c. 1852) on the grounds contains many relics, and a large-scale model of the fort stands before it.

TITUSVILLE
Drake Well Park near here is devoted to the early days of the oil industry, which was born in this town in August, 1859. Drake's derrick has been restored.

SWARTHMORE
Benjamin West House (1724, restored 1875) Birthplace of the noted Quaker artist, a founder of England's Royal Academy.

TRAPPE
Augustus Lutheran Church (1743) The oldest unaltered Lutheran church in America.

TULLYTOWN
Pennsbury Manor Restoration of William Penn's Mansion (*see p. 80-81*).

VALLEY FORGE STATE PARK
The *Grand Parade Grounds* and several redoubts are still visible, and the houses occupied by the various commanders remain, notably that occupied by Washington. There are accurate reproductions of a field hospital and soldiers' and officers' huts, and the *Old Camp Schoolhouse*, built by William Penn's daughter Letitia in 1705 and used as a hospital during the encampment, has been restored. A museum on private property near the park contains Revolutionary relics (*see pp. 94-95*).

WASHINGTON CROSSING STATE PARK
The *Thompson-Neely House*, quarters of Lord Stirling and Lieutenant James Monroe before the Battle of Trenton, is furnished with appropriate pre-Revolutionary pieces, and the *Old Ferry House* (1757) marks the place where the crossing of the Delaware began (*see p. 93*). Nearby, but all privately owned, are the *Keith House*, used by Washington; the *Merrick House* (1764), headquarters of General Greene; and the *Dr. Chapman House*, where General Knox and Captain Alexander Hamilton were quartered.

WATERFORD
Fort Le Boeuf (1753) Site of the old French fort is here, along with *Judson House*, used as a state museum.

WOMELSDORF
In *Conrad Weiser Park* is the 1751 home of the noted Indian interpreter and treaty maker. The house is a museum.

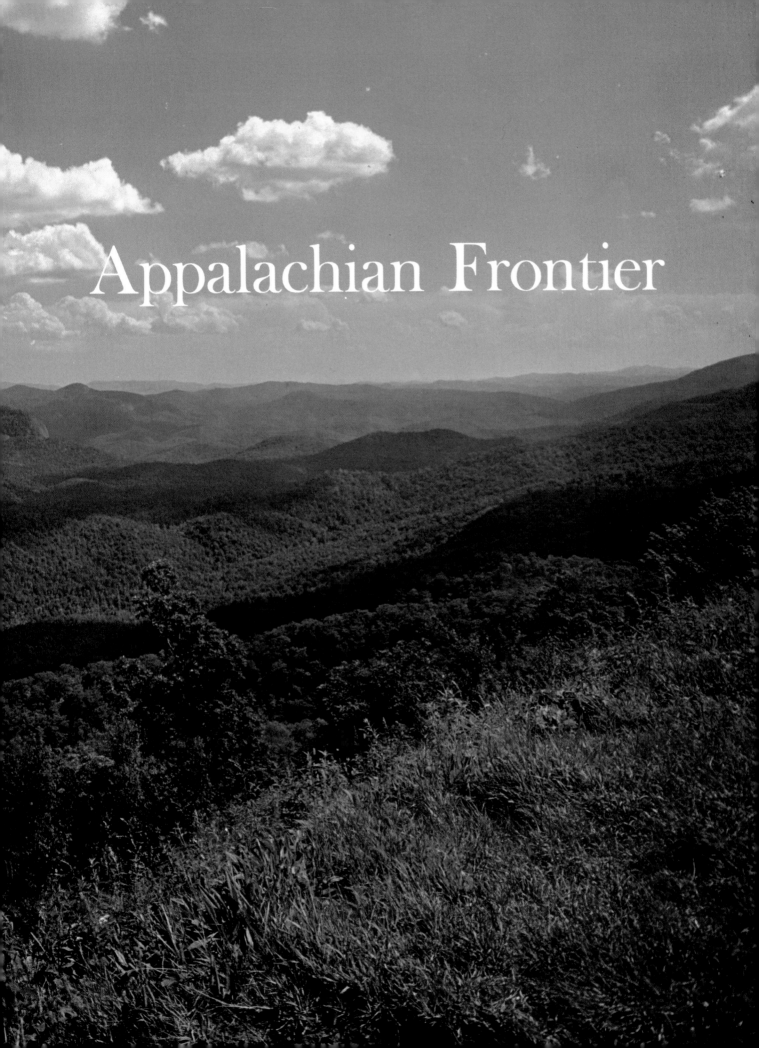

Appalachian Frontier

In George Caleb Bingham's idyllic painting, Daniel Boone leads a group of pioneers along the mountain trail known as Cumberland Gap. Originally discovered by buffalo, this passage was followed later by Indians and white men. The Indian threat was always present, and in some years as many as one hundred settlers were killed on the Wilderness Road.

Many settlers began the westward trek in sturdy Conestoga wagons, named for the Pennsylvania valley where they originated. The wagons were useless, however, on the Wilderness Road, which was not much more than a rough trail, so pioneers bound for the mountain frontier often transferred their belongings to pack trains or floated down the Ohio.

The Land Beyond the Mountains

TENNESSEE CONSERVATION DEPARTMENT

A modern highway hugs the steep slopes of Cumberland Gap, crossing mountains still wild and heavily timbered.

Long before the first white man found his way into the wilderness beyond the Appalachian Mountains and brought back stories of the wondrous land that was there, the Indians knew it as a place almost mystically beautiful. The region between the Ohio and Tennessee rivers inspired a feeling of reverence, a belief that it was almost too good for man to inhabit. There is still splendid countryside in Kentucky, Tennessee, and West Virginia, as anyone who has been there knows, but it can hardly compare with the sight which greeted the first frontiersmen.

Sparkling clear rivers, teeming with fish, flowed through valleys surrounded by the boundless primeval forest. Buffalo and elk crisscrossed the land in vast numbers, trampling the earth into traces which formed roads for the Indians, and which, to this day, are followed by modern highways. Birds so numerous that they darkened the sun filled the forest's enormous roof, and vale and hillside were covered with an unimaginable profusion of wild flowers. Wherever the forest was broken, the ground was covered with a green, jointed cane which grew to a height of twelve feet; and in the woods there were sycamores, oaks, chestnuts, and tulip poplars from six to ten feet in diameter.

Strangely enough, this marvelous land was almost completely uninhabited when the first frontiersmen arrived. Until the Revolution there was almost continuous warfare between the Iroquois Indians of the north and the southern tribes, and no group from either faction could survive in the no man's land of Kentucky or Tennessee, which was known as the Middle Ground or the Dark and Bloody Ground. Hunters and war parties moved about in the region, especially on the famous Warriors' Path which ran from the Cherokee settlements south of Knoxville up through the Cumberland Gap, north across the Ohio River where it is joined by the Scioto, and from there through Shawnee country to Lake Erie, near the present city of Sandusky. As long as fifty years before the first white hunters moved in, a few intrepid traders had pushed into the deep woods in search of Indian commerce. But essentially, the long hunters—so called because of their two- and three-year absences—were the first whites to learn much about the mountains of Kentucky and Tennessee.

Their stories were something to kindle the imagination, and a young teamster on Braddock's ill-fated expedition of 1755 never forgot wilderness scout John Finley's description of the wonders of "Kentucke." That young man was Daniel Boone, whose life began in 1734 near Reading, Pennsylvania. In 1750 his family moved down into the Shenandoah Valley, then on to the Yadkin in North Carolina, whence Boone pushed off on his many exploration trips.

Daniel Boone did not discover the Cumberland Gap —his old friend John Finley showed him the pass through which thousands of settlers would cross the mountains—but more than any other man, it was Boone who led the way along the Wilderness Road. Like the name Cumberland Gap, the words Wilderness Road make it sound rather easy. Both were misnomers, and the Wilderness Road was at best a pack trail which climbed countless ridges, ran through almost impenetrable valleys, across rushing streams— and it was twenty years before it could be negotiated by anything on wheels. Yet in this period a human tidal wave of 100,000 restless, courageous people took themselves and their possessions on foot and on horseback over the mountains to Kentucky.

Like so many early trails, this one had been broken

CONTINUED ON PAGE 146

145

CONTINUED FROM PAGE 145

by enormous herds of buffalo, traveling their ancestral routes from north to south each year. A long section of the Wilderness Road followed the "buffalo trace," which slanted across four modern states. Keeping away from lowlands or marshes where their vast weight would cause them to sink as the mastodons had in the Kentucky salt licks centuries earlier, the buffalo had discovered Cumberland Gap, at the point where Kentucky, Tennessee, and Virginia come together. After the hard climb up over the rocks, they paused to pant and blow at the top before thundering down the slopes into Kentucky. From Cumberland Gap their track went northwest, crossing the Ohio between New Albany and Louisville, slanting across Indiana and crossing the Wabash at Vincennes—the ancient route followed almost exactly by Abraham Lincoln's family. From here the trace went straight over Illinois flatlands through the waving turkey-foot grass of the wet prairies to the Mississippi River near St. Louis.

Boone had made two scouting expeditions for Colonel Richard Henderson, on the second of which Boone's son was tortured and killed by Indians. Then, in 1775, Colonel Henderson hired him to cut a path to Kentucky for the new Transylvania Company—a road which can be followed today with considerably more ease. Setting out from Long Island (now Kingsport, Tennessee), Boone and thirty men traveled north to Moccasin Gap, Virginia, then on to Natural Tunnel, where they turned left to "an important stopping place"—the site of the Duffield schoolhouse. Here they headed west along the route known today as 25 E to the Cumberland Gap. From the Gap, moving west and north along the buffalo trace to Rockcastle River and up Roundstone Creek, the men cut and fought their way through unexplored territory up to Big Hill, where they caught their first vista of the Kentucky plains. This was the end of the mountain wilderness, and they moved into gently rolling forest three miles

south of modern Richmond—fifteen miles from the place on the Kentucky River where Boone planned to build the first fort. In the night the Indians came, killing two of Boone's party, and the survivors had to wait twelve days before moving on to the place which became Boonesborough. Nothing but a monument marks the site of the fort at Boonesborough, but at Harrodsburg a fine reconstruction of another settlement Boone helped lay out shows clearly what these frontier communities were like.

There was another important segment of the thoroughfare which became known in its entirety as the Wilderness Road. Blazed by Ben Logan, this trail branched off from Boone's at an intersection in the thick brush known as Hazel Patch, eight miles north of today's London, Kentucky, and continued along the buffalo route (U.S. 150 today) from Mt. Vernon to the Falls of the Ohio (Louisville).

A man living in Philadelphia at the close of the eighteenth century had two choices of routes to the West. One, of course, led down into Virginia, and over the Wilderness Road. The other meant buying horses and a wagon to pack his family and belongings nearly 300 miles over the Pennsylvania mountains to the Monongahela, then building or buying a flat-bottomed boat for the equally hazardous trip down the Ohio. Whether he drifted downstream in a wallowing flatboat or walked across the mountains, the settler was spared almost no form of insecurity—Indian attacks; malaria, smallpox, or the strange milk sickness; the back-breaking toil of clearing the virgin wilderness; and the terrible loneliness.

Although the battle of Yorktown is generally considered the end of the Revolution, the fighting went on west of the mountains for thirteen more years, during which more Americans were killed than in all the major Revolutionary battles combined. The men and women and children who fought (and all of them did)

CONTINUED ON PAGE 148

Westbound wagons gather at a Maryland inn. The Great Smokies wilderness, even today, retains a feeling of the primeval forest seen by the first white men to venture beyond the Appalachians.

On Blennerhassett Island in the Ohio River are the overgrown ruins of
the mansion where Aaron Burr laid his plans for a southwestern empire.

CONTINUED FROM PAGE 146

were utterly on their own, without support from the
states they left behind or the country then in the making. Interminably besieged by French, English, Spanish, and the omnipresent Indians, they also had to
govern themselves, work out their own laws, and survive. Not only did they manage to do so, but became,
in the process, a new breed of American—as tough and
durable a people as any the world has seen.

Everywhere in the new West, leaders sprang up—
men of brilliance, ambition, eloquence—good men and
bad. There was James Wilkinson, a scheming, influential man; John Sevier, "Nolichucky Jack," that
ideal of frontiersmen who never fought an unsuccessful campaign; James Robertson, the courageous
builder of the Cumberland settlement; George Rogers
Clark, the outstanding hero of them all, who was

almost single-handedly responsible for the frontier's
survival during the Revolution and who, aside from
George Washington, probably contributed more to his
nation's future than any Revolutionary soldier.

That there are no more early architectural survivals
in this mountain frontier is explained by the fact that
the buildings themselves were usually log cabins, subject to attack and the ravages of time. The most rewarding places to see date from a later period, like
Henry Clay's Ashland, at Lexington, Kentucky, in the
lush, rolling bluegrass country. Here, today, mile after
mile of trim white fences line the borders of estates
whose sole purpose is to produce the finest race horses
in the world. And there is Belle Meade, the lovely old
mansion in Nashville alongside the Natchez Trace,
where the breeding of thoroughbred horses in the U.S.

148

began. But the construction of Belle Meade and the great bluegrass plantation homes did not begin until the families coming over the Wilderness Road found themselves with security and leisure time.

One way to glimpse America's first West is to see that great overland entry—the Wilderness Road, which runs for almost 700 miles across the Appalachian barrier, much of it along modern highways. There is Cumberland Gap, where Henry Clay is supposed to have stood, listening, as he said, "to the tread of the coming millions." About two miles south of Parkersburg, West Virginia, is the 507-acre Blennerhassett Island, where several ruined houses and some building stones hidden in the overgrowth of willow trees are all that remain of Harman Blennerhassett's magnificent estate. This was where Aaron Burr came after his duel with Alexander Hamilton, to plot with Blennerhassett an empire in the Southwest.

In Kentucky, near the town of Crab Orchard, a station on the Wilderness Road, is Walnut Flat, and the first brick house in Kentucky. It was built about 1783 by Colonel William Whitley, a steel-eyed, long-nosed Irishman who was one of the most fearless Indian fighters. At a time when the countryside swarmed with savages Whitley calmly decided to erect the finest house in the state—and the tall, two-and-a-half-story structure with his own initials set over the front door (his wife's are in the rear) is remarkably elegant inside. In addition to a ballroom there is a secret place where women and children could hide in the event of attack, a handsome paneled mantel, and a hall stairway on which an eagle's head with olive branch is carved on each step. In all his years as an Indian fighter Whitley was never taken prisoner or wounded (except when the tip of his nose was clipped off by a bullet). Then, at the age of 64, he enlisted as a private in the War of 1812, and fell in a furious battle with the great Shawnee chief, Tecumseh.

Throughout this area are other reminders of its most famous frontiersman, Daniel Boone. Near Elizabethton, Tennessee, is Sycamore Shoals Monument, a three-sided shaft of river rocks which marks the site where Boone negotiated a treaty with the Cherokees in 1775. Boone Creek and Boone Hill, near Jenkins, Kentucky, are traditional haunts of the explorer. At the present Blue Licks Battlefield State Park Boone was making salt in February, 1778, when he was captured by Indians. Taken to Et-Nah Woods near Chillicothe, Ohio, he was held captive and adopted by the Shawnees, but escaped to travel 160 miles to warn Boonesborough of an impending attack. A few years later, on August 19, 1782, "the last battle of the Revolution" was fought, at the Blue Licks, and peace finally came to this first American West.

Henry Clay's bedroom at his home, Ashland

James Polk's family home, Columbia, Tennessee

These log cabins are part of the reconstructed fort at Harrodsburg, the first permanent settlement in Kentucky.

149

Jackson's Hermitage

O nce the way had been shown them by Daniel Boone and other frontiersmen, the unending stream of settlers poured into the new West—a great migration of poor, adventurous men, restless and land-hungry, cutting into the forest like a horde of beavers. Long before the frontier was settled these men, confronted by obstacles the like of which had seldom been faced, made a decision which was to affect for all time the future of America's opening frontier. Just over a month after shots were exchanged at Lexington and Concord, seventeen settlers gathered under a huge elm at Boonesborough and announced their right to govern themselves as they saw fit. Before them, English, French, and Spanish had moved into virgin territory, founding settlements; but never before had one of these colonies announced so boldly its independence or demonstrated so vociferously the belief that no man was superior to any other.

To the West, in particular, and slowly to the rest of the burgeoning nation, came the realization that one man—Andrew Jackson—somehow personified this new spirit, this new set of values. Born in 1767 in the Waxhaw settlements claimed by both North and South Carolina, he fought in the Revolutionary battle of Hanging Rock at the age of thirteen, and was slashed with a saber for refusing to clean a British officer's boots. During the War of 1812 he fought the Creek Indians, and in 1815, after the peace treaty had been signed, he won the greatest American victory of the war at New Orleans. Known as Old Hickory, he was swept into the presidency in 1828 as "the favorite of the people," the "last of the Revolutionary patriots," who had "slain the Indians and flogged the British."

Andrew Jackson grew up in the Carolinas, and after he became famous an old resident remembered him as "the most roaring, rollicking, game-cocking, card-playing fellow that ever lived in Salisbury"; but in Tennessee the long, thin shadow of the man is more tangible, even at this date. In Jonesboro, the state's oldest town, there is a gaunt, two-story log house sheathed in clapboards where Jackson boarded when he was first practicing law. Just outside of Kingsport

This portrait of Old Hickory shows the tall, lean frame which concealed energy, courage, and a fiery temper.

is the site of one of the hot-tempered General's many duels. And Greasy Cove Race Track, near Erwin, and Clover Bottom, where the highway crosses Stone's River outside Nashville, were two places where Jackson raced his horses.

And there is the Hermitage. This lovely old mansion is one of the few important historic houses furnished completely with original pieces, and because it is so little changed it reflects clearly the personality and times of Andrew Jackson and his family. In 1804, when Jackson bought the property, a cluster of log cabins stood on the grounds, and here Andrew and Rachel Jackson lived and entertained for fifteen years. By 1819 the Jacksons had outgrown the log-house style of living, and thanks to three good years of cotton prices, he was able to begin work on their new home. Jackson had just returned from the Seminole wars, so ill that he did not believe he could live long, but he showed a friend the site where he had determined to build—a level spot in a large flat field. When the

friend suggested another, higher location, Jackson replied: "No, Mrs. Jackson chose this spot, and she shall have her wish. I am going to build this house for *her*. I don't expect to live in it myself." But live in it he did, until his death in 1845—some seventeen years after Rachel Jackson had died.

In the beautiful garden are the tombs of Old Hickory and his wife, the smokehouse, carriage house, and a cabin which belonged to Alfred, Jackson's manservant. The Hermitage is the home of a man who grew beyond his frontier beginnings, yet never forgot their strength. One of the former President's neighbors told James Parton, the biographer, what kind of house this was: "Put down in your book," he said, "that the General was the prince of hospitality; not only because he entertained a great many people but because the poor, belated peddler was as welcome at the Hermitage as the President of the United States and made so much at his ease that he felt as though he had got home."

Cotton profits made it possible for Jackson to build the Hermitage in 1819, replacing the log house in which he had lived previously. Although the Hermitage burned in 1834, it was rebuilt in his lifetime.

151

DAVID E. SCHERMAN, REPRINTED FROM *Holiday*

A Confederate cannon on Lookout Mountain, overlooking Chattanooga, surveys the Moccasin Bend of the Tennessee River. In 1863 Hooker's men struggled up the steep mountain to rout the Southerners in a spectacular "battle above the clouds."

The Battles for the West

When the lines of Federal troops crossed the Ohio River in 1861 and headed south, the slow strangulation of the Confederacy had begun. Somehow, whatever glamour the war possessed remained in the east, focusing on the Army of the Potomac and Robert E. Lee's Army of Northern Virginia; but the struggle which took place on the far side of the Allegheny Mountains was no less terrible or fierce; and because of what happened there, William Tecumseh Sherman and his tough westerners were finally able to sweep vengefully across the southern heartland, cutting it in two.

The long roll call of Civil War battles fought in

Tennessee—upwards of 300 engagements—began with Ulysses S. Grant's capture of Fort Henry on the Tennessee River and Fort Donelson on the Cumberland, and then exploded in the bloody struggle at Shiloh. This was a battle no one quite expected to happen here, a battle fought by 80,000 young men who hardly knew how to fire their guns, which ended only after nearly one-fourth of them had been shot. Today Shiloh is a national military park—acres of sleepy wooded hills and little fields, tied together with roads which take the visitor to all the important landmarks of the desperate engagement which neither side quite won. The little road from Pittsburg Landing leads past the cemetery and on to a church which stands on the site of the original frame building which gave Shiloh its name. Not far from the famous Peach Orchard is the Hornet's Nest, where several thousand backwoodsmen held out just long enough to save the entire Federal Army. In the park is a battle-scarred log cabin which stood in the midst of heavy fighting; and Bloody Pond, a shallow pool where wounded from both sides crawled to quench their thirst.

There are dozens of other battlefields to see in Tennessee—Murfreesboro, Franklin and Nashville—and Chickamauga, in Georgia, that tangled mountain wilderness south of Chattanooga where the Union armies took a fearful beating and "the pale river of death ran blood"; but none are more spectacularly visible or more interesting than Chattanooga.

The disorganized, demoralized Yankees who piled back into the town after the rout at Chickamauga in September, 1863, were in a box. To the east lay enemy territory, to the north were impassable mountains, to the south along Missionary Ridge was Bragg's Confederate army, and to the west the only road to safety was controlled by Rebels stationed on top of the great mass of Lookout Mountain. Today, standing alongside the Civil War cannon on this eminence, the visitor surveys the panorama that lay at the feet of the Confederates late in November, 1863. Everything about this fight was visible, and to the Southerners in their impregnable position, it must have seemed utterly impossible that Grant and the Union armies could fight their way out of the beleaguered town. Yet that is exactly what happened.

Off to the northeast, at the upper end of Missionary Ridge, Sherman hit the Confederate right, while Hooker surprisingly dislodged the Rebels above the clouds wreathing Lookout Mountain. But there things bogged down, and the Army of the Cumberland—the same men who were smoldering from the defeat at

From this point 20,000 fresh Union troops crossed the Tennessee River to support Grant's hard-pressed troops at Shiloh.

Chickamauga—were ordered to make a feint at the Confederate center on Missionary Ridge to ease things for the flanking movements. Thoroughly rankled by the implication that they were not good enough to carry one of the main attacks, these men, who had a score to settle with the Rebels, marched forward in a battle line two miles wide, flags fluttering in the wind, toward the great mountain wall held by the Confederates. They seized the first line of Southern trenches, looked up at the crest of the mountain, 500 feet above them, and, to the utter astonishment of the onlooking generals, began climbing. To the Confederates it must have seemed that men who would dare so much would stop at nothing, and as the irresistible line swept up toward them the Southern defense simply withered away. When the Army of the Cumberland reached the summit and saw the Rebels tumbling down the other side, incredible victory was in their hands, and from this moment on the Confederate cause itself would be all downhill, moving inexorably toward the little village of Appomattox Court House in southern Virginia.

JERRY COOKE, *Time*

Back-Country Folk

In the 1880's a well-armed group of Hatfields posed for a picture with the family patriarch, "Devil Anse," seated at center.

At Thacker Creek "Devil Anse" and five Hatfields were ambushed by 42 McCoys. They shot 17 of them, then escaped.

Before he died of natural causes at the age of 83, "Devil Anse" ordered this marble statue of himself carved in Italy.

Tucked away in isolated backwashes of the Appalachian Mountains are a few people whose origins go back to the first pioneers and frontiersmen to settle this region. In the mountain fastnesses are pure Anglo-Saxons who cling to phrases out of Chaucer and Elizabethan England, whose ancient ballads date from Tudor times. Inevitably, civilization has encroached on the manners and mores of these mountain folk; sons who have been off to the wars have returned dissatisfied with the old ways; but there remain, here and there, touches of Elizabethan speech, curious superstitions, and many of the old carols and ballads. It is a simple, primitive life, set against the backdrop of age-old blue mountains and quiet valleys, in little clearings carved out of virgin forest two centuries ago.

One of the best approximations of frontier conditions in America is preserved in the Great Smoky Mountains National Park, where many log cabins remain in surroundings of magnificent natural beauty. The log huts, barns, and implements at Cades Cove, an isolated, oval valley rimmed with mountains, and at the Pioneer Museum near Cherokee, North Carolina, are authentic remains of America's first West.

It is not so many years since these same mountain families were engaged in feuds which have become part of the nation's folklore. The Kentucky-West Virginia border carries the dark scars of the Hatfield-McCoy feud, a battle which began in the bitter strife of the Civil War and continued unabated for more than thirty years. Hatfields still farm the West Virginia side of the Big Sandy River as they did when "Devil Anse" Hatfield, a Confederate, killed Harmon McCoy, a Union soldier, in battle. The McCoys were landowners on the Kentucky bank of the Big Sandy, and when Devil Anse returned from the war, he quarreled with Randall McCoy over a stolen pig. When Anse's boy decided to marry Randall's daughter, Anse refused permission, and the young couple decided to live together anyway. From then on it was open war, erupting in cold-blooded murders, savage raids, and ambushes. Along the banks of Tug Fork, three McCoy boys were tied to the bushes and killed to avenge the knifing of Ellison Hatfield; and up Grapevine Creek is the spot where Lark McCoy and his cronies ambushed forty Hatfields, killing fourteen of them. A flat wooden bridge has replaced the protective drawbridge over Island Creek to Devil Anse's home, and the Hatfields and McCoys no longer live in dread of each other, but people still remember "the trouble" which hatred and fear brought to the mountains.

154

Like most mountaineers, the family who live in the rough board shanty above are devout, God-fearing people. Below, young girls stand waist-deep in water while a companion gets a baptismal ducking in a group immersion. Such ceremonies are usually followed by music and dancing. At left, an old man displays his battered banjo; below, another mountaineer plays on the jawbone of an ass.

155

PARKERSBURG

WES[T]

BLUE LICKS BATTLEFIELD

WINFIEL[D]

FRANKFORT   PARIS

CHARLESTON

LOUISVILLE   LEXINGTON   WARRIORS' PATH

Ohio   River

BARDSTOWN   HARRODSBURG   BOONESBOROUGH

ELIZABETHTOWN   SPRINGFIELD   DANVILLE

HODGENVILLE

K E N T U C K Y

Kentucky   River

WICKCLIFFE

FAIRVIEW   LEVI JACKSON WILDERNESS
                                                ROAD STATE PARK

COLUMBUS—BELMONT MEMORIAL
STATE PARK

CUMBERLAND GAP   BRISTOL

FORT DONELSON
NAT'L MILITARY PARK   ROGERSVILLE   ELIZABETHTON
FORT HENRY   JONESBORO

NATHAN BEDFORD FORREST   GREENEVILLE
PARK   NASHVILLE

HURRICANE   FRANKLIN   STONE'S RIVER   KNOXVILLE
MILLS   NAT'L MILITARY PARK

T E N N E S S E E

COLUMBIA

PINSON   MERIWETHER LEWIS   MANCHESTER   GREAT SMOKY MTS.
                  NAT'L PARK   NAT'L PARK

MEMPHIS   SHILOH NAT'L
               MILITARY PARK

NATCHEZ TRACE

CHATTANOOGA

Tennessee   River

KEY:

EARLY HOUSE

PLANTATION HOUSE

PIONEER SITE

CIVIL WAR SITE

ABRAHAM LINCOLN LANDMARK

BLUEGRASS REGION

INDIAN MOUND

APPALACHIAN FRONTIER

KENTUCKY

BARDSTOWN

Federal Hill (completed 1818) The house that inspired "My Old Kentucky Home."

John Fitch Monument Memorial to the man who invented a successful steamboat 20 years before Fulton's *Clermont*.

St. Joseph's Cathedral (1819) A Greco-Roman church built of local materials, containing paintings brought here from the sacked churches of Belgium and France during the Napoleonic period. These, the altarpiece, and the bell are supposedly gifts of King Louis Philippe of France.

Talbott Hotel (c. 1800) In continuous use since it was built.

Wickland (1813) This house, near Bardstown, is known as the "Home of Three Governors." It is a brick mansion with fine doorways and handcarved woodwork.

BEREA

Near this college town is **Indian Fort Mountain,** a prehistoric stronghold with 200 caves used for defense. Stone walls guard the summit. Close by is **Basin Mountain,** a similar Indian fort. Both were strategically located near the famous **Warrior's Path,** which passed through **Boone's Gap,** south of Berea.

BIG BONE LICK

This town of a few houses and a deserted hotel is in the valley where one of the most famous finds of prehistoric bones was made. Mastodons, giant sloths, and other mammals, attracted by the sulphur springs and salt deposits, were mired in the soft soil, to be preserved for thousands of years. Indians and settlers used the mastodon ribs for tent poles, and found tusks 11 feet long.

BLUE LICKS BATTLEFIELD STATE PARK

The bloody battle between British-led Indians and American settlers, including Daniel Boone, occurred here in 1782, and ended the Revolution in the West. A granite shaft records the names of those who fell in battle, and the *Pioneer Museum* houses many relics, as well as the Hunter Collection of prehistoric remains unearthed here.

BOONE CREEK

In this section, near Jenkins where Daniel Boone once hunted, many of the old customs survive among the mountain people.

BOONESBOROUGH

A granite monument marks the site of the fort laid out by Boone in 1775. A small graveyard is all that remains of this famous frontier settlement (*see* pp. 144-49).

BOWLING GREEN

Kentucky Library of Folklore and a museum of Indian and pioneer relics are in the *Kentucky Building.*

BRANDENBURG

Buckner House (1855) Noted for hand-carved woodwork and winding staircase; headquarters of General John Hunt Morgan for a time during the Civil War .

COLUMBUS-BELMONT MEMORIAL STATE PARK

Confederate General Leonidas Polk fortified the bluffs known as Iron Banks, near Columbus, and had a huge chain more than a mile long stretched across the Mississippi to prevent passage of Union gunboats. When Grant captured Forts Henry and Donelson, the Confederates evacuated Columbus. Fortifications and trenches have been restored, and some 15-lb. links of Polk's chain are in the park. About 1780 George Rogers Clark built a blockhouse here, and a reproduction houses some relics.

COVINGTON

Carneal House (1815) A two-story Georgian Colonial mansion. The owner helped slaves cross the river into Ohio. One of them is said to have been the prototype of Eliza in *Uncle Tom's Cabin*. Private.

Dan Carter Beard Home Boyhood home of founder of Boy Scouts of America. Private.

John W. Stevenson Home (c. 1820) Brick structure which has subterranean cellars once used for hiding slaves. Private.

Clayton House (1839) Private.

CYNTHIANA

Harrison County Courthouse (1851) Stately old brick building. Back of the courthouse square is a log house built in 1790. The town was the site of a Civil War battle.

Nearby at Lair, is the *Ewalt House* (1794) built by a Revolutionary soldier.

DANVILLE

Old Centre The administration building at Centre College is a striking example of Greek Revival architecture.

Ephraim McDowell Memorial (1802) Handsome house which was the home of the "father of abdominal surgery." Restored and furnished in the period.

ELIZABETHTOWN

Here Abraham Lincoln's father, Thomas, unsuccessfully courted Sarah Bush. After Nancy Hanks' death in 1818, Thomas returned and finally married Sarah, who was then a widow. The *Hardin County Courthouse* has a room of Lincolniana.

FAIRVIEW

Jefferson Davis Memorial Park Contains a monument to the Confederate president, and a reproduction of the log cabin in which he was born. Site of the original cabin is now occupied by the Bethel Baptist Church.

FORT KNOX

The graves of some of Lincoln's relations are in *Mill Creek Cemetery,* not far from the government reservation.

FRANKFORT

Boone Memorial A limestone shaft marks the graves of Daniel Boone and his wife.

Liberty Hall (1796) Monroe, Lafayette, and Jackson were among the distinguished visitors to this house, home of John Brown, first U.S. Senator from Kentucky.

Old Capitol (1827-29) One of finest examples of Greek Revival style. Houses the Kentucky Historical Society, with rich collection of Kentuckiana.

Orlando Brown House (1835) Built by Senator John Brown for his son.

GEORGETOWN

Shropshire House A handsome Greek Revival house with beautiful doorway.

Showalter House Stands on site of a slave market whose auction block is still in the yard.

GREAT CROSSINGS

Named for buffalo trace from interior Kentucky to the Ohio River. Between here and Stamping Ground (named for the herds of buffalo that stamped down the soil around its salt lick) is Blue Spring, where some buildings of a Choctaw Indian school established in 1825 still stand.

HARLAN COUNTY

The area around the West Virginia-Kentucky line, near Tug Fork, was the site of the Hatfield-McCoy feud (*see* pp. 154-55).

HARRODSBURG

In 1774 James Harrod established the first permanent white settlement in Kentucky here. A replica of *Harrod's Fort* is in *Pioneer Memorial State Park* (*see* p. 149). Also in the park are the cabin in which Lincoln's parents were married; a pioneer cemetery; the *George Rogers Clark Memorial;* the *Doctor Shop,* a memorial to pioneer physicians; and the *Mansion Mu-*

seum (1830), with historic relics. Among numerous fine private houses in the town are **Diamond Point** (1840), **Burford Hill** (1820), and **Clay Hill** (1812). **Fair Oaks** is an unusually handsome home, built about 1845 by a Shaker doctor. Near Harrodsburg is the **McAfee House** (1790), with thick fieldstone walls and handcarved woodwork, built by an early pioneer family. A few miles from town is the **Mud Meeting House** (1800), originally a Dutch Reformed church, now the property of the Harrodsburg Historical Society. A well-preserved building, its construction of timbers, hand-split hickory, clay, and straw is unique. Not far away is Perryville, scene of a decisive Civil War battle in 1862, after which the Confederates abandoned efforts to occupy the state.

HENDERSON

Audubon Memorial State Park Once a favorite haunt of the ornithologist, who roamed Kentucky from 1808 to 1826. The **Audubon Museum** has a collection of his prints and stuffed birds. A Kentucky room contains pioneer relics.

HODGENVILLE

Abraham Lincoln National Historical Park includes about 100 acres of **Sinking Spring Farm**, where Lincoln was born. A **Memorial Building** houses a log cabin believed to be his birthplace, and near Hodgenville a reproduction of the cabin has been constructed on the site of **Knob Creek Farm**, where Lincoln lived for a few years as a child.

LANCASTER

Near here is the foundation of the **Kennedy House**, one of the largest southern plantations, which once had 200 slaves. Harriet Beecher Stowe visited here, and later patterned a number of the *Uncle Tom's Cabin* characters on members of the family and their slaves. A few miles away is the **William Owsley House** (1813) on a hill overlooking the Wilderness Road.

LEVI JACKSON WILDERNESS ROAD STATE PARK

A reproduction of a pioneer village and a fine museum are in this park, near London.

LEXINGTON

Some of the most famous horse farms in America are located in this lovely area.

William Whitley House, Stanford, Ky.

The city's most famous house is Henry Clay's **Ashland** (c. 1810), designed by Latrobe (*see* p. 149). Although architectural details were altered when the house was rebuilt by Clay's son in 1857, the plan remains essentially the same, and it contains many of Clay's possessions. The garden behind the house was laid out by Pierre L'Enfant. Among the noteworthy private dwellings are **Hopemont** (c. 1812), a post-Colonial mansion built by the grandfather of John Hunt Morgan, Confederate hero; the **Mary Todd Lincoln House,** where she lived at the time of her marriage to Abraham Lincoln; the **Thomas Hart Home** (1794); the **Benjamin Gratz House** (1806); the **William Morton Home** (1810); and **Rose Hill** (1818), which has an entrance copied from the Temple of Minerva at Nîmes, France. Near Lexington is Shakertown, locally called Pleasant Hill, which has a large number of interesting buildings dating back to the important Shaker community founded in 1805. Among them are the **Women's Work Shop;** the **East Family House** (1817), now the Shakertown Inn; the **Farm Manager's House** (1809); and the **Guest House,** now a museum, which has two lovely spiral stairways. Near Lexington is **Old Keene Place,** built about 1790 by a kinsman of Patrick Henry, and near it is the stone **Pisgah Presbyterian Church** (1812, later remodeled). Also near Lexington are the fine **Bryan Station House** (1797), and the Bryan Station spring used by pioneers.

LOUISVILLE

In 1773 a settlement was made here, at the Great Falls of the Ohio, and it was one of the important early communities west of the Alleghenies. Now, of course, it is best known to the tourist as the home of Churchill Downs and the Kentucky Derby, held here since 1875, but the city has a number of interesting historic houses as well. Among them are the **Grayson House** (1810), the oldest brick house in the city (private); the **Benjamin Smith Home** (1827), an imposing Classical Revival residence; and the **Ford Mansion** (1858), now the YWCA. The **Filson Club** contains a large collection of books, manuscripts, and pioneer relics of Kentucky.

MAYSVILLE

Samuel Frazee House (1795) Built by an Indian fighter and scout.

MILL SPRINGS

A roadside park commemorates a Civil War battle here (January 19-20, 1862). A water-power gristmill (c. 1818) is still in operation.

PARIS

Cane Ridge Meeting House (1791) A revival meeting held here in 1801 was described as the "most remarkable religious assemblage ever known on the continent." **Duncan Tavern** (1788) A handsome building restored and furnished in the period. **The Grange** (1816) Near Paris, in Millersburg, is this handsome house with slightly

Andrew Johnson Tailor Shop, Greeneville, Tenn.

curved pavilions and Palladian windows. It was built for Ned Stone, a slave dealer, and close to the house is an old brick building used for slaves, with a stone dungeon beneath its central hall.

Mount Lebanon (1786) This stone house was built near Paris for Governor James Garrard, and stands amid ancient cedar trees. Across a little creek is **Fairfield,** another stone house built by Garrard.

POPE'S LANDING

Birthplace of Carry Nation

PROSPECT

Zachary Taylor House Private.

SHELBYVILLE

Long Run Baptist Church Although some historians believe Abraham Lincoln's grandfather died near Springfield, he is generally believed to be buried beneath this church on Long Run Creek, so named because of the long flight down the valley by those escaping Indian attack.

SPRINGFIELD

In **Lincoln Homestead Park** are a reproduction of Lincoln's grandmother's home; a memorial to Nancy Hanks; and a monument on what is thought to be the site where Lincoln's grandfather was killed by Indians. The **Washington County Courthouse** (1814) has records concerning the Lincoln family.

STANFORD

William Whitley House Begun in 1787, this home of the famous pioneer scout and Indian fighter was the first brick house built west of the Alleghenies, and certainly an imposing one for its time (*see* pp. 144-49). Many unusual features include a dungeon, a hidden stairway, and the initials of William Whitley set in bricks in front of the house (his wife's are in the rear).

WASHINGTON

The Hill (1800) A Georgian house built by John Marshall's brother.
Marshall Key House Harriet Beecher Stowe, visiting here, saw slaves sold on the auction block which still stands on the courthouse green.

WICKLIFFE

Buried City Some mounds made by prehistoric Indians here are still intact; others have been opened so carefully that the remains are visible in their original positions.

TENNESSEE

BENTON

Old Fort Tennessee Blockhouse An early fort of hewn pine logs, with loopholes, has been moved to the center of town.

BRICK MILL

Fort Loudoun A reconstruction of the fort built by the British in 1756.

CAMDEN

Near Camden is *Nathan Bedford Forrest Park,* a reminder of an 1864 attack by Confederate cavalrymen which destroyed large quantities of Union supplies. A park museum contains war relics.

CARSON SPRINGS

Pritchett Home Contains military relics, curios, and old books.

CHATTANOOGA

Chickamauga and Chattanooga National Military Park is on the site of the 1863 battle (*see* pp. 152-53). Among the many memorials, the *Georgia Monument* and the *Monument of the First Wisconsin Cavalry* are outstanding. There are reconstructions of the *Kelly House,* the *Brotherton House,* and the *Blacksmith Shop,* all scenes of heavy fighting. On Orchard Knob, where Generals Grant and Thomas directed the Union forces, the earthworks are well preserved, and the guns are mounted as nearly as possible in the position of Grant's signal guns. The *Cravens House* (c. 1850) on Lookout Mountain is on the site of the "Battle Above the Clouds." In Chattanooga, *General Grant's Headquarters* (1839) is an interesting house, probably the oldest one remaining in the town. It contains valuable relics. Preserved in *Union Station* is the *General,* the wood-burning locomotive which made a spectacular run in 1862 in an attempt to cut Confederate communications. Near Chattanooga are an old *Indian Cabin* (c. 1748), said to be the only one of its kind left in the state; and *Brown's Tavern* (1803), built by an officer of Gideon Morgan's Cherokee regiment in the War of 1812. *Nickajack Cave,* where Tennessee, Alabama, and Georgia meet, was a hideout of the river pirates.

CHEROKEE COMMUNITY

The Young's Building (c. 1796) A log structure, first courthouse of Grainger County.

CHEROKEE NATIONAL FOREST

A wild, mountainous region abounding in game. The town of Tellico Plains is on the site of an old Cherokee town. Nearby is *The Mansion* (private) built around a cabin erected by John Sevier.

COLUMBIA

The James K. Polk Ancestral Home (1816), built by the father of the President, is maintained in its original condition (*see* p. 149), and several other Polk family homes are here. *St. John's Church* (1842), built by four Polk brothers, and *St. Peter's Church* (1861), with its unusual handcarving, are noteworthy. *Beechlawn* (1852) is a handsome plantation house surrounded by beau-

tiful old beech trees (private). It was headquarters for both Union and Confederate generals in the Civil War. Near town is *Clifton Place,* a beautiful house (1812) with magnificent gardens. West of Columbia is the *Meriwether Lewis National Monument,* which includes a section of the *Natchez Trace;* the site of *Grinders* (or Griners) *Stand,* where Lewis met his violent and mysterious death; and Lewis' grave. Also near Columbia is *Rattle and Snap* (private), built in 1845 by a member of the Polk family.

COOKEVILLE

Ann Trigg Robinson House Contains a notable collection of family relics.

CUMBERLAND GAP

U.S. 25, following much of the famous Wilderness Road, crosses the mountains at this historic passage (*see* p. 145).

DANDRIDGE

Near this old town is the *Branner Gristmill* (c. 1850), on the site of a mill built by a Revolutionary soldier. The *McSpadden House* (1804) is a two-story brick residence with heavy doors and fine interior craftsmanship, built by another Revolutionary veteran. Nearby is *Island Mound,* once an Indian ceremonial building.

DAYTON

Near here is Hiwassee Island, once the home of Oo-loo-te-ka, the Cherokee who adopted Sam Houston as his son. This was a large Indian village, and recent excavations have unearthed artifacts, pottery, and other remains of prehistoric and late Indian culture. The famous Scopes trial was held in Dayton in 1925.

DENMARK

John A. Murrell House Ruined home of the famous Natchez Trace outlaw.

DOVER

Fort Donelson National Military Park, near Dover, commemorates one of the most crucial Civil War battles, the capture of the fort by General Grant in 1862. In the park are examples of Civil War defenses: the old fort, earthworks, and rifle pits. There is a *Confederate Monument* and a *National Cemetery.* The *Fort Donelson Museum* (1826) in Dover was formerly a tavern; General Simon Bolivar Buckner surrendered to Grant on the front porch.

ELIZABETHTON

Sycamore Shoals Monument Marks the site where Daniel Boone helped negotiate a treaty with the Cherokee Indians in 1775.

FRANKLIN

One of the bloodiest battles of the Civil War, ending in Confederate defeat, was fought in and around Franklin on November 30, 1864. About 8,500 men fell in 55 minutes. On the hills to the east of town are traces of the Union breastworks. In town are a *Confederate Cemetery,* and the private *Carnton House* (c. 1824), whose porch held the bodies of five Confederate

generals after the battle. The *De Graffenried Works* nearby are Indian mounds named for the farm on which they stand. The *John Eaton Home* in Franklin (open by request) is where Eaton, Jackson's secretary of war, lived with his wife Peggy, storm center of a social feud in Jackson's Administration. The *Carter House* (private) was built here about 1830.

GALLATIN

Rock Castle Begun in 1784, this is one of the first stone houses built west of the southern Alleghenies (private). Nearby are *Fairview* (1832, private) and *Trousdale Place,* which is now operated as a museum.

GATLINBURG

Headquarters of the *Great Smoky Mountains National Park* is here, and among the interesting places to see are the *Great Smoky Mountains Museum;* the *Mountain Farm Museum,* with a collection of old domestic and agricultural implements and other articles; and the *Barnes Cherokee Indian Museum,* with a fine collection of Cherokee artifacts.

GREENEVILLE

Andrew Johnson Tailor Shop A small frame structure now enclosed in a brick building. At the shop one can make arrangements to visit the *Johnson Home* (1851). The site of the capitol of the state of Franklin is at the courthouse. The *Sevier-O'Keefe House,* originally a log cabin, is the oldest building in town.

HURRICANE MILLS

Located near Hurricane Mills are a group of early Indian mounds, known as the *Link Site* and the *Slayden Site.* The latter revealed traces of an Indian village which is thought to be pre-Columbian.

JOHNSON CITY

South of here is the *Haynes House,* built of logs about 1770, and later clapboarded.

JONESBORO

Jonesboro is the oldest town in Tennessee and retains much of its original character. Andrew Jackson boarded in the *Christopher Taylor House* while practicing law.

KINGSPORT

Between Kingsport and Johnson City, U.S. 23 crosses the region of the *Watauga Settlement,* passes the site of the first house built by a permanent settler in the region, and covers territory explored by Daniel Boone on scouting trips. Not far away is the first Tennessee gristmill (c. 1772).

KNOXVILLE

William Blount Mansion (1792) This has been called the most important historic site in the state. Blount, a delegate to the Constitutional Convention, was appointed governor of the territory by Washington, and through his efforts Tennessee was admitted to the Union in 1796.

Chisholm's Tavern (1792)

Hunter-Kennedy House (1820) A brick

house (private) once the center of a self-sustaining economic community. Remains of a gristmill stand nearby, and there is still a huge smokehouse on the property.

Jackson House (1800) Fine old house with secret stairway, and unusual "witch door." Open by request.

Longueval (1823) A post-Colonial house with noteworthy gardens.

Swan Pond (1797) A house built of rough pink marble.

Near Knoxville is the site of the Battle of Boyd's Creek, between John Sevier's frontiersmen, returning from Kings Mountain, and the Cherokees. On the battlefield is the *John Chandler House* (1825) which has never been remodeled.

LIMESTONE

Old Stone House (1792) Early house with thick walls and apertures for muskets.

Birthplace of Davy Crockett The site is on the banks of the Nolichucky River.

MANCHESTER

The *Old Stone Fort,* near Manchester, is an unusually fine example of prehistoric defense works. The earth walls are 20 feet thick, and the inner defenses were evidently built by skilled engineers. Some believe the structure was built by De Soto, but examination of tree rings indicates that it was old when he landed. If the fortifications were built by a prehistoric tribe, their culture must have been more advanced than any known north of Mexico.

MARYVILLE

Barclay McGhee Home (1790)

Maryville College (founded 1819)

Sam Houston School A little log cabin where the leader of the Texas revolution taught when he lived here.

MEMPHIS

Auction Square (1819) One of the original squares where slaves were once auctioned.

Beale Street The street made famous by W. C. Handy, Negro composer.

De Soto Park Where De Soto and his followers are said to have discovered the Mississippi River, in 1541. Under an Indian mound is a cave used as a powder magazine during the Civil War.

Jefferson Davis Park Occupies the site of De Soto's shipyard, where the Spanish explorer is said to have built barges to transport his men across the Mississippi.

Gayoso Hotel (1844) Union and Confederate headquarters in the Civil War.

Hunt-Phelan Home (1835) An impressive brick house with Ionic portico. Private.

Robertson-Topp Home (1837-38) A massive structure with Corinthian pillars. Private.

NASHVILLE

The *State Capitol* (1855) is a handsome Classic Revival building designed by the noted architect William Strickland. He is thought to have had a hand in the rebuilding of *Belle Meade* (c. 1853), one of the loveliest plantations in Tennessee, once famous for its thoroughbred horses Andrew Jacksons' *Hermitage* (*see* pp. 150-51), begun in 1819 and rebuilt in 1835, contains many of his own furnishings, and flowers he planted still bloom in the beautiful garden where he is buried with his wife. Other things to see in Nashville are *Fort Nashborough,* a model of the fort built in 1780 by James Robertson, whom Jackson called the "father of Tennessee"; the restoration of *Fort Negley* (1862), whose guns opened the Battle of Nashville in 1864; and the *Natchez Trace Marker,* which indicates the junction of the Trace with the old Wilderness Road.

NEW PROVIDENCE

Old Stone Blockhouse (1789) Built by John Sevier's brother Valentine.

PINSON

Cisco Indian Village, near Pinson, is the site of an ancient fortified city; 35 mounds and other defense works extending for six miles are well preserved.

PULASKI

Colonial Hall (c. 1840) is an interesting Greek Revival house (private). The town reservoir is on the site of a Civil War fort, and some earthworks remain.

REELFOOT LAKE

Once a thick forest, the lake bed was created by the New Madrid earthquake in 1811; waters of the Mississippi flowed into a depression caused by the tremor. Davy Crockett settled on the Rutherford Fork of the Obion River near here in 1821 and hunted around the lake.

ROGERSVILLE

Andrew Jackson Inn (1856) Has a notable unsupported circular stairway.

Presbyterian Church (c. 1835) The slave gallery and handcarved woodwork are particularly interesting.

RUTHERFORD

Davy Crockett Home Site and Barn (1822)

SHILOH NATIONAL MILITARY PARK

The park commemorates the bloody battle fought near the little country church called Shiloh on April 6-7, 1862 (*see* p. 153). A museum is in the park; there are old cannon in the fields and a military cemetery.

SMYRNA

Sam Davis Home and Grave Davis, a 19-year-old Confederate scout, was hanged by Federal troops in 1863.

SPRING CITY

Near here is the *Hampton Group* of Indian mounds, part of a chain that extended through the Tennessee River Valley.

STONES RIVER NATIONAL MILITARY PARK

The Civil War battle fought here, near Murfreesboro in 1863, was costly but indecisive. In the park, a pyramid of cannon balls marks the site of the temporary headquarters of General Bragg. *Redoubt Brannan,* built by Union troops, is well preserved. The *Murfreesboro Courthouse* was raided on July 13, 1862, by Nathan Bedford Forrest's men, who rescued civilians held there by Federal troops.

WEST VIRGINIA

BARBOURSVILLE

D.A.R. Toll House Museum (1837) Originally a turnpike way station.

BERKELEY SPRINGS

One of the oldest spas in the region, the warm springs here were regarded by Indians as a gift of the Great Spirit. In 1748 Washington "call'd to see ye Fam'd Warm Springs," and returned often, bringing his family. He is supposed to have planted the "Washington Elm" in the town. One of the most interesting homes here is the private *Allen House,* built before 1800 of logs and later clapboarded. It was a tavern for many years and contains some of the original glass and timbers. *The Castle* (private) is a gray stone structure modeled after a Norman castle and built in 1887. *Port James*

Rumsey is a small park dedicated to the man who experimented with an early steamboat at the mouth of Sir Johns Run here in 1784.

BETHANY

Alexander Campbell Homestead Home of the founder of the Disciples of Christ.

BEVERLY

Rich Mountain Battlefield Near Beverly is the scene of a decisive Union victory in 1861. An apple orchard now surrounds the ruins of the *Hart House* (built by the son of a signer of the Declaration of Independence) used as a hospital after the battle.

BUNKER HILL

A monument marks the site of the cabin built in 1826 by Morgan Morgan, first white settler in this area.

CARNIFEX FERRY BATTLEFIELD STATE PARK

The site of an 1861 battle which led to Federal control of the lower Kanawha.

CHARLES TOWN

The town was founded by George Washington's brother Charles, whose home, *Happy Retreat* (1780), now called Mordington, is in an excellent state of preservation (private). Another brother, Colonel Samuel Washington, built *Harewood* (1771), where James and Dolly Madison were married in 1794; George Washington is said to have designed the house. *Claymont Court* (1820), near Charles Town, was built by the grandnephew of George Washington. It is private and may be visited by appointment only. Part of the *White House Tavern* was built in 1742, with stout construction and secret passages in the event of Indian attacks. John Brown's trial took place in the **Jefferson County Courthouse** in 1859; the site of the gallows is marked. The **Tiffin House** (private) was the home of the first governor of Ohio from 1789 to 1796, and the **Crane House** (private) was built before 1800.

CHARLESTON

Site of Fort Lee (1788)

Holly Grove (1815) This gray brick house was first called the Ruffner Mansion. Later a tavern where notables like Andrew Jackson, Henry Clay, Sam Houston, and John Audubon stopped. It is private.

Stalnaker Drugstore (1840) This old pharmacy contains historic relics.

State Capitol Includes the **State Museum** of pioneer relics like Daniel Boone's rifle, Lewis Wetzel's rifle, Aaron Burr's spectacles, and models of Rumsey's steamboat and Blennerhassett Mansion.

DROOP MOUNTAIN BATTLEFIELD STATE PARK

Site of a Confederate defeat in 1863.

FORT ASHBY

Fort Ashby (c. 1756) Sole survivor of a chain of frontier outposts built under the direction of George Washington.

GAP MILL

Rehoboth Church (1784) A log building; the oldest extant Methodist church west of the Alleghenies.

GLEN FERRIS

Glen Ferris Inn A popular stopping place on the James River and Kanawha Turnpike during the mid-19th century.

HARPERS FERRY

The original site of the engine house in which John Brown made his last stand is marked by a simple monument; the engine house itself has been moved to the campus of Storer College, on a cliff overlooking the Shenandoah (see p. 112). The site of the government armory is also marked.

HAWKS NEST STATE PARK

Cabin Museum Contains a collection of items relating to the settlement of the state.

JANE LEW

The **Jackson Farm** (now the state 4-H Camp), near Jane Lew, belonged to the grandfather of General "Stonewall" Jackson, who lived here from 1830 to 1842. A mill (1837) still stands; the site of the Jackson house is occupied by the **McWhorter Cabin** (1793), built by a Revolutionary veteran and moved from its original site.

LEETOWN

After his court-martial in 1778 General Charles Lee lived in eccentric retirement in the house known as **Prato Rio.** The ground floor had no partitions; Lee divided the space into quarters with chalk lines on the floor, and in one "room" kept his books, in the next his bed, etc. Washington, hoping for a reconciliation, wrote to say that he would call, but on arrival found this sign on the door: "No meat cook'd here today." Another cashiered general, Horatio Gates,

lived in **Traveler's Rest** nearby.

LEWISBURG

Old Stone Church (1796) The oldest unaltered church in continuous use west of the Alleghenies.

LOGAN

Near here, in Omar, is the Hatfield cemetery, where "Devil Anse" Hatfield is buried (see pp. 154-55). In this area the bitter Hatfield-McCoy feud took place between the Hatfield family of West Virginia and the McCoys of Kentucky.

LOST RIVER STATE PARK

Lee Cabin Built by "Light Horse" Harry Lee, father of Robert E. Lee. The area was once known as Lee's White Sulphur Springs and was a popular resort. Lost River disappears under a mountain and emerges on the other side as the Cacapon River.

MARTINSBURG

Tuscarora Presbyterian Church Contains part of original church, built c. 1745.

MIDDLE WHEELING CREEK

Monument Place (1798) A Georgian Colonial mansion; restored; period furniture.

Old Stone Mill (c. 1826)

MORGANTOWN

The first settlement, made in 1758, was destroyed by Indians, and in 1767 Zackquill Morgan, son of Morgan Morgan, erected log houses and two forts here. In 1793 Morgantown was the terminus of a road opened by the Pittsburgh *Gazette* for distribution of its papers. The **McCleery House** (1790) is probably the oldest house in the city. The **Old Stone House** (before 1813) is now an antique shop.

MOUNDSVILLE

Grave Creek Mound One of the largest Indian burial mounds in America. Museum.

OLD FIELDS

Fort Pleasant (1823) A mansion built by an early settler; named for the frontier fort which stood near here in 1756.

PARKERSBURG

Blennerhassett Island This island in the Ohio River, south of Parkersburg, was a wilderness paradise in 1805, when Harman Blennerhassett, a wealthy and eccentric Irishman, was persuaded to join Aaron Burr in his scheme for an empire in the Southwest. The collapse of the plot ruined Blennerhassett, although he was never brought to trial; a heap of stones is all that remains of his mansion (see p. 148).

Centennial Cabin Museum Contains relics of settlement days.

Oakland This private house was begun in 1833. The woodwork was carved by slaves.

The Point Site of the first settlement.

Stratford Hotel (1812)

Tavenner House (1800) Another private house, erected by Colonel Hugh Phelps.

PHILIPPI

This town was the scene of what has been called the first land battle of the Civil War, known as the "Philippi Races" because of the rapid Confederate retreat. A two-way covered bridge (1852) is still in use here.

POINT PLEASANT

Tu-Endie-Wei Park A monument marks the site of the Battle of Point Pleasant (1774) which local historians call the "first battle of the Revolution. **Mansion Museum,** a log building, contains battle relics.

SHEPHERDSTOWN

This is the oldest continuously settled community in the state and has expanded little since its founding in 1762. In 1790 George Washington considered it a possible location for the national capital. The **Richard ap Morgan House** has been called the oldest in the state, but records indicate it was built after 1764. In the early 19th century the **Old Market House** was an open pavilion where farmers kept their stalls. **Rumsey State Park** overlooks the stretch of the Potomac River where James Rumsey successfully demonstrated his steamboat in 1787.

ST. ALBANS

River Lawn (c. 1832) Once a tavern on the James River and Kanawha Turnpike.

SNOW HILL

Daniel Boone Cave Said to have been used as a shelter by Boone on hunting trips. On the bluff across the river he built a cabin about 1788, where he lived for several years.

WEIRTON

Peter Tarr Furnace (late 1700's) Ruins of first iron furnace west of the Alleghenies.

WHEELING

The first known white visitor was Céleron de Bienville who buried a lead plate here claiming the area for France. The name Wheeling came from the Indian word *weeling* (place of the skull), after Delaware Indians beheaded some whites as a warning to other settlers. The site of **Fort Henry** (1774) is marked, and near the B&O railroad tunnel is **Wetzel's Cave,** hideout for Lewis Wetzel, the most noted Indian killer in the area. **Washington Farms** includes a small house built by Washington's nephew about 1817. The **Mansion House** (1835) was the most impressive house of its day, and has rooms illustrating the furniture of several periods. **Monument Place** (1798) is notable for its doorway and woodwork. Near Wheeling, at Triadelphia, is the **Green Hotel** (c. 1800) a former tavern on the National Road. Also nearby are a stone mill (c. 1826), still in operation; and the **Stone House** (c. 1820), once a stagecoach station. On the crest of Wheeling Hill is the **McCulloch's Leap Marker** which commemorates the traditional escape of the scout who rode his horse down the 150-foot precipice to elude a band of Indians.

WHITE SULPHUR SPRINGS

Mementos of this famous resort's colorful past are preserved in the **President's Cottage** (1816), which served as a summer retreat for Presidents Van Buren, Tyler, and Fillmore. General Robert E. Lee and his family spent several summers in the **Lee Cottage.**

WINFIELD

Morgan's Museum Contains many relics of the Indian wars and the Civil War.

The Old South

The Mysteries
of the Mounds

In discussing American history it is fairly common practice to begin with a fleeting reference to hardy Norse adventurers, recount the voyage of Christopher Columbus, mention some of the more remarkable Spanish explorations, and then settle down to business with the colonies at Jamestown and Plymouth. What is often forgotten is the fact that America has a fascinating prehistoric story of its own.

Humans had been in the New World for as much as 25,000 years before the white men came, and it is hard to realize that these people, and the enormous reach of land from sea to sea, enjoyed thousands of years of complete isolation; yet except for the handful of Norsemen who touched the coast of North America a few centuries before Columbus, there was no contact whatever. Within the great continent, no Indian tribe had any real knowledge of the land or its neighbors beyond a range of several hundred miles. Although there was a network of trails all over the country, long voyages of any sort had to be made by lake or river. There is nothing to indicate that Indian society discovered or made use of the wheel, and the only beast of burden (aside from the squaw) was the dog. Yet anyone who thinks of these natives simply as barbaric

A Master Farmer artisan fashioned this white-faced effigy in clay almost a thousand years ago. Such objects, often left with the dead in mound graves, had a religious significance.

savages must reckon, among other things, with their elaborate social structures, some of the finest modeling and carving ever to exist in North America, and genuine cultures which were well on their way toward true civilizations when the first white man appeared on the scene.

Down in central Georgia, on the bluffs overlooking the muddy, wandering Ocmulgee River, are the remains of a nomadic people who were here when giant ground sloths, three-toed horses, camels, and mammoths still roamed the continent. Of the six successive civilizations unearthed at Ocmulgee, the earliest may date back to 8000 B.C.; the most recent one came to an end fifteen years before George Washington was born.

Probably the first Indians to live at Ocmulgee were the almost unknown creatures of the Stone Age who are called Wandering Hunters because of their social pattern. These were descendants of men who crossed Bering Strait to America from Asia as the last of the great ice sheets retreated, and moved across the continent killing game with their distinctive grooved

JOHN E. THIERMAN

Boulders at Trackrock Gap, near Blairsville, Georgia, are etched with prehistoric symbols and animal-track carvings.

164

spears. It is estimated that these Indians lived in Georgia for as long as 5,000 years. After them came the Shellfish Eaters, attracted to the region by the mussel beds in the rivers and by the deer and bear. Remains of their pottery—made of clay mixed with moss fibers or grass—have been found at Ocmulgee, along with spear points and net sinkers. After they left the region—around 100 B.C.—the Early Farmers moved in, to stay for something like 900 years. Like their predecessors these Indians subsisted largely on game, but they also raised a few crops, probably beans and pumpkins, and found enough leisure time to make beautiful pottery which they decorated with elaborate designs. Then, in this inexorable procession of civilizations, the Early Farmers were pushed out by the invasion of the Master Farmers. These were highly skilled fellows; in addition to growing beans and pumpkins they raised corn and tobacco, and devoted their extra energies to the construction of temples, placed on large mounds of earth, and of circular earth lodges used for religious ceremonies and tribal government councils. A corn field once used by them has been perfectly preserved by a thick layer of red clay; and there are oval pits, surrounding a prehistoric village, which probably served as fortifications.

The Funeral Mound at Ocmulgee—a conical structure thirty feet high and over 250 feet long—was once a combined temple and burial place, formed of five different kinds of clay, each marking the summit of an earlier mound. From the ornaments, tools, clay pipes, and bowls of food found here, we know that the Master Farmers believed in an afterlife. And here, as in so many other mounds and stone graves found in the southeast and through the Mississippi Valley, one can see the striking similarity between their flat-topped mounds of earth, crowned with a wood and thatch temple, and the stone temple-topped pyramids of Central America.

The largest monument at Ocmulgee is the Great Temple Mound, also built by the Master Farmers, which was originally 40 feet high and 300 feet across at the base. It is pyramidal in shape, and was made sometime between A.D. 1350 and 1500 by the laborious process of carrying dirt and clay to the scene in baskets. At least four times during construction the project was "completed," a caplike layer of clay was laid on, and a ceremonial structure built on top. Then someone with a grander dream came along, and work began again.

Eventually, like all the others, the Master Farmers were driven out—this time by their old enemies the Early Farmers, who returned, acquiring from archaeologists the name Reconquerors. The Indians of this fifth civilization—ancestors of the Creeks and Cherokees—lived in small villages in the swamps, protected from attack by palisades of upright logs. They went on making pottery, they continued to build mounds. Then around 1690 white men built a trading post nearby, and the civilization of the Mound Builders, like that of so many other Indians in America, was about to be destroyed once and for all. Creek society, for example, degenerated sharply at this time. Once a group of independent farmers, they became hunters to reap the quick rewards of bartering deerskins for the copper bells, knives, guns, and rum so thoughtfully supplied by the traders. It was inevitable that they would finally take a stand against the white invaders, and this they did in 1715, when Emperor Brim of the Creeks decided to drive the English out of Carolina and then polish off the Spanish and the French. His "Yamassee War" lasted until 1717 when he was defeated; then the Creek nation moved west, and the mounds of Ocmulgee were deserted. Deserted, that is, by the living—but populated with silent remains which could tell in their own way the story of a people who had miraculously crossed and established their homes on this continent thousands of years before a European knew of its existence.

Temple mounds like this one at Ocmulgee not only served as burying places but were also civic and religious centers.

Spanish Florida

It was a time of fantastic dreams, of adventure and the lust for riches. Within a century the waters of the Atlantic, once peopled with demons and monsters and ending in an abyss, became a traveled highway over which Spanish treasure galleons hauled the plunder of a virgin continent intended to make the King of Spain master of all Europe. Columbus had shown the way, and the Castilians, toughened by eight centuries of struggle with the Moors, saw a golden vision that called for courage whose like the world had seldom seen. Off into the unknown they went, and there has never been a conquest like it. In one generation Spain acquired more territory than Rome overran in 500 years, and by the time Philip II ascended the thrones of Portugal and Spain in 1580, nearly ninety years after Columbus' first voyage, no other nation had yet planted a single permanent settlement in the New World.

The first Spanish colonies were nothing but headquarters for a gold hunt, and because no treasure was found on the seaboard of America no one settled there until 1565. Tales of a magic spring which brought eternal youth to the aged took Ponce de Leon to the balmy "island" of Florida in 1513, and although he failed to find the fountain he discovered the Bahama Channel which became the route of the treasure galleons. In 1521 he returned to colonize Florida but was attacked by Indians on the day he landed and received a fatal wound. Next to try was the red-bearded, one-eyed Pánfilo de Narváez, victim of one of the most harrowing expeditions on record. Narváez landed in 1528 at St. Clement's Point just north of Tampa Bay, and when he found a little gold ornament in a deserted Indian hut, set off at once on a frantic search for treasure. For three months Narváez and 300 men, weighted down with armor, staggered through the swampy, miasmic jungles, beset by Indians, reptiles, and insects, weakened by hunger and the terrible heat. Finally they ate their horses, managed somehow to put together five crude boats, and set sail—for where, no one quite knew. Two of the craft were captured and the men killed by Indians, Narváez was lost in a storm, but two other boats reached Texas. Unbelievably, Cabeza de Vaca and three companions kept alive for six years, to be found by a Spanish patrol in the deserts north of the Rio Grande.

In 1539 the iron-willed Hernando de Soto came through Florida on one leg of another frightful journey. Starting with 620 knights and soldiers in armor, 223 horses, and hundreds of hogs on the hoof, he fought his way through the wilderness of Florida, Georgia, up into the Carolinas, Tennessee, Alabama, and after two years, to the bank of the Mississippi River.

In 1564 a group of French Protestants fleeing from persecution at home built Fort Caroline at the mouth of the St. John's River, near present Jacksonville. As the first European settlement north of Mexico, this was a real threat to Spain, and Don Pedro Menéndez de Avilés was sent to destroy the French. Arriving on St. Augustine's Day in 1565, he wiped out Fort Caroline by land attack and the French fleet in a naval battle, then sailed down the coast to establish a base at the Indian village of Seloy. There he fortified a barnlike Indian house, and this was the forerunner of the Castillo de San Marcos, seat of Spanish power in Florida.

San Augustín was formally established on September 8, 1565—the oldest permanent white settlement in the United States. The peninsular site selected by Don Pedro as a strategic point for defense was capital of a territory stretching north to Labrador and west to the Mississippi; but for years no one seemed to realize the importance of Spanish North America, and the tiny settlement of three or four hundred people struggled along with little attention from anyone. In 1586 Sir Francis Drake deemed it worthy of consideration and sacked and burned the town; but there was little further activity until 1672, when English settlement of Charles Town (South Carolina) goaded the Spanish into action. On the site of St. Augustine's old wooden fort they started building the castle that would protect Florida, and for the next 84 years Spaniards, slaves, and Indian laborers worked unceasingly on the great fortification. When, in 1702, Governor James Moore of South Carolina appeared with an army and occupied the town, the Spanish population simply moved into the castle and raised the drawbridge: the English cannon were useless against the thick coquina walls. After Moore's forces were repulsed, the Spaniards decided to build walls around their town, too, and these withstood attacks by Colonel William Palmer in 1728, James Oglethorpe in 1740, and others. Finally, with Spain's decline as a world power, Florida became part of the United States in 1821.

Along the narrow streets of St. Augustine there are still many reminders of its centuries under the Spanish flag—a thick-walled house which is probably the oldest in the country, an old Spanish inn, the Spanish treasury, and numerous others. But none of them can quite equal Castillo de San Marcos, symbol of all that Spain once held, and lost, in the New World.

H. W. HANNAU

H. W. HANNAU

These three buildings in St. Augustine are reminders of two centuries of Spanish rule in Florida. The vine-covered clapboard building above is a schoolhouse built in 1778. At right, the St. Augustine Cathedral, built in 1793-97, is the only church in Florida surviving from the Spanish period. Below, the coquina walls of Castillo de San Marcos overlook Matanzas Bay. Spaniards, slaves, and Indians worked for 84 years constructing the fort, which cost thirty million dollars. The King of Spain was prompted to remark that its "bastions must be made of solid silver," but it served the Spaniards well, withstanding a number of English assaults.

ELIOT ELISOFON, *Life*

The Lost Colony

The Englishmen who landed at Roanoke in 1584 found fertile land and friendly natives.

The mystery of the settlement known as the Lost Colony is somehow heightened by the wonderful place names which mark that windswept coast of North Carolina. Starting south from the edge of the great Dismal Swamp and moving toward the "graveyard of the Atlantic," past the whistling swans of Currituck Sound, the visitor sees Kitty Hawk, Kill Devil Hill, Nags Head, Manteo, then Roanoke Island; and beyond lie Cape Hatteras, the treacherous Diamond Shoals, and Ocracoke. The beaches that shimmer with laughter and sunlight and dancing waves are accursed to the sailor with his long memory for tragedy: "If Tortugas let you pass, You beware of Hatteras." Here in the shifting sands are the skeletons of countless ships blown ashore in the wild fury of a howling gale; the hiding place of Blackbeard and other rascals who preyed on Atlantic shipping; and the spot where nearly 150 colonists—including the first English child born in the New World—disappeared, never to be seen again.

In 1578 Sir Humphrey Gilbert, a man with a little pointed beard and soulful eyes who wanted very badly to found an English empire in America, was granted a charter by Queen Elizabeth allowing him to discover and colonize "remote heathen and barbarous lands" not already owned by a Christian prince. After landing in Newfoundland, which he claimed for the Queen, Sir Humphrey sailed south, encountered "many stormes and perils," and on the way back to England was drowned.

His young half brother, Sir Walter Raleigh, a very good friend of the Virgin Queen, thus fell heir to Sir Humphrey's rights, and in 1584 dispatched two ships to explore the North American coast. On July 13 of that year the party landed in North Carolina, somewhere near Roanoke Island, and went into ecstasies over "the goodliest land under the cope of heaven." Captain Barlowe, one of the leaders, thought "in all the world the like abundance is not to be found," and described in detail the "most pleasant and fertile ground, replenished with goodly Cedars, and divers other sweete woods, full of Corrants, flaxe, and many other notable commodities." He also mentioned the "gentle, loving, and faithfull" Indians they had encountered.

On the heels of this expedition another, composed of 108 persons and including geographer Thomas Hariot and the artist John White, went to Roanoke to settle; but within a year's time they had antagonized the loving and faithful Indians to a point where it seemed prudent to accept a ride home offered them by Sir Francis Drake, who was passing by. Soon after their departure in June, 1586, Sir Richard Grenville, cousin to Sir Walter, arrived to find the settlement deserted; and being "unwilling to loose the possession of the country," he left fifteen men on Roanoke Island with provisions for two years.

The following summer some 150 "planters" sent out by Raleigh arrived at Roanoke, but the only trace of the fifteen men was one skeleton. Master Ralfe Lane's fort (a palisaded structure recently reconstructed) had been razed, although the "sundry necessary and decent dwelling houses" around it were still standing. For some reason, despite orders to press on to Chesapeake Bay, the settlers stayed on Roanoke Island, and here on August 18 Governor John White's daughter Eleanor Dare gave birth to a child whom she named Virginia.

When trouble with the Indians flared up, Governor White decided to teach the natives a lesson by a sneak attack on the town of Dasamonquepeuc. The raid could not have been more unfortunate, for the hostile Roanoke Indians, sensing what was in the wind, had decamped, and the only people there were peace-loving Croatoans who were outraged at being subjected to fire and sword. With considerable difficulty the situation was patched up—at least the Croatoans pretended to forgive the white men—and in August Governor White sailed for England and provisions.

He had no end of trouble getting away from home, for 1588 was the year of the Spanish Armada, and there were no ships to be had. Not until August, 1590, did White return to Roanoke, and when he arrived it was to find the settlers vanished completely. Searching the island in sorrow, he did discover one clue—the word

A Roanoke colonist, John White, painted these watercolors, two of the earliest pictures of Indians by a European. The breechclouted native shown here was a Virginia chieftain. Below, White's sketch of the town of Secoton reveals a sedentary agrarian life unlike the popular stereotype of the nomadic, tepee-dwelling hunters of the Plains. Cornfields are seen, and in the foreground a ceremonial dance is in progress. The large hut at lower left was a tomb where bodies of kings were kept.

CROATOAN carved on a post of the fort. White had arranged for the settlers to use a distress sign or a Maltese cross if they were forced to leave, but there was no trace of such a mark. White decided to go to Croatoan Island (now called Ocracoke) to look for his family and the other colonists, but bad weather blew his ship south and he finally had to return to England. Lacking personal funds to finance another expedition, and unable to raise money elsewhere, White finally gave up, but his last recorded words were: "I would to God my wealth were answerable to my will." Sir Walter Raleigh also kept hoping to find some trace of the colonists, and in 1602 he sent out a search expedition. But nothing was discovered.

For generations men have sought to solve the mystery of Roanoke Island, but nothing further has ever been learned of the Lost Colony. It is likely that they were all killed by Indians, although some believe they mingled with the natives and that the so-called Croatoans of present-day Robeson County are their descendants. Others maintain that the Spaniards in Florida destroyed the colony, and there is evidence that Spanish officials in St. Augustine were planning just that. And finally, there is a possibility that the colonists, despairing of relief, sailed for England in a boat left them by White, and were lost at sea. Whatever the answer, men will always ponder what lay behind that one word, CROATOAN—all that remained of England's first real effort to establish a foothold in America.

Jamestown

Today Jamestown, Virginia, is a flat, wooded island nearly three miles long, separated from the mainland by a marshy inlet. There were many things about this place no one could have foreseen, 350 years ago, including the fact that it would one day be an island; but the men who landed there in May, 1607, thought it a fine anchorage, a place not overrun by Indians, and out of range of the Spanish—and decided to stay, making it the first permanent English settlement in America. Yet were it not for the mute evidence of ivy-covered church ruins, an ancient graveyard, and resto-

rations of some of the first buildings, one might doubt its survival.

The first of many mistakes these colonists made was the site itself, surrounded by mosquito-infested swamps, with an unreliable water supply and unhealthy climate. Inside a triangular fort they built a church, storehouses, and some flimsy living quarters, and here trouble broke out almost immediately. There was mutiny, malaria, and the menace of Indians whom the colonists had treated unwisely. Then a real leader, Captain John Smith, turned up in their midst. Smith learned to speak Algonkian, bargained with the Indians for corn, and began to create organization out of chaos. Late in 1607, while out exploring, he was captured by Powhatan and saved, according to his story, by Pocahontas. When he returned to the colony the settlers were starving. A fire in January, 1608, destroyed nearly all their buildings, but Smith managed to get the colony through the winter. He begged the London sponsors to send carpenters, masons, and "diggers up of trees," but in September more gentlemen-settlers arrived. Miraculously, they survived yet another winter; then in August came 400 new, inexperienced settlers, with damaged supplies, fever, and plague. That autumn Smith was injured and sent back to England—probably because others coveted his position. His departure was followed by the "Starving Time," the terrible winter of 1609–10 which only sixty of the 500 colonists survived.

Lord Delaware had been appointed governor of the colony, and his advance agent was so appalled by what he saw at Jamestown that he decided to abandon the settlement. But Delaware determined to salvage the effort. Under his able rule Jamestown finally became a going concern, and the community began to spill out into the lovely James River Valley. Then in 1698 Jamestown burned, and it was decided to move the capital to Middle Plantation, or Williamsburg.

Near the site of the first fort, an ivy-draped church tower is the last standing ruin of seventeenth-century Jamestown. Excavators have found delft tiles (top) which colonists used to adorn their homes. At right, John Smith's statue surveys the James River from the location of the first landing.

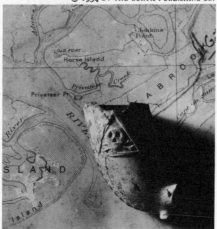

Pirate's pipe bowl, found at Charleston.

Skull and Crossbones
Off the Carolinas

If there is any one place to seek out the haunts of pirates, it is that shoreline extending roughly 75 miles in either direction from Charleston, South Carolina, known as the Debatable Coast. So named because Spain, France, and England all claimed it, this picturesque mosaic of islands, inlets, marshes, and harbors once served as the ideal hiding place for seagoing cutthroats, murderers, and thieves.

It is not difficult to draw a parallel between pirates of the seventeenth century and racketeers of the twentieth. Both had a predatory outlook toward other people's property and a cheerful willingness to eliminate anyone who got in the way. Both enjoyed the protection of merchants and certain civic officials. Like latter-day rackets, piracy had its economic formula. The buccaneers disposed of their loot to favored merchants at bargain rates, far lower than those paid for goods legitimately landed. The merchants, in turn, put political and financial pressure on royal governors and their minions to look the other way.

The years 1550 to 1700 and 1714 to 1725 were the golden ages of international piracy, and as early as 1685 these outlaws swaggered through Charles Town, as it was then called. There were men like the satanic Edward Low, who once cut off and cooked a captured Rhode Islander's ears and forced his victim to eat them. There was "Gentleman Pirate" Stede Bonnet, a wealthy Barbados landowner who reputedly turned pirate to escape a nagging wife. One of the few known to have made captives walk the plank, he was captured in 1718 and hanged in Charles Town.

But the most fearsome scoundrel of all was the man who was born Edward Teach, or Thatch, in Bristol, England, and was known up and down the coast as Blackbeard. A contemporary explains that his sobriquet came "from that large quantity of hair, which, like a frightful meteor, covered his whole face, and frightened America more than any comet that has appeared in a long time." Blackbeard liked to tuck long hemp matches under his hat, then ignite them for the joy of the fire crackling against his hair. A privateer in Queen Anne's War, by 1716 he was an apprentice pirate to Benjamin Hornigold. When Hornigold took the King's Pardon, Blackbeard struck out on his own. With Stede Bonnet, he blockaded Charles Town in May, 1718, took five ships, and prevented anyone from entering or leaving the harbor until he had been paid off handsomely. Later he arrived in Bath, North Carolina, accepted a pardon from his friend Governor Charles Eden, married his fourteenth wife (a lass of sixteen), and set sail again, unreformed and unrepentant. Eventually some of the North Carolina merchants and planters whose businesses were being ruined by Teach made plans to do him in. Since their own governor was his friend, they appealed to Alexander Spotswood of Virginia—that rare creature, an honest royal governor. At his own expense, Spotswood fitted out two sloops commanded by Lieutenant Robert Maynard and Captain Ellis Brand, and on the evening of November 21, 1718, they slipped into Ocracoke Inlet, where Blackbeard tarred and caulked his ships. Blackbeard appears to have had warnings of the expedition, including one from South Carolina's secretary, but he pooh-poohed them as rumor and spent the night carousing. Brand's vessel was damaged in the attack next morning, and when Maynard closed, the pirates boarded his sloop. In the hand-to-hand combat Blackbeard, a walking arsenal, fought like a madman, and Maynard emptied his pistol twice into his seemingly indestructible body. Then, in the act of reaching for a pistol, the pirate fell to the deck, dead. His body bore 25 wounds, five from pistols, and Maynard's men finished the grisly business by cutting off his head, which they hung from the bowsprit on their return to Hampton Roads. That year the Carolinas were finally rid of the pirate trade.

172

At left, an old etching shows the satanic Blackbeard amusing himself by burning lighted matches under his hat. Below is the rotting hulk of one of the many ships wrecked on the treacherous shoals of Cape Hatteras, the "graveyard of the Atlantic". In colonial times the Hatteras coast was a notorious pirate haven. Ocracoke Inlet, shown above, was the place where Blackbeard tarred and caulked his boats; here the pirate was surprised and killed by Spotswood's men in 1718.

Colonial Williamsburg

At left is a street of restored colonial homes and shops. Ornate wrought-iron gates frame the Governor's Palace (center), and the formal gardens at right belong to the George Wythe House.

If the remnants of Blackbeard's crew had time for such thoughts before they were hanged in Williamsburg, they must have been impressed by the splendor of the colony's capital. This seat of royal authority was something to awe the most sophisticated colonial. Yet no one who saw it in 1718 would dream that the town would be practically deserted eighty years later, its buildings in a state of decay.

When Jamestown burned, many of its settlers removed to Middle Plantation, as the huddle of crude buildings near the College of William and Mary was called, and in 1699 Williamsburg became Virginia's capital. Alexander Spotswood, that energetic soul who had seen to Blackbeard's demise, was responsible for much of the town's growth. Arriving in 1710, he directed a good part of the construction program, including several college buildings and the present Bruton Parish Church. By the time the bedraggled pirates were herded into town, the magnificent brick Governor's Palace was almost complete; the general assembly was meeting in the building Christopher Wren designed for the college (the only one of his design in America, and the nation's oldest academic structure); and the octagonal public magazine was newly finished. Although Williamsburg's colonial population never exceeded 2,000, it was filled from the very beginning with planters and statesmen whose personal and political convictions were to shape American history. For 81 influential years it was the capital of the colony of Virginia, playing host to George Washington, Patrick

The Capitol where Patrick Henry defied George III has been reconstructed exactly as it looked upon completion in 1705.

Henry, George Wythe, Thomas Jefferson, George Mason, and many others. Here, on May 29, 1765, Patrick Henry rose in the House of Burgesses to condemn the Stamp Act, crying "Caesar had his Brutus; Charles the First his Cromwell; and George the Third ["Treason!" shouted the Speaker] *may profit by their example. If this be treason, make the most of it.*" Henry apologized to the shocked House for his outburst, but the seed had been sown, and before long he, Jefferson, and other patriots were meeting at the Raleigh Tavern to develop inter-colonial committees of correspondence. Williamsburg was the scene of George Mason's Virginia Declaration of Rights; the May 15, 1776, Resolution for Independence which led directly to July 4; the framing of a Virginia constitution on which most other states patterned theirs; and Jefferson's famous Statute for Religious Freedom. Before and during the siege of Yorktown, Williamsburg was headquarters first for British, then for Continental and French forces. Both Washington and Rochambeau stayed in the handsome Wythe House, and American wounded were quartered in the Governor's Palace. Williamsburg had begun to decline when the capital was moved to Richmond in 1780 to escape the British. By 1795 its population was only half what it had been in 1779, and nine years later it was "very decayed."

Then, in 1926, John D. Rockefeller, Jr., came to Williamsburg at the invitation of Dr. W. A. R. Goodwin, rector of Bruton Parish Church, who had plans to restore the entire town. The result of their vision and generosity is the magnificent restoration which transports visitors back 200 years through time to see, in accurate detail, the once-great colonial capital.

175

A sketch from Benjamin Latrobe's journal shows Martha Washington serving tea at Mount Vernon.

George Washington's Virginia

Had it not been for a determined South Carolinian named Ann Pamela Cunningham, it is quite doubtful if George Washington's beautiful Mount Vernon would have survived to delight the millions of Americans who look to it as one of the nation's great shrines.

Washington had inherited the estate in 1754 and during his lifetime increased its acreage from 2,126 to something over 8,000. In his will he divided up the property, leaving the mansion and 4,000 acres to his nephew Bushrod Washington, but with the passing years Mount Vernon's owners found it impossible to maintain the disintegrating buildings and unproductive land on which they stood. One of them tried to interest the State of Virginia or the Federal Government in buying the property, and when neither expressed interest it began to look as if the estate would crumble into decay.

In 1853 Miss Cunningham stepped into the breach and penned her first appeal—a plea to the women of America to "guard and protect" this hallowed spot. When she retired from this work of love 21 years later, she could take pride in what she had bequeathed to her countrymen.

It is unfair to single out the work of the Mount Vernon Ladies' Association; yet it is worth reminding Americans, through this example, that the preservation of most of their treasured historic possessions has often been possible only when groups of private individuals have been willing to do something about it.

CONTINUED ON PAGE 178

This 1793 map of the five farms comprising Mount Vernon was drawn from field notes by Washington, an accomplished surveyor. What he termed the "Mansion House Farm," where his countryseat still stands, is at bottom center on the map. As the photograph at right indicates, the view of the Potomac has changed so little since Washington's time that the family might survey the same peaceful scene from their tea table.

CONTINUED FROM PAGE 176

The manner in which Mount Vernon is maintained today would probably surprise and gratify its most illustrious owner. Washington was well aware of its possibilities: "No estate in United America is more pleasantly situated than this," he wrote. But in 1759 when he brought his bride Martha Custis there to live, the plantation was shabby and run-down, with endless repairs needed, indoors and out. It was a large and fairly typical Virginia plantation, and by the standards of the time Washington was a wealthy man; yet the apparent wealth of plantation society was sometimes deceiving—as noted by the Duc de La Rochefoucauld. "The Virginians are not generally rich," he said, "especially in net revenue. Thus one often finds a well-served table, covered with silver, in a room where for ten years half the window panes have been missing, and where they will be missed for ten years more. There are few houses in a passable state of repair, and of all parts of the establishment those best cared for are the stables."

Washington Irving, in his biography of Washington, hit on an apt description of plantation life. "A large Virginia estate," he said, "was a little empire. The mansion-house was the seat of government, with its numerous dependencies, such as kitchens, smoke-house, workshops and stables." At Mount Vernon, as at so many similar establishments of the time and place, the area immediately surrounding the manor house was designed as a gentleman's countryseat—an American copy of the English country estate, with meadows, sweeping views, rows of trees, and carefully tended gardens. Between house and river there was a sizable park, and those small areas which were under cultivation near the house were devoted mainly to testing new crops and improved methods of agriculture.

Economically speaking, Mount Vernon was far less profitable than one might expect. Partially this was due to the land itself, which failed to produce good tobacco, the cash crop on which so many relied. Various alternatives were tried—wheat, flax, hemp—and Washington attempted to make money out of his still or derive some profit from the Potomac's abundant shad and herring; but the odds were against him. The plantation system required close supervision to produce prosperity. In 1786 nearly ninety people were living in and about the main house, with 150 more

CONTINUED ON PAGE 180

In Edward Savage's portrait, the Washingtons are pictured with their two wards, Martha's grandchildren by her first marriage. At the right is Mount Vernon, where Washington retired to enjoy "domestic ease under the shadow of my own vine, and my own fig tree . . . with the implements of husbandry, and Lambkins around me."

178

Martha's dressing table

Parlor card table

Washington's desk and chair

CONTINUED FROM PAGE 178

on its adjacent farms. All these people had to be clothed and fed, and nothing which could be produced on the estate was bought elsewhere. The managerial responsibilities in this self-contained community were enormous, but Washington was too much needed in public affairs for him to give them the time they required. From 1759 on he served in the Virginia House of Burgesses, and more and more played the part of counselor, executor, and private banker to his friends and neighbors. And when he wrote, several months after his retirement from the presidency, that he and his wife were sitting down to dinner alone for the first time in twenty years, it gives us an idea of the amount of entertaining involved in plantation life.

After he was commissioned commander in chief of the Continental Army in 1775, Washington was away from Mount Vernon for over eight years, except for brief visits en route to and from Yorktown in 1781. Inaugurated President in 1789, he visited his home only fifteen times during his eight years of office, and when he finally came home, only two and a half years of life remained to him.

Seeing Mount Vernon today, it is apparent that if plantation life had its drawbacks, it also had its charms. The beautiful parlors, the music room, the banquet hall, and the library were scenes of a life which was socially and intellectually stimulating. Nearby were the estates of Belvoir and Gunston Hall, whose owners, the Fairfaxes and George Mason, were frequent guests. Social position was the privilege of the highly gifted as much as the well born, and those whom the Duc de La Rochefoucauld calls "men of the first class" were certainly equal to any such group in history. Every plantation was attached to an Epis-

PRATT, *Ladies' Home Journal*

Prince Street in Alexandria has changed little since Washington's time. Its handsome homes are a reminder of the years when the town was a prosperous Potomac tobacco port.

copal parish, and nearly all Virginia gentlemen were closely associated with the established church. Philip Vickers Fithian, who tutored the Carter children at Nomini Hall, reported the "general custom on Sundays here with Gentlemen to invite one another to dine, after Church; and to consult about, determine their common business, either before or after Service— it is not the custom for Gentlemen to go into Church til Service is beginning, when they enter in a Body, in the same manner as they come out; I have known the Clerk to come out and call them in to prayers."

If the mansion at Mount Vernon reflects a leisurely life whose all-consuming topics of conversation were law and politics, the neat white outbuildings bespeak an era of handicrafts and the extent to which society depended upon the work of slaves. There is no activity today in the kitchen, smokehouse, or laundry yard, but these and the other service buildings make it possible to understand the problems of self-sufficiency at a time when nearly everything that was eaten or worn was produced within the borders of the plantation.

Standing on the white-columned piazza, the visitor surveys the same placid view George Washington looked out on two centuries ago. This home has more associations with the nation's beginnings than any other in the United States—a place whose tangible and emotional memories reveal the man beloved in his time and in our own. For George Washington, Mount Vernon was an island of peace in a world beset with troubles, and it remains a place where all Americans are privileged to experience the same feeling.

Washington drew plans for Pohick Church, located six miles from Mount Vernon. Construction was completed in 1774.

On Sundays the colonial planters gathered at churches like Bruton Parish in Williamsburg to worship and talk business.

Tidewater Golden Age

The half century preceding the Revolution was the Golden Age in Virginia. Third- and fourth-generation families, reaping the benefit of ancestral foresight and business acumen, lived on estates of thousands of acres. They were farmers, businessmen, and merchants; they collected great libraries, listened to music, danced and entertained endlessly. They held banquets, balls, and boat races; barbecues, musicales, and horse races. They hunted and went to church and were as insistent on their children's good manners as they were upon their education. But for all their success in the New World, for all their devotion to the colony, they still called England "home."

One of the most distinguished men of his time was William Byrd II, a handsome, dashing man known as the "Black Swan," who built his home "two miles above where the great ships ride" on the James River. This was Westover—one of the first houses on the grand scale in Virginia.

There was Gunston Hall, a simple, story-and-a-half Colonial house built on 5,000 acres along the Potomac near Alexandria by George Mason, fourth of his name and line in Virginia. A man who preferred to work behind the scenes, Mason framed Virginia's Declaration of Rights and most of its Constitution—two documents which profoundly influenced the Declaration of Independence and the Bill of Rights.

A gaunt shell of vast empty walls on the York River is all that remains of Mann Page's Rosewell, the estate which consumed most of his own and his wife's fortunes. The house had 23 rooms in its central portion and six in each wing, a wainscoting of carved mahogany, and a staircase which could accommodate eight persons walking abreast.

Of the surviving plantation houses among the best are Benjamin Harrison's Berkeley, near Charles City; William Byrd Harrison's Brandon, with its formal gardens of gigantic boxwood, yews, and cucumber trees;

CONTINUED ON PAGE 185

BRADLEY SMITH

This is the view from the front door of Stratford, Robert E. Lee's birthplace, which was begun about 1725 by an ancestor, Thomas Lee, an important colonial leader and native Virginian.

The great wealth of planter William Byrd II was reflected in the opulence of Westover. Built in the 1730's, this elegant Georgian mansion was one of the first of the great Virginia plantation homes.

One of the showpieces at Shirley is a handsome carved walnut staircase which climbs a square well three stories high. The Palladian Room of Gunston Hall (below) is an excellent example of a gracious colonial drawing room. Many of these houses are private; the reader should refer to the listings on pages 206-19 to see which are open to the public.

Cotton, rice, tobacco, and indigo, the traditional money crops of the seaboard South, all depended on slave labor.

CONTINUED FROM PAGE 182

and Shirley, one of the largest Tidewater mansions. In Shirley's huge hall, which occupies more than a quarter of the main floor, is a "hanging stair" which seems to have no support on its way up a square well three stories high.

One spectacular house is Carter's Grove, set behind a row of giant tulip poplars overlooking the James River. It was begun for his daughter by "King" Carter, who owned more than 300,000 acres of land and 700 slaves, and completed by his grandson, Carter Burwell. The entrance to this beautiful estate lies between ancient cedars and locusts, and the rose-brick Georgian mansion is a perfect monument to a way of life which has gone from the scene forever.

Imported English artisans fashioned the graceful carved stairway and pine-paneled main hallway of Carter's Grove.

The grand proportions of Carter's Grove conformed to the refined but expensive tastes of planter Carter Burwell.

Low Country Aristocracy

All along the southern seaboard, wrote George Washington, "the lands are low, sandy, and unhealthy; [and] as I should not choose to be an inhabitant of them myself, I ought not to say anything that would induce others to be so. . . ." Obviously, there were those who disagreed with this view, and in the years before the Revolution Charleston was dominated by as exclusive and aristocratic a society as could be found in the colonies. Their remarkable wealth came from two easy-to-grow, easy-to-sell crops—rice and indigo. And if the owners of the great plantations had to spend several months in Charleston to escape the miasmic fumes and disease which resulted from the annual flooding of rice fields (Washington was right about the climate, it seemed), this served to make Charleston a glittering, civilized oasis on the barren southern coast line. English visitors thought the city the most agreeable in America, and by 1800, Henry Adams wrote, "Nowhere in the Union was intelligence, wealth, and education greater in proportion to numbers than in the little society of cotton and rice planters who ruled South Carolina."

Charleston today is full of eighteenth-century architecture, including some of the best English work of its time. Concessions were made to the climate, in galleries and in high basements which formed a full story on the ground level, and many houses were built flush with the sidewalk, turning their backs, as it were, to the street to insure the occupants' privacy. Beyond the colorful homes, the delicate grillwork, and the gardens of old Charleston are the outlying plantations, many of them carefully restored like Hampton, whose acreage along the Santee River has belonged to the Rutledge family since 1686.

Ironically enough, the guns they themselves set off in Charleston Harbor in 1861 began the end of this society and its counterparts in Savannah, Mobile, and elsewhere in the South. Yet in the homes that remain—some crumbled beyond repair, a few, like the handsome Wormsloe Plantation near Savannah, still in the possession of families whose forbears built them two centuries ago—one finds the echo of that other world, hanging in the air, unforgotten.

Wormsloe House (left) near Savannah stands on plantation land owned by the same family for two hundred years. At right is Charleston's Rainbow Row. These pastel-colored homes are typical of the city's beautifully preserved houses.

The World Turned Upside Down

At St. John's Church in Richmond, speaking before a revolutionary assembly in March, 1775, Patrick Henry made a plea for armed resistance to British misrule.

It was March, 1775, a month before men would die on Lexington Green, and a convention of Virginians was meeting at St. John's Episcopal Church in Richmond. In this serene clapboard building, Patrick Henry rose to make one of America's most impassioned pleas for freedom: "Is life so dear, or peace so sweet, as to be purchased at the price of chains and slavery? Forbid it, Almighty God! I know not what course others may take, but as for me, give me liberty, or give me death!"

At the time he spoke, the idea of revolt was confined to a small group. But as the tide of revolution swept across the land, it affected the relationships of all classes to each other and to their established institutions, so that revolution became, in many places, civil war. Nowhere was this more apparent, or the struggle more bitter, than in the South. Upcountry frontier was a very different world from Tidewater aristocracy. In the mountain communities, Germans, French Huguenots, Dutch, Scotch Highlanders, Scotch-Irish, English, Welsh, and Swiss pioneers began to ex-

press their differences through violent action.

In the back country one of the bitterest and most crucial battles of the war was fought at King's Mountain, where Southern patriots—many of them "overmountain" frontiersmen—shattered a Tory force whose leader, Major Patrick Ferguson, was the only non-American on either side.

There are few surviving landmarks of this all-but-forgotten war, largely because the war was one of quick thrusts, marches, maneuvers, and raids. When the able Nathanael Greene was given command of Continental forces in the South, his chief object was survival. He could do little more than harass Cornwallis' flanks, harry his outposts, and encourage the guerrilla operations of "Swamp Fox" Francis Marion, Andrew Pickens, and Thomas Sumter, the "Carolina Game Cock." Among the few victories was the one which Saratoga veteran Dan Morgan fashioned in a backwoods cattle pasture, called the Cowpens; but mostly it was a campaign described by Greene as "fight, get beat, rise and fight again." In no other battle could he claim victory

In the painting above, Francis Marion and his partisans cross the Pee Dee River in South Carolina during a guerrilla raid on the British. At right is a section of the reconstructed Grand French Battery at Yorktown. During the siege, heavy allied bombardment silenced most of the British batteries and eventually pounded Cornwallis' forces into submission.

—at Guilford Court House, Hobkirk's Hill, Ninety-Six, or Eutaw Springs—yet each achieved Greene's goal of inflicting such damage on the enemy that they would be compelled to retreat.

Although Greene's half-naked, ill-fed troops fought on for another year, the climax came elsewhere, suddenly, at the old tobacco port of Yorktown, Virginia. In 1781 the town consisted of about sixty houses, a few of which, like the Somerwell, Digges, Nelson, and Sessions houses, still stand. Near here are the restored British and American earthworks, and outside of town, near the battlefield, is the frame Moore House, where representatives of Washington and Cornwallis negotiated the final surrender. But the enduring memory of Yorktown is also to be found in the echoing words of Patrick Henry, and in the thrilling picture (next page) of British troops in new uniforms, marching out between lines of French and Americans. In one of those wonderful ironic touches, the British bands played them out to the tune of an old march called "The World Turned Upside Down."

189

Louis Van Blarenberghe based his painting of the British surrender at Yorktown on sketches made on the spot. Marching out of their lines of defense, measured ranks of brilliantly redcoated English soldiers pass between rows of Frenchmen,

n blue uniforms, and Americans, whose backs are toward the viewer. At upper left, some British are already stacking
heir arms. Lord Cornwallis, however, did not march with his troops that day, excusing himself on account of illness.

Jefferson's Monticello

From the summit of the "little mountain" the long hills roll off toward the smoky haze of the Blue Ridge, little swatches of cultivated land patterning the earth where forests stood two centuries ago. When Thomas Jefferson came here in 1766 to clear the land and level his mountaintop he knew exactly what he wanted, and sixty years of his life were spent making it into an embodiment of his personal tastes and philosophy. Monticello became, after the death of his wife, his great love; the place where a man whose reputation was that of a warm, friendly man of the people could be what he was—remote, aloof, a democrat at a distance.

From the beginning Thomas Jefferson set his heart on a house unlike anything in America, and the beautiful symmetry of his mansion, capturing in soft warm brick the classic elegance he admired, was the forerunner of a new style in American architecture. The house is full of his inventions and innovations—a revolving chair which can be made into a chaise longue; a revolving tabletop to facilitate writing and record-keeping; a system of air shafts for ventilation; the first dumb-waiter; a porch-ceiling weather vane; the famous hall clock with cannon balls to mark off days of the week; a bed between study and bedroom which can be raised to make a passage through the suite.

These things and others reveal the scientist and inventor who inherited the mantle of Franklin. Here is the architect, farmer, author of the Declaration of Independence, President of the United States. Yet anyone willing to approach Monticello leisurely, and with care, will find also the personality and individuality of its remarkable owner. That story begins with a boy who dreamed of living on top of the mountain; it leads to college, where architectural books opened the path; to a law practice whose fees paid for clearing the land, planting gardens and trees. The big, sandy-haired man, "straight as a gun barrel," was as much the lord of the manor as any Hudson River patroon. He could have been merely that, but he chose not to limit outlook or intellect, and Monticello is the perfect reflection of his choice.

In New England, on July 4, 1826, John Adams lay dying, happy with the thought that "Thomas Jefferson survives." But Jefferson had died, too, a few hours earlier on that great fiftieth anniversary, leaving an epitaph for the little graveyard at Monticello which stated the three accomplishments of which he was proudest: "Author of the Declaration of American Independence, of the Statute of Virginia for Religious Freedom, and Father of the University of Virginia."

Inside Monticello (left) are such Jeffersonian inventions as his pulley-lift bed, a quartet music stand, and a calendar clock.

James Madison

James Monroe

William Henry Harrison

The Virginia Dynasty

Virginia's great outpouring of political genius during the early years of the Republic was no accident. The Virginia planters were for the most part men who continued the conditions of life they had left behind in Europe; they kept in touch with that society, importing its literature and ideas along with the prevailing London fashions. They read the best books, sent their sons to Europe's universities, nurtured the traditions of scholarship, and gave themselves wholeheartedly to public life.

There were, of course, men of equal caliber in New England; but most of these gentlemen were absorbed in theological and philosophical studies. Unlike New England, with its democratic town meeting which made a political unit of each township, Virginia adopted the parish system. This system was forced upon it by the distances which existed between neighbors; and it meant, inevitably, government by a small group of men who were in the beginning representative, but who later filled any vacancies from within their own ranks and tended to become a closed corporation.

Virginia's parish system produced four of the young nation's first five Presidents—Washington, Jefferson, Madison, and Monroe—four men who served a total of 32 years in the country's first 36 years of life. Except for Jefferson, they were conservatives—men with a vision of an aristocratic republic governed by superior individuals. In founding the University of Virginia in the foothills of the Blue Ridge Mountains,

Jefferson too sought to produce individuals of the same superior quality, but on a much broader base, and within the social atmosphere of a democracy.

After the first succession of Virginia Presidents ended with Monroe, America turned for a time to John Quincy Adams and then, having encountered on its frontiers conditions which no longer fitted the confines of conservative leadership, to Andrew Jackson, a man of the new West. To the nation's and to Virginia's credit, men of stature had been found in the Old Dominion when the struggling colonies needed them most; and the country would turn again to Virginia for William Henry Harrison, for John Tyler and Zachary Taylor, and, in the twentieth century, for Woodrow Wilson.

The homes of most of these Virginia Presidents survive today, reflecting gracefully the way of life of the men who occupied them. Washington's Mount Vernon and Jefferson's Monticello are perfect mirrors of their masters, and the same thing is true of Madison's Montpelier, in Orange County, and of James Monroe's two homes—Ash Lawn in Charlottesville, and Oak Hill at Leesburg.

The beautiful red brick Berkeley Plantation on the James River was the ancestral home of the Harrison family and it remains one of the great Tidewater mansions. Not far from it is Sherwood Forest, where John Tyler lived. In Staunton, the visitor may see the modest Manse where Woodrow Wilson was born.

John Tyler

Zachary Taylor

Woodrow Wilson

The colonnaded dormitory rows of the University of Virginia were designed by Jefferson along classical lines. As the University's architect and builder, the aging ex-President viewed its construction through a spyglass from Monticello.

A "mass of throbbing nerves," Jefferson Davis had intense, somewhat Lincolnesque features.

From Bull Run
to Appomattox

Time was running out in the spring of 1861, one event piling on another with dismaying speed, rushing the nation to disaster. Even as a train carried Abraham Lincoln from Springfield, Illinois, toward Washington, an erect, tough-minded Jefferson Davis stood on the colonnaded portico of the Alabama capitol to take an oath of office, and a southern actress danced on the Stars and Stripes. Davis, the grandson of an illiterate Welsh peasant, was "ambitious as Lucifer," and his wife called him "a mere mass of throbbing nerves"; but neither of these traits was strong enough to make him want war, just then. A West Pointer, he knew what war meant, and he had a healthy respect for the North's industrial resources. Needless to say, a fight was the last thing Abraham Lincoln wanted, but when April came the guns in Charleston Harbor opened fire on a pentagon of stone called Fort Sumter, and it did not much matter what anyone wanted any more. The thing had happened.

There would be four long, terrible years of bloodshed on the North American continent—four years the nation could never forget—and it is a good thing for Americans to go, now and again, to see where this happened and try to understand it all. An enormous lot of fighting took place outside the state of Virginia, but partly because Richmond was for so long the goal of the Federal armies, and Robert E. Lee and Stonewall Jackson their principal opponents, this state has more associations with the Civil War than any other, in the popular mind. Here the real fighting began, here it ended, and here is where the Confederacy's greatest heroes were made.

A good place to begin an understanding of what the South was fighting for is down on Virginia's Northern Neck at a place called Stratford Hall, Lee's birth-

place. Lee was only three years old in 1810 when his father, "Light Horse" Harry Lee, Revolutionary hero and friend of Washington, and his mother Ann Carter Lee, daughter of the distinguished Carters of Shirley, packed the children and a few belongings into a coach and headed out the long drive. The Lees had fallen on hard, humiliating times and were forced to leave Stratford, the massive, H-shaped brick structure which is one of the finest Georgian mansions in America. The once-rich fields lay fallow, slaves had gone, the great house was on its way to neglect and ruin, and for the rest of his days Lee would long for what had been lost. There is a picture of Lee leaving another great, well-loved home—this one the columned Greek Revival house across the Potomac from Washington,

Severe fighting in both Bull Run battles centered around an old tavern called the Stone House, seen in a wartime photo.

A Union shell explodes in the rubble-clogged parade of Fort Sumter during the siege of Charleston in the fall of 1863.

where Lee had married the daughter of George Washington Parke Custis, adopted son of the first President. Arlington, when Lee saw it for the last time in April, 1861, had also grown shabby; the grounds were rundown and the fields only partially cultivated. Beautifully restored now, these two proud, lovely houses speak eloquently of family and position, explaining much of Lee the gentleman. For the rest of the gentleman-soldier combination, Virginia's battlegrounds hold the key.

War in earnest began 25 miles southwest of the nation's capital, near Manassas, an important railroad junction. Along the steep banks of Bull Run, the little stream that meanders through the gentle countryside, the North in particular discovered for the first time that nothing about this war would be easy. There are still two buildings at Manassas that survived two battles where about 25,000 Americans were shot—the Stone House, which was right in the center of action, and the Dogan House, a weather-beaten, one-room log hut. On top of a little rise is the famous equestrian statue of Thomas J. Jackson, looking out over the fields where he won his nickname for standing there "like a stone wall." The first battle began on the morning of July 21, 1861, when unlucky General Irvin McDowell, goaded by the public cry of "On to Richmond!" took 35,000 pathetically untrained boys in blue out to dislodge Beauregard's equally untrained Confederates. The felony was compounded by a near-army of Congressmen, sightseers, and correspondents who tagged along to see the fun begin. When McDowell's men began what was a fairly orderly retreat, Confederate artillery blocked a bridge across their escape route, and in the ensuing traffic jam the civilians panicked. Before long there was a full-scale rout, with soldiers and civilians turned into a helpless, completely disorganized mob that stumbled back to Washington for the next 24 hours.

A little over a year later, at the end of August, 1862, Union General Pope learned at Bull Run what it was to run afoul of what Robert E. Lee and Stonewall Jackson had planned for him. For a full day he mounted a furious attack against the entrenched Jackson, and somehow, next morning, he got the idea that Jackson was retreating. Not only was he totally in error on this score, but he was unaware that James Longstreet's veterans had come up to join Stonewall. Just as Pope was assaulting Jackson, Longstreet wheeled his gray line forward toward Bald Hill, rolling up the Union left flank as he drove along the Warrenton Pike. Second Manassas was another crushing defeat for the North, but the boys had come of age in a year's time. After this one the troops picked themselves up and were ready to fight again at Antietam, only seventeen days later.

Off to the west of Bull Run lies the lovely Shenandoah Valley, a fertile land where Dutch, Scotch-Irish, and Quakers began to settle in the 1730's, leaving their mark in prosperous little farms and a tradition of independent self-sufficiency. Once a gateway to the western frontier and a scene of George Washington's first military assignment, the valley in 1862 was the South's great "covered way" leading to the Yankee fortress. Confederates coming down the valley were headed for the heart of the Union; while Federals moving up the valley were going the wrong way, if they wanted to get to Richmond. The great valley was a strategic artery and an incomparable source of food and forage for southern armies, but above all it was Stonewall Jackson country.

Between the tiers of blue mountains the quiet Shenandoah winds through pleasant little towns, pastures, and woodland which the silent, dour Jackson made his own against all comers. Sucking a lemon, the harsh disciplinarian in the worn, mud-spattered uniform rode at the head of a gray column of men who would

CONTINUED ON PAGE 199

At left, Stonewall Jackson reviews his weary but cheering troops. Although he drove them at a killing pace, his men were devoted to this dour, Cromwell-like man. They moved so swiftly that they were nicknamed "Stonewall's foot cavalry." In the Shenandoah Valley (below), Jackson's lightning-stroke attacks ran the Union forces ragged in the spring of 1862, securing the Confederacy's breadbasket until Sheridan devastated it two years later.

The American Wars, BY ROY MEREDITH
WORLD PUBLISHING CO.

Confederate artist Allen Redwood sketched this Rebel sharpshooter.

ALVIN JOSEPHY, *Time*

Protected by a stone wall, Confederates stood along the sunken road below Marye's Heights and slaughtered Federals advancing across the open fields of Fredericksburg. Burnside lost 12,653 men before he called off the assault.

CONTINUED FROM PAGE 197

march and fight like fools for him, giving the art of warfare a new concept of mobility. Beginning with Kernstown, the site of one of Jackson's few defeats, Stonewall's trail runs north to Winchester, oldest city in the valley, where earthworks remain from some of the battles fought here. It includes Harpers Ferry, winds down to Front Royal, Strasburg, and Cross Keys; and finally to the college town of Lexington, where Jackson taught at the Virginia Military Institute, and where he is buried.

For a concentrated dose of the Civil War as it was fought by the Army of the Potomac and the Army of Northern Virginia, few places can rival that wedge-shaped chunk of land bounded roughly by the Rapidan River in the north, the James in the south, and the foothills of the Blue Ridge Mountains to the west. Here Union armies pounded on the gates of Richmond, sometimes nearly destroying themselves in the process; and here the efforts of the southern states to establish themselves as an entity apart from the Union came to an end. From the standpoint of what can still be seen, the most rewarding section of this area is in and around Fredericksburg, Virginia.

The town itself goes back to the roots of America, to John Smith who visited there in 1608, to a group of early settlers who built a little fort on the Rappahannock River in 1671. Located at the foot of rolling hills at the head of tidewater and navigation on the Rappahannock, Fredericksburg was a trading center for rich cargoes of Virginia tobacco until the Civil War, when it found itself strategically located midway between Washington and Richmond, situated on major rail and road routes north and south.

In November, 1862, General Ambrose Burnside arrived on the north bank of the Rappahannock and surveyed a scene which has changed little since—a pleasant town of colonial houses and tree-shaded streets, just beyond which lay an open plain, three-quarters of a mile wide. On the far side of the plain is a long, low hill called Marye's Heights, running parallel with the course of the river. At its foot, behind a four-foot stone wall, is a road, and when the Federal attack began on the chill, foggy morning of December 13, 1862, that road was full of Confederate veterans, four to five ranks deep. Behind them on the hill was their artillery, which could crisscross the whole plain with fire, making this an almost perfect defensive position. All that day and long into the hours of darkness, wave after wave of Federal troops broke against Lee's position until the Confederates wondered why their fire "did not absolutely sweep them from the face of the earth." Never once did the Union troops falter, but not one man got within thirty yards of the fateful stone wall. And when it was over at last, the North had lost nearly 13,000 men.

That winter the two armies faced each other across the Rappahannock, and Joe Hooker, who had replaced Burnside, worked out a plan to outflank Lee

CONTINUED ON PAGE 200

Civil War trenches still crisscross Virginia's Wilderness. Here the two armies slugged blindly through a jungle of second-growth timber in the battles of Chancellorsville and the Wilderness. The horror of both fights was compounded when the woods caught fire, incinerating hundreds of wounded.

dense brush and forest. All day Lee waited, not knowing if Hooker would assault his thin lines, or if Jackson would reach Hooker's right flank undetected. Then, at five fifteen in the afternoon, Jackson's men stormed out of the woods, red battle flags flying in the dusk, 28,000 men in a line more than a mile wide and three divisions deep. Against them there was nothing the Federals could do. In a matter of minutes a whole Union corps had collapsed, and the broken remnants of Hooker's right wing fell back on Chancellorsville in utter confusion. Next day the South resumed the attack, and the Union army was forced back to a position north of the town. Chancellorsville, however, was the costliest victory the Confederacy was to win; casualties were near 13,000, and Stonewall Jackson, surveying his position after dark, had been shot by his own men. A stone slab near the battlefield marks the place where his left arm was buried, and in the Chandler farmhouse south of Fredericksburg he died a week later. Lee, refusing to believe that he would not live, sent word that although "he has lost his left arm, I have lost my right"; but hours later Stonewall died, murmuring, "Let us cross over the river, and rest under the shade of the trees."

Twelve months after the southern victory at Chancellorsville, war returned to the deep, silent Wilderness. The tide had turned: Grant's victory at Vicksburg had opened up the Mississippi; Lee's defeat at Gettysburg had ended the threat of invasion; and the Union

CONTINUED FROM PAGE 199

and drive toward Richmond. It was a good plan, and it might possibly have worked. Hooker divided his army into two groups, sending Sedgwick and 40,000 men to cross the river below Fredericksburg while Hooker and 80,000 men moved to the west around Lee's left flank. Not for two days did Lee discover the movement, but when he did he acted with characteristic initiative, setting in motion the last and most daring of all the Lee-Jackson maneuvers—one which brought dramatic victory out of apparent defeat. Hooker had reached Chancellorsville when he felt Lee's resistance for the first time, and he decided to set up a defensive position there and await attack. Chancellorsville was in that dismal dense tangle of second-growth forest, nearly fifteen miles square, called the Wilderness.

On the night of May 1, Lee and Jackson sat on a cracker box discussing their situation and working out a plan which, for sheer audacity, has scarcely been equaled. Although they had only 45,000 troops to nearly twice that many for Hooker, they split their forces to launch a surprise attack. Lee, with less than 20,000 men, was to hold off Hooker, while Jackson, on the morning of the second, took off through the

As the Confederates evacuated Richmond, valuable supplies were put to the torch. In the confusion, however, the flames spread and most of the southern capital was burned. When the Union army entered the city which it had fought so long to capture, the place was in ruins; nowhere was there "sound of life, but the stillness of a catacomb." These gutted buildings were photographed by Mathew Brady after the surrender.

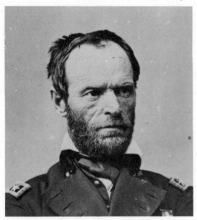

Sherman, Sheridan, and Grant (left to right) were the three Union generals who contributed most to the Confederate defeat.

triumph at Chattanooga had put the western armies in position to cross Georgia to the sea, cutting the South in half. Ulysses S. Grant, now the general in chief of all Union armies, assumed personal direction of the campaign against Lee, to "hammer continuously against the armed force of the enemy and his resources, until by mere attrition, if in no other way, there should be nothing left to him. . . ."

Grant had no intention of fighting again in the tangled woods near Chancellorsville, but Lee was a man devilishly clever at making his enemies fight exactly when and where they chose not to. Lee struck, and for two horrible days thousands of men fought and died in the flaming underbrush. A high wind whipped

brush fires into a blazing inferno, and the entire area seemed to be aflame. When the fighting played itself out on the morning of May 8, both armies were just about where they had been at the start; but unlike Chancellorsville, when Union troops had withdrawn to the north to lick their wounds, they now headed south. This time there would be no turning back.

The next day the two armies hit each other again at Spotsylvania Court House. For ten days the savage hand-to-hand struggle went on, culminating in the Bloody Angle, a hideous, writhing death struggle that was the most terrible 24 hours of the war. Two weeks after Grant crossed the Rapidan he had lost 33,000 men—an average of 2,000 casualties every 24 hours.

CONTINUED ON PAGE 202

CONTINUED FROM PAGE 201

Further south, in the Petersburg National Military Park, well-preserved remains of Union and Confederate earthworks and trenches speak of those ten months the two armies spent here, facing each other. Petersburg was an important supply depot for the Richmond area, and the point where five railway lines, vital to the Confederacy, converged. Between June, 1864, and April of the next year, the Union forces assaulted or jabbed at the southern defenders, at one point tunneling nearly 600 feet underground to blow up a huge section of the Confederate lines, forming a great crater which the visitor may still see today. Here also are the sites of batteries, the remains of earthen forts and embankments built as the Federal noose slowly tightened around the city's defenses. As the southern plight became more and more desperate, Lee, almost completely encircled, pulled out of the city his men had defended so bravely, and headed west along the north bank of the Appomattox River, hoping to join General Johnston in North Carolina.

The little crossroads village of Appomattox Courthouse is about 22 miles east of Lynchburg in rolling farm country near the headwaters of the Appomattox River. In 1863 a newcomer named Wilmer McLean had come to town and bought a modest red-brick house in the middle of a locust grove. McLean was fed up with the war; he had owned a farm in northern Virginia which bordered a stream called Bull Run,

Brady took this photo of Lee one week after Appomattox.

and when his property was overrun with soldiers in the war's first battle, he sold out. Now, by a queer twist of fate, the same armies he had tried to avoid were returning to his very door. Lee's ragged troops, near starvation and outnumbered four to one, just could not go any farther. Phil Sheridan had cut off their escape path, and Grant was moving up with the main forces. Shortly after sending a letter to Grant proposing a meeting, Lee and an aide were riding toward Appomattox Court House, when they met Wilmer McLean. The farmer offered his house as a meeting place, they accepted, and the war had come full circle—from Bull Run to a modest parlor in Appomattox. In the simple brick house the two great soldiers—personifying the two opposing civilizations and philosophies—met and decided on surrender terms. After it was over, Lee stood on the porch steps for a moment, absently striking his hands together as he looked off to the hillside where his army was camped, and then mounted his horse Traveller to face his worst ordeal—breaking the news to what was left of his great army, and bidding them farewell. Across the nation church bells were pealing. It was Palm Sunday.

At Harrison's Landing near Brandon on the river James, the Union Army entrenched after the 1862 Seven Days' Battle.

The old tavern shown at right was there when Lee and Grant met on Palm Sunday, 1865, at Appomattox Court House.

202

APPOMATTOX
HERE ON SUNDAY APRIL 9, 1865,
AFTER FOUR YEARS OF HEROIC STRUGGLE
IN DEFENSE OF PRINCIPLES BELIEVED FUNDAMENTAL
TO THE EXISTENCE OF OUR GOVERNMENT
LEE SURRENDERED 9,000 MEN THE REMNANT
OF AN ARMY STILL UNCONQUERED IN SPIRIT
TO 118,000 MEN UNDER GRANT.

Near this pylon on Kill Devil Hill, the Wrights made man's first powered heavier-than-air flight.

Birth of an Age

From Appomattox Courthouse to the barren dunes of Kitty Hawk, North Carolina, is a far cry; but an old civilization yielded to a new one just as completely on these sand hills as it had in Wilmer Mc-Lean's parlor. In 1900 the postmistress of the isolated village of Kitty Hawk received a letter from two Dayton, Ohio, bicycle mechanics named Wright, inquiring about the area's topography. Orville and Wilbur Wright wanted to make some "scientific kite-flying experiments," and U.S. Weather Bureau reports of steady winds in the area had prompted their inquiry.

Six hundred feet from a triangular pylon honoring the Wright brothers, a granite boulder marks the spot where, on December 17, 1903, a contraption of bicycle chains, wood, cloth, and wire left the ground in man's first powered flight. Only three newspapers covered that event, and even five years later, when a reporter telegraphed the Cleveland *Leader* that he had seen a Wright machine leave the ground, his editor wired back angrily: "Cut out the wildcat stuff. We can't handle it."

As Wilbur Wright watches, his brother Orville pilots their contraption in the 120-foot flight which opened the Air Age.

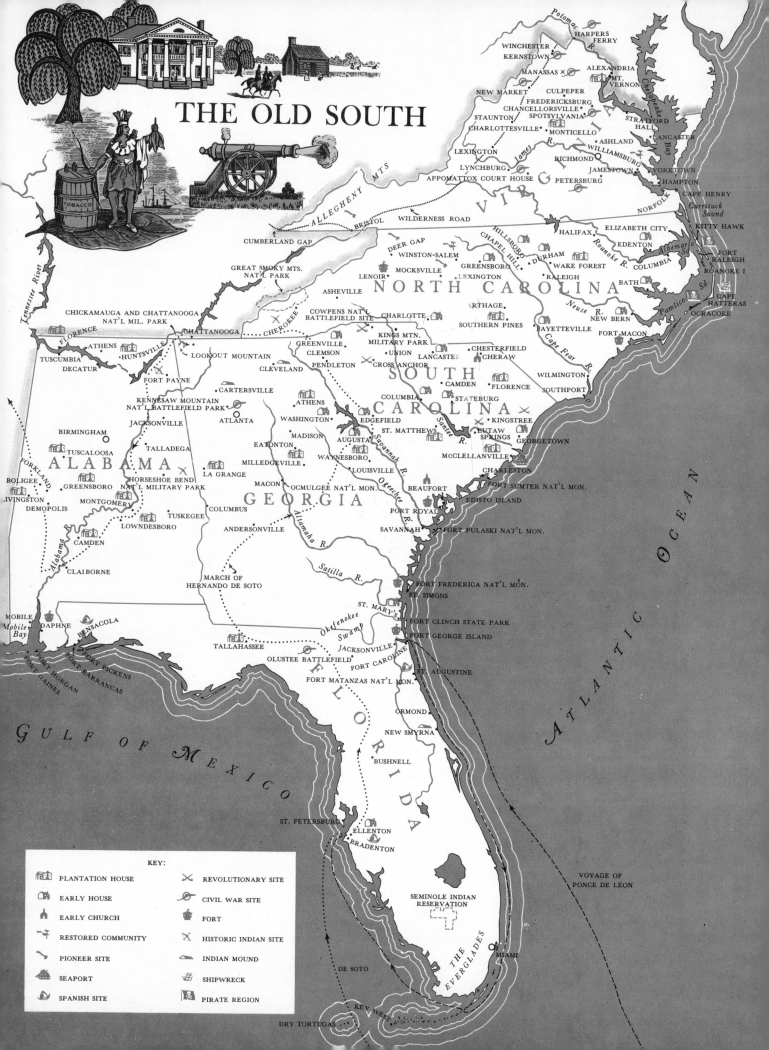

THE OLD SOUTH

TOBACCO

POTOMAX R.

HARPERS FERRY
WINCHESTER
KERNSTOWN
NEW MARKET
MANASSAS ×
ALEXANDRIA
MT. VERNON
CULPEPER
FREDERICKSBURG
CHANCELLORSVILLE
SPOTSYLVANIA
STAUNTON
CHARLOTTESVILLE
MONTICELLO
STRATFORD HALL
LANCASTER
LEXINGTON
ASHLAND
WILLIAMSBURG
RICHMOND
LYNCHBURG
JAMESTOWN
YORKTOWN
APPOMATTOX COURT HOUSE
PETERSBURG
HAMPTON
CAPE HENRY
NORFOLK
Currituck Sound

ALLEGHENY MTS

BRISTOL
WILDERNESS ROAD
HALIFAX
ELIZABETH CITY
EDENTON
COLUMBIA
KITTY HAWK

CUMBERLAND GAP

DEER GAP
HILLSBORO
CHAPEL HILL
DURHAM
WAKE FOREST
FORT RALEIGH
ROANOKE I.
WINSTON-SALEM
GREENSBORO
BATH

GREAT SMOKY MTS. NAT'L PARK
LENOIR
MOCKSVILLE
LEXINGTON
RALEIGH
CAPE HATTERAS

ASHEVILLE
NORTH CAROLINA
NEW BERN
OCRACOKE

CHICKAMAUGA AND CHATTANOOGA NAT'L MIL. PARK
COWPENS NAT'L BATTLEFIELD SITE
CHARLOTTE
CARTHAGE
SOUTHERN PINES
FAYETTEVILLE
FORT MACON

CHEROKEE
CHATTANOOGA
FLORENCE
KINGS MTN. MILITARY PARK
CHESTERFIELD
CHERAW

ATHENS
HUNTSVILLE
GREENVILLE
CLEMSON
PENDLETON
UNION
LANCASTER
WILMINGTON

TUSCUMBIA
DECATUR
LOOKOUT MOUNTAIN
CLEVELAND
CROSS ANCHOR
SOUTH
CAMDEN
FLORENCE
SOUTHPORT

FORT PAYNE
CARTERSVILLE
COLUMBIA
CAROLINA
STATEBURG

KENNESAW MOUNTAIN NAT'L BATTLEFIELD PARK
ATHENS
EDGEFIELD
KINGSTREE

BIRMINGHAM
JACKSONVILLE
ATLANTA
WASHINGTON
ST. MATTHEWS
EUTAW SPRINGS
GEORGETOWN

TUSCALOOSA
TALLADEGA
MADISON
AUGUSTA
McCLELLANVILLE

ALABAMA
LA GRANGE
EATONTON
WAYNESBORO
LOUISVILLE
CHARLESTON

BOLIGEE
GREENSBORO
HORSESHOE BEND NAT'L MILITARY PARK
MILLEDGEVILLE
MACON
OCMULGEE NAT'L MON.
BEAUFORT
FORT SUMTER NAT'L MON.

LIVINGSTON
MONTGOMERY
GEORGIA
EDISTO ISLAND

DEMOPOLIS
TUSKEGEE
COLUMBUS
PORT ROYAL

CAMDEN
LOWNDESBORO
ANDERSONVILLE
SAVANNAH
FORT PULASKI NAT'L MON.

CLAIBORNE
MARCH OF HERNANDO DE SOTO
Satilla R.

FORT FREDERICA NAT'L MON.
ST. SIMONS

MOBILE
Mobile Bay
DAPHNE
PENSACOLA
ST. MARY'S
FORT CLINCH STATE PARK

FORT FICKENS
Okefenokee Swamp
FORT GEORGE ISLAND

FORT MORGAN
FORT BARRANCAS
FORT GAINES
TALLAHASSEE
JACKSONVILLE

OLUSTEE BATTLEFIELD
FORT CAROLINE

FORT MATANZAS NAT'L MON.
ST. AUGUSTINE

GULF OF MEXICO
FLORIDA
ORMOND

NEW SMYRNA

ATLANTIC OCEAN

BUSHNELL

VOYAGE OF PONCE DE LEON

ST. PETERSBURG
ELLENTON
BRADENTON

SEMINOLE INDIAN RESERVATION

DE SOTO

THE EVERGLADES
MIAMI

KEY WEST
DRY TORTUGAS

KEY:

🏠	PLANTATION HOUSE	✕	REVOLUTIONARY SITE
🏠	EARLY HOUSE	⚓	CIVIL WAR SITE
⛪	EARLY CHURCH	🏰	FORT
⚒	RESTORED COMMUNITY	✕	HISTORIC INDIAN SITE
⚒	PIONEER SITE	⛰	INDIAN MOUND
⛵	SEAPORT	🚢	SHIPWRECK
⚑	SPANISH SITE	☠	PIRATE REGION

ALABAMA

ANNISTON

Regar Museum of Natural History Contains Civil War relics and Indian items.

ATHENS

Cary House (1857) Has notable stairway.
Frasier-Brown Plantation Good example of an old plantation residence.
Mason Home (1826) Pioneer residence.
Pryor Home (c. 1826) Greek Revival house.

BIRMINGHAM

Arlington Historical Shrine (1842) A typical ante-bellum house, furnished in the period.
Mudd-Munger House (c. 1842) An impressive mansion with period furnishings.

BOLIGEE

Rosemount Mansion (1830) A fine Greek Revival dwelling.
Hill of Howth (1816) A log house, oldest in the western section of the state.

CAMDEN

Camden Courthouse Ante-bellum structure.
General Jones House
Old Female Academy (c. 1840) An interesting early southern school.
Tait Plantation

CLAIBORNE

James Dellet House (1835) Interesting home with original furnishings.
Deer's Store Oldest post office in state.

DAPHNE

Site of Civil War engagement near Blakely, where some earthworks remain. The *Old Spanish Fort* (1799) is now in ruins.

DECATUR

Hinds House An imposing plantation home.
Old State Bank (1832) Now known as Leila C. Seton Hall, it houses a museum.
Rocky Hill An ante-bellum mansion.
General Joe Wheeler House (1818, 1860's)

DEMOPOLIS

Gaineswood (c. 1844) An imposing Greek Revival southern mansion. Private.
Vine and Olive Colony A log house and some olive trees remain from a 19th-century colony established by French exiles.

FLORENCE

Courtview (1854) Open by permission.
James Hood Plantation Beautiful pre-Civil War residence.
Forks of Cypress (c. 1819) Plantation house with 24 massive columns.
Simpson-Irvine House (c. 1830) Contains old furniture, documents. By permission.

FORKLAND

Old Inn Pioneer tavern now a residence.
Strawberry Hill Ante-bellum plantation.
Thornhill (c. 1845) Oldest schoolhouse in Alabama is on the plantation grounds.

FORT PAYNE

Kershaw House A country residence built around an old Indian blockhouse.

GREENSBORO

Japonica Path Beautiful ante-bellum home with splendid gardens.
Magnolia Grove (1838) Home of Richmond P. Hobson, Spanish-American War naval hero.
Otts Place A fine urban residence.
Governor Seay House
Umbria Charming plantation residence.

HORSESHOE BEND NATIONAL MILITARY PARK

The site where Andrew Jackson decisively defeated the Creek Nation in March, 1814; near Dadeville.

HUNTSVILLE

Ewing-Thornton House or Cedarhurst (1825) An exceptionally fine example of a plantation home. Open April and October.
First National Bank An institution which once took shoes as collateral for loans.
Green Bottom Inn A restored tavern.
Leroy Pope House (c. 1815) The palatial home of the town's founder.
The Towers (c. 1820) Birthplace of Confederate General John Hunt Morgan. Open by appointment.

JACKSONVILLE

The Magnolias (1850) Has Civil War memorabilia. Open by permission.

LIVINGSTON

Oak Manor Interesting architecturally.
Old Inn Pre-Civil War.
Sherrard Home Lovely old plantation house.

LOWNDESBORO

The Colonnade (1852) A Greek Revival home which is open by request.
Haygood House An impressive mansion.
Lewis Home (1842) Preserved as a memorial to Dixon Lewis, Alabama statesman.
Wooten Place (1855) French Colonial style.

MARION

Judson College The second oldest girls' school in the U.S.
Judge Porter King House (1865) A distinguished architectural specimen.
Lea-Stewart House Sam Houston married here.
Marion Institute Ante-bellum military academy, with old barracks still in use.

MOBILE

In this city's narrow, short streets, old houses with lacework balconies and sharply hipped roofs remind the visitor of its Spanish and French background. Among its notable features is a 17-mile-long azalea trail. The first plants were brought from France in 1754. On Dauphin Island in Mobile Bay are shell mounds built by Indians over 500 years ago, but the first white settlement was made in 1702 by Jean Baptiste Le Moyne, Sieur de Bienville. *Fort Gaines*, in the bay, was built by the Spanish in 1720. The so-called *Oldest Building*, a small Creole-style structure of stucco-covered brick (private), dates from about 1795. The *Kirkbridge House*, begun in 1820, contains portions of old *Fort Conde* (1717). *Fort Morgan*, which played a part in the War of 1812 and the Civil War, is practically intact. Among the interesting homes are the *House of Two Cities*, built in 1820 at Blakely, dismantled, and brought in rowboats by slaves to Mobile; *Eslava House*, a showplace with beautiful gardens; *Goldsby House* (1837), with one of the finest wrought-iron gates in the country (private); and the *Gliddon House* (1840), which shows the Spanish and French influences. The homes of two Confederate heroes are here: the *General Braxton Bragg House* (private) and the *Admiral Raphael Semmes House* (1858). The *Dr. G. G. Oswalt Home* (1870) has a fine collection of antiques, and is open on request, as is *Georgia Cottage* (1840), a Greek Revival house. Among the fine public buildings are *City Hall* (1855), originally built as a market and used as a

ALABAMA DEPT. OF ARCHIVES AND HISTORY

First White House of the Confederacy, Montgomery

Confederate armory, and *Barton Academy*, the first public school in Alabama.

MONTGOMERY

Probably the most famous historic building in this state capital is the *First White House of the Confederacy* (c. 1852), a two-story white frame house occupied by Jefferson Davis and his family. Today it houses war relics and some of Davis' personal belongings, brought from his home at Beauvoir, Mississippi. The *Archives and History Building* deserves mention as the first department of its kind established by any state. The *Capitol* is certainly one of the handsomest Greek Revival structures of its kind. Among the monuments on the grounds is the *Confederate Monument*, whose cornerstone was laid by Jefferson Davis in 1886. Davis worshiped at *St. John's Episcopal Church* in the city. The *Winter Building* (1841) is an early Victorian structure which contained the offices of the Southern Telegraph Company in 1861. From a corner room on the second floor, the Confederate secretary of war sent his famous message to General Beauregard, giving him discretionary power to fire on Fort Sumter. Also to be seen in Montgomery are the *Museum of Fine Arts'* collection of Indian relics and historical material, and *Jasmine Hill,* a plantation noted for its elaborate gardens. An exceptional example of the Greek Revival southern mansion is *St. Mary of Loretto Academy* (1851), on one of the city's many hills.

MOORESVILLE

Old Tavern Early stagecoach stop.
Zeitler Collection Exhibits of old weapons, Indian relics, and rare ante-bellum household articles.

RIVER ROAD

Along the route usually called the River Road, from Columbus, Ga., south to Eufaula, Ala., are the following beautiful private houses: the *Mott House* (formerly Bass Plantation, 1842), 12 miles west of Columbus; the *Comer House* (formerly Mitchell Mansion), 15 miles farther south; and still farther south, the *Toney Plantation Home,* once in the family of George Walton, a signer of the Declaration.

SELMA

Kenen Place (1826) is a fine ante-bellum house, open by appointment. Ten miles south of Selma are the ruins of Cahaba, state capital from 1820 to 1826.

TALLADEGA

Mount Ida (1830) Imposing mansion. Open by appointment.
Orangevale or Lawler Place An early

19th-century home with much of its original furniture.
Salter Place One of the best Greek Revival houses in the state. By appointment.
Talladega College Oldest Alabama college for Negroes.

TUSCALOOSA

Dearing-Swain House (1837) Private.
Friedman-Battle House (1835) A classic example of Georgian style.
Governor's Mansion (c. 1835) Housed the governor when Tuscaloosa was the state capital. Now a faculty club, it is open on request. Also in the town are the ruins of the former state capitol.
Moundville State Monument Some of the most extensive remains of aboriginal culture in the South. Museum displays relics found in the burial mounds.
Stafford School (1832) One of the earliest schoolhouses still in use in the area.
University of Alabama One of the loveliest campuses in the country. *Gorgas House* (1829) on the campus was the home of Confederate General Josiah Gorgas, father of William C. Gorgas, one of the conquerors of yellow fever. The house is in the Southern raised-portico style. The *President's Mansion* (1840), open on request, is a stately Greek Revival home.

TUSCUMBIA

Ivy Green Birthplace of Helen Keller.

TUSKEGEE

Cobb House Greek Revival residence.
Harris House or Thompson House Elaborate ironwork. Private.

ALABAMA DEPT. OF ARCHIVES AND HISTORY

Gorgas House, Tuscaloosa

Old Fort Decatur Near Tuskegee, in a bend of the Tallapoosa River, is this well-preserved earthwork built in 1814, supposedly on an Indian mound.
Tuskegee Institute Outstanding Negro college established 1881 by Booker T. Washington. Later the distinguished scientist George Washington Carver worked and taught here.
Varner-Alexander House (1854) Greek Revival home, original furniture. Private.

UNIONTOWN

Cedar Grove An imposing old house with many of the original furnishings.

FLORIDA

BRADENTON

De Soto National Memorial commemorates De Soto's 1539 landing in Florida. On Terra Ceia Island is the *Madira Bickel Mound State Monument*—site of an Indian temple mound and village of Ucita where De Soto first camped.

BULOWVILLE

Bulow Plantation (c. 1820) Ruins of a sugar-indigo-rice plantation and a large sugar mill once used as a base by Major Benjamin Putnam in the Seminole War. Near here the Indian leader Osceola was captured in 1837.

ELLENTON

Judah P. Benjamin Memorial (Gamble Mansion) Greek Revival house where Confederate secretary of state took refuge after the Civil War. House was built 1842-45.

EVERGLADES NATIONAL PARK

Seminole Indians live near this fascinating swamp area, and around Collier City are remains of canals, artificial basins, and harbors of an ancient civilization. At Caxambas many shell mounds remain.

FERNANDINA

Fort Clinch State Park Brick fort completed in 1861, captured by Confederates, and seized by the Federals in 1862.

FORT JEFFERSON NATIONAL MONUMENT

A tremendous ghost fortress which is as interesting as it is difficult to reach. It is located on one of the Dry Tortugas, 68 miles west of Key West, once the haunt of pirates and smugglers, and still a paradise

FLORIDA STATE NEWS BUREAU

Thomas Edison House, Fort Myers

of bird and marine life. The hexagonal brick fort is half a mile in perimeter, surrounded by a deep moat. In 1865 four men involved in Lincoln's assassination were imprisoned here, among them Dr. Mudd.

FORT MYERS

Thomas Edison Estate For almost 50 years the inventor wintered here. Private.

JACKSONVILLE

Fort Caroline Early French fort and town at the mouth of the St. John's River. A National Monument overlooks the site.
Fort George Island Before 1567 the Spanish built a blockhouse here. In 1743 General Oglethorpe, founder of Georgia, invaded Florida and camped on the island. Some buildings erected by Zephaniah Kingsley, a slave trader, including his plantation house, are still here.

KEY WEST

Watlington The only "open" house in Key West is typical of many old Bahama-type homes to be seen here.

MIAMI

Vizcaya-Dade County Art Museum

NEW SMYRNA

In the old town are an Indian mound, foundations of what may have been a

Spanish fort, and part of a canal built by a colony of Minorcans.

OLUSTEE
Olustee Battlefield Scene of a bloody Civil War battle.

PANAMA CITY
Site of *Confederate Salt Works* is nearby.

PENSACOLA
A town rich in history, it was visited in 1539 by one of De Soto's captains. Tristan de Luna attempted to found a colony here in 1559, but a permanent settlement was not established until 1698. Ceded to England in 1763, it was an important British base in the Revolution. Andrew Jackson captured it in 1814. In the town are the *Barclay House* (late 1700's), the *Dorothy Walton House* (1805), and the *Plaza Ferdinand VII*, a remnant of the original Spanish square. *Fort Pickens*, on Santa Rosa Island, was built 1829-34, and nearby are ruins of two Spanish forts, *Barrancas* and *San Carlos*.

ST. AUGUSTINE
In addition to the fascinating *Castillo de San Marcos* (see pp. 166-67), begun in 1672, this ancient city of quaint narrow streets has many well-preserved buildings dating back to the Spanish settlement. The *"Oldest House,"* built in the late 1500's, is one of the most interesting structures. The

Don Toledo House, another coquina building, is typical of the second Spanish occupation and contains heirlooms of former residents. The *Fatio House* (1806) has a 1750 slave kitchen and fine furnishings (open on request). Recently restored, the *Llambias House* (before 1763) is one of a handful of dwellings in St. Augustine dating from the first Spanish period. The date of the *Old Spanish Treasury* is uncertain, but it is notable for its fine furnishings. The thick-walled treasury room

Fort Jefferson in the Dry Tortugas

contains an authentic Spanish chest, a collection of old coins, and two ghoulish figures used for intimidation by the Spanish Court of the Inquisition. Open weekdays. The *Casa de Cannonosa* (House of the Cannon Ball) was so named because one of its walls was pierced by Oglethorpe's cannon fire in 1740. It was used as a tavern during the early American occupation. For many years the *City Gates* (1804) guarded a drawbridge over a moat, part of the city's defense system, and some sections of the outer walls still remain. In the *Fountain of Youth Park* is an Indian burial ground and a museum of 16th-century relics. An *Old Spanish Inn,* built of coquina covered with stucco, dates from the 1700's. *Fort Matanzas* (1737), 40 feet square and 30 feet high, stands near the site where Menendez massacred French Huguenots in 1565, making Florida Spanish, rather than French territory.

TALLAHASSEE
Goodwood Plantation (1839) Square, simple house of late Colonial style.

The Grove (1836) A Greek Revival house built by Richard Call, an early territorial governor. Open on request.

Murat House Near Tallahassee, this home was built in the early 1800's for Prince Achille Murat and his wife.

GEORGIA

ANDERSONVILLE
Site of Confederate prison where 13,000 Union men died during 13 months. In the National Cemetery are graves of many of these men.

ATHENS
The Greek Revival style, which reached full flower in Georgia, is nowhere better expressed than in this old university town. The *University of Georgia* (1785), was the first chartered state university in the U.S. A partial list of the many fine houses includes the *Brumby House* (1818), *Crane House* (1842), *Dearing House* (1856), and the *Henry Grady House* (1845), all open by appointment. Some of the older buildings on the university campus predate the Classic Revival, such as *Old College* (1805) and *Demosthenian Hall* (1824). The *Mell House* (1845) has classic lines with restrained Victorian trimmings, and is open by appointment. *Magnolia Hall,* or Upson House (1840), is a superb residence with old family furnishings. The *President's House* (1854) is one of the loveliest mansions in the South, with a peristyle of 16 Corinthian columns raised half a story above the ground (open by appointment).

ATLANTA
Grant Park A remarkable presentation of the Battle of Atlanta (1864) may be seen here, in the cyclorama painted by a number of German artists in 1885. Preliminary sketches for the painting, one of the largest

in the world, were done by an eyewitness.

McElreath Hall This handsome Georgian house contains the collections of the Atlanta Historical Society, including a remarkable picture collection of this area.

Stone Mountain A huge granite dome once used by Indians as a signal tower. Now a Confederate memorial.

Wren's Nest Home of Joel Chandler Harris, where he wrote the Uncle Remus stories.

AUGUSTA
A charming town founded by James Oglethorpe two years after the settlement of Savannah. Some of its fine houses are the *White House* (1750), oldest in the city, which was a trading post before and during the Revolution; *Kilpatrick House* (1751), another former inn, open on request; *Meadow Garden* (c. 1800), home of George Walton, signer of the Declaration; *Old Government House,* an elegant mansion with elaborate ironwork; and *Ware's Folly* (1818), now the Gertrude Herbert Institute of Art, which cost $140,000 to build—a tremendous sum in its day. Open daily by appointment.

BIRDSVILLE
Jones Plantation (1762) A white clapboard Colonial house with Greek Revival front and Victorian porches. Four lanes of live oaks lead to the house, and the coaching inn, log dining house, and coach house remain nearby.

CARTERSVILLE
Etowah Indian Mounds Six mounds here have yielded Indian objects of great beauty. The largest one, covering 3 acres, is second in size only to the Cahokia Mound in Illinois.

CHATSWORTH
Chief Joseph Vann House (1804-9) The brick home built by the half-Cherokee, half-Scot Vann has been beautifully restored. Vann owned thousands of acres here and supported the nearby Moravian mis-

The Executive Mansion, Milledgeville

sion. In 1838, when the dispossessed Cherokees moved west, he gave up his house and joined them.

CHATTAHOOCHEE NATIONAL FOREST

Soapstone boulders at *Trackrock Gap* near Blairsville bear petroglyphs probably carved by earlier Indians than the Cherokees (*see* p. 164). The *Nacoochee Indian Mound,* near Cleveland, is said to have been visited by De Soto in 1540, and gold mines nearby worked by some of his men.

CHICKAMAUGA BATTLEFIELD

One of the bloodiest battles of the Civil War was fought here, near Rossville, on September 19-20, 1863. The battlefield is now part of the *Chickamauga and Chattanooga National Military Park,* oldest and largest in the U.S.

CRAWFORDVILLE

Liberty Hall Home of Alexander Stephens, Confederate vice-president.

CUMBERLAND ISLAND

Dungeness Plantation Ruins of famous

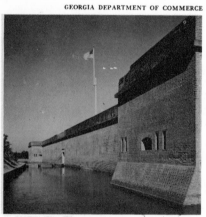

Fort Pulaski, Savannah

plantation owned by General Nathanael Greene. Here "Light Horse" Harry Lee, father of Robert E. Lee, died. In 1893 T. M. Carnegie built a Victorian mansion on the foundations of the Greene House. Private.

EATONTON

Birthplace of Joel Chandler Harris, who heard here the tales of an old slave, Uncle George Terrell, prototype of Uncle Remus. Near Eatonton is the *Indian Eagle Mound,* built in the shape of an eagle and, in the opinion of many, "the most perfect effigy mound in North America."

IRWINVILLE

Jefferson Davis Memorial Park Where the Confederate president was taken prisoner at the end of the Civil War.

JEKYLL ISLAND

Settled by Spanish in 1566, this beautiful island was once the site of a millionaires' club, and is now a state park. The tabby ruins of an early plantation house are here.

KENNESAW MOUNTAIN NATIONAL BATTLEFIELD PARK

Scene of battle between Sherman's Union troops and Confederates led by Joseph Johnston in 1863, in which the Federals flanked the Southern forces and cleared the way for capture of Atlanta.

LA GRANGE

Bellevue (1853) Stately mansion with Ionic pillars at front and sides.

LOUISVILLE

Old Market House (1758) Older than the town, this structure of great oak timbers is also called the Old Slave Market.

MACON

The Columns (c. 1850) Greek Revival house remodeled in 1895, now an inn.
Cowles-Bond House
Cowles Cottage (1829)
Goode-Holt House (1840)
Sidney Lanier Cottage (before 1842) An early house, once the home of the South's most popular poet.
Skelton-Napier-Small House (c. 1850) A showplace of the Greek Revival style.
Wesleyan College One of the first colleges to grant degrees to women.

MADISON

Bonar Hall (1832) Brick manor house.
Boxwood (c. 1851) An elegant Victorian house; fine boxwood. Open on request.
Honeymoon Restored 19th-century home.
McHenry Home (c. 1820) Fine period house.
The Oaks Plantation Outside of town.
Snowhill Home of Lancelot Johnson, inventor of a machine for crushing cottonseed.

MILLEDGEVILLE

State capital from 1804 to 1868, the city has some excellent Greek Revival homes, of which these are open on request: *The Cedars* (1825), notable for its gardens; *Executive Mansion* (1838), a magnificent three-story house modeled on Palladio's Italian villa; the *John W. Gordon House* (1820); the *Elizabeth Jones House* (1820), furnished with 18th-century pieces; the *Methodist Parsonage;* the *Rockwell House* (1834); and the *Sanford House* (1820), scarcely altered, now an inn.

OCMULGEE NATIONAL MONUMENT

One of the most impressive Indian mounds found in the U.S. (*see* pp. 162-63). Among the examples to be seen are the *Ceremonial Earth Lodge; Corn Field Mound;* the *Great Temple Mound,* largest in the area; and a *Funeral Mound.* Also here is a *Trading Post* from the Creek-Colonial period, possibly built by the English sometime after 1690.

OKEFENOKEE WILDLIFE REFUGE

This primeval swamp, once the hunting ground of Creeks and Seminoles, has changed little since William Bartram visited it in the 1770's. Indian mounds are visible on several islands, and Billy's Island was the refuge of the Seminole chief, Billy Bowlegs.

ST. MARYS

Until Florida was annexed by the U.S. this was the southernmost port of the country.

House in Savannah

Many French *émigrés* settled in the community, and still standing are the home, built in 1802, of Major Archibald Clark, who entertained Aaron Burr and General Winfield Scott here; the *Presbyterian Church* (1808); and *Orange Hall* (c. 1833).

ST. SIMONS ISLAND

Fort Frederica (1736) Built by James Oglethorpe, founder of Georgia, to protect the colony from the Spanish. Near here in 1742 the Battle of Bloody Marsh was fought, which turned a Spanish thrust against Charleston. The picturesque ruins of the fortified town are a National Monument. Part of the old military road is still in use, and the site of Oglethorpe's house is among groves of ancient live oaks. Ruins of Major Pierce Butler's plantation are on the northern end of the island. Here Aaron Burr took refuge after shooting Alexander Hamilton, and it was the house actress Fanny Kemble, Butler's English wife, described in her *Journal of a Residence on a Georgian Plantation. West Point Plantation* includes a private "Pink Chapel" (c. 1840). Slave cabins (c. 1770) are preserved at *Hamilton Plantation.*

SAVANNAH

Savannah is an interesting mixture of styles from Colonial to Gothic Revival. On *Factors Walk* may be seen old red brick buildings once used as cotton warehouses, and *Bull Street* is another interesting architectural sight. The *Owens-Thomas House* (1816-19) is a combination of Regency and Greek Revival. *Lafayette's Balcony,* where he greeted the public in 1825, is an unusual wrought-iron structure. It is owned and operated as a house museum by the *Telfair Academy of Arts and Sciences* (1818) which also has interesting furnishings and paintings. The *Herb House* is said to be the oldest in the city, and according to tradition it was here that John Flint, villainous pirate of *Treasure Island,* died. *Low House* (1849), a Greek Revival brownstone mansion, is now headquarters of the Georgia Society of Colonial Dames. The *Eppinger-Robinson House,* erroneously known as the Lachlan McIntosh House, is the oldest brick house in the state. Now private, it was originally a tavern, built in the 1760's. The *Green-Meldrim House* (1850-61) was Sherman's headquarters in 1864 and is now the St. John's Episcopal Church parish house. *Christ Church* (1838) is the third on its site. Nathanael Greene, Revolutionary hero, is buried in Johnson Square, beneath a monument whose cornerstone Lafayette laid in 1825. *Fort Pulaski National Monument* was begun in 1829 and completed in 1847. It is the third fort on Cockspur Island. The huge fortress of rose brick was captured by Union forces in 1862, and the fort, moat, and drawbridge have been beautifully restored. Near Savannah is the site of Mulberry Grove, presented to General Nathanael Greene by Georgia, where Eli Whitney, encouraged by the General's widow, invented a cotton gin. *Wild Heron Plantation* (1756) is about 12 miles from Savannah Grove River. Possibly the oldest plantation house in the state, it contains bricks brought from England, original hand-hewn timbers and paneling. The house is private but is open by appointment 2 weeks in advance. Between Savannah and Darien is *Midway Church* (1792), on the site of an earlier one built by Puritans who emigrated from South Carolina in 1752. On the Isle of Hope near Savannah

is *Wormsloe Plantation* (c. 1850), an estate which has been in the same family since 1733. The grounds are considered the most impressive in Georgia, with a mile-long avenue of oaks leading to a 20-acre park, and camellias and azaleas as tall as young trees. The house is private, but on the grounds are ruins of *Fort Wimberly*, built by the family in 1741, and open by request. Northwest of Savannah was New Ebenezer,

GEORGIA DEPARTMENT OF COMMERCE

The President's House, Athens

a Lutheran settlement founded by Salzburgers in 1736; *Jerusalem Church* is all that remains.

SEA ISLAND
Retreat Plantation (c. 1760) The gardens, approached by an avenue of live oaks, remain although the house is gone. The old barn now forms the central part of the Sea Island Golf Club, and one of the original slave cabins is preserved.

WARM SPRINGS
Little White House The Georgia home of President Franklin D. Roosevelt.

WASHINGTON
Campbell-Lindsay House (c. 1800) Noteworthy Greek Revival. Open on request.
The Cedars (1790) A richly furnished, 28-room house built by a French *émigré*. Open on request.
Holly Court (1825-51) Open by appointment.
Toombs Mansion (1794-1837) Home of the secretary of state of the Confederacy.

WAYNESBORO
Bellevue (1768) A perfectly preserved pioneer house which has been in the same family for two centuries. Built of hand-hewn pine and cypress. Open by appointment.

NORTH CAROLINA

ASHEVILLE
Biltmore (1890-95) The enormous mansion built for George Vanderbilt in the French Renaissance style. Covering four acres, the mansion is a treasure house of tapestries, furniture, and works of art. Superbly landscaped grounds.
Thomas Wolfe Memorial Home The author's house, described as Dixieland in his novel *Look Homeward, Angel*.

BATH
Founded in 1705, Bath was the first town of the province. Five royal governors lived here and several pre-Revolutionary houses

STANDARD OIL COMPANY, N.J.

Cape Hatteras Lighthouse

are preserved in the town. The *Marsh House* has a chimney 17 feet wide, containing windows and closets. *St. Thomas Episcopal Church* (1734) is the oldest house of worship in the state, and one of the oldest in the U.S. It is a simple, dignified brick building, containing silver candlesticks presented by George II and a 1732 bell. The *Glebe House* has been restored as the St. Thomas parish house.

BLUE RIDGE PARKWAY
Between Asheville and the Virginia line are a number of early pioneer dwellings, such as the *Brinegar Cabin* and the *Caudle Cabin*.

CAPE HATTERAS
Hatteras Lighthouse (1869) Tallest lighthouse in the U.S., it guards this most dangerous cape on the eastern seaboard, the "graveyard of the Atlantic" (*see* pp. 172-73).

CARTHAGE
House in the Horseshoe Pre-Revolutionary frame house with bullet holes in the weather-boarding from a 1781 skirmish.

CHAPEL HILL
Seat of the University of North Carolina, chartered 1789, opened 1795. Among the town's many old buildings are *Old East Building* (1793); *South Building* (1798) with Ionic porch and two-story columns; *Person Hall* (1797), now an art museum; and *Playmakers Theater* (1849), a Greek Revival structure.

CHARLOTTE
Founded in mid-18th century, Charlotte

was the center of an early gold rush and until the discovery of gold in California this area was the country's chief source of that metal. The *Mint* (c. 1837) was the first branch of the U.S. Mint, and bears an enormous golden eagle over the pediment. The city was named for Queen Charlotte of Mecklenburg-Schwerin, and the famous Mecklenburg Resolves were signed here on May 31, 1775. Cornwallis named the city "The Hornet's Nest" because of the hard time its patriots gave him during his occupation in 1780. Jefferson Davis convened his cabinet here for the last time in 1865. In the vicinity of Charlotte are the *Hezekiah Alexander House* (1774); the *Potts House* (1811), built of hand-hewn logs (open on request); *Mill Hill* (1821), built by a cabinetmaker (open by appointment); and the *Michael Brown House* (1766), early Pennsylvania-style stone.

CHEROKEE
Oconaluftee Indian Village An authentic reproduction of a Cherokee village of 200 years ago, with council house, dwellings.

DEEP GAP
Mountain Pass Where Daniel Boone crossed the Blue Ridge into the wilderness.

DURHAM
Bennett Place Memorial Six miles west of town is the spot where General Joseph Johnston surrendered to General Sherman on April 26, 1865, virtually ending the Civil War.
Fairntosh Plantation (1802) Twelve miles

211

St. Paul's Episcopal Church, Edenton

north of Durham, the house has much of its original furniture, and slave cabins, schoolhouse, and chapel are preserved.

EDENTON

Along with Bath and New Bern, Edenton was one of the province's earliest communities, settled about 1658 by colonists from Jamestown, Va. *Chowan County Courthouse* (1767) is a magnificent Georgian building of red brick with white trim, typical of Tidewater Virginia. The *Barker House* was the home of the London agent for the colony, and his wife presided over the Edenton Tea Party, October 25, 1774. *St. Paul's Episcopal Church* (1736-60) is almost unrivaled for its type and period. The *Cupola House* (c. 1712) is one of the most striking Jacobean buildings in the U.S., with great brick chimneys and octagonal cupola, once used as a lookout for ships. Also in the town are the *Littlejohn House* (1769), with beautiful paneling; the *Iredell House* (1759); *Booth House* (c. 1756), a charming residence with unusual Chippendale stairway and period furniture (by appointment); *Pembroke Hall* (1841); *Albania; Paxton House* (c. 1790); *Ellison House;* and *Edmund Hatch House* (1744). Near Edenton, close to Albemarle Sound, are *Sycamore Plantation* (before 1775), typical of the plantation dwellings of the period; *Greenfield* (c. 1752), famous for its double galleries; and *Mulberry Hill* (1784), a distinguished four-story brick house. Also in this vicinity are *Clement Hall* (c. 1758); *Bandon* (c. 1800), one of the finest plantation houses in the region; and *Somerset* (1830), on a plantation which once had its private race track.

ELIZABETH CITY

Brick House Reputed haunt of Blackbeard. *Fearing House* (c. 1740) Enlarged in the Greek Revival era. Still in the same family.

FAYETTEVILLE

Founded in 1739 by Scots, whose "Campbelltown" is in the eastern part of town. Scottish refugees fled here after their defeat at Culloden, and in 1774 the famous Flora

MacDonald, who helped "Bonnie Prince Charlie" escape, lived here with her husband. *Market House* (1838) was originally built as the statehouse in 1780, and destroyed by fire in 1831.

FORT MACON

The deeply-moated, pentagonal fort was built in 1826-34, and is beautifully restored.

GREAT SMOKY MOUNTAINS NATIONAL PARK

This 800-square-mile tract is the best preservation of the vast forest which once stretched from the Atlantic to the prairies. In Cades Cove and near the Oconaluftee Ranger Station some of the old log cabins of the pioneers are preserved, to show how people lived on the mountain frontier.

GREENSBORO

Old McNairy House (1761) Near the town is the house where Andrew Jackson lived while studying law in Salisbury.
Dolly Madison Well Site of birthplace of Dolly Payne in 1768, in the Quaker community of New Garden, west of Greensboro. *Guilford Courthouse National Military Park* Six miles northwest of Greensboro, where General Nathanael Greene allowed Cornwallis a nominal victory which led to his eventual downfall.

HALIFAX

Colonial Clerk of Court's Office Now used for a county library.
Constitution House A small, clapboarded building (restored and moved from the original site) where a committee drafted the state constitution late in 1776.
Old Gaol (c. 1764) Where Highland Scottish leaders who fought patriots in the battle of Moore's Creek were imprisoned. Contains a museum.

HILLSBORO

Founded about 1754, and once a summer capital for low-country planters. The *Colonial Inn* dates from the 18th century, and stands on the route Boone took to Kentucky in 1776. *Old Courthouse* (1845) is a Greek Revival building with low square tower. The *Lloyd House* (1754) is the one remaining wing of a house where Governor Tryon summered. The *Presbyterian Church Cemetery* contains the graves of several signers of the Declaration of Independence. The *Nash-Hooper House* (1772) was the home of the Revolutionary hero Francis Nash for whom Nashville is named, and later of a signer of the Declaration, William Hooper. *Ayr Mount, Sans Souci,* and other old houses are also open during the annual Garden Club tour. Near Hillsboro is *Alamance Battleground,* a state historic site, where patriots known as Regulators were defeated by the governor's militia on May 16, 1771.

KITTY HAWK

In this picturesque town and on nearby Kill Devil Hill, Orville and Wilbur Wright perfected their first airplane (*see* pp. 204-5).

LENOIR

Fort Defiance (1788) Not a fort, but a big old farmhouse named for one which stood

on the site. Built by General William Lenoir, a leader in the Kings Mountain battle.

LEXINGTON

Boone Memorial Park Near Lexington is a *Museum of Relics* and a cave thought to have been used by Boone.

MOCKSVILLE

Grave of Squire and Sarah Boone The original 18th-century headstones of Daniel Boone's parents are preserved near here.

MOORE'S CREEK NATIONAL MILITARY PARK

Scene of battle, February 27, 1776, in which North Carolina patriots defeated a force of loyalists.

NEW BERN

Tryon Palace (1767-70) Built for Royal Governor William Tryon, whose extravagance caused a small war by the patriot "Regulators" in 1771, this great two-story mansion is being rebuilt. Called the "most beautiful building in colonial America," it also served as the statehouse, where the first provincial congress met.
Smallwood-Ward House (1810) A charming house of golden brick, with portico. Private.
John Wright Stanley House (c. 1780)
Stanley-Green-Winfield House (1850)
Taylor-Ward House (c. 1792) An unusual three-story house. Private.
A two-day tour of other private houses in this old town (founded 1710) is usually held the first week in April. Among many

Barker House, Edenton

fine private houses are the *Lively-Vail-Moulton House* (1776), the *Jarvis-Hand House* (1810), the *Fulshire-Ives House* (1775), and the *Bryan-Ashford House* (1802) with fine early furniture.

OCRACOKE INLET

Favorite resort of pirates and smugglers (*see* pp. 172-73). *Teach's Hole,* inside the Outer Banks, is the traditional hideout of Blackbeard. During the Revolution Americans smuggled munitions and supplies into Pamlico Sound, to be carried overland.

PETTIGREW STATE PARK

Somerset Place (1830) Near Columbia, this

restored plantation includes the mansion house, kitchen, laundry, and smokehouse.

RALEIGH

Andrew Johnson Birthplace Moved about two miles from the place where the seventeenth President was born in 1808.

Haywood Hall (1793) Notable white clapboard house furnished with heirlooms.

Joel Lane House (1760) Oldest in Raleigh, it was the home of a pioneer settler.

State Capitol (1833-40) A beautifully-proportioned building.

Wakestone Home of the late Josephus Daniels. Owned by Masonic Grand Lodge.

ROANOKE ISLAND

Fort Raleigh National Historic Site The area where the first English settlements were attempted, 1585-87 (*see* pp. 168-69), has reconstructed earthworks of the original fort, museum, and outdoor theater.

SOUTHERN PINES

Shaw House Early dwelling, restored cabin.

SOUTHPORT

The Cape Fear area once had some of the noblest plantation houses in the country. Some of the survivors are: *Orton Plantation* (1725-1840), on a bluff overlooking Cape Fear River, surrounded by live oaks perhaps 500 years old, and gardens with hundreds of varieties of azaleas and camellias in bloom January to May. At the entrance are massive gray stone pillars topped with spread eagles. Half a mile southeast is *Old Palace Field,* with the ruins of Russelborough, burned by the British in 1776, where Governor Tryon once lived. South of here is the location of Old Brunswick, now a state historic site. The ruins of *St. Philip's Church* (1754-68) are all that remain of a town which once shipped large quantities of naval stores. Nearby is the site of *Fort Anderson,* part of the Confederate defense line of Wilmington, now marked by grassy ruins.

WAKE FOREST

Calvin Jones House (before 1820) Plantation house now being restored.

WILMINGTON

Bellamy Mansion (1859) Original furnishings.

Moravian Church, Winston-Salem

Cornwallis House (1771) Beautiful mansion with colonnaded porches, Palladian doorway, and period furnishings. The headquarters of Cornwallis in 1781.

St. James' Church (1839) On the site of a 1751 church. Thomas Godfrey, author of the first American play produced professionally, is buried here.

Moore's Creek National Military Park Site of the battle (February 27, 1776) between patriots and Tories, most of whom were Scottish Highlanders, which resulted in a great patriot victory and determined North Carolina's stand in the Revolution.

WINSTON-SALEM

Old Salem (1766) A pioneer village of great charm founded by Moravians who lived a communal life here for 60 years. Almost all the buildings are of handmade brick and reveal great craftsmanship. Set flush with the sidewalks, they have hooded doorways, arched windows, graceful iron railings, and steep gabled roofs. Among the restored buildings are the *Home Moravian Church* (1798-1800), with octagonal bell tower; the *Lick-Boner House* (1787), with traditional furnishings; the *Brothers House* (1769), used for unmarried brethren; *Salem Tavern* (1784); *Warden's House* (1797); and *Wachovia Museum* (1794). The *John Vogler House* (1819) has been restored as it was when the home and shop of a clockmaker and silversmith. West of town is Bethabara Village, the original Moravian settlement, with a fine church.

SOUTH CAROLINA

BEAUFORT

A town with a long and turbulent history, at times occupied by Spanish, French, English, Scottish, and West Indian planters, destroyed by Yamassee Indians, conquered by the British in the Revolution, the Union in the Civil War, and wrecked by two great hurricanes. In spite of its history the pleasant town contains many fine old buildings, among them *Verdier House* (1795), a plantation-style home; and the following houses, open by appointment: *Tabby Manse* (1768); *Secession House* (1850's), supposedly where the first draft of the Ordinance of Secession was drawn up; the *Johnson-Danner House* (1850); *Palmetto Hall* (1790), a beautifully built and furnished plantation house; and the *McLeod House* (1813), with tall Doric columns. Here also are the *St. Helena Episcopal Church* (1724); *Beaufort Arsenal,* built in 1795 and rebuilt in 1852; and the *Oldest House* (c. 1720), believed to antedate the Yamassee War of 1715.

CAMDEN

Old Courthouse (1826)

CHARLESTON

The place William Allen White called "the most civilized city in America" has not only witnessed a great deal of history, but has so many fine buildings that it would be impossible to enumerate all of them here (*see* pp. 186-87). One of the city's most impressive sights is *Rainbow Row,* with its 18th-century houses, iron fences, and magnificent gardens. Charleston contains "single" houses with gable end toward the street and side entrance, and "double" houses, with the entrance on the street. The larger mansions had kitchen, carriage house, and servants' quarters in separate outbuildings to the rear. *St. Michael's Episcopal Church* (1752-61) which has a superb tower, was the only great church in the colonies when it was built; and *St. Philip's Episcopal Church* (1835-38), with its old graveyard, and the *Huguenot Church* (1845), last remaining Huguenot church in the U.S., are well worth visiting. The *First Baptist Church* (1822) was designed by one of America's first native-born architects, Robert Mills, who was Jefferson's draftsman at Monticello. Some of the fine public buildings are the *South Carolina Society Hall* (1804); the *Charleston Museum,* oldest in the U.S.; *Dock Street Theater* and *Planters Hotel,* restorations of the first theater in the country and the hotel built around its ruins soon after 1809. The "Catfish Row" of *Porgy and Bess* is on Church Street. One of the most splendid houses in America is the *Miles Brewton House* (1769), a Georgian-style "double" house enclosed with a handsome iron fence. Another showplace is the *William Gibbes House* (c. 1772), a three-story clapboarded house built for a wealthy merchant. Its furnishings are superb, and may be seen during the House and Garden Tour. The *Joseph Manigault House* (c. 1790) is a masterpiece designed by the

St. Helena's Episcopal Church, Beaufort

native Charleston architect, Gabriel Manigault, for his brother. Probably the finest house of the city's Federal era is the *Nathaniel Russell House* (1811), an odd-shaped three-story structure with exquisite mantels and paneling. It is now the quarters of the Charleston Historic Foundation. The *Branford-Horry House* (c. 1751) contains some of the most impressive woodwork in Charleston, and is usually open during the tour, as are the *John Stuart House* (1772), a delightful Georgian home; *Thomas Rose's House* (c. 1735), built of brick 29 inches thick, covered with oyster-shell stucco, and paneled throughout; the *Capers-Huger House* (c. 1745), one of the earliest "double" houses, restored since it was bombarded in the Civil War; *George Eveleigh's House* (c. 1738); the *Thomas Legare House* (1750); *William Rhett House* (1712); *Othniel Beale Home* (1740); and the *Heyward House* (c. 1789). The so-called *Pirate House* on Church Street is not authentic, but the building is interesting in itself. The *Old Exchange* (1771) stands

HERBERT LOEBEL

Nathaniel Russell House, Charleston

where the pirate Stede Bonnet was imprisoned in 1718, and the *Pirate Monument* on the Battery marks the spot where he and a number of his crew were hanged. The *Heyward-Washington House* (1770) is an early Georgian brick residence built by a signer of the Declaration. It is beautifully restored and furnished with museum pieces. In the rear are the old brick kitchen, carriage house, and servants' quarters; owned by the Carolina Art Association. On Broad Street are the *Izard House* (1757) and *John Rutledge House* (1760). *Sword Gate House* (1776) is of brick, with later wood sections, and has a wrought-iron gateway which is one of the city's wonders. *Ashley Hall* (1816) is a magnificent Regency house; and the *Young-Johnson House* (1770) is a small, lovely brick Colonial house, full of works of art (private). Near Charleston is *Drayton Hall* (c. 1738) a massive Georgian mansion on the Ashley River (private). Its adjoining *Magnolia Gardens* were called the "most beautiful in the world" by John Galsworthy. A neighboring

plantation is *Middleton Place* (1738-55), of which one wing remains. Henry Middleton, who built it, owned 20 plantations, 50,000 acres, and 800 slaves. What may have been the first landscaped garden in America may still be seen here, and the *Middleton Oak* at the river's edge is said to be 900 years old. Middleton Place is open from February to May.

CHERAW

St. David's Episcopal Church (1770-73) Built by a group of Welsh settlers, this served as a Revolution and Civil War hospital.
Hartsell House (1780) Sherman's headquarters, 1865; contains period furniture.
Old Market Hall (1836)

CHESTERFIELD

Craig House (1798) Georgian Colonial.

CLEMSON

Fort Hill (1803-25) Home of John C. Calhoun, who brought his family here in 1825 and enlarged the original house, named for a fort which once stood on the site. Contains much original furniture.

COLUMBIA

There are many points of interest in this town which became the state capital in 1786. The oldest buildings on the university quadrangle were completed in 1801, and the *University Library,* the first college library in the U.S., was built in 1840. The *Crawford-Clarkson House* (c. 1837) has notable ironwork, and is open on request. Woodrow Wilson's boyhood home is here, as is the *Chesnut Cottage,* home of Mary Boykin Chesnut, whose *Diary from Dixie* is the best account of the Civil War from the viewpoint of a southern woman. Lafayette stayed at a house in the town, and the Secession Convention of December 17, 1860, was held at the *First Baptist Church* (1856). Other fine houses are the *Seibels House* (1796), the *Governor's House* (1855), *Boylston House* (1822), and *Ainsley Hall Place* (c. 1818).

COWPENS NATIONAL BATTLEFIELD SITE

Site of a brilliant victory by General Daniel Morgan over a superior British force, January 17, 1781.

CROSS ANCHOR

Near the site of the Battle of Musgrove's Mill, an American victory over the British.

EDGEFIELD

Halcyon Grove (c. 1810) was home of Governor Andrew Pickens. Nearby is *Becky's Pool,* where Becky Cotton deposited the bodies of her first three husbands, whom she murdered. A ravishing beauty, she was acquitted, and one of the jurymen became her fourth husband.

EDISTO ISLAND

Seabrook Plantation (1810) A delightful white clapboard house with double staircase.

EUTAW SPRINGS BATTLEFIELD PARK

Where General Nathanael Greene's ragged Americans tried to delay the British from joining Cornwallis on September 8, 1781.

FLORENCE

The Columns (1850-56) A tremendous Greek Revival house with 22 free-standing columns, near Florence.

FORT SUMTER NATIONAL MONUMENT

The shot which began the Civil War burst over Fort Sumter on April 12, 1861. The fort has been partially restored.

GEORGETOWN

Once a busy indigo and rice port, it was founded in 1735, and has many interesting old buildings. Near here is *Murrells Inlet,* a pirate refuge. *Brookgreen Gardens* is an unusual open-air museum on the site of a plantation where the poet, artist, and composer Washington Allston was born. The *Prince George Protestant Episcopal Church* (c. 1750) shows the Wren influence, and the *County Courthouse* (1824) is a fine Greek Revival structure. The *Pyatt House* (c. 1790), the *Winyah Indigo Society Hall* (1857), and the *Masonic Temple* (1735), once a bank, are also worth visiting.

GOOSE CREEK

This is a region of old plantations. Among them are *Medway* (1686), a one-story Dutch house of handmade brick, covered with stucco; *Dean Hall Plantation* (1821), whose gardens are open; *The Bluff* (c. 1790), *Exeter* (1726), and *Lewisfield* (1774), all with old slave cabins and gardens; and *St. James Church* (1711), a most interesting church of pink stuccoed brick. Near Moncks Corner are *Gippy* (1821), named for an old slave; and *Mulberry Plantation* (1714), one of the most elaborate mansions in the colonies (private). During the Yamassee War it was a fortified stronghold.

GREENVILLE

Rock House Built early in the 19th century by one of "Swamp Fox" Marion's lieutenants.

GREENWOOD

Nearby is the site of *Ninety Six,* oldest white community in the Up Country, named erroneously for its distance from Keowee. Near it is the site of *Star Fort* where Nathanael Greene besieged the Brit-

STATE DEVELOPMENT BOARD, COLUMBIA

St. David's Episcopal Church, Cheraw

Sword Gates, Legare House, Charleston

ish. A tunnel which the Polish engineer Thaddeus Kosciusko began to dig under the fort may still be seen.

INDIANTOWN
Presbyterian Church (1830)
Springbank Plantation (1783)

KINGS MOUNTAIN NATIONAL MILITARY PARK
Scene of the battle between patriots and Tories, October 7, 1780.

KINGSTREE
One of the state's early inland settlements. Near here General Francis Marion hid his men. Traces of Revolutionary breastworks still remain at the site of Lower Bridge Battle.

LANCASTER
Eleven miles north of town is a site claimed as Andrew Jackson's birthplace.

McCLELLANVILLE
Hampton Plantation (1735) One of the finest examples of Georgian Colonial architecture. Eliza Lucas Pinckney, credited with introducing indigo cultivation to South Carolina, lived here with her son-in-law.
Fairfield Plantation (1730-66) White frame house, once the home of Thomas Pinckney.
Hopsewee (1749) A restored house where

Thomas Lynch, Jr., a signer of the Declaration, was born.
St. James Episcopal Church (c. 1768) A fine Georgian building.

PENDLETON
Hopewell Plantation (late 1700's) Home of General Andrew Pickens, the Revolutionary hero. On the grounds the Treaty of Hopewell was signed in 1785 between Pickens and several Indian tribes, who innocently surrendered their rights to about one third of Georgia and of Tennessee.
Maverick Place or Mont Pelier (c. 1850) Typical Up Country plantation house and home of Samuel Maverick, a lawyer who moved to Texas, where he was given a herd of 600 cattle as a fee. His ignorance of the range is immortalized by the word "maverick," applied to unbranded cattle.
Farmers' Society Hall (1826) The society, organized in 1815, still meets here.
Old Stone Church (1797-1802) Presbyterian church for a community dominated by the Pickens family. Pickens and many Scotch-Irish church members who followed him at the battles of Ninety Six, Cowpens, and Eutaw Springs are buried here.
Governor Andrew Pickens Home (1812) Home of the General's son.
St. Paul's Episcopal Church (1822) Mrs. John C. Calhoun and children buried here.

PORT ROYAL
Fort Frederick (1731) Built by English; largest tabby fort in America. Restored.

SALUDA
Old Town Where Old Hop, a Cherokee king, ceded lands to Americans in 1777.

STATEBURG
Borough House (1754) In the town founded by General Thomas Sumter, "Gamecock of the Revolution," this impressive house was used by Generals Greene and Cornwallis in the Revolution, and contains valuable relics and furniture. On the grounds are the 400-year-old *Spy Oak*, from which Tory spies were hanged, and a beautiful pre-Revolutionary garden. General Sumter's grave is nearby.
Millwood Vine-covered columns stand

above the ashes of this house, burned during Sherman's march to the sea. This was the boyhood home of Wade Hampton, who became Confederate cavalry commander upon J. E. B. Stuart's death.

SULLIVAN'S ISLAND
Fort Moultrie The log fort was sucessfully defended against the British in 1776, during the Revolution. Edgar Allan Poe served as a soldier here in 1828, and later used the island as the scene for *The Gold Bug.* Osceola, chief of the Seminoles, died in prison here in 1838.

SUMMERTON
Fort Watson Memorial During the Revolution the British built this fort atop an Indian mound 50 feet high. In 1780 General Francis Marion had his men build, in a single night, a log tower higher than the fort, and at dawn they poured a shower of lead into Fort Watson which surrendered.

UNION
The town has several good Greek Revival houses. Among them are *Meng* (1832), *Culp* (c. 1857), *Jeter* (1859), and *Herndon Terrace* (1848). The *Sawyer House* (1812) is open by appointment, as is *Duncan Home* (1854). *Gist Mansion* (1832), near the town, is a lovely Greek Revival plantation house with particularly fine wrought-iron work.

Fort Hill, Clemson

VIRGINIA

ALEXANDRIA
A town familiar to the Washington, Custis, and Lee families, where whole streets of Colonial and Federal houses survive (*see* p. 180). Many of George Washington's personal Masonic relics are in the *Masonic Museum,* which also has several fine early portraits. Most of the 18th-century houses are private, but several are open during fall and spring tours. The *Benjamin Dulany House* and the *Holland House* may be seen at these times. Some of the fine dwellings lining the old cobblestone streets are the *Lloyd House* (1793); the *Carlyle House* (1752), where General Braddock planned his disastrous campaign, and scene of the

Fairfax Resolves, drawn by George Mason to protest British taxation; and the privately-owned *Lord Fairfax House* (1816). The *Stabler-Leadbeater Apothecary Shop* (1792) was a dispensary for the Washingtons and other families of the vicinity, and is now a museum. In 1859 Robert E. Lee was making a purchase here when Lt. J. E. B. Stuart delivered his orders to suppress John Brown's raid at Harpers Ferry. The *Old Presbyterian Meeting House* (1774-90) has a graveyard in which many Revolutionary figures are buried. *Christ Church* (1767-73), a building with a fine Palladian window, is where Washington and Robert E. Lee worshiped. Washington

paid for the wrought-brass and crystal chandelier. *Friendship Fire Engine House* (1775) is now a museum of early fire-fighting equipment. *Gadsby's Tavern* (1752) is a famous old inn where Washington's military career began, recruiting his first command in 1754, and ended, with his review of the Alexandria troops from the steps in 1799.

APPOMATTOX COURT HOUSE
McLean House Reconstruction of the house where on April 9, 1865, General Lee surrendered the Army of Northern Virginia to General Grant (*see* pp. 202-3).

ARLINGTON
Custis-Lee Mansion (1802-20) A proud,

Custis-Lee Mansion, Arlington

pillared mansion which was the home of George Washington Parke Custis, foster son of the first President. Robert E. Lee married Mary Ann Custis here in 1831 and six of their children were born in the house.

ASHLAND
Henry Clay Birthplace Clay was born on a farm at Clay Spring, four miles east.
Old Fork Church (1735) Near Scotchtown, this is where Patrick Henry and Dolly Madison once worshiped.
Scotchtown About nine miles northwest of Ashland, this was Patrick Henry's home from 1771 to 1777, and was later sold to John Payne, father of Dolly Payne Madison.

BACON'S CASTLE
Bacon's Castle (1655) Said to be the only true Jacobean house in the country, where some of Nathaniel Bacon's followers took refuge after their rebellion against Governor Berkeley and the burning of Jamestown. (Not open to the public.)

BRISTOL
Once the northern gateway to the Tennessee Valley and the Great Smokies. In a stockade where the *Presbyterian Church* now stands the frontiersmen planned the campaign which ended in the British defeat at Kings Mountain.

CAPE HENRY
Memorial Cross Marks the approximate site of the Jamestown colonists' first landing.
Old Lighthouse (1791) Oldest in America.
Adam Thoroughgood House (c. 1636) A Jacobean reminder of early Virginia.

CHANCELLORSVILLE
Scene of Lee's victory over Hooker in May, 1863, where Stonewall Jackson was fatally wounded. Jackson's amputated arm is buried here.

CHARLOTTESVILLE
This is "Mr. Jefferson's town." As creator of the *University of Virginia,* he designed its campus and buildings (*see* p. 195), including the Palladian structures on the highest ground with the *Rotunda* as the focal point. The high serpentine brick walls were also his design. *West Range* ("Rowdy

Row") houses the Jefferson Society Room, whose members included Madison, Monroe, Lafayette, and Edgar Allan Poe. The *President's House* on Carr's Hill, and the *James Monroe House* (1790) and his office are open during Historic Garden Week. Near Charlottesville is *Monticello,* the beautiful house which Jefferson built, rebuilt, enlarged, and perfected between 1769 and 1809 (*see* pp. 192-93). Between Monticello and the town is the *Michie Tavern* (1753), a colonial inn which has one of the few original colonial bars, and a ballroom (open March 15 to December 1). The *Old Swan Tavern* (c. 1773) was built by John Jouett, whose son rode to Monticello to warn Jefferson that Tarleton's cavalry was on the way to capture him in 1781. The *Old Courthouse* (1803 and 1860), once used as a church, is where Jefferson, Madison, and Monroe worshiped. In the vicinity of Charlottesville are many other historic places, among them *Shadwell,* Jefferson's birthplace, and *Edgehill* (1818), built by Jefferson's grandson. *Colle* (c. 1770) is on a tract of land given by Jefferson to Filippo Mazzei, the Italian liberal. *Castle Hill* (1764) was built by Jefferson's guardian, an early pioneer who made the first trip into Kentucky. *Edgemont* (1796) is a lovely frame house designed by Jefferson (open by appointment). *Bremo Plantation* (c. 1803) was designed by Jefferson. *Ash Lawn* (1799) is the home Jefferson designed for his friend James Monroe; now furnished with Monroe treasures. Nearby, George Rogers Clark and Meriwether Lewis were born, and *Franklin* (late 1700's) is a clapboard house where Benjamin Franklin's grandson, and also Meriwether Lewis, lived. *Morven* (1820) is a white frame cottage owned by Jefferson's great friend William Short.

CULPEPER
General A. P. Hill Birthplace

FALLS CHURCH
The Falls Church (1733 and 1769) Washington was a vestryman here. A recruiting station in the Revolution, and a Civil War hospital.

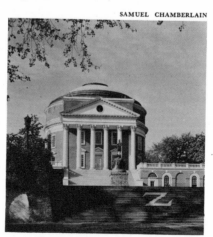

University of Virginia Rotunda, Charlottesville

FREDERICKSBURG
An interesting town long before the Civil War battle with which it is usually associated. In the *James Monroe Law Office* (1758) the future President practiced. The house contains furniture the Monroes bought in France for the White House. The *Hugh Mercer Apothecary Shop* (mid-18th century) and the *Rising Sun Tavern* (c. 1760) are interesting old buildings, the latter being a scene of Revolutionary activity. On Fauquier Street one old horse-chestnut tree is left of the 13 Washington planted there as a symbol of the 13 original states. Washington's mother lived in the *Mary Washington House* (1772) and he often visited her there. His sister Betty and her husband Colonel Fielding Lewis lived at *Kenmore* (1752), a superb period house. Other sites of interest include *Federal Hill,* the *John Paul Jones House,* and *Marmion,* 17 miles from Fredericksburg, which belonged to the Fitzhugh family and was bought by Washington's nephew. Pecan trees here were planted by the first President. The *Fredericksburg and Spotsylvania National Military Park* includes the battlefields of Chancellorsville, Fredericksburg, Spotsylvania Courthouse, the Wilderness (*see* pp. 196-203), and the *Jackson Shrine* where "Stonewall" died. It preserves earthworks, gun emplacements, and other defenses used by both armies.

GLOUCESTER
In the heart of Tidewater Virginia, the town has many pre-Revolutionary buildings, including a debtor's prison, ordinary (1732), courthouse (1766), and *Ware Church,* built before 1723. *Belroi,* three miles away, was the birthplace of Walter Reed.

GLOUCESTER COUNTY
Abingdon Church (1775) Beautiful cruciform church set in a walnut grove.
Powhatan's Chimney Near Abingdon Church is the probable site of the chief's main village, where Captain John Smith was taken after his capture. The marl chimney may have belonged to a house built for Powhatan by white settlers.
Rosewell (1726) Nothing but ruins remain of the most magnificent house built in the colonial period. Built by Mann Page, it had 35 rooms, three great halls, and a giant staircase. The house burned in 1916.

GORDONSVILLE
Montebello Birthplace of Zachary Taylor.

GREAT FALLS OF THE POTOMAC
Ash Grove (1790) Near the Falls is the old house with hunting lodge built by Thomas, Lord Fairfax. Holly and boxwood gardens.
Washington's Iron Foundry Ruined mill on the old Potomac Canal.

HAMPTON
Blackbeard's Point Here in 1718 Blackbeard's head was hoisted on a pole.
St. John's Church (1728)

HANOVER
County Courthouse (1733) Scene of Patrick Henry's first important legal victory.

Hanover Tavern (c. 1723) Where Henry lived while pleading his case. He was married at **Rural Plains**, a late 17th-century brick house, and the site of his birthplace is nearby, where foundations of the **Studley House** remain.

JAMES RIVER PLANTATIONS
Berkeley (1726) Main seat of the Harrison family, which gave the U.S. its ninth and twenty-third Presidents. Benjamin Harrison IV bought the plantation, part of Berkeley Hundred, and his son began the brick mansion which stands above the James. Interior has hand-carved woodwork, period furnishings.
Brandon (1755) Near Hopewell is one of

Upper Brandon, on the James River

the homes which belonged to the Harrison family, an imposing house with two wings and beautiful paneling. **Upper Brandon**, a mile farther up the James, also belonged to the family. It is open during Garden Week.
Carter's Grove (1751-53) One of the great examples of colonial craftsmanship, completed by Carter Burwell, grandson of "King" Carter, who began it in 1690 (*see* p. 182). Exquisite paneling and superb entrance hall and stairway. Open during spring.
Sherwood Forest (1780 and 1840's) A rambling clapboard house a mile back from the river, bought by John Tyler in 1842. Members of the President's family still live here. Open daily except Sundays.
Shirley (rebuilt 1769) Tall brick house with dormers which was altered by Charles Carter, grandfather of Robert E. Lee (*see* p. 185).
Westover (1790) One of the nation's most famous houses is this red brick mansion built by Col. William Byrd II (*see* p. 185). The doorways of Portland stone are in the Palladian tradition, and the size and setting are spectacular. House open during Garden Week, grounds and gardens daily.

JAMESTOWN
The original foundations, streets, and fences are visible in this site of the first permanent English settlement in the New World (*see* pp. 170-71). The town is now

joined to the mainland by a causeway; and *James Fort, Chief Powhatan's Lodge,* and three of the colonists' ships have been reconstructed. Many objects on display were found in excavated ruins. A glass factory has been rebuilt. The **Jamestown Church Tower** was part of the settlement's fifth church, which has been reconstructed behind the tower. The **Jacquelin-Ambler House** ruins stand at the eastern end of the island. It was begun about 1710, burned during the Revolution and Civil War, finally destroyed in 1895. Also on the island are the **Jamestown Tercentenary Monument,** statues of John Smith and Pocahontas, and a monument to the chaplain who celebrated the first Anglican communion service in America.

KERNSTOWN
Site of the first battle of Stonewall Jackson's Valley Campaign.

LANCASTER COUNTY
Christ Church (1732) Built by "King" Carter, who died the year it was completed, leaving 300,000 acres and 1,000 slaves. Largely intact, including Palladian doorways and wine-glass pulpit, it is the finest Greek cruciform church in Virginia.
Corotoman The site of the Carter's mansion, with ruins of one outbuilding, is near the church.
Epping Forest Birthplace of Mary Ball, George Washington's mother.
St. Mary's White Chapel (1740, restored 1830) An exquisite little church used by the Ball family. Washington's grandfather's will is in the Lancaster courthouse.

LEESBURG
Oak Hill (1821) Home of James Monroe, where he spent much time during his terms as President, and where he commuted from Washington with state papers in his saddlebags. Gardens and furnishings are as beautiful as the house, which is open by appointment. During the War of 1812 President Madison and his cabinet fled to Leesburg with 22 wagonloads of priceless documents, including the Declaration of Independence and the Constitution.

LEXINGTON
Lee Memorial Chapel is on the lovely campus of **Washington and Lee University**, where Robert E. Lee was president from the end of the Civil War until his death in 1870. His office and tomb are here, and Stonewall Jackson is buried in **Lexington Presbyterian Cemetery**, along with other Confederate soldiers. **Jackson's home** has been restored, and is now a museum. The **Jail** (1777) and **Old Blue Tavern** (1785) are relics of the 18th century. *Virginia Military Institute,* opened in 1839, includes **Stonewall Jackson Memorial Hall,** with a huge canvas of the battle of New Market. Matthew Maury was another faculty member, and his house is here. The **Natural Bridge** near Lexington is the natural wonder which intrigued Jefferson to the extent of building a log cabin near it for visitors.

LYNCHBURG
Fort Early Breastworks used by defenders

of the city under Gen. Jubal A. Early, when Union troops tried to take the city, 1864.
Miller-Claytor House (1791) Open by appointment.
Oldest House (c. 1757)
Terrell-Langhorne House (c. 1800)
Poplar Forest Near Lynchburg is this octagonal brick country house built by Jefferson about 1806. Private.

MANASSAS
National Battlefield Park Scene of the First and Second Battles of Bull Run: July 21, 1861, and August 29-30, 1862. The **Old Stone Bridge** and the **Stone House,** used as a hospital, are original landmarks (*see* pp. 196-203).

MARSHALL
Oak Hill (1773) Home of Chief Justice John Marshall. Private.

MIDDLETOWN
Belle Grove (1794) James and Dolly Madison honeymooned here, and General Sheridan used it as headquarters in 1864. On the grounds his army was surprised by a Confederate attack.

MOCCASIN GAP
Through this pass Daniel Boone crossed the Clinch Mountains in 1769.

MOUNT VERNON-POTOMAC RIVER AREA
Belvoir Ruins near Pohick Church mark the site of the home of G. W. Fairfax, intimate friend of Washington. Built in 1741,

Berkeley, on the James River

the house was destroyed in the War of 1812.
Gunston Hall (1775-78) About 10 miles from Mount Vernon, this Georgian brick building has a magnificent old boxwood garden and beautiful interiors with handsome woodcarving by William Buckland, an indentured servant. This was the home of George Mason, friend of Washington and statesman whose Virginia Resolves were the basis for the Declaration of Independence and the Bill of Rights (*see* p. 185).
Mount Vernon The noble mansion which was George Washington's home (*see* pp. 176-81).
Pohick Church (1774) Parish church of

Mount Vernon, Gunston Hall, and Belvoir. Restored.

Woodlawn Plantation (1805) About five miles from Mount Vernon, this estate was a wedding gift from Washington to his adopted daughter, Nelly Custis. Fine late Georgian mansion, furnished with family and period pieces. Fascinating children's rooms.

NEW KENT

This town is not much larger than it was in 1691, when it became the county seat. ***White House Plantation*** was the home of Martha Dandridge Custis at the time of her marriage to George Washington, and was left by George Washington Parke Custis to his grandson, Robert E. Lee's second son. It was burned by Union troops in the Civil War. ***St. Peter's Church*** (1701-3) is an early Colonial-style building. Across the river is ***Elsing Green*** (c. 1719), a plantation which has been worked since 1690. Inside the huge Georgian Colonial house is the mahogany table on which Cornwallis signed his surrender. The house is open by appointment, as is ***Windsor Shades*** (c. 1745).

NORFOLK

Fort Norfolk (1796) Important defense post for many years.

Hampton Roads Opposite Norfolk is the scene of the *Monitor-Merrimac* battle.

Myers House (1791) Excellent Georgian house with rare furniture, relics.

St. Paul's Church (1739) A British cannon ball is still embedded in the wall.

ORANGE

Montpelier (1760) The Madison family homestead to which James and Dolly retired after they left the White House. The portico was added at Jefferson's suggestion. As many as 100 guests were entertained at some affairs. The formal garden, which Lafayette helped design, is open, but the house is private.

PETERSBURG

Blandford Church and Cemetery Soldiers from six wars are buried near the ivy-covered church, begun in 1735. Some 30,000 Confederate graves are here.

SAMUEL CHAMBERLAIN

Kenmore, Fredericksburg

SAMUEL CHAMBERLAIN

Abingdon Church, Gloucester County

National Military Park Many miles of earthworks from the 10-month Union siege of Lee's forces are preserved, as is the *Crater,* where Federals blew up the Confederate position. A museum and national cemetery are on the site.

RAPPAHANNOCK RIVER PLANTATIONS

Menokin Francis Lightfoot Lee, a signer of the Declaration, lived here. The house is ruined except for one dependency.

Mount Airy (1751) A dark sandstone house built by John Tayloe II, whose daughters married into the Carter, Lee, and Lloyd families. Tayloe had a private race track here.

Sabine Hall (c. 1730) A brick mansion with long low wings, and beautiful gardens. Fine interior woodwork and early furnishings. The estate was presented by "King" Carter to his son Landon.

RICHMOND

In 1737 the city of Richmond was laid out by Colonel William Byrd on a site purchased by Captain John Smith from Powhatan in 1609. The *Capitol* (1785-92), designed by Jefferson, is the first American building in the form of a classic temple, and contains Houdon's statue of Washington, the only one made from life. Here Aaron Burr was tried for treason, Lee was commissioned commander of the Virginia forces, and the Confederate House of Representatives met. *Hollywood Cemetery* is the burial place of many famous Virginians, including Presidents Tyler and Monroe, and Jefferson Davis. Robert E. Lee's family lived in the ***Lee House*** (1844) in 1864-65; and the handsome ***John Marshall House*** (c. 1790) is almost unchanged since the first Chief Justice lived there. The *National Battlefield Park* preserves a number of defense positions involved in the struggle for the Confederate capital. The ***Poe Shrine*** (1680's) oldest house in the city, has a large collection of the poet's manuscripts. ***Tuckahoe*** (1700-10) is a beautifully preserved, H-shaped house with fine interiors, which was the ancestral home of William Randolph. On the grounds is a small brick

schoolhouse where Jefferson studied as a child (open by appointment). ***Virginia House,*** owned by the Virginia Historical Society, is a reconstructed Tudor manor house surrounded by English gardens. The ***White House of the Confederacy*** (1818) is where Jefferson Davis and his family stayed during the Civil War. John Wickham, who defended Aaron Burr in his treason trial, lived in the ***Wickham House*** (1812). ***Wilton*** (1750) is a superb Queen Anne mansion moved to the city in 1935 and beautifully restored and furnished.

SMITHFIELD

St. Luke's Church (c. 1650) Like an English village church; built in the early 17th century.

SPOTSYLVANIA

Site of the Battle of Spotsylvania Courthouse, May 8-19, 1864.

STAUNTON

Stuart House (1791) Built by a friend of Thomas Jefferson.

Woodrow Wilson Birthplace Formerly the manse of the Presbyterian Church, of which Wilson's father was pastor.

SURRY

Thomas Rolfe House (1652) On the site

SAMUEL CHAMBERLAIN

The Capitol, Richmond

of Smith's Fort Plantation, which belonged to the son of John Rolfe and Pocahontas.

TAPPAHANNOCK

Old Clerk's Office (before 1750)

Old Courthouse (1728) Now part of church.

Debtor's Prison Dates from the time the town was a port called Hobs Hole.

WESTMORELAND COUNTY

George Washington Birthplace National Monument This is a representation of *Wakefield*, where Washington was born February 22, 1732. When Washington was three his father moved the family to Hunting Creek Plantation, now Mount Vernon, and Wakefield burned in 1779. About a mile from here is the family cemetery.

Grounds of Nomini Hall The brick house built by "King" Carter about 1752 burned in 1850. Here Philip Vickers Fithian wrote his descriptions of plantation life.

Stratford Hall (1725) One of the great houses of America, this was the home of the Lee family and birthplace of the five sons of Thomas Lee (two of them signers of the Declaration), and of Robert E. Lee. The massive, H-shaped brick house stands in a beech grove above the Potomac, and contains fine paneling and period furniture. Open daily, April 15 to October 1 (*see* p. 184).

Yeocomico Church (1706) One of the most picturesque Virginia churches, where Washington's mother attended services.

WILLIAMSBURG

The restorations and reconstructions which have taken place in this historic community make it one of the most rewarding sites in the country to visit (*see* pp. 174-75). Among the most outstanding reconstructions are the **Governor's Palace,** a magnificent edifice with gardens and outbuildings; and the beautiful pink brick **Colonial Capitol,** erected on the original foundations of the "best and most commodious pile" in colonial America. **Bruton Parish Church** is a mellow red brick colonial structure where many distinguished Virginians worshiped. Some of the most important public buildings are **Dr. Blair's Apothecary Shop,** one of the earliest American drug stores; the **Old Courthouse** (1770); the **Public Gaol,** Virginia's first penitentiary; the **Public Magazine** (1715-16), an octagonal building from which Gov. Dunmore removed the powder on April 20, 1775, precipitating the outbreak of the Revolution in Virginia; and the beautiful **Raleigh Tavern,** a frequent meeting place of patriots. Probably the finest dwelling is the **Wythe House** (1755), home of George Wythe, patriot and statesman who taught law to Jefferson, John Marshall, James Monroe, and Henry Clay. The house was Washington's headquarters before Yorktown, and Rochambeau's afterward. Among the other interesting houses are the **Coke-Garrett House** (before 1750), the **Ludwell-Paradise House** (c. 1717), **Sir John**

NATIONAL PARK SERVICE

Grace Episcopal Church, Yorktown

and Peyton Randolph House (c. 1715), **Semple House, Tazewell Hall** (c. 1760), **Bassett Hall** (before 1753), and the **John Blair House** (c. 1747). At the **College of William and Mary** is the **Wren Building** (begun 1695), the oldest academic building in America and the only structure here designed by Wren. In front of it is the statue of Lord Botetourt, a royal governor. The **Brafferton Building** (1723) housed the first permanent Indian school in the colonies, and the **President's House** (1732) was Cornwallis' headquarters during the Revolution.

WINCHESTER

This beautiful spot near the northern entrance to the Shenandoah Valley is the oldest Virginia city west of the Blue Ridge. Among the many historic sites are **George Washington's Office,** a clapboarded log building used while he was surveying for Lord Fairfax; the **Land Office,** where Lord Fairfax conducted the business of his vast realm; and **Christ Church** (1828), where Fairfax is buried. The town was the site of **Fort Loudon,** built by Washington in

1756-57, and part of the southwest bastion still stands. The **Red Lion Tavern,** where Washington stopped, is now a private house. The ruins of the **Old Lutheran Church** (1764) here mark the site of a Revolutionary barracks, burned during the Civil War. More than 100 engagements of that war occurred near here, and Stonewall Jackson's headquarters house is in the town. In the vicinity are many homes built by old Virginia families, like **Long Branch** (early 1830's), designed by Benjamin Latrobe for Robert Carter Burwell, great-grandson of "King" Carter (open by appointment); and Nathaniel Burwell's **Carter Hall** (1790). During Historic Garden Week in May many fine houses, such as **Elmington, Llewelyn, Riverside, Norwood, Red Gate, Saratoga,** and **Spring Hill** are open. **Abrams Delight** (1754) is being restored as a house museum. In the churchyard of the **Old Chapel** (c. 1790) near Winchester many prominent Virginians are buried. **Fairfield** (c. 1770), near Berryville, is open by appointment, as is **Annfield** (1790), birthplace of Mary Custis, Robert E. Lee's wife.

YORKTOWN

In the **Colonial National Historical Park** are fortifications from the climactic Revolutionary engagement, the site of Washington's and Rochambeau's headquarters, and **Moore House** where, on October 18, 1781, General Cornwallis' terms of surrender were drawn up (*see* pp. 188-91). Also worth seeing in this historic town are the restored **Custom House** (1706), **Grace Episcopal Church** (1697), the **Shield House** (1699), and **Lightfoot House** (1725). The **Swan Tavern Group** is a restoration of the inn, kitchen, smokehouse, and stable, dating from about 1722. The private **York Hall** or Nelson House (1725-40) is an impressive Georgian brick house, home of a signer of the Declaration. During the siege of Yorktown the house was Cornwallis' headquarters, and General Nelson directed a cannonade against his own home.

OVERLEAF: DAVID E. SCHERMAN

The Great River

France's Claim

When Charles Dickens visited St. Louis in 1842, he was struck by the remnants of old French culture he encountered there. "Some of these ancient habitations," he wrote, "with high garret gable windows perking into the roofs, have a kind of French shrug to them; and being lop-sided with age, appear to hold their heads askew, besides, as if they were grimacing in astonishment at the American improvements." St. Louis, at the time of Dickens' visit, was being transformed from a French provincial town into an American river city; but like so many other points on the Mississippi, its roots went deep into the past of France's empire in the New World.

The French truce with the Iroquois Indians in 1666 enabled the French to send explorers to the great river which cuts through the heart of America. Along with the adventurers and *voyageurs* who came to North America were the missionaries—mostly Jesuits and a few Récollet fathers, who set out into the wilderness. One of the Jesuits was Père Jacques Marquette who, with a young explorer named Louis Joliet, was sent in 1673 by Governor Frontenac to see if the river ran west toward China, or emptied into the Gulf of Mexico. With five companions, traveling in two birchbark canoes, they journeyed south as far as the mouth of the Arkansas River, just above the present Arkansas-Louisiana line, where Indians told them they were only ten days' travel from the point at which the Mississippi emptied into the Gulf. With this discovery, the Mississippi and all it commanded was linked to Quebec and the St. Lawrence.

Nine years later, Robert Cavelier, Sieur de La Salle, embarked on a voyage of exploration. On April 9, 1682, after reaching the Mississippi delta, he took formal possession of the territory for France, naming it Louisiana in honor of King Louis XIV. On that day, wrote Francis Parkman, "The fertile plains of Texas; the vast basin of the Mississippi from its

VEUË DU CAMP DE LA CONCESSION DE MONSEIGNEUR LAW AU NOUVEAU BILOXY, COSTE DE LA LOUISIANNE

frozen northern springs to the sultry borders of the Gulf; from the woody ridges of the Alleghenies to the bare peaks of the Rocky Mountains—a region of savannas and forests, sun-cracked deserts and grassy prairies, watered by a thousand rivers . . . passed beneath the scepter of the Sultan of Versailles; and all by virtue of a feeble voice, inaudible half a mile."

One of the few French efforts at colonization was fostered by the Scottish promoter, John Law, who managed to lure over seven thousand settlers to communities like New Biloxi and Natchez, Mississippi, before his "Mississippi Bubble" collapsed. One offshoot of his real estate project was the establishment of La Nouvelle Orléans, the city which, more than any other in America, retains its French flavor. But there are others, too, like Ste. Genevieve, Missouri, a quiet, eighteenth-century town on the riverbank, in which DuBourg Place, the walled convent, and old Creole houses of squared upright logs, remind the visitor of a time when half the continent belonged to the King of France.

John Law's colonists had begun building the settlement at Biloxi by December, 1720, when this drawing was made. Until Law's grandiose venture collapsed, leaving them stranded, the settlers lived in tents and bark huts. The main building at upper left was built of upright posts with clay filling, like the 1737 dwelling at Cahokia, Illinois (below), one of the few surviving French frontier houses in America.

223

The Natchez Trace

Today broad ribbons of concrete reach out to link Nashville, Tennessee, and Natchez, Mississippi, following what was the dark, fearsome route of the storied Natchez Trace. Like many of our ancient roads, this one was beaten into a path by the hoofs of countless buffalo, returning year after year to their historic feeding grounds and salt licks. With nothing but instinct to guide them, the huge beasts created an artery followed, in time, by Choctaw and Chickasaw, frontiersmen, highwaymen, armies, and the U.S. mails, not to mention modern surveyors. Settlers from the East came by Avery's Trace to Nashville, turned south onto the Natchez Trace, and moved along the stump-infested track into Mississippi and Louisiana territory. Original sections of the Trace still remain, some of them cut deep into the clay bed by the numberless feet tramping the pathway which slanted five hundred miles through the wilderness.

In the early nineteenth century, flatboats by the score floated down the Mississippi, carrying goods southward. These bulky boats could not be poled against the current, and once they drifted downstream they were usually scrapped and sold for lumber. The boatmen needed a way to get back north again, and the first and most famous of their roads was the Natchez Trace. Except in the vicinity of its northern and southern terminals, it was a gloomy, forested path, ideal for predatory bandits who made it their hunting grounds. A man who had pocketed his profits

in New Orleans could sleep along the way back at an inn or tavern for twelve and a half cents a night, but his pocketbook and his life were at the mercy of land pirates who swarmed the area. One of them was Samuel Mason, who moved in and out of Spanish territory, posing as a respectable citizen, and occasionally hanging placards on his murdered victims, lettered "Mason of the Woods." Joseph Hare, who made the transition from pickpocket to highwayman, was another bad one; and Big and Little Harpe were known as "the scourge of the frontier," operating from the Cumberland to the Mississippi. Probably the worst of the lot was John Murrell, who became a thief at ten, and a murderer before he was twenty-one. Describing him in *Life on the Mississippi,* Mark Twain wrote: "It is a mistake to compare [Murrell] with Jesse James. Murrell was his equal in boldness, in pluck, in rapacity; in cruelty, brutality . . . and much his superior in larger aspects." In Denmark, Tennessee, there is a stone house with a cellar conveniently large for hiding stolen Negroes, which Murrell used as headquarters for a while; but beyond this, nothing survives but the legend of his evil-doing.

At the southern end of the Trace is Natchez, for a time one of the busiest, most prosperous ports in America. On the bluff, within sight of the old road, are the city's incomparable mansions, eloquent reminders of the wealth men derived from cotton. Below, on a narrow ledge of land, is a single, dusty street of shabby buildings—all that remains of Natchez-under-the-Hill, the riotous haven of flatboatmen, Indians, gamblers, and bandits in the days when the river front was the wildest, roughest place on the American frontier.

The greatest riddle of the Natchez Trace may be encountered at the site of Grinder's Stand, the Tennessee tavern where Meriwether Lewis met death in a mystery unsolved since 1809. His grave is still here, where the tavern once stood, and a museum has been constructed nearby, in a style typical of the old inns along the Trace.

Over this historic road, many other famous Americans traveled long ago. Andrew Jackson and his Tennesseeans followed the Trace on their way to meet the British at New Orleans; and the traveler may still see a grove of giant oak trees at Washington, Mississippi, where Aaron Burr was arrested for treason in 1807.

DAVID E. SCHERMAN

Aaron Burr was arrested for treason beneath these oak trees on the Natchez Trace near Washington, Mississippi.

Original sections of the historic route to Mississippi and the Southwest remain at places like this, near Jackson.

Intricate ironwork balconies frame the view from many Vieux Carré houses. At the end of Orleans Street is St. Louis Cathedral, built when Spain ruled the city.

The City of Three Nations

St. Louis Cathedral on the Place d'Armes is on the site of a church built here by Bienville.

One hundred and seven miles by water from the mouth of the Mississippi, in a majestic bend of the river, is a city which owes its character to three nations and the great waterway which gave it birth. In 1718 Sieur de Bienville, the French explorer, founded New Orleans as a trading center for New France. Levees were built, a town laid out in a rectangle of narrow streets, and thanks to John Law's grandiose real estate project, the settlement prospered. The first hastily-built houses of cypress slabs were replaced by low-roofed, story-and-a-half brick structures, many combining shop and residence like those in European towns. Two of these old buildings can be seen in New Orleans today—the Ursuline Convent, begun in 1727, and a private dwelling called Madame John's Legacy, built about the same time.

In 1763, eighty-one years after La Salle took possession of the Mississippi Valley, New Orleans—along

The eagle and motto on this charming 1803 painting of New Orleans reflect the possessive, confident American attitude toward the city immediately after the Louisiana Purchase.

with all Louisiana territory west of the river—was ceded to Spain. The Spanish flag flew over the Place d'Armes for forty years, a period which produced not only the stuccoed brick Cabildo with its massive arches and wrought-iron balconies, but a marriage of French and Spanish cultures—the blend known as Creole. In the midst of lush tropical wilderness, eighteenth-century New Orleans was elegant, with operas and lavish balls, Creole aristocracy and emigrés from the French Revolution—and it was brutal. Frontiersmen, soldiers, and slaves mixed with pirates and smugglers, with explosive results.

Then came 1803 and Thomas Jefferson's Louisiana Purchase, adding New Orleans, along with the vast, fabulous lands west to the Rockies, to the United States. Disdaining their new rulers, the Creoles withdrew into the Vieux Carré, whose narrow streets and picturesque French and Spanish buildings with patios and intricate wrought-iron balconies, are among America's most interesting architectural sights. Upstream, the Americans began building a new, distinctly different section of the city, the Garden District.

Despite its unwelcome reception, U.S. rule ushered in a period of remarkable prosperity and growth that lasted until the Civil War. Nowhere was it reflected so well as in the Garden District, where Greek Revival mansions and handsome gardens were created on the foundations of New Orleans' burgeoning riches. Gateway to a huge, bountiful interior, the city was the outlet for Illinois lead, Kentucky tobacco, furs from the upper Missouri, grain and meat from midwest farms, cotton and sugar from neighboring plantations. And when the *New Orleans,* first steamboat on western waters, arrived from Pittsburgh in 1812, the city's greatest era began.

The West's natural resources were visible along miles of New Orleans docks, and in 1815, just six miles south of the city, Andrew Jackson and 5,000 tough westerners demonstrated the quality of the area's human resources. Jackson assembled a motley crew of Kentucky and Tennessee militia, the New Orleans garrison, and Jean Lafitte and his pirate crew, and awaited the assault of the British expeditionary force led by Sir Edward Pakenham, brother-in-law of the Duke of Wellington. In the fields known today as Chalmette National Historical Park, Jackson lost 71 men while inflicting 2,000 casualties on a British army which outnumbered him two to one. Not long afterward, a popular song told, in true riverman style, how they threw up entrenchments, and—

> *Behind it stood our little force—*
> *None wished it to be greater;*
> *For ev'ry man was half a horse,*
> *And half an alligator.*

Cajun Country

West of New Orleans, fringing the Gulf of Mexico, is a region crisscrossed by endless stretches of swampland and watered by innumerable streams or bayous. It is a place of haunting, moss-draped beauty, a luxuriant maze of water and swamp where turtles and alligators sun themselves on logs, birds of every description flutter among the entangled cypress, magnolia, and live oaks, and winding roads follow the meandering bayous past slumbering, white-columned plantation houses at the end of tree-lined avenues.

This is Cajun country—home of descendants of the refugees from Nova Scotia, which was the first permanent French colony in Canada. After 1755, when the British seized their lands and turned them out, more than four thousand Acadians came to Louisiana to settle, and since that time, physically isolated and set

In the village of St. Martinville on Bayou Teche is the statue of Emmeline Labiche, supposedly the Evangeline of Longfellow's poem. According to the Acadian version of the legend, she went mad after finding her lover married.

BRADLEY SMITH

The tradition is that this white house belonged to Louis Arceneaux, the faithless lover of Emmeline. Now it is a museum near St. Martinville. At right, young Acadians prepare a shrimp boat for the annual blessing of the bayou fleet.

apart from the main currents of American life, they have clung to their old ways, remaining one of the least assimilated peoples in the United States. Speaking an ancient French dialect which few outsiders can follow, mixing little with the modern world, they earn a living by fishing, boating, trapping, and by selling hand-woven baskets and cloth. In a region of few roads, they live on simple wooden houseboats, dependent on the waterways and the pirogue—a slender, graceful canoe hollowed out of a single cypress log—for transportation.

A New England poet who never visited Louisiana preserved for American folklore the legend of the Acadians—the tragic story of Evangeline making the long trek from Nova Scotia to Louisiana in search of her sweetheart. According to legend, Longfellow's poem was based on the story of Emmeline Labiche, whose statue now stands in the St. Martinville churchyard, near the old Acadian cottage which belonged to her lover. St. Martinville, on Bayou Teche, enjoyed a brief period of glamour and prosperity when refugees from the French Revolution made it "a pretty little village . . . full of barons, marquises, counts and countesses," but in the middle of the nineteenth century a yellow fever epidemic, the Civil War, and the diversion of trade from bayou to railroad combined to bring about its decline as the "little Paris."

The Bayou Teche and Bayou LaFourche regions are as lovely as any in Louisiana, and the people with the musical names who live along the waterways have preserved their old customs and a simplicity of life which suits the serenity of their surroundings.

In single file, Admiral Porter's fleet ran the gantlet of Vicksburg's guns after midnight of April 16, 1863. Two weeks later, below the Confederate citadel, Porter ferried Grant's army across the river.

Citadel of the Mississippi

The visitor who goes to Vicksburg today, expecting to see a town which was, during the Civil War, one of the South's most vital strategic positions, is in for something of a surprise. For the Mississippi River, which once flowed past the town on the high bluff, making it a citadel whose master commanded the river and its valley, is no longer there. In 1876 the Mississippi, whose crossing and control had been for so long objects of Ulysses S. Grant's undivided attention, broke through a narrow tongue of land north of Vicksburg, made a new channel for itself, and left the town high and dry. Although Vicksburg is fronted once again by water, now it is the Yazoo River, whose flow was diverted into the old riverbed early in the present century.

In 1862 the Confederate stronghold at Vicksburg was the key to control of the Mississippi Valley. Its powerful batteries commanded a five-mile stretch of river, giving the South access to troops and supplies from the west, and prohibiting the uninterrupted passage of Union shipments from the north to New Orleans. As Grant commented after the war, "Vicksburg was the only channel . . . connecting the part of the Confederacy divided by the Mississippi. So long as it was held by the enemy, the free navigation of the river was prevented." Vicksburg's strategic location defied easy capture: from the north it was protected by the soggy land of the Yazoo delta, stretching northward for 175 miles; to the south, well-fortified bluffs barred

invasion; across the river the land was marshy and treacherous. The only access to the city was from the rear, over the high, dry land to the east. From this direction, after a number of other attacks met disaster, General Grant finally approached in what was probably his most brilliant campaign.

Early in 1863, Grant had taken personal command of the Army of the Tennessee and stationed himself at Milliken's Bend, on the Louisiana side of the river. Throughout the winter months he made several movements in the marshy lands around Vicksburg. In one attempt he had his men begin a canal across a peninsula opposite the city. Twice he tried without success to cut his way through the alluvial swampland north and west of Vicksburg and secure a foothold on the east bank, out of range of the city's batteries. Each of these operations failed, but they kept Grant's men occupied during the winter, and served to confuse General John Pemberton, the Confederate commander at Vicksburg.

By spring the rainy season had passed and the waters had subsided; but there was criticism of Grant in the North, from politicians demanding either a speedy victory or his removal. Lincoln defended his general with the classic remark: "I can't spare the man—he fights." And Grant embarked on the daring plan he had conceived.

Moving his men down the west bank of the river through Louisiana, Grant waited for Admiral David

D. Porter to run the gantlet of Vicksburg's guns, join him south of the city, and ferry the army across. After midnight on April 16, 1863, Porter's vessels, piled high with bales of cotton and hay for added protection, got under way. As row after row of Confederate batteries cut loose, the fleet steamed past the city in single file, so close that those aboard could hear the clatter of falling bricks on the streets. Somehow, they made it without the loss of a single man, and two weeks later Grant captured Port Gibson on the east bank of the Mississippi. To keep Confederate General Joe Johnston from joining Pemberton at Vicksburg, Grant purposely cut himself off from his supplies, marched east, and in quick succession, won the battles of Raymond, Jackson, Champion's Hill, and Big Black River—a seventeen-day campaign which was one of the most successful of the entire war.

Turning now to Vicksburg, Grant took a position along a series of ridges which circled the city for nearly fifteen miles. And what the visitor sees today in the Vicksburg National Military Park is the elaborate system of offensive and defensive positions with which Vicksburg was ringed during the forty-seven-

day siege. Opposing the Union approaches are Confederate lines of defense—redoubts and trench lines extending in an arc to the north, east, and south, strengthened by a system of parallel ridges about seven miles long. In the city, on a terraced square overlooking the business district, is the Greek Revival Court House from whose tower Union troops finally hauled down the Stars and Bars on July 4, 1863, a building which contains one of the largest collections of Confederate relics in the South. And in the park itself are the statues, the stately monuments to the brave men who died here, and the redoubts where this crucial battle was fought.

That July 4, 1863, the nation's eyes were focused on Lee's retreat from Gettysburg; but Vicksburg was the Confederacy's point of no return. As a result, Lincoln said, "The father of waters rolls unvexed to the sea," and one month later the first Union merchant steamboat safely completed the thousand-mile passage from St. Louis to New Orleans.

In 1876 the Mississippi River (rear) changed course, and today the Yazoo River flows past Vicksburg, at upper left.

Before the steamboat, Mississippi cargoes traveled by raft and flatboat, piloted by colorful rivermen such as these.

River Plantations

In the 1840's what seemed like an endless procession of boats was moving up and down the Mississippi. There were flatboats and keelboats, operated by tall, big-boned pioneers—the "most rip-roaring of all sons of perdition"—who brawled, bragged, and sang their way into one of the most colorful chapters of American folklore. Across the water came the haunting note of a boatman's horn, or snatches of songs like "Some rows up, but we rows down; All the way to Shawnee town; Pull away—pull away!" When the riverman went ashore after the long passage, it was to "out-run, out-hop, out-jump . . . and lick any man in the country," for the men and the stories they told were as big and unruly as the river which was their world. The steamboat had come, too—the "floating palace" that belched steam and smoke and gave every boy along the river a vehicle for his dreams.

What a man could see from one of these boats when he came within 200 miles of New Orleans was one of the great spectacles of the American scene. Within sight of each other, on both sides of the river and along the bayous, were the magnificent plantation houses—tall, pillared white residences built by the wealth derived from cotton and sugar. Cultivated fields of tassel-topped sugar cane and long, low rows of grayish-white cotton balls came down to the levee's

edge, and all around was the lush foliage of the semitropics—clumps of live oak and cypress hung with Spanish moss, huge flowering bushes of camellias and magnolias, hedges of roses, and the sharp-pointed palmettos and Spanish dagger.

Although cotton had been planted in Louisiana in 1718 and sugar cane as early as 1700, not until the last decade of the eighteenth century were the potentials of these two crops fully realized, with the invention of the cotton gin and the development of sugar refining on a commercial scale. The mild climate and fertile soil were well suited to both crops, there was plenty of slave labor, and the Mississippi and its complex network of waterways provided economical transportation to New Orleans, where vessels from all over the world were tied up two and three deep along the miles of water front.

The years between 1820 and the Civil War were the opulent ones for the river plantations, and nothing reflects that fact better than the houses themselves. In general, plantation architecture was of two kinds: the early houses built by French and Spanish before the Louisiana Purchase of 1803; and the later, American adaptation of Greek Revival style, which dominated the years from 1820 to the war.

French planters of the late eighteenth century built

CONTINUED ON PAGE 234

A fine Greek Revival mansion in Natchez is D'Evereux, which has classic
columns, hipped roof and a belvedere from which the fields were inspected.

Greenwood's beautiful proportions are reflected in an artificial lake dug
by its first owner so that he could enjoy the sight of his mansion twice.

CONTINUED FROM PAGE 232

homes well suited to the hot, damp climate, following a tradition already established in the West Indies estates. The main floor stood well above the ground, supported by pillars eight or nine feet high to provide protection against floods and heat. Ground-floor walls, columns, and floor were made of plastered brick, while the upper story was of cypress, held together with clay and Spanish moss. A *galerie* encircled the house, and slender wooden columns supported a steep hipped roof. Inside, the house was simply laid out— two or three rooms wide, and one or two deep—all of the rooms opening out onto the *galerie* through shuttered French doors. Seldom was there a central hall, since access to the rooms could be achieved from the broad porch. Darby, on Bayou Teche, and the Keller Plantation in St. Charles Parish, are good examples of the French style, as is Parlange, built in 1750 by the Marquis Vincent de Ternant of Dansville-sur-Meuse. Another is Ormond, built before 1790, which is quite reminiscent of the West Indies plantation homes. This house, whose owner disappeared mysteriously in 1798, has been restored recently, and is one of the most striking examples of a plantation house snatched from the edge of ruin.

When Americans moved into this region in great numbers after the Louisiana Purchase, they brought with them the new, popular Greek Revival style, and soon adapted it into one of the most original architectural forms of the nineteenth century. This was what is known as Louisiana Classic, a completely indigenous house which was usually square, with a tremendous hipped roof and a great attic for insula-

CONTINUED ON PAGE 236

CLARENCE JOHN LAUGHLIN

ARTHUR GRIFFIN, FPG

In a seashell spiral, this unusual staircase climbs a Gothic turret of Afton Villa, near Bains, Louisiana.

234

A tunnel of live oaks 300 yards long leads from the Mississippi River to Oak Alley. Thought to have been planted by a French pioneer about 1690, they were fully grown when the house was built in 1832.

Behind the river plantation houses were formal gardens, like these at Evergreen. Farther back were the slave quarters (right) and fields. The decorative white structure seen here is a Greek Revival privy.

CONTINUED FROM PAGE 234

tion against the sun's heat. Below were two floors of large, high-ceilinged rooms which opened onto both a central hall and a deep gallery which circled the house. The gallery shaded the rooms from all but the early morning and late afternoon sun, and there was a maximum of cross-ventilation.

Most of the Classic plantations were laid out along a similar pattern. The main house faced the Mississippi, which was the route to the outside world and its markets, and between house and landing there was frequently an *allée* of magnificent trees, like the one at Oak Alley, shown on page 235. On either side of the house, in front, were *garçonnières* for guests. To the rear were the gardens, flanked by *pigeonniers*, or dovecotes; then the carriage houses, the long rows of

slave quarters, and the cotton gin or sugar mill.

Although the basic building materials came from the surrounding area, the embellishments were from Europe: silver hinges, hand-painted Dresden doorknobs, French tile for the roofs, and ceilings and panels decorated by European artists. As the scale of life expanded, houses became bigger and grander. Belle Grove, which was destroyed by fire in 1952, had 75 rooms and could accommodate fifty guests at a time. One of the best-preserved plantation homes is Houmas, which was once a 12,000-acre estate worked by 550 slaves. An English visitor reported that the view from Houmas was "one of the most striking of its kind in the world," and went on to say that "If an English horticulturist could see six thousand acres of the

236

finest land in one field, unbroken by hedge and sprouting sugar cane, as level as a billiard table, he would surely doubt his sense." Here, a visitor's morning bath of tepid Mississippi water was cooled with ice, and three mint juleps before breakfast was the limit.

Not all the plantation homes are Louisiana Classic, of course. There are houses in Natchez, and elsewhere in Mississippi, like ruined Windsor near Port Gibson, which are almost pure Greek Revival. On the east bank of the river, between New Orleans and Baton Rouge, is San Francisco, the apogee of a style called "steamboat Gothic"; and Afton Villa, near St. Francisville, above Baton Rouge, is a curious Gothic type.

Fifty miles from New Orleans is Evergreen, one of the most beautifully designed plantations in Louisiana, and near St. Francisville is Greenwood, often considered the finest remaining example of a large plantation house. Built in 1830, Greenwood once had 12,000 acres, including a deer enclosure and a private race track; and inside the house are central hallways twenty feet wide and seventy feet long.

Social and economic changes brought about by the Civil War killed the prosperous plantation era, and gradually many of the great mansions went, too—some lost in the shifting river's course, some abandoned to slow decay. Some which remain are listed on pages 240 through 245, and while a few are in ruins, enough have been preserved so that one may still see what is left of America's last great non-urban culture.

CLARENCE JOHN LAUGHLIN

Nothing but stark columns remain of the once-lovely Windsor Plantation, built in 1861 near Port Gibson, Mississippi.

JEROME ZERBE

Fifty miles north of New Orleans, Evergreen was built in the 1830's at the height of the classic revival. Beautifully designed, the handsome house has 18-inch walls and floors and timbers of cypress. Behind the restored house are the plantation's 25,000 acres.

Midstream in the "monstrous big" Mississippi is Turtle Island, where Tom Sawyer and Huck Finn played. Mark Twain grew up in Hannibal, Missouri, in the house below at right. Next to it is a replica of the "thirty yards of board fence nine feet high," which Tom Sawyer's Aunt Polly wanted whitewashed. Here Tom learned that "in order to make a . . . boy covet a thing, it is only necessary to make the thing difficult to attain." At left, he tests his discovery.

Mark Twain's Mississippi

It was not much more than a hundred years ago—a short time, as history goes, but a time almost beyond recall, in American tempo—that Mark Twain experienced the thrill of boyhood in small-town America. Beyond Hannibal, Missouri, were sunlit prairies and cool dark woods; at its doorstep was the life-giving river; and in its dusty, unhurried streets boys went barefoot, dreaming of the day when each and every one would be a steamboat captain. "Once a day a cheap and gaudy packet arrived upward from St.

One of the last packet boats on the Mississippi River, the *Gordon C. Greene* turns downstream toward New Orleans.

Louis, and another downstream from Keokuk. Before these events, the day was glorious with expectancy; after them, the day was a dead and empty thing. "I can picture," Twain wrote, "the white town drowsing in the sunshine of a summer's morning; the streets empty, or pretty nearly so; one or two clerks sitting in front of the Water Street stores, with their splint-bottomed chairs tilted back against the walls . . . a sow and a litter of pigs loafing along the sidewalk. . . . Presently a film of dark smoke appears above one of those remote 'points'; instantly a Negro drayman, famous for his quick eye and prodigious voice, lifts up the cry, 'S-t-e-a-m-boat a-comin'!' and the scene changes! . . . Every house and store pours out a human contribution, and all in a twinkling the dead town is alive and moving. . . . Ten minutes later the steamer is under way . . . After ten more minutes the town is dead again, and the town drunkard asleep by the skids once more."

Hannibal's story is the story of dozens of other river towns that grew and dwindled and grew again, dependent on the winding river's whims. Yet the town still retains much of what Twain knew there. The river between it and St. Louis has altered but little

since Huck Finn floated downstream. Around a bend north of town is Turtle Island, and south is Jackson Island, where Tom Sawyer and Huck used to swim, and decided to become pirates. At its northern edge is Holliday Hill—"Cardiff Hill" to Tom—which still yields, as it did to Twain, "the most extensive view up and down the river, and wide over the wooded expanses of Illinois." On the south is the higher point of Lover's Leap, and the cave where Injun Joe died.

The house where Mark Twain lived is a plain, two-story frame house built by his father in 1844, typical of the unpretentious pre-Civil War homes along the Mississippi. To one side of it stands a replica of the famous "thirty yards of board fence nine feet high," which Tom's Aunt Polly told him to whitewash. Nearby is a modest frame structure where the Hawkins family lived in Twain's youth, home of the Becky Thatcher who was Laura Hawkins in real life. A tablet marks the site of the house where Tom Blankenship, Huck's prototype, lived with his father and older brother. Where Hannibal has changed, so has America; but it is possible to recapture here some of the long, long dreams of youth which were Tom Sawyer's and every boy's, not so very long ago.

IKE VERN. REPRINTED FROM *Holiday*; © 1949 BY THE CURTIS PUBLISHING CO.

THE GREAT RIVER

ST JOSEPH

HANNIBAL

FLORIDA

SIBLEY

LEXINGTON

KANSAS CITY

INDEPENDENCE

BOONVILLE

HERMANN

O'FALLON

ST CHARLES

JEFFERSON CITY

DEFIANCE

ST LOUIS

MISSOURI

STE. GENEVIEVE

PILOT KNOB

SPRINGFIELD

DIAMOND

CAPE GIRARDEAU

PEA RIDGE

NEW MADRID

FAYETTEVILLE

BLYTHEVILLE

FORT SMITH

ARKANSAS

CORINTH

HOLLY SPRINGS

BALDWYN

LITTLE ROCK

HOT SPRINGS

PONTOTOC   TUPELO

PINE BLUFF

ABERDEEN

ARKANSAS POST
STATE PARK

COLUMBUS

STARKVILLE

WASHINGTON

GREENVILLE

MISSISSIPPI

NOXAPATER

SHREVEPORT

LOUISIANA

VICKSBURG

JACKSON

NATCHITOCHES

PORT GIBSON

NATCHEZ

WOODVILLE

KEY

🏠 EARLY HOUSE

🏛 PLANTATION HOUSE

⚒ PIONEER SITE

🛻 PIONEER TRAIL

⛴ SEAPORT

⚜ FRENCH SITE

⚙ CIVIL WAR SITE

🏰 FORT

🔺 INDIAN MOUND

CLINTON

ST FRANCISVILLE

PASS
CHRISTIAN

OPELOUSAS

BATON ROUGE

BILOXI

LAFAYETTE

PLAQUEMINE

SHIP ISLAND

ST MARTINVILLE

NEW IBERIA

VACHERIE   NEW ORLEANS

FRANKLIN

NAPOLEONVILLE

THIBODAUX

GULF   OF   MEXICO

ARKANSAS

ARKANSAS POST

Arkansas Post State Park Site of the oldest white settlement in the state (1686), and in 1819 the first capital of the Arkansas Territory.

FAYETTEVILLE

Tebbetts House (c. 1854) A one-story Greek Revival house, one of a few fine houses which survived destruction during the Civil War. Used as Federal headquarters in 1863, it still bears the mark of Confederate musket balls. Open on request. *William Quesenbury House* (1854) Open on request.
Walker-Stone House (1847)

FORT SMITH

Site of old *Fort Smith,* constructed in 1818, an important outpost and a starting point for California-bound caravans during the Gold Rush days. The *Old Commissary* (1839) houses a museum. The famous "Hanging Judge," Isaac C. Parker, came here in 1875 to restore order to the lawless frontier. During his 21-year judgeship he condemned 160 men to death. Parker's courtroom and the gallows are restored.

HELENA

As Arkansas' only important Mississippi River port, Helena was a lively community during its steamboat days and later served as a vital link in the line of Union fortifications along the river. Places of interest include the *Joseph Cantrell Barlow Home,* the *Phillips County Museum,* and nearby *Confederate Hill* memorial.

HOT SPRINGS

Hot Springs National Park De Soto probably visited here in 1541.

LITTLE ROCK

The *Arkansas Territorial Capitol Restora-* *tion* is a group of 13 brick and frame structures carefully reconstructed to resemble the town when it was a rural county seat in the early 1800's. The group includes the *Henderliter House,* a simple building of hand-hewn logs covered with cypress siding; the *Noland House* (1830), a handsome territorial residence with a formal garden bordered with boxwood from Mount Vernon; the *Woodruff House* (1824), containing the printing shop of the Arkansas *Gazette,* the oldest newspaper west of the Mississippi; the *Conway House,* with original hand-carved mantels and doors; and the *Old State House* (1836), a distinguished white building with columned portico. It houses exhibits of the *State History Museum.* The *Pike-Fletcher-Terry House* (1840) is a handsome Greek Revival residence of one of Arkansas' most distinguished early citizens (open Tuesday and Thursday afternoons). The *Old Stage Coach Inn* (1836), located 10 miles from Little Rock on the old Southwest Trail,

PHELPS

Territorial Capitol, Little Rock

is a carefully restored red brick building.

MAGNOLIA

Frog Level or Frazier Plantation (1852) Beautifully preserved ante-bellum residence (open on request).

NORFOLK

Major Jacob Wolf House (1809) Built on an impressive site overlooking the White River by Indians and Negro slaves for Major Wolf who came here as Indian agent, trader, and blacksmith. Now a pioneer museum.

OSCEOLA

Mound Builders Museum, on Nodena Plantation. Contains Indian relics.

PEA RIDGE

Site of the Battle of Pea Ridge (March 6-8, 1862), Arkansas' most important engagement of the Civil War. Here an attacking Confederate force was badly beaten and two Confederate generals were killed. The Northern victory led to Union control of the state of Missouri.

PINE BLUFF

The second oldest town in Arkansas. Among the fine old houses are the *Bocage House* (1865), the *Bell-Robinson House* (1852), and the *Thompson House* (1860).

POTTSVILLE

Kirkbride Potts Plantation House (1855) Well-preserved former station of Butterfield Overland Mail route. Open on request.

PRAIRIE GROVE BATTLEFIELD PARK

Battlefield Museum

WASHINGTON

Confederate capital from 1863 to 1865 when Union forces occupied Little Rock. The *Confederate State Capitol* (1833) has been restored as a Southern shrine.

LOUISIANA

BATON ROUGE

Old State Capitol (1847-50) A turreted, castle-like Gothic structure, destroyed during the Civil War and rebuilt in 1882. *Louisiana State University* The Anthropology Department's museum contains a collection of Indian relics.

BAYOU LaFOURCHE

Along this winding waterway Cajuns still cling to their French ways. One of the many fine old homes and plantations is *Armelise* (1804, restored 1946), north of Paincourtville. This is a typical early bayou home constructed of brick filled in with moss and mud, built by an Acadian *émigré.* Open by appointment. *Madewood* (1844-48), near Napoleonville, is a distinguished Greek Revival mansion of stuccoed white brick. Open by appointment. *White Plantation* (c. 1790), north of Thibodaux, is a typical early raised cottage built of hand-hewn timber held together with wooden

pegs. *Magnolia* (1858), south of Thibodaux, an 18-room plantation residence, served as a hospital during the Civil War. *Acadia Plantation* (1828-30), east of Thibodaux, is open on request. *Rienzi Plantation* (late 19th century), near Thibodaux, is a handsome brick home with double front curved stairway and colonnaded second-story gallery. According to legend it was built for Queen Maria Louisa, consort of Charles IV. Private.

CHALMETTE NATIONAL HISTORICAL PARK

Scene of part of Battle of New Orleans, Jackson's brilliant victory in the War of 1812.

CLINTON

This quiet little town is noted for its fine Greek Revival buildings. The *Courthouse* (1841, restored 1936) is an imposing brick structure encircled by tall columns. *Lawyer's Row* (1825-29) is a group of five pil-

lared offices on Courthouse Square originally occupied by 12 prominent barristers. Other distinctive buildings include the *Chase House* (1830), *William Bennett Home* (1825), *Marston House* (1837), and the *Stone House* (1806). All are private. *Richland Plantation* (1820-24), near Clinton, is open by permission. *The Shades* (1808), near Jackson, is a lovely red brick house in a setting of boxwood; and *Hickory Hill* (1810), near Jackson, is a tall red brick columned residence. Also of interest in the Clinton area are *Asphodel* (1821 and 1833); *Bonnie Burn* (1850); and *Kernan Grove* (1836). These are open by appointment.

FORT MACOMB and FORT PIKE

East of New Orleans, on Lake Pontchartrain, are the ruins of ramparts built by Andrew Jackson during the War of 1812.

FRANKLIN

Oaklawn Manor (before 1816, restored 1926). This handsome Greek Revival mansion is a showplace of the Bayou Teche country.

JEANERETTE

Albania (1842) An enormous, well-preserved sugar plantation home on Bayou Teche; antique furnishings. Open on request.

LAFAYETTE

Lafayette Museum (c. 1848) Built by Charles Mouton, well-known jurist and member of the Acadian family who founded the town. The recently restored home is now a museum.

MISSISSIPPI RIVER PLANTATIONS

The following sites north of New Orleans on the West Bank are listed from north to south:

St. Louis Plantation (1858), 10 miles south of Plaquemine. Green-shuttered white frame house with wide, columned gallery. Lovely formal garden. Open on request.

Mulberry Grove Plantation (1836), in Hohen Solms. Antique furnishings.

Ruins of Belle Grove (1857), near Hohen Solms. Once the most lavish and ornate of all Louisiana mansions, its marble ruins remain an impressive sight.

Oak Alley (1836), Vacherie in St. James Parish. Noted chiefly for magnificent avenue of oaks leading from the river landing to the Greek Revival residence (*see* p. 235). Beautifully restored.

Evergreen (1830's), 18 miles below Vacherie. Greek Revival mansion with well preserved *garçonnières*, carriage houses, plantation office, slave cabins, and gardens (*see* pp. 236-37). Open on request.

The Cottage (1830's), near Hahnville. Raised cottage plantation home. Open on request.

The following sites on the East Bank are listed from south to north:

Old River Road On the east bank of the Mississippi between New Orleans and Baton Rouge; winds through the state's oldest plantation district.

Destrehan (1790) Being restored.

Ormond (1780's), near Destrehan. Good example of early Spanish Provincial architecture; beautifully restored. Private.

Voisin Place (1785), near Reserve. An unpretentious raised cottage.

San Francisco Plantation (1850), near Reserve. A whimsical gingerbread-trimmed home built by an imaginative Creole who copied the "Steamboat Gothic" style of the Mississippi steamboats. Private.

Tezcuco Plantation (1855-61), near Burnside. Small raised cottage in a grove of moss-hung oaks. Open on request.

Houmas (c. 1840), near Burnside. Beautifully restored columned mansion flanked by hexagonal *garçonnières* amid great oak trees; choice furnishings. Open on request.

The Hermitage (1812), in Darrow. Square brick residence; being restored. Open on request.

Belle Hélène, formerly Ashland (1841), above Darrow. A splendid home surrounded by square pillars; being restored. Open on request.

The Cottage (1824), 8 miles south of Baton Rouge. The 22 huge rooms in this enormous Greek Revival mansion belie its name.

NATCHITOCHES

The oldest town in the Louisiana Purchase, Natchitoches is the site of *Fort St. Jean Baptiste,* built in 1721 by the French explorer Louis de Saint Denis. The earthworks of the old fort are in the American Cemetery. Interesting old houses in the town may be seen during the annual tour arranged by the Chamber of Commerce and Garden Club. They include the *André Chamard House* (1735), the *Lemée House* (c. 1830), *House of Brides* (c. 1775), *Joseph Tauzin House* (1840), *Lauve House* (1806), *Old Neville Prudhomme House* (c. 1850); and the *Williams House* (1776). The latter is built of cypress logs filled in with clay bound by deer hair, instead of the usual moss. In the Cane River country south of Natchitoches are some particularly interesting old homes: *Melrose* (1835); *Yucca House* and *African House* (1750), two unique structures of mud, brick, and cypress built by a freed slave woman. The *Alphonse Prudhomme Home,* or Oakland Plantation (1818-21), is a few miles south of Natchitoches. The plantation was founded in 1718 by Emanuel Prudhomme, who planted Louisiana's first cotton crop.

NEW IBERIA

The Shadows (1830) A beautiful, well-preserved house with lovely gardens, located on Bayou Teche.

NEW ORLEANS

Founded by the French in 1718, the colorful city was ceded to Spain in 1762, won by the French in 1800, and finally acquired by the United States in 1803 (*see* pp. 226-27). The *French Quarter* in downtown New Orleans is the original settlement where a blend of French and Spanish cultures has been preserved. It is a section of narrow streets, courtyard gardens, old houses, cafés, and shops with decorative ironwork balconies. *Jackson Square,* a central plaza facing the river, was formerly known as the Place d'Armes and was the city's main meeting place and parade ground. Facing the square is the *Cabildo* (1795), once the seat of Spanish rule and scene of the formal transfer of Louisiana from France to the

LA. DEPT. OF COMMERCE & INDUSTRY

Houmas House, near Burnside

United States. It is the property of the *State Museum* which has a fine collection of historical material. Also on Jackson Square is the *Presbytère* (1794-1813), which now contains the *Louisiana Museum of Natural History.* Between the Cabildo and Presbytère is *St. Louis Cathedral,* a Spanish Gothic church built in 1794 and remodeled in 1851 and 1916 (*see* p. 226). *Madame John's Legacy* is a small house, probably the oldest in the Mississippi Valley. Part of the original structure (1726) remains. The *Ursuline Convent* (1734) was the first nunnery in Louisiana. *Beauregard House* (1826) was for a time the residence of General P. G. T. Beauregard (open on request). The *U.S. Customs House,* begun in 1849, was used as a military prison after Union forces occupied the city. Other sites of interest are the restored *French Market, Lafitte's Blacksmith Shop,* the *Old Absinthe House* (c. 1806), *Patio Royal* (c. 1801), *Labranche House* (1830's), *Grima House* (1820's), with one of the loveliest courtyards in the district, and *619 Peter Street.* The latter is a reproduction of an early 19th-century house owned by the State Museum. Throughout the French Quarter, especially along Royal Street, are countless other interesting houses, courtyards, and shops. Most of the Quarter's historic homes are privately owned and only a few are open for special tours. The *Garden District* was a residential section for Americans who, finding the Creoles antagonistic, settled outside the old town. This area, which extends from Jackson to Louisiana avenues between Magazine Street and St. Charles Avenue, contains many handsome ante-bellum homes set in old gardens. Of special interest are the *Short Home* (1859), the *Hero Home* (1850's), the *Ogden* or "Iron Lacework" House (1838), the *Jordon House* (1840's), the *Mehurin Home* (1830's), the *Westfeldt House* (1830), *Wisdom House* (1840), and the *Strachan House* (1848) where Jefferson Davis died while visiting his daughter. All are private. The city's old French cemeteries have white stuccoed vaults built above ground because of the moist soil. Below New Orleans on the Mississippi these three fine houses are in the process of restoration: the *Judge René Beauregard Home* (1840), on the *Chalmette Battlefield,* a Greek Revival mansion which will be open to the public; *Magnolia Plantation House* (1795), a large residence formerly the home of Reconstruction Governor Henry Clay Warmoth (open on request); and *Bellechase* (before 1844), the famous home of Judah P. Benjamin, Confederacy cabinet member, which is now under reconstruction as a Civil War museum.

OPELOUSAS

Opelousas retains much of the charm of its early French-Spanish days. The *Governor Mouton House* (1848) was the seat of state government when Opelousas served briefly as the capital during the Civil War (open on request). *Ringrose Plantation* (1810-30) is a beautifully preserved home (private). The *Wartelle House* (1839) was built by a captain in Napoleon's army (open on request). *Magnolia Ridge Mansion* (c. 1831) is an impressive brick residence (open on request).

ST. FRANCISVILLE
This small West Feliciana Parish town lies in the center of a region north of Baton Rouge which is noted for its many handsome plantation homes. John James Audubon painted some of his best bird pictures here. *Virginia* (1839 and 1852) is a town house built by French political *émigrés*. Among the many fine houses north of St. Francisville are the following: *The Oaks*, a late Victorian residence with handsome gardens and family antiques (open when the gardens are in bloom); *Waverly* (1821), a fine Georgian Colonial home, recently restored, where Audubon taught dancing to augment his income (open on request); *Afton Villa* (1830's), a Victorian-Gothic mansion fashioned after a villa in Tours,

France, with hexagonal turrets, stained-glass cathedral windows, flamboyant woodwork, and a magnificent spiral staircase (*see* p. 234); *The Cottage* (1795-1859), a Spanish-style plantation with original school, slave quarters, and offices; *Greenwood* (1830-35), a classic Colonial mansion surrounded by 28 enormous Doric columns, once part of a luxurious 12,000-acre establishment which included 40-odd buildings, 100 brick slave cabins, an artificial lake, a race track, and a deer park (*see* p. 233); and *Highland* (1799), a fine house built of virgin cypress with handsome interior woodwork. *Oakley Plantation* (1799-1810), south of St. Francisville, is the *Audubon Museum* in Audubon Memorial State Park. John James Audubon visited here in 1832 to tutor the owner's daughter and paint the surrounding birdlife. House and park are being restored as an Audubon shrine and bird preserve. *Parlange* (1750), across from St. Francisville, is one of the oldest and most charming Louisiana plan-

tation homes. Octagonal brick *pigeonniers* flank the drive, and it has a beautifully furnished interior.

ST. MARTINVILLE
This picturesque town on Bayou Teche was settled in the late 18th century by Acadians, Creoles, and French *émigrés* (*see* pp. 228-29). The *Acadian House Museum* in Longfellow-Evangeline Memorial Park is a cottage associated with Louis Arceneaux, supposed lover of Evangeline. In the yard of *St. Martin's Catholic Church* (1832) is a monument marking the grave of Emmeline Labiche, thought to be the Evangeline of Longfellow's poem. Other early St. Martinville buildings include the old *Courthouse* (1853); the *Post Office*, remodeled from an ante-bellum home; *Old Government House* (now a school); and the *Castillo Hotel*, now a convent, which dates from the days of Spanish rule. Outside the town is *St. John Plantation* (1828), a large columned house built by one of the early commandants at Poste des Attakapas.

MISSISSIPPI

ABERDEEN
The center of a prosperous ante-bellum cotton-growing region, this area has a number of homes which are open upon request.

BALDWYN
Brice's Crossroads National Battlefield Site Here on June 10, 1864, a Union force under General S. D. Sturgis was beaten by General Nathan Bedford Forrest.

BILOXI
Founded by Pierre le Moyne d'Iberville in 1699, Biloxi is the oldest permanent white settlement in Mississippi (*see* pp. 222-23). Across the bay on the site of Old Biloxi a marker indicates where Fort Maurepas once stood, the first European settlement in the Mississippi Valley. *Fort Massachusetts* was begun by Federal troops before the Civil War on Ship Island, which commands the entrance to Biloxi Bay; the fort was an important Northern prison. *Beauvoir* (1852-54), a typical raised West Indian style cottage, was the last home of Jefferson Davis; it is furnished with many original Davis family pieces and preserved as a Confederate museum.

COLUMBIA
Old Ford Home (c. 1812) Scene of a convention which met in 1816 to draw up plans for Mississippi's statehood.

COLUMBUS
A handsome town distinguished by many fine homes built in the period 1830-50. Some are open during the annual spring tour; others may be seen throughout the year by making arrangements with the Chamber of Commerce.

HOLLY SPRINGS
Arrangements may be made with the Garden Club to see some of the town's handsome ante-bellum homes.

JACKSON
Battlefield Park Confederate trenches used in the city's defense may be seen.
Governor's Mansion (1839-41) Its portico is a copy of the east entrance to the White House in Washington. Open on request.
Old State Capitol (1833-42) Mississippi voted to secede from the Union here on January 9, 1861. In the central rotunda is a statue of Jefferson Davis, who made his last public appearance when he spoke to the legislature in 1884.

NATCHEZ
By the early 1800's the town founded by Bienville in 1716 was one of the busiest and most prosperous cotton ports on the Mississippi, and southern terminus of the *Natchez Trace* (*see* pp. 224-25). Today the city has one of the finest concentrations of well-preserved ante-bellum homes in the country. Each spring during the Natchez Pilgrimage many homes and gardens are open to the public. At other times arrangements for house tours may be made with the local Garden Clubs or the Chamber of Commerce. Among the fine houses are *Arlington* (1816), a beautifully proportioned square red brick house with an outstanding collection of old glass, rare books, and fine portraits; and *Auburn* (1812), which has a fine spiral stairway. Below the Natchez bluffs along the river's edge is a narrow strip of eroded land called the *Batture*. This was once the rough and bawdy port where flatboats tied up 14 deep for a stretch of two miles. A few dilapidated buildings are the only reminders of the taverns, dives, and gambling dens which once thrived here. *Bontura* (1790-1830) is a typical Creole residence, and *The Briars* (1812) is a fine example of southern plantation architecture. One of the oldest Natchez houses, with period furnishings,

is *Cherokee* (1794); and *Connelly's Tavern* (c. 1795) was a well-known inn on the Natchez Trace. Here Andrew Ellicott, defying the Spanish, raised the first American flag over the lower Mississippi Valley (1797). The restored building is a fine example of Spanish Provincial architecture with raised brick foundation, long narrow double galleries supported by slender posts, and low-ceilinged rooms. The *Conti House* (1788) is a Spanish Colonial stuccoed brick town house, residence of the last territorial governor and first state governor of Mississippi. One of the finest examples of Greek Revival style is *D'Evereux* (1840), impressively set among enormous live oaks and magnolias (*see* p. 233). Other splendid houses are *Dunleith* (1847); *Elgin Plantation* (1812), with two-story, 90-foot gallery; *The Elms* (1782), of Spanish origin; and *Elmscourt* (1810). *Gloucester* (c. 1802), an early Natchez mansion, was the residence of Winthrop Sargent, first territorial governor. *Green Leaves* is notable for its delicate ironwork, carved woodwork, and fine period furnishings; and *Holly Hedges* (1795) is one of the most elegant 18th-century town houses in Natchez, with handsome antique furnishings. *Hope Farm* (1774-89) is actually two houses connected by a gallery. The front portion, added in 1789 by Don Carlos de Grandpré, Spanish governor, reflects the Spanish Colonial influence. *Lansdowne* (1853) is a huge house with six tall chimneys and a central hallway nearly 90 feet long. *Linden* (1790) and *Longwood* are well worth seeing, and *Melrose* (1840's) has furnishings and grounds almost unchanged since ante-bellum days. *Monteigne* (1853) has handsome antique furnishings; and *Oakland* (1835) has been restored with original furnishings, including a large collection of

Sèvres, Spode, and majolica. *Richmond,* built in three stages (1784, 1832, and 1860) reflects Spanish Provincial, Greek Revival, and modified Empire styles. *Rosalie* (c. 1820) is a red brick Georgian mansion used as Union headquarters in 1863, and restored and maintained by the D.A.R. Behind the house is the site of old Fort Rosalie, scene of an Indian massacre in 1729. *St. Mary's Cathedral* (1841-51) was the first cathedral in Mississippi; and *Stanton Hall* (1852-57) is one of the most palatial houses in Natchez. The luxurious furnishings were brought from Europe in a ship chartered by the builder. The house, which contains a 72-foot-long ballroom, is headquarters for the Natchez Garden Club.

NATCHEZ TRACE PARKWAY
The partially completed parkway follows the general route of the Natchez Trace, famous colonial overland trail which angled 500 miles southwestward from Nashville, Tennessee, to Natchez (*see* pp. 224-25). The trace was used by Indians, settlers, and outlaws, and by bands of northbound rivermen returning from lower Mississippi ports.

NOXAPATER
Near here, in the heart of Choctaw Indian country, is *Nanih Waiya,* sacred "mother mount" of the Mississippi Choctaws and Chickasaws. The mound is regarded by the Indians as the birthplace of their race.

PASCAGOULA
Old Spanish Fort A low wooden dwelling resembling a farmhouse, built by the French in 1718. Later occupied by English and Spanish.

PASS CHRISTIAN
Dixie White House (1854) This low white mansion acquired its name when President Woodrow Wilson stayed here in 1913. Antique furnishings. Open by permission. *Ossian Hall* (1848) Two-story Greek Revival mansion. Extensive gardens.

PHILADELPHIA
Choctaw Indian Agency

PONTOTOC
Lochinvar (1836) A hilltop mansion with

eight large square rooms and a graceful spiral stairway which extends three stories into the observatory. Open on request.

PORT GIBSON
Ten miles from here are the remains of *Windsor* (1861), considered in its time the handsomest home in Mississippi. It had five stories topped by an observatory and was luxuriously furnished. All that remains today are 22 gigantic Corinthian columns which form a perfect outline of the house (*see* p. 237). *Magnolia Church Battlefield,* four miles southwest, marks the Battle of Port Gibson, May 1, 1863. In the spring the Port Gibson Pilgrimage arranges tours of old houses, gardens, and historic places in the vicinity.

SELSERTOWN
Selsertown Indian Mound Covering nearly six acres, it is one of the largest mounds in the state. Apparently built by the Indians as a signal tower and dwelling site, and for protection against floods and enemies.

STARKVILLE
Four fine ante-bellum residences (all private) are *Montgomery House, Rice House, Outlaw House,* and the *Dr. James Gillespie House.*

TUPELO
Ackia Battleground National Monument This 49-acre tract, on the site of an old Chickasaw village, was the scene of a 1736

MISS. AGRICULTURAL & INDUSTRIAL BOARD

Connelly's Tavern, Natchez

battle where the French were decisively beaten by the Chickasaws.
Tupelo National Battlefield Site of a Confederate defeat on July 14-15, 1864, the last major battle fought in Mississippi and one of the bloodiest.

VICKSBURG
During the Civil War Vicksburg became a prime objective of the North for control of the Mississippi Valley (*see* pp. 230-31). The city finally capitulated after a 47-day siege on July 4, 1863. The *Duff Green House* (1840's) is a red brick home noted for its fine iron lacework galleries. From the tower of the *Old Courthouse* (1856-61), a distinctive Greek Revival building which is now a museum, victorious Union soldiers hauled down the Confederate flag and raised the Stars and Stripes. An extensive collection of Confederate and other historic relics is on display. The well-preserved *Podesta-Klein Home* (c. 1838) boasts a reception hall, banquet room, and ballroom on its first floor. A cannon ball fired from a Union gunboat is imbedded in one of the walls. The *Sprague,* largest sternwheel towboat in the world, is now a museum depicting life on the Mississippi. The 1,300 acres of *Vicksburg National Military Park* form a crescent on the hills behind the city. Many old breastworks and trenches are still visible, and there are remains of nine major Confederate forts and ten Union approaches. A park museum contains information on the battle and material about old Vicksburg. In *Vicksburg National Cemetery,* two miles north of the city, are buried over 17,000 soldiers, nearly 13,000 of them unknown.

WASHINGTON
Under a group of gigantic oak trees Aaron Burr was arrested here for treason on January 10, 1807, as a result of his involvement in a mysterious enterprise to separate the western states from the Union (*see* p. 224).

WOODVILLE
Hampton Hall (1832) and the *General Posey Home* (1842) are open by appointment. *Rosemont Plantation* (early 1800's) was the boyhood home of Jefferson Davis.

MISSOURI

ALTENBURG
Log Cabin College Originally a Concordia Seminary building, now a museum.

BOONVILLE
One of the oldest Missouri towns and once a thriving supply center for wagon trains heading west, Boonville was the scene of one of the first land battles of the Civil War (June 17, 1861), when state troops were routed by a Federal force. *Arrow Rock Tavern* (c. 1834), on the site of an important river crossing near Boonville, is now a museum and inn, carefully restored with furnishings of the period. The *George Caleb Bingham House* in Arrow Rock State

Park is a reconstructed brick house built by the famous pioneer painter shortly after his marriage in 1837.

BOWLING GREEN
Honey Shuck Home of J. B. "Champ" Clark, famous Speaker of the House of Representatives. Open by request.

CAPE GIRARDEAU
Founded as an Indian trading post in 1793 on a rocky ledge over the Mississippi, it later prospered as a riverboat town. During the Civil War it was occupied by Union troops. The earthworks and a moat surrounding a small parade ground at *Fort D,* one of the area's chief defenses, have been

preserved in a public park. Several fine ante-bellum houses serve as reminders of the town's early days.

COLUMBIA
State Historical Society Fine library and historical art collections.
University of Missouri First state university west of the Mississippi. Columns of the first building still stand.

DEFIANCE
In 1799 Daniel Boone came from Kentucky with his family to settle in the lovely Femme Osage Valley. His farm can be seen near here. Boone sold the farm in 1815 to pay off his creditors and after that lived off

and on with his son, Nathan Boone. The *Nathan Boone House* (1810) is a blue lime-stone country dwelling which the elder pioneer helped build. Open on request.

DIAMOND
George Washington Carver National Monument Honors the distinguished scientist and teacher, born of slave parents. The monument consists of 210 acres, formerly the old Diamond Grove Plantation where Dr. Carver was reared. Eventually there will be a museum dedicated to the scientist's accomplishments.

FLORIDA
Mark Twain State Park In the park is the *Clemens Home*, a small frame structure, now a museum.

HANNIBAL
Samuel Clemens House Boyhood home of Clemens (Mark Twain) and setting for events described in *The Adventures of Tom Sawyer* and *Huckleberry Finn* (see pp. 238-39). Adjoining the modest dwelling is a museum of Mark Twain memorabilia.

HERMANN
A Missouri Valley community settled by German immigrants in 1837. Among the interesting German-style buildings are the *Gentner House* (1850) and the *Strehley House* (1845), both open by permission. A museum is maintained by Historic Hermann, Inc., in the old school building.

INDEPENDENCE
Old Jackson County Courthouse Replica of the one-story log house which was built in 1827 at a cost of $150. This town was one of the chief starting points for the Santa Fe and Oregon Trails (see p. 281). *Harry S. Truman Home* (c. 1865) Residence of the former President. Private. *Harry S. Truman Library*

IRONTON
Battle-scarred earthworks mark the ruins of *Fort Davidson*, built during the Civil War to protect nearby mineral deposits. Scene of the Battle of Pilot Knob (September 26-27, 1864).

JEFFERSON CITY
Cole County Historical Society Museum *State Capitol* Contains paintings and murals of Missouri history.

KANSAS CITY
Kansas City began as a lively frontier town and fur-trading post. It later absorbed nearby Westport Landing, important starting point for wagon trains heading west (see p. 281). The *Alexander Major Home* (1855) is the former residence of the organizer of the Pony Express; restored as a museum. The *William Rockhill Nelson Gallery of Fine Arts* and *Mary Atkins Museum of Fine Arts* contain a fine collection of early American rooms. The *Kansas City Museum* has historical exhibits.

KEARNEY
Boyhood home of Jesse James, famous outlaw and bandit is near here.

LEXINGTON
The *Lafayette County Courthouse* (1847-9) is the oldest Missouri county courthouse

MASSIE, MISSOURI RESOURCES DIV.

Fort Osage, near Sibley

still in use today. Embedded in one of its portico columns is a cannon ball fired during the Battle of Lexington (1861). The *Anderson House,* now a museum, was used during the Civil War as a hospital by both Confederate and Union troops. Under the auspices of the local Garden Club a yearly tour of ante-bellum houses is conducted which includes *Linwood Lawn* (1850), the *Remely-Ardinger House* (1839), and the *Stalling Home* (1844).

NEW LONDON
Ralls County Courthouse (1858) A handsome Classic Revival building.

O'FALLON
Fort Zumwalt State Park Site of old Fort Zumwalt, built during the War of 1812. In the park are remains of a log cabin built by pioneer Jacob Zumwalt in 1798, later incorporated into the fort.

ST. CHARLES
Settled in 1769, this is one of the oldest communities in Missouri. Served as state capital from 1821 until 1826. A group of three buildings, now used as offices and residences, includes the original capitol. *Sibley Hall* (1857) is a large brick mansion on the campus of Lindenwood College.

STE. GENEVIEVE
Founded by the French about 1735, it is the oldest settlement in Missouri. Its early Gallic origins are reflected in the town's several 18th-century houses, its central *Du Bourg Place* dominated by a large church and walled convent, and its old French cemetery. The *Louis Bolduc House* (1784) is a typical Creole dwelling with long, sloping roof, massive chimney, and four-sided gallery. Restored, it is now a historic house museum. The *Jean Baptiste Vallé House* (1785) was the home of the Spanish commandant. When American rule was established in 1804 and Vallé was put in charge of the district, his home became in effect the statehouse for Upper Louisiana (private). Other old buildings include the *Vital de St. Gemme de Beauvais House* (c. 1791) and the *Misplait House,* both open on request. In the *Ste. Genevieve Cemetery* many early pioneers are buried. The *Price House* (c. 1800) is one of the region's earliest brick dwellings (open by request). The

Bequet-Ribault House (private) shows French influence, and the *Janis-Zeigler House* (private) was once the Green Tree Tavern.

ST. JOSEPH
Founded as a fur trading post in 1826 by Joseph Robidoux, the town was later an important center of trade for the Oregon Trail traffic. In 1860 it became the starting point for the Pony Express. The *Sylvanie Robidoux House* (1840's) is a 15-room home with eight fireplaces, built for the daughter of the town's founder. Also of interest are the *Pony Express Stables* (open on request), and the *Jesse James House,* where the notorious outlaw was shot by a former associate who wanted the $10,000 reward. The *Joseph Robidoux House* (private), built in the 1840's, is probably the oldest house in the town. The *Patee House* was headquarters for Russell, Majors and Waddell, the firm that launched the Pony Express.

ST. LOUIS
The city was founded by Pierre Laclede in 1764 as a fur post and later became one of the chief Mississippi River ports. Although most of the original water-front area was destroyed by fire in 1849, three early St. Louis buildings have been preserved in the *Jefferson National Expansion Monument.* The *Old Rock House* (1819), built by fur trader Manuel Lisa, was once a warehouse for John Jacob Astor's company. The *Old Courthouse* (1862), a fine Greek Revival structure with an impressive dome, served as a public forum as well as a courthouse. Here Henry Clay attended court and sold real estate, Ulysses S. Grant came to apply for a job and sold his only slave, and Dred Scott first sued for his freedom. The *Old Cathedral of St. Louis of France* (1834) is the fourth church to occupy this site since 1764. The *Dent-Grant House* (1845) was the scene of Ulysses S. Grant's marriage to Julia Dent (private). The *Campbell House* is a three-story ante-bellum brick residence, now a museum, complete with many of its original furnishings of the 1860's. The *City Art Museum* includes several beautifully furnished period rooms. Also in St. Louis is the *Eugene Field House* (1845), home of the children's poet. The *Jefferson Memorial* in Forest Park houses state and local relics and original Louisiana Purchase documents.

SIBLEY
Fort Osage (1808) Early U.S. outpost in the Louisiana Territory, established to enforce American authority over the region and to promote trade with the Indians. Its block-houses, soldiers' quarters, and trading post have been reconstructed.

SPRINGFIELD
Wilson's Creek Battlefield Southwest of Springfield is the scene of a bloody battle (August 10, 1861) won by the Confederates under General Price. The Union commander, General Nathaniel Lyon, was killed. The battle site, where 2,500 men lost their lives, is being restored.

245

OVERLEAF: ANDREAS FEININGER

Lakes and Prairie

Heartland of a Nation

Of the many thousands of visitors to this region of lakes and prairies, none had a more lasting effect on its geography and history than the huge, inanimate ice sheets which paid their final call about 25,000 years ago. Out of the north the inexorable glaciers moved across Canada, gouging off the tops of hills, mixing topsoil with pulverized rocks and minerals, scooping out the basins of the Great Lakes from old river beds, and finally depositing the whole rich mixture over the land as far south as the Missouri and Ohio rivers. Not only did the glaciers determine the size and drainage of the Great Lakes and change the direction of the Missouri River, but they created an agricultural heartland which is one of the richest farming areas in the world.

In a very real sense, this central prairie land became the crossroads of America, marked by the paths of nearly all the diverse peoples who have made a nation's history. Here are the curious monuments left by prehistoric Indians, the hunting grounds of the red men encountered by the first settlers, the outposts and water routes of French *coureurs de bois*. In Alexandria, Minnesota, is the mysterious Kensington Runestone, discovered by a farmer in 1898. The subject of heated controversy ever since, the stone is inscribed with runic characters which, if genuine, would indicate the presence of a band of Vikings in the area as early as 1362.

Into this heartland came the first waves of settlers from the eastern seaboard, most of them Anglo-Saxon or Scotch-Irish in origin. Later the Germans arrived, followed by Irish, by people from the Mediterranean's shores, by Russians, Poles, and Balkan and Baltic immigrants. And they were followed in turn by the great influx of Scandinavians who selected the northlands of Michigan, Minnesota, and Wisconsin that resembled so closely their homelands.

At first there were only individuals moving in, then came little communities, each group adding its unique patch to this quilt of American life. Colonies of Frenchmen established Gallipolis in Ohio and pockets of settlement in Illinois and Iowa; Amish, Mennonites, Mormons, and other religious sects built communal societies which still dot the region; southerners imported Jefferson's Greek Revival ideas to towns like Gambier and Mount Vernon, Ohio; Swiss came to Indiana; Dutch to Michigan; Cornishmen and Germans to Wisconsin; and New Englanders deposited their architecture and village greens almost intact in places like Canfield, Norwalk, Milan, Copley, and

Chicago was located on the French portage from Lake Michigan to the Mississippi. In 1803 the U.S. constructed Fort Dearborn here.

Voyageurs and trappers bought supplies at Grand Portage on Lake Superior, Minnesota's first white settlement.

Traces of ancient Indian copper mines may be seen at Isle Royale, Michigan. Shown above is a reconstruction of Fort Recovery in Ohio, on the site of the fort Anthony Wayne erected here in 1793.

Sault Ste. Marie was a French outpost until 1762. The British built the first locks here about 1797.

Galena, Illinois, never lived up to the promise it seemed to have in 1856. At right is the mysterious Kensington Runestone, center of a controversy since its discovery by a farmer in 1898.

A magazine and foundations of French Fort de Chartres are in Illinois.

New London. These Ohio towns were part of the Western Reserve, claimed by Connecticut, and even today they retain the atmosphere of New England villages, complete with a traditional "common" and white-steepled church nearby.

Gradually the cities began to grow, in a manner no one could have predicted. There is Galena, in Illinois, whose future was bright with promise a century ago, which today has less than half its 1856 population and remains an almost perfect prototype of the mid-nineteenth-century Middle Western town. Or there is Chicago, a sleepy village on the banks of the Chicago River in 1833, today the second city in the nation, and possibly as representative of modern America as any metropolitan area in the land.

For almost the first two hundred years of life in America, the only way to create a farm was the hard way—by the back-breaking toil of clearing the forest. In the early nineteenth century, frontier farmers had reached the western edge of the wooded Appalachian Plateau. Before them, in what is now western Ohio and the state of Illinois, lay the eastern pocket of the prairie where they could see for the first time the horizon and the full sweep of sky. Because they had never known farmland where trees did not grow, they settled for a time, stubbornly, in the forest at the edge of the grass. Perhaps a generation passed before any of them moved onto the tempting open land, and not until 1833, when the first steel plow was made, could they do much with the deep, thickly-matted sod. Then, very quickly, this region came into its own as a marvelously productive area.

The chain of inland fresh-water seas, together with the Ohio and Mississippi and their tributaries, were the lines of communication and of trade in the early years. The marketable foodstuffs went south, over the Mississippi's natural highway. Then the Erie Canal and the National Road put this region into contact with the thickly-populated East, and by the time of the Civil War all the movement seemed to be an east-west flow. That was the route of the wagon trains and the railroads, and when whole mountains of iron ore were discovered in Minnesota, and the Sault Ste. Marie canal opened, this whole sector became a nexus of an overpowering change in American life, as well as a connecting link between the cities of the East and the beckoning West.

For the man who had his back to the Appalachian Mountains and his face toward the Mississippi River, the vastness of the prairie made other continents seem unreal, or relatively unimportant. Throughout its history, the land of lakes and prairie has had a sense of security, in the heart of its natural riches, which has given it a character all its own.

Objects like these, found in prehistoric burial mounds in Ohio, Indiana, and Illinois, indicate the skilled craftsmanship of the ancient peoples who made them. The most famous example of their handiwork is the Adena pipe, made in the form of a man's figure.

Prehistoric Mound Builders

During the same period when nomads on the other side of the world were exploring and settling the Nile Valley, when the first farmers in lower Mesopotamia were inventing the wheel, wandering people were filtering into the eastern half of America. For several thousand years these descendants of Asiatic migrants lived along the river banks, subsisting on shellfish, small game, roots, and nuts, and left behind, for the speculation of archaeologists and anthropologists, shell heaps, village sites, and stone implements.

About the beginning of the Christian era a more advanced people appeared in the Ohio Valley, called the Adena Indians. The present state of Ohio was a center of their activity, and even today there are more than 5,000 mounds, fortifications, and village ruins within its borders, the evidence of several ancient civilizations. Still others may be seen in Wisconsin and in Illinois, at the famous Cahokia and Dickson Mound sites. These Adena people, known for their construction of funeral mounds like the huge one near Miamisburg, Ohio, buried ornaments of hammered copper, mica, beads, woven fabrics, and carvings with their dead. The most famous example of their handiwork is the Adena pipe. They also made the first grit-tempered pottery, built large ceremonial earthworks, and constructed circular homes and community halls.

They were followed by the most advanced prehistoric society in Ohio, the Hopewell people, who roamed as far east as New York and west to Kansas. Remains of this civilization were found first at the Hopewell site near Chillicothe, but the most remarkable earthworks are Seip Mound State Park, near Bainbridge, and the Mound City Group near Chillicothe. Over twenty burial mounds stand in the thirteen-acre Mound City area—enough to provide considerable information about the habits of these people. The site of each mound was probably occupied first by a wooden structure, where the last rites for honored Hopewell dead were conducted. It is believed that these structures were later burned, perhaps with the idea of purification, or to allow the spirit of the dead person to escape, and then, after offerings were left, the site was covered by a mound. Since the only tools available to the Hopewells were sticks, or hoes of shell or bone, this must have been a formidable task.

Skilled craftsmen in wood, stone, copper, and bone, the Hopewell people were also skilled pottery makers, and conducted an extensive "foreign" trade. In one Hopewell site excavations revealed copper from the Lake Superior region, obsidian from the Rocky Mountains, ocean shells from the Gulf of Mexico, and mica from the southern Alleghenies.

In addition to the many burial mounds still existing in Ohio, there are fortifications built by the Hopewell Indians. One of the best examples of these is at Fort Ancient, near Wilmington, where some 100 acres enclosed by earthworks are situated on a bluff that rises high above the Little Miami River. At Glenford near Somerset, there is a rocky plateau once circled by a stone wall seven to ten feet high, and over a mile long. At intervals along the ruined parapet causeways were cut from the sandstone of the plateau, and a moat protected what was a vulnerable section of the fort. Another mound-builders' fort is at Fort Hill State Park, near the site of a prehistoric village.

After the decline of the Hopewell people, the next important group to appear was the Late Woodland civilization, Indians who occupied the Ohio Valley perhaps four hundred years before the white man arrived, and who may have been related to the Shawnees. Various centers of their activity may be seen today near Lebanon, Cincinnati, and in Ross and Scioto counties.

Most mysterious of all the remains left by these Indians are the so-called effigy mounds, constructed in the shape of a bird, beast, or serpent. A number of these effigy mounds exist in Wisconsin, but the largest and finest in the country is Ohio's Great Serpent Mound. This is an embankment of earth near Fort Hall and Hillsboro, nearly a quarter of a mile long, which represents a gigantic serpent in the act of uncoiling. The greater part of the snake's body is extended in seven deep curves, and partly within the monster's open jaws is an oval wall of earth resembling an egg. The average width of the serpent is about twenty feet, and its height along tail and body is four or five feet. No man-made objects have been found in Serpent Mound itself, and although some scientists believe that it is the burial place of priests or medicine men, one can only guess at its purpose.

Whatever secret the mounds may hold, their meaning for the Indians was eloquently suggested by a man who may never have seen one. Speaking at the signing of a treaty with the white men in 1855, Chief Seattle said: "Every part of this soil is sacred. . . . Every hillside, every valley, every plain and grove, has been hallowed by some sad or happy event in days long vanished. Even the rocks, which seem to be dumb and dead as they swelter in the sun . . . thrill with the memories of stirring events connected with the lives of my people. . . . When your children's children think themselves alone in the field, the store, the shop, upon the highway, or in the silence of the pathless woods, they will not be alone. . . . At night when the streets of your cities and villages are silent and you think them deserted, they will throng with the returning hosts that once filled them and still love this beautiful land. The white man will never be alone."

Ohio's remarkable Great Serpent Mound may be seen best from the air, as in this photograph. Nearly a quarter of a mile long, the uncoiling serpent holds what seems to be an egg in his jaws (upper right).

La Salle

Père Marquette

Empire in the Wilderness

In 1534 Jacques Cartier made the first of his three trips to the New World in search of a passage to the Orient. Although he discovered the rock of Quebec, gave a name to Mont Real, and prowled into the interior, he found neither passage nor gold, and France paid scant attention to his discoveries. The royal point of view toward ventures of this kind was expressed by the Duc de Sully, who observed: "Far-off possessions are not suited to the temperament or to the genius of Frenchmen, who to my great regret have neither the perseverance nor the foresight for such enterprises, but who ordinarily apply their vigor, minds, and courage to things which are immediately before their hand and constantly before their eyes."

But the Duc reckoned without such men as Samuel de Champlain, who gave France a footing in the St. Lawrence Valley which would last for 150 years. From this base the *voyageurs* and *coureurs de bois* set out on their explorations into the wilderness, and side by side with them went missionaries—mostly Jesuits,

and a few Récollet fathers. Sharing the Indians' lodges, hopefully teaching the children, and stoically eating the lichen *tripe de roche,* these adventurous missionaries frequently suffered unspeakable tortures and death with quiet courage.

Best known of the French "Blackrobes" was Père Jacques Marquette, who arrived in Quebec in 1666, studied Indian languages, and was sent to the mission at Sault Ste. Marie—a place once described by Henry Clay as "the remotest settlement in the United States, if not in the moon." In 1672 he was joined by the young French explorer Louis Joliet, and the next May they and five companions set off in canoes to find the "great river" about which the Indians told them.

From St. Ignace on the Straits of Mackinac they went to Green Bay, traveled southwest to Portage, where a marker commemorates their passage into the Wisconsin River, and a month later they had gone down the Mississippi as far as the mouth of the Arkansas. Learning from Indians that the river flowed into the Gulf of Mexico, they decided to return, and headed up the Illinois River. Passing Buffalo Rock, near the present site of Père Marquette State Park, they stopped at Starved Rock, the principal Illinois Indian village. Now a state park, this was the site of a mission founded by Marquette two years later, and the base of La Salle's operations in 1683.

After leaving the Illinois River, they paddled up the Des Plaines, portaged across a swampy tract in the southwest section of present-day Chicago, then headed down the South Branch and the Chicago River into Lake Michigan. In four months they had traveled more than 2,500 miles and established a trade route between the Great Lakes and the Mississippi (the Fox-Wisconsin waterway) which for 150 years would be the main artery of travel in the old Northwest.

Today, except for place names throughout the area, almost all tangible evidence of such heroic men as Marquette, Joliet, La Salle, Tonti, Du Lhut, and others has vanished, like France's New World empire.

An Illinois Indian village was at Starved Rock, above, when Marquette and Joliet visited here in 1673. The British took Fort Michilimackinac from France in 1761, later built the fort shown below.

An old map shows Cartier landing in Canada where he claimed the St. Lawrence area for France in 1534. North is at the bottom of the map.

From the Revolution through the War of 1812, the Northwest Territory was almost constantly in the throes of Indian warfare led by such chiefs as (left to right) Logan, a Mingo; Little Turtle, a Miami; and the Shawnee Tecumseh.

The Old Northwest

It was late in 1776, and Kentuckians, crowded into isolated little forts like Boonesborough and Harrodsburg, could sense the mounting pressure of Indian attacks. Warfare had been a habit in this region since the first red inhabitants fought each other for its possession, but in 1776 the outcome of skirmishes in the wilderness was being watched across the seas, in the capitals of Europe. In fact, the increased tempo of attacks on the colonial frontier had been planned in London to gain control of the Northwest Territory, and they were organized by Lieutenant Governor Henry Hamilton, "The Hair Buyer," in Detroit.

Fortunately for the Americans, there was one man who seemed to know what to do, and after telling Governor Patrick Henry and the Virginia Assembly "if a country is not worth protecting, it is not worth claiming," he had persuaded them to contribute 500 pounds of powder for Kentucky's defense. In 1778 George Rogers Clark was 26 years old, and he was as determined as the British to take control of the Northwest. He collected 175 men, and on a late spring day they set out to conquer the Illinois territory. They went first to Fort Massac (where you can see a reconstructed portion of the old French fort), camped the next night at Indian Point, the forested bluff near Vienna, Illinois, and after a six-day march arrived at Kaskaskia, which they took on July 4, 1778. By August, Clark had captured Cahokia and Vincennes, and began making plans to take Detroit.

Governor Hamilton, outraged to hear of Vincennes' fall, headed an expedition to recapture the fort, and arrived there in December of 1778. The town was held

This is the way Detroit looked in 1796, at the time the British surrendered the outpost to the U.S.
Long after the Revolution the British here abetted Indian attacks on American frontier settlements.

by only twenty men under Captain Leonard Helm, who could do little but surrender to Hamilton's 700 whites and Indians. Hamilton knew there were only 80 Americans at Kaskaskia and half that many at Cahokia, but for some reason he decided to settle down for the winter at Vincennes.

Two hundred miles away, in Kaskaskia, George Rogers Clark heard of Hamilton's victory at Vincennes, and knowing he could not defend his own position, decided to divide his tiny force, recruit some French, and attack the enemy. Few campaigns in history, on which so much depended, have been conducted with more resourcefulness or daring, and even Hamilton, contemplating Clark's campaign in his cell at Williamsburg some time later, wrote that it was a military feat "unequalled perhaps in History."

Across plains, forests, and swollen, icy rivers Clark and his 170 men marched. One of Clark's men wrote: "Set off to cross . . . Horse-Show Plain, all covered with water breast high. Here we expected some of our brave men must certainly perish, having froze in the night, and so long fasting. Having no other resource but wading this . . . lake of water, we plunged into it with courage, Col. Clark being first." By the time they crossed the Wabash, west of Vincennes, they had been eighteen days on the march, and without food for the last two. At dusk Clark had twenty American flags attached to poles, spaced them at wide intervals along his line of march, and started his handful of men off on a zigzag course toward the town. The defenders at Vincennes, believing they were attacked by twenty companies, held out through the night but gave up by morning, and formally surrendered to Clark the next day, February 25, 1779. It was the first significant

CONTINUED ON PAGE 256

General Rufus Putnam's house at Marietta, Ohio, formed a part of Campus Martius, the colony's fortified stockade.

The Northwest Territory Land Office, built in 1788, is located near the Campus Martius Museum at Marietta.

William Henry Harrison occupied an office in the old Territorial Capitol at Vincennes (left). His home, Grouseland, appears in the background. At right is a restoration of Elihu Stout's print shop.

255

At Fallen Timbers, Little Turtle's Indians were concealed within a two-mile treefall; but Wayne's well-drilled infantry flushed them out with a bayonet charge, and his cavalry routed them.

CONTINUED FROM PAGE 255

American victory in the old Northwest.

George Rogers Clark was thirty years old when his western campaign ended, and for 36 years more he lived, deep in debt, his claims and services ignored by his country, watching civilization bear down like a steamroller on the forests and plains he had loved and conquered. Late in life the state of Virginia sent the sick old man a sword engraved with words of honor, but Clark said, "Damn the sword! I had enough of that—a purse well filled would have done me more service!" Not until 1936 was the handsome monument to one of the West's outstanding heroes dedicated in Vincennes, Indiana's oldest town. Inside the columned building on the site of his victory are the ironic words Clark wrote to Patrick Henry: "Great things have been effected by a few men well conducted—our cause is just—our country will be grateful."

Vincennes is, in fact, one of the few places in this region where it is still possible to see some of the historic buildings of the Northwest Territory. Here is the Territorial Capitol, a frame building which was from 1800 to 1813 the seat of government of an area which now includes Indiana, Illinois, Michigan, Wisconsin, and the part of Minnesota which is east of the Mississippi. The first occupant of the governor's office was William Henry Harrison, who defeated Tecumseh at Tippecanoe in 1811. His stately home, known as Grouseland, or the White House of the West, is near

the old Territorial Capitol, and is well worth visiting.

At Marietta, Ohio, a few buildings date back to the first organized settlement in the territory under the Northwest Ordinance of 1787. General Rufus Putnam's house, which was part of the fortification called Campus Martius, is enclosed in a wing of the Campus Martius Museum. Nearby is the Northwest Territory Land Office, built in 1788, and the oldest surviving building in the state.

Today if you follow Route 127 north from Cincinnati you will be retracing the approximate road taken by General Anthony Wayne in 1793 and 1794, on his way to and from the crucial battle of Fallen Timbers. It passes the sites of Forts Hamilton, St. Clair, Jefferson, and Greenville, where the Treaty of 1795 was signed with the Indians. To the west of the road is a reconstruction of Fort Recovery, where Little Turtle defeated General Arthur St. Clair in 1791 and attacked Wayne's men in 1794. A few earthworks of Fort Defiance remain in the city of Defiance, Ohio, and there are remains of Fort Miamis, in Maumee. Near here a monument marks the site of Wayne's victory at Fallen Timbers in the Maumee Valley.

But mostly what remains here are the memories of a time when this was part of America's first West, occupied by a handful of courageous men and women, who saw in it a land of promise, and who were willing to fight, and fight again, and frequently die for it.

In 1792 U.S. control of the Northwest depended on Anthony Wayne.

George Rogers Clark and his "Long Knives" captured Vincennes in 1779.

William Henry Harrison, later President, was the victor at Tippecanoe.

A rare contemporary painting shows Wayne and his officers negotiating with Indians near Fort Greenville. The long-winded proceedings lasted for two months in the summer of 1795, but resulted in U.S. control of the Northwest Territory.

War on the Lakes

Although we are often inclined to think of the War of 1812 as one which was fought to preserve freedom of the seas, it is entirely possible that it would never have happened at all had it not been for the bumptious Americans in frontier settlements who coveted land along their northern boundary still held by Indians and the British. Urged on by "war hawks" like Henry Clay, John Sevier, and John C. Calhoun, Congress declared war on June 18, 1812.

Nearly all the land battles in that war were disastrous from the American point of view, and only when General William Hull surrendered Detroit to the British did it occur to the government that control of the Great Lakes was going to be important. During the spring and summer of 1813, 28-year-old Oliver Hazard Perry, stationed at Erie, Pennsylvania, hastily built and equipped ten ships with supplies hauled over the Alleghenies to Pittsburgh and poled up the French River. The largest vessels were the sister-brigs *Lawrence* and *Niagara*, 480 tons each.

Until August of 1813, British Commander R. H. Barclay blockaded Perry's little fleet in Erie Harbor and then, for a reason which has never been clear, he sailed away. On August 4, Barclay returned to discover that Perry had got his vessels over the harbor bar and was out on the lake.

Put-in-Bay in the Bass Islands was Perry's base of operations, and from here, at sunrise on September 10 he sighted Barclay and sailed out to meet him. By 10 A.M. the *Lawrence* was cleared for action and flying a battle flag which carried the words of the dying Captain James Lawrence: "Don't Give Up the Ship." Less than two hours later the *Detroit*, Barclay's flagship, opened on her, and after two hours of fighting,

Oliver Hazard Perry and his twelve-year-old brother, a midshipman, were rowed from the flagship *Lawrence* to the undamaged *Niagara* under heavy enemy fire.

The painting above shows British and Americans burying their dead after the Battle of Lake Erie in 1813. Years later the bodies of three men from each side were buried beneath the floor of the rotunda of the Perry Monument (below), which stands near the site of the important 1813 victory at Put-in-Bay.

every gun was out of action and most of the crew dead or wounded. By 2:30 that afternoon the ships on both sides were in such dreadful condition that it looked as though the battle would go to the first one who could produce an undamaged ship.

Fortunately for the Americans, the *Niagara* was behind and was almost untouched. As she neared the scene, Perry climbed into an open boat and rowed over to her. By this time the *Lawrence* had struck her colors, but the British were unable to take possession because of the *Niagara's* approach. Fifteen minutes later the battle was over; Perry reboarded the *Lawrence,* received Barclay's surrender on her deck, and sat down to write his famous message to General William Henry Harrison: "We have met the enemy, and they are ours."

His victory not only had an electric effect on the nation's morale, but it changed the entire complexion of the war. It meant the end of the British occupation of Detroit; it shook the British-Indian alliance; and it opened the road to Canada for Harrison, who defeated the British and Indians at the Battle of the Thames in October.

Today a massive pink granite column stands at Put-in-Bay in South Bass Island, Ohio, looking out over the waters where Perry's great victory took place. The *Lawrence* and the *Niagara* were scuttled after the Battle of Lake Erie, but in 1913 the *Niagara* was raised, and in 1931 she was moved to Pennsylvania State Park on Presque Isle peninsula, where the historic vessel has been restored.

MRS. HAROLD SMOOT, PHOTOGRAPH COURTESY *Life*

About 1860 A. F. Phillips painted New Salem's first mill (center) as it looked in the 1830's.

CHICAGO HISTORICAL SOCIETY, PHOTOGRAPH COURTESY GJON MILI, *Life*

Land of Lincoln

The baby who was born on Sunday morning, February 12, was named Abraham, after the grandfather who had been killed by Indians only 23 years earlier. One window shed light on the dirt floor of the log cabin, and a twig-and-clay chimney carried the smoke out of a room that looked like all the others on the Kentucky frontier. It was 1809, and the child who began life here would, from the beginning, draw his ideals and his strength from a land that was still rough and new, and almost always difficult.

To follow the early years of Abraham Lincoln one begins in Hodgenville, Kentucky, at a spring and a giant white oak which mark the site of Thomas Lincoln's Sinking Spring Farm. This is a national park now, and a cabin like the one in which the child was born is enclosed within a columned marble building. Ten miles to the northeast, in a region of rolling, wooded farmland, a similar cabin stands on the site of Knob Creek Farm, where the Lincoln family moved in 1811. Near this place of "high hills and deep gorges," not far from the old Cumberland Pike, Lincoln first attended school, trudging four miles to learn reading, writing, and ciphering. CONTINUED ON PAGE 262

This life-size painting, probably done during the Lincoln-Douglas debates, was used as a Republican campaign poster.

Near Lincoln's Kentucky birthplace is the reconstructed Knob Creek cabin, with split-rail fence such as Lincoln built.

From their cabin doorway in Decatur, Illinois, the Lincolns saw this view of the Sangamon River. When he was 22, Abraham set out on the stream for New Orleans, but was halted accidentally at New Salem.

CONTINUED FROM PAGE 260

Five years later, like so many other restless frontier families, they were on the move again—this time to the forested southwest corner of Indiana where Lincoln said they spent some "pretty pinching times." Much of the natural landscape in Lincoln State Park has remained relatively untouched, and in this lonely, unspoiled place, a simple stone marks the grave of Nancy Hanks Lincoln, who died when her son was nine, and a low stone wall outlines the site of their cabin.

Indiana life fell short of Thomas Lincoln's expectations, and in 1830 he and his new wife set out with the family in ox-drawn wagons, crossing the Wabash into Illinois at the spot where the Lincoln Memorial Bridge now stands. The family first settled on the Sangamon River about ten miles from Decatur, but after a severe winter they moved on to Coles County, where the transient Lincoln settled three more farms before his death. A reconstructed log cabin marks the site of the home where he died in 1851.

In the spring of 1831 Abraham Lincoln left home, the compelling mark of the frontier on him, etched by a life he described as "the short and simple annals of the poor." Near Springfield, he and his cousin and a step-brother set off on a flatboat for New Orleans, carrying a load of produce for Denton Offut, a local promoter. Twenty-five miles downstream the raft stuck on a milldam near the little hamlet of New Salem. Offut, who had accompanied them this far, liked the looks of the little town and offered Lincoln a job there after he returned from New Orleans. So it was that Lincoln arrived, as he said, like "a piece of floating driftwood" in the village overlooking the narrow, muddy Sangamon River.

262

All but one of the buildings in New Salem have been reconstructed since Lincoln's time, but this state park is an authentic re-creation of what life was like in a midwestern pioneer town of the 1830's. The Onstot Cooper Shop, built in 1835, is the only original structure, and here Lincoln and Isaac Onstot often studied together by the light of a fire kindled by the cooper's shavings. Other buildings in the park are log cabins, shops, the Lincoln-Berry store, and a saw-and-gristmill by the dam which caught Lincoln's raft and brought him to New Salem.

The town was only three years old when Lincoln arrived, and here, near the edge of the prairie, he educated himself, became an effective speaker, acquired an interest in the law and politics, joined the militia to fight in the Black Hawk War, became storekeeper, surveyor, postmaster, and ran for the state legislature. Here he knew Ann Rutledge, the pretty young girl with whom legend has linked him in a "lost love." But most important, here he derived much of the frontier's raw, rich strength, made valuable friendships, and equipped himself to make a living with his brain instead of his hands. By the time he was admitted to the bar in 1837, New Salem no longer held enough opportunities for a wider career. Not only had Lincoln grown beyond the town, but New Salem itself had passed its prime, only eight years after its founding. It could never rival Springfield as a trading center, and by 1840 only ten buildings remained in a town which had ceased to exist.

For the next 24 years, Springfield was Abraham Lincoln's home. When he arrived in 1837 to practice law in the new capital, homes of some elegance and crude log cabins sprawled off in all directions from the public square by the unfinished statehouse, and the streets were filled with mud and hogs. For a time Lincoln was "quite as lonesome here as I ever was any-

CONTINUED ON PAGE 264

This reconstructed mill stands by the dam which stopped Lincoln's flatboat at New Salem and interrupted his journey.

The only structure at New Salem State Park which dates back to Lincoln's time is the Onstot Cooper Shop, shown below. Inside the log building Lincoln is said to have studied by the light of the fire, teaching himself the law. Near here are the reconstructed Rutledge Tavern, the Lincoln-Berry store, and other log cabins. Several miles away, on the outskirts of Petersburg, is the grave of Ann Rutledge.

263

RALPH CRANE, *Life*

Lincoln practiced law in this primitive courtroom in Decatur while he was riding the circuit. His home in Springfield is still much as it was when he lived there. In the parlor below he received the Republican nominating committee in 1860.

RALPH CRANE, *Life*

Lincoln could see the old state capitol building through this wavy pane of glass in the Lincoln-Herndon law offices.

CONTINUED FROM PAGE 263

where in my life," but before long he was riding from one county seat to another for sessions of the circuit court, and in spite of the hardships, enjoying his life and his companions, and becoming a distinguished lawyer. One of the places where he practiced may still be seen in Decatur—the two-story Lincoln Log Cabin Courthouse of notched hewn logs, chinked with cement.

In Springfield he had three different law partners, and his last office, the firm of Lincoln and Herndon, looks out upon the stately yellowish-brown Sangamon County Courthouse (then the capitol) where Lincoln tried cases, served in the state legislature, and delivered his famous "House Divided" speech. In a third-floor office of this building, he learned of his election as President of the United States.

In 1842 he married the plump, impulsive Mary Todd, and two years later they bought the unpretentious frame house on the northeast corner of Eighth and Jackson streets. Shaded by trees now, in those days it was bare and treeless, a place where the tall, badly-dressed lawyer could be seen playing with his boys in front, or chopping wood out back. Inside, where three of their sons were born, the horsehair sofa and marble-topped tables reflect the taste of the period. Lincoln's rocker and other pieces of their furniture are in the parlor where he received the nominating committee of the Republican Party in 1860.

After his election, the Lincolns held a reception in their home for 700 friends who came to bid them farewell. Then Lincoln tied up the trunks and addressed them to the White House, and on the cold, drizzly morning of February 11, 1861, he and his party sat in the Great Western station, waiting for the single-car train which would take him east.

A crowd gathered around the rear platform, umbrellas raised against the rain, and Lincoln looked for the last time at the faces of his neighbors. "My friends," he said quietly, "no one, not in my situation, can appreciate my feelings of sadness at this parting. To this place, and the kindness of these people, I owe everything. Here I have lived a quarter of a century, and have passed from a young to an old man. Here my children have been born, and one is buried. I now leave, not knowing when, or whether ever, I may return. . . ." Then, thinking of the task that lay before him, he asked their prayers and God's help in all that was ahead, and bid them farewell. The engine whistle blew, Lincoln turned and went into the car, and the train started off toward Washington and immortality.

Utopias on the Prairie

It is interesting to consider how many early American communities were founded by people seeking a haven for religious and intellectual principles. All through the eastern and central states are remains of distinctive settlements which grew from the labors of religious or utopian societies. Each added something unique to the landscape, and each reflects the character of its founders.

There is the village of Zoar, Ohio, a tidy place of low rambling cottages and picket fences, founded in 1817 by Joseph Bimeler and a group of German Separatists. Like some other groups, the Zoarites thought that the best way to preserve their unity and beliefs, while conquering the frontier, was to form a society where all members shared in the ownership, labor, and fruits of the community. Here the visitor may still see well-preserved homes, the old hotel, village store, and the beautiful two-and-a-half-acre garden which follows the Bible's directions for the New Jerusalem. The Number One House, once a business office and quarters for the aged and infirm, is now a museum of the Zoarites' handiwork; and on a hill overlooking the town is the lovely Meeting House they built.

In Iowa are the seven villages of the Amana Society, led to America in 1843 by Christian Metz. Many of the old shops, homes, and mills are still in use, as are the plain churches with bare floors and whitewashed walls; and descendants of the first colonists live along the quiet streets of the towns. Oldest of the communities, the town of Amana is also the most reminiscent of a German village.

On the banks of the Wabash is New Harmony, Indiana, with its memories of two utopian colonies. The first, called Harmonie, was settled by Father George Rapp and his German followers whom he kept working in the fields, without pay, from sunrise to sunset, blowing a horn at them if they relaxed. In 1825 Rapp and his flock sold their community to Robert Owen and headed east, to found Economy, Pennsylvania. Although it lasted only three years, Owen's colony established the first U.S. kindergarten, a scientific laboratory, and other educational innovations. Today one may still see in this quiet town the Rappites' stone granary; Gabriel's Rock where the angel supposedly spoke to Father Rapp; a men's dormitory; and Father Rapp's mansion. There is also a fine restoration of an intricate maze Rapp designed, a hedge labyrinth through which his followers wandered in the only amusement permitted them.

Father Rapp blew this horn at slackers in the fields. At right is the restored hedge labyrinth at New Harmony. In the center, a stone tower symbolizes the heaven which Rappites would gain after a tortuous journey through life.

THE OHIO HISTORICAL SOCIETY

At Zoar older children minded the babies, since women were expected to work in the fields. For a while celibacy was enforced, because childbearing interfered with work.

The Iowa villages founded by the Amana Society retain many of the original buildings, and descendants of Christian Metz's followers live in old communities.

One of the few buildings in New Harmony which date from the Owenite era is the odd structure built by Robert Owen's son to house an experimental laboratory.

267

LAKES AND PRAIRIE

ITASCA
STATE PARK

CHISHOLM

GRAND PORTAGE NAT'L
HISTORIC SITE

ISLE ROYALE
NATIONAL PARK

Lake Superior

COPPER HARBOR

SAULT STE. MARIE

ST. IGNACE

MACKINAC
ISLAND

DULUTH

M I N N E S O T A

ALEXANDRIA   • LITTLE FALLS   HAYWARD

BEAVER
ISLAND

Mississippi River

RHINELANDER

ELK RIVER

W I S C O N S I N

ST. PAUL

MINNEAPOLIS
MENDOTA

SLEEPY EYE   LE SUEUR   FRONTENAC

GREEN BAY

KAUKAUNA
NEENAH

Lake Michigan

MUSKEGON

PIPESTONE

RIPON

PORTAGE

Wisconsin R.

GRAND RAPIDS

LANSING
SPILLVILLE   DECORAH
FORT ATKINSON

Des Moines R.

WATERTOWN

MADISON

LAKE MILLS

LANSING

Missouri River

PRAIRIE DU CHIEN

MILWAUKEE

MARQUETTE

MINERAL POINT   NEW
GLARUS   MILTON

BELMONT
CASSVILLE   JANESVILLE   BURLINGTON

CAMBRIDGE
JUNCTION

BELOIT

ADRIAN

I O W A

GALENA

FREEPORT   ROCKFORD

MOORHEAD

ANDREW

EVANSTON

CASSOPOLIS

AMANA   WEST
BRANCH

GRAND
DETOUR

NAPERVILLE
AURORA

CHICAGO

SOUTH BEND

DES MOINES

IOWA CITY
DAVENPORT

KINGSBURY

DEFIANCE

MUSCATINE

ROCK ISLAND

COLUMBIA CITY

FORT WAYNE

COUNCIL BLUFFS

OSKALOOSA

BISHOP HILL
STATE PARK

STARVED ROCK
STATE PARK

KANKAKEE

BURLINGTON

I L L I N O I S

METAMORA

ANTHONY WAYNE
ROUTE

NAUVOO

LEWISTON

BLOOMINGTON

LAFAYETTE

I N D I A N A

PIQUA

KEOKUK   CARTHAGE

DICKSON MOUNDS
STATE PARK

COVINGTON

CRAWFORDSVILLE

ANDERSON

FOUNTAIN CITY

JEFFERS

BEARDSTOWN

MOUNT PULASKI

DAYTO

Illinois R.

NEW SALEM   DECATUR

INDIANAPOLIS

GREENFIELD

CENTERVILLE

MIAMISBURG

SPRINGFIELD

OXFORD   LEBA

LINCOLN LOG CABIN
STATE PARK

TERRE HAUTE

BROOKVILLE

CINCINN

PERE MARQUETTE
STATE PARK

POINT
PLEASANT

ALTON

VANDALIA

MITCHELL   MADISON

VEVAY

CAHOKIA

SALEM

VINCENNES   SALEM

Wabash R.

CORYDON   NEW ALBANY

FORT DE CHARTRES
STATE PARK

NEW HARMONY   GENTRYVILLE

KASKASKIA

CARMI

Mississippi River

SHAWNEETOWN

EVANSVILLE   ROCKPORT

Ohio R.

FORT MASSAC
STATE PARK

CAIRO

ILLINOIS

KEY:

EARLY HOUSE

PIONEER SITE

FORT

RESTORED COMMUNITY

FRENCH SITE

ABRAHAM LINCOLN LANDMARK

HISTORIC INDIAN SITE

INDIAN MOUND

BEARDSTOWN
City Hall (1845) Where Lincoln successfully defended Duff Armstrong in 1858.

BISHOP HILL
In *Bishop Hill State Park* are many buildings built by a Swedish religious sect here in 1846. Among them are: *Old Colony Church* (1848); the *Steeple Building;* and three former communal dwellings.

BLOOMINGTON
David Davis Home
McLean County Historical Society Museum A collection of Lincolniana.

BRYANT COTTAGE MEMORIAL
Between Decatur and Champaign is the small frame house where Lincoln and Douglas supposedly met on July 29, 1858, to arrange their series of debates.

CAHOKIA
Oldest town in Illinois, now in the industrial area of East St. Louis. The *Old Church of the Holy Family* (1799) is now a parish meeting hall. The *Jarrot Mansion* (c. 1803), perhaps the oldest brick house in the state, has been restored. *Cahokia Courthouse* (c. 1737), a state memorial, is the oldest house in Illinois (*see p. 223*). The interior has been restored.

CAHOKIA MOUNDS STATE PARK
Near East St. Louis are remains of a Mound Builder village which extended about eight miles along Cahokia and Canteen creeks, covering most of what is now East St. Louis.

CAIRO
This "steamboat metropolis" of a century ago is virtually a museum town of the great days of Mississippi traffic. *Magnolia Manor* (1869-72) is furnished as an example of the gaslight era. The *Rendelman House* (1865), open by appointment, was built by a river captain. The *Ohio Building* (c. 1858) was one of General Grant's headquarters.

CARTHAGE
Old Jail Where Mormon founder Joseph Smith and his brother Hyrum were killed by a mob in 1844.

CHICAGO
The Great Fire of 1871 destroyed most of early Chicago, and the visitor today will find few reminders of the past. A reproduction of *Fort Dearborn* (1803) stands in Burnham Park. Some of Chicago's older buildings are: the *Widow Clark Home* (1836) on the South Side (private); *St. Mary's Church* (1865); *Hull House,* one of the first settlement houses in the country, which has as its center the Charles J. Hull residence, built in 1856; and the *Marshall Field House* (1873). The *Chicago Historical Society* in Lincoln Park has a library, museum, and period rooms. A portion of the famous portage discovered by Marquette and Joliet, linking the Great Lakes with the Mississippi, is preserved in *Chicago Portage National Historic Site.*

DECATUR
Lincoln Log Cabin Courthouse Begun in 1829, the first in the county.

DICKSON MOUNDS STATE PARK
Six miles northwest of Havana, this is one of 800 Indian mounds in Fulton County.

FORT DE CHARTRES STATE PARK
One of the few remains of the French period, the stone fort was built in 1756. Still preserved are the powder magazine and original stone foundations. A careful restoration has been made of the gateway, chapel-guardhouse, and barracks.

FORT KASKASKIA STATE PARK
The only original buildings from the first Illinois capital are the *Pierre Menard House* (1802) and earthworks and foundations of the fort captured by George Rogers Clark in 1778.

FORT MASSAC STATE PARK
Moat and foundations (1757) of the fort from which George Rogers Clark launched his attack on Kaskaskia.

FREEPORT
Site of the second Lincoln-Douglas debate.

GALENA
This was a boom town when lead was being mined, and Greek Revival houses of stone and brick remain from that period. Before the Civil War, U. S. Grant worked in his brother's leather-goods store, which is still standing, as is the house on High Street where the Grants lived. Their post-war house is now a state memorial, with many original furnishings. Among old houses to be visited by appointment are the *Elihu Washburn House* (1830's), the *General John E. Smith Home* (1845), and the *Joseph Hoge House* (1844).

LEWISTON
The town immortalized in the *Spoon River Anthology,* it was the boyhood home of Edgar Lee Masters. The *Phelps Store* (1825) was an Indian trading post. The 17-room brick mansion of Major O. M. Ross was built about 1822, and the *Major Newton Walker House* a decade later.

LINCOLN LOG CABIN STATE PARK
Eight miles south of Charleston is a reconstruction of the cabin, built in 1837, where Lincoln's father Thomas lived until his death in 1851. Graves of Thomas and his second wife Sarah are three miles away.

METAMORA
Metamora Courthouse (1845) A Greek Revival building on the Lincoln law circuit.

MOUNT PULASKI
Mount Pulaski Courthouse Lincoln practiced law here, northeast of Springfield.

NAPERVILLE
There are many early buildings in this town and in nearby Downer's Grove and Hinsdale, including the *New York House* built as a hotel (1849); the *Bailey Johnson Town House* (1840); and in Downer's Grove, the *Blodgett Homestead* (1836); and the *Rogers Pioneer Homestead* (1845); and in Hinsdale the *Fullersburg Inn* (c. 1836).

NAUVOO STATE PARK
The home of Joseph Smith, *Mansion House,* and many early buildings have been preserved.

NEW SALEM STATE PARK
North of Springfield, an authentic reproduction of the village of New Salem as it was in Lincoln's time (*see* pp. 260-64).

PÈRE MARQUETTE STATE PARK
A cross marks the point where Marquette and Joliet turned up the Illinois River.

ROCKFORD
One of the rare Indian effigy mounds is in *Beattie Park.* The *Richard Mandeville Home* (1837), *Swiss Cottage,* and the *Swedish Historical Museum* are of interest.

ROCK ISLAND
Black Hawk State Park The principal settlement of the Sauk and Fox nation, and site of the Watch Tower above Rock River.

The park museum has many exhibits of Indian life and the Black Hawk War. On an island in the river is a reproduction of the blockhouse of *Fort Armstrong,* and the *Colonel Davenport House* (1833).

SALEM
The birthplace and boyhood home of William Jennings Bryan is a museum.

SHAWNEETOWN STATE MEMORIAL
Along the Ohio River are the *Dockers Riverside Hotel* (1870); the oldest bank building in Illinois (1839); the *Rawlings Hotel* (1820's); the *Posey Building* with Robert Ingersoll's law office; and the *Old Slave House* (1834).

SPRINGFIELD
Capital of the state, and of Lincoln country (*see* pp. 260-265), the city contains the *Lincoln Home* with many original furnishings; the *Sangamon County Courthouse* (1837),

formerly the capitol, where Lincoln tried many cases; and *Oak Ridge Cemetery,* with the tomb of the Lincolns and three of their children. The *Illinois State Historical Library* has much Lincolniana.

STARVED ROCK STATE PARK
Site of the principal village of the Illinois Indians. The first white men here were Joliet and Marquette in 1673; two years later Marquette founded a mission here. In 1679 La Salle made this his base, and built Fort Louis. At the head of French Canyon are remains of a Shawnee village which flourished at the time of La Salle.

VANDALIA
Vandalia was the capital of Illinois from 1820 to 1839, and the *State House* (1836) is the third on the site. Lincoln was in the legislature here and stayed at the *Morey Rooming House.*

INDIANA

ANDERSON
Mounds State Park Largest prehistoric earthwork in the state.

BROOKVILLE
Little Cedar Grove Baptist Church (1812)

CENTERVILLE
Morton House Home of Oliver P. Morton, Indiana's Civil War governor. Private.

COLUMBIA CITY
East of town are remains of Miami Chief Little Turtle's *Eel River Trading Post.*

CORYDON
Indiana's first state capital (1816-25) and scene of its only Civil War engagement. The *Old State Capitol* (1812) has been restored, and the *Old State Treasury* (1817) is now a private home. The brick *Posey House* (c. 1817) has a large collection of pioneer relics, and the *Hendricks-Porter-Griffin House* (1817) is almost unchanged (open on request).

CRAWFORDSVILLE
Lane Place (1836) Belonged to Henry S. Lane, a prime mover in Lincoln's 1860 nomination. Now houses Montgomery County Historical Society.
Lew Wallace Study A Victorian brick building which belonged to the Civil War general, author of *Ben Hur.*

EVANSVILLE
Willard Carpenter Homestead (1848)

FORT WAYNE
A marker indicates the site of Fort Wayne, built by Anthony Wayne in 1794. In the *Fort Wayne-Allen County Museum* are archaeological and pioneer relics.

FOUNTAIN CITY
Levi Coffin House (1820's) Famous Underground Railroad station. Private.

GENTRYVILLE
Lincoln State Park In the backwoods country where Abraham Lincoln's father had a tract of 160 acres. The site of the one-room

Lincoln cabin is marked by hearthstones.

GREENFIELD
Riley Homestead (1849) Where poet James Whitcomb Riley was born.

INDIANAPOLIS
Benjamin Harrison House (1872)
James Whitcomb Riley Home (1872)
State Library and Historical Building Indiana historical material.

JEFFERSONVILLE
William Henry Harrison laid out the town in 1802 according to a plan suggested by Thomas Jefferson. Many of the early Mississippi River packets were built here.

LAFAYETTE
Site of Fort Ouiatenon West of Lafayette, a blockhouse reconstruction stands on the site of the French trading post.
Tippecanoe Battlefield Where William Henry Harrison defeated the Indians in 1811.
Tippecanoe County Historical Museum Battlefield mementos, paintings of Indians.

MADISON
Lanier House (1844) Fine Greek Revival.
Shrewsbury House (1849) Brick mansion with spiral staircase. Several other mansions of distinction are the *Paul House* (1809), *Schofield Mansion* (1817), and the *Sullivan House* (1818), open on request.

MITCHELL
Spring Mill Village Re-creation of a typical Indiana village of the period 1815-30.

NEWBURGH
Angel Mounds State Memorial The largest group of Indian mounds in the state.

NEW HARMONY
In this unusually interesting community George Rapp and Robert Owen carried on two famous Utopian experiments in the 19th century (*see* pp. 266-67).

ROCKPORT
Lincoln Pioneer Village Careful replicas of the rude log homes and buildings belong-

ing to Lincoln's Indiana friends.

SOUTH BEND
La Salle Oak Said to be the site of La Salle's council with Indians in 1681.
Leeper Park Log homestead of Pierre Navarre, first permanent white settler here.
Museum of the Studebaker Corporation Many interesting vehicles are exhibited here, including the carriage in which Lincoln rode the night he was assassinated.
Old Courthouse (1855) Now a museum.
University of Notre Dame Founded in 1842 by Father Edward Sorin. A log building erected that year still stands.

TERRE HAUTE
Eugene V. Debs House Modest home of the famous labor leader. Private.
Dresser (Dreiser) House Childhood home of novelist Theodore Dreiser. Private.

VEVAY
The *Henry House,* the *Dumont House,* and the *Morerod House,* built between 1810-20, are open by request. Also here is the *Birthplace of Edward Eggleston,* author of *The Hoosier Schoolmaster.*

VINCENNES
Once the capital of Indiana Territory, Vincennes is the oldest town in the state. The *George Rogers Clark Memorial Building* stands on the site of his famous victory. The seat of government for Indiana Territory was the *Territorial Capitol* (1800); nearby is *Grouseland* (1804), the home of William Henry Harrison, governor of the territory (*see* p. 255). Lincoln was entertained frequently in the *Ellis Mansion* (1830), and once spent a night in the *Bonner-Allen Mansion* (1842). Near the Clark Memorial is *St. Francis Xavier Cathedral* (1825-41), a Greek Revival structure on the site of the first log chapel in the settlement. A replica has been made of *Elihu Stout's Office* where the first newspaper in Indiana Territory was printed in 1804.

IOWA

AMANA
Seven villages settled in the 1850's by German immigrants (*see* pp. 266-67).

ANDREW
Butterworth Tavern (1852) Home of Ansel Briggs, Iowa's first governor.

BURLINGTON
Log Cabin (1833) Built by Jeremiah Smith, Jr., this was a haven for trappers and for families on their way West. Private.

COUNCIL BLUFFS
Lewis and Clark Monument Erected to commemorate Lewis and Clark's council with the Oto and Missouri Indians in 1804, held across the river.
Log Cabin Museum Historical and Indian material may be seen in Lincoln Park.

DAVENPORT
Blockhouse On Rock Island is a reproduction of Fort Armstrong, built here in 1816.
Antoine Le Claire Home (1833). Constructed by a founder of the town, it is on the grounds of the *Davenport Public Museum*, which contains an important Mound Builder collection, a pioneer wagon brought to Iowa in 1840, and other relics.

Log Cabin Store Replica of Captain John Litch's store, built in 1836.

DECORAH
Norwegian American Historical Museum A group of typical pioneer buildings—houses, a schoolhouse, and a parsonage—have been built on Luther College campus. Open April to November.

DES MOINES
State Historical, Memorial, and Art Building Collections include manuscripts and Civil War and pioneer relics.

DUBUQUE
Shot Tower (1855) Eight-story stone tower once used for molding lead shot.

FORT ATKINSON STATE PARK
Near the village of Fort Atkinson is a restoration of the fort built in 1837. Part of a barracks, two blockhouses, and a magazine remain.

IOWA CITY
Old Capitol Greek Revival structure with beautiful hanging staircase.
Plum Grove Farm (1844) Built by the first governor of Iowa Territory, it is restored and furnished in the period.

KEOKUK
Old Ivins House (Hawkeye Hotel, 1850)

LANSING
Fish Farm Indian Mound Group Near the town are Indian burial mounds.

MARQUETTE
Effigy Mounds National Monument On the bluffs of the Mississippi are more than a hundred burial mounds of the Hopewell culture (about A.D. 1000). Many are in the shape of animals and birds. Notable are the *Great Bear Mound* and the *Marching Bear Group.*

MUSCATINE
Mark Twain House Small home where the author lived, 1853-54. Private.

OSKALOOSA
Morgan Cabin A hewn-log cabin, built in the 1840's. Furnished in pioneer style.

SPILLVILLE
Bernatz Mill Picturesque stone mill.
Dvořák House A brick and stone house where composer Anton Dvořák lived while working on his New World Symphony.

WEST BRANCH
Herbert Hoover Birthplace

MICHIGAN

MICHIGAN HISTORICAL COMMISSION

Schoolcraft House, Sault Ste. Marie

ADRIAN
Governor Croswell House (c. 1840) Period furnishings. Open on request.

BEAVER ISLAND
Site of a Mormon colony founded by James Jesse Strang.

CAMBRIDGE JUNCTION
Walker Tavern (1833) Restored stagecoach tavern with original furnishings.
Walker Brick Tavern (1854)

COPPER HARBOR
Fort Wilkins State Park Restored stockade and garrison of *Fort Wilkins*, now a historical museum.

DEARBORN
Greenfield Village A reconstruction of a typical American village of the 1850's includes more than 90 buildings: courthouse where Lincoln practiced law; Menlo Park laboratory of Thomas Edison; homes of Luther Burbank, Stephen Foster, Noah Webster, Henry Ford, and others. There is a typical village green, the Wright Brothers' Cycle Shop moved from Dayton, a small Mississippi paddlewheel steamer. All the authentic buildings were moved here from their original sites.
Henry Ford Museum Built by Henry Ford and dedicated to his friend Thomas A. Edison, it contains exhibit halls, replicas of Independence Hall, Congress Hall, and the old City Hall of Philadelphia. Exhibits cover the history and development of American industry, agriculture, transportation, science, and education.

DETROIT
Botsford Tavern (1836) Northwest of Detroit, this restored white frame building is furnished with period pieces.
Detroit Historical Museum Displays on the early history of the city and state.
Fort Wayne Military Museum Completed in 1848 and recently restored.
Ulysses S. Grant House House occupied by Grant and his bride, 1849-50. Open Sept.

ISLE ROYALE NATIONAL PARK
One of the few remaining tracts of wilderness in the country. Frequented by man since prehistoric times, this is probably the first place where copper was mined in America. Evidence of prehistoric mine workings are still visible (*see* p. 248).

LANSING
State Historical Society Fine exhibits dealing with Michigan's early history.

MACKINAC ISLAND
A picturesque island in the Straits of Mackinac, first visited by Jean Nicolet in 1634 while seeking a waterway to the Orient. *Fort Mackinac* is a well-preserved limestone fortress built by the British in 1780. *Fort Holmes* is a reconstruction of the log fortress built by the English during the War of 1812. *The Astor House* (1822), served as headquarters for John Jacob Astor's American Fur Company. Also restored are the *Fur Agent's House* (1817); the *Store, Employees' Residence,* and *Warehouse;* the *Beaumont House* (1820); and *Old Mission Church* (1830), one of the oldest buildings in the Northwest.

MACKINAW CITY
In *Michilimackinac State Park* is a replica of the old fort's stockade, scene of 1763 Indian massacre.

MUSKEGON
Muskegon County Museum Displays relics of early lumber and fur trading days.

ST. IGNACE
Near here are earthworks of *Fort de Buade,* built by the French in 1671.

SAULT STE. MARIE
The *John Johnston House* was built in 1795 by a pioneer fur trader. The *Schoolcraft House* (1826-27) is a beautifully restored pioneer home constructed by Henry R. Schoolcraft, the Indian agent.

MINNESOTA

ALEXANDRIA
Kensington Runestone A curiously inscribed stone discovered by a local farmer in 1898 (*see* p. 249).

BRAINERD
Lumbertown USA Reconstruction of a typical logging town of the 1870's.

CHISHOLM
Minnesota Museum of Mining Mine cutaways and mining equipment of the past.

DULUTH
St. Louis County Historical Society Mementos of Duluth's early days.

ELK RIVER
Oliver Hudson Kelley House (1896) Farmhouse of the founder of the Grange. Now a museum.

FRONTENAC
St. Hubert's Lodge (1855) Rambling building with southern-style porches and galleries, once a luxurious lodge. Private.

GRAND PORTAGE NATIONAL HISTORIC SITE
The nine-mile portage trail from Lake Superior to the Pigeon River, once used by explorers and fur traders, is still clearly defined. At the river end of the trail is the site of Fort Charlotte, a fur-trading post of the British XY Company in the late 18th century. Along Grand Portage Bay on the lake is a reconstruction of the North West Company's trading post of the same era.

ITASCA STATE PARK
Indian mounds are scattered throughout the park.

LE SUEUR
Mayo House (1859) Early home of famous family of doctors.

MENDOTA
The first permanent white settlement in Minnesota. Three restored houses, all built in the state's territorial period, are of special interest: the *Sibley Home* (1835), the first stone house in Minnesota; *Faribault House* (1837); and the *Du Puis House* (1854).

MINNEAPOLIS
A marker in *Morris Park* indicates the place where Father Louis Hennepin discovered the Falls of St. Anthony in 1680. Two of the oldest houses in the city, both built in Minnesota's territorial period, have been carefully restored: the *Godfrey House* (1848), and the *Stevens House* (1849).

PIPESTONE
Pipestone National Monument The quarries were the source of stone which Plains Indians used for ceremonial pipes.

ST. PAUL
About twelve miles away is *Fort Snelling* (1819), an early U.S. Army post.
James J. Hill House (1887) Romanesque mansion built by the railroad tycoon. Private.
Indian Mounds Park Several large prehistoric burial mounds on a high bluff overlooking the Mississippi.
State Historical Society Building Exhibits of Minnesota frontier history.

SLEEPY EYE
In *Fort Ridgely State Park* are the remains of *Fort Ridgely*, scene of a fierce encounter in the Sioux uprising of 1862.

OHIO

CANFIELD
Elisha Whittlesey Homestead and Law Office Two lovely brick buildings in a Western Reserve settlement.
Elijah Wadsworth House (1800) Home of one of Washington's aides.

CHILLICOTHE
Adena (1807) Designed by Benjamin Latrobe for Thomas Worthington, a United States senator and sixth governor of Ohio. This lovely stone mansion has been completely restored.
Headquarters of Governor Arthur St. Clair (1798) Home of the governor of the Northwest Territory when Chillicothe was its capital. Hand-carved interior woodwork.
Mound City Group National Monument Contains 24 burial mounds, built by Hopewell peoples. *Hopeton Earthworks* are across the river, and *Harness Mound* is 8 miles away (*see* pp. 250-51).
Ross County Historical Museum Local museum in Greek Revival home (c. 1838).

CINCINNATI
Harriet Beecher Stowe House Home of Reverend Dr. Lyman Beecher; today a museum dedicated to his daughter, the author of *Uncle Tom's Cabin*.
Taft House Museum (1820) One of the finest remaining Federal-style houses.

CLEVELAND
Dunham Tavern Museum (1842) Restored; houses a Western Reserve collection.
Weddell House (1847)
The Western Reserve Historical Society Interesting museum collection of pioneer material, and fine Americana library.

COLUMBUS
Ohio State Museum Large collections concerning prehistoric Indians and state history may be seen here. This is headquarters of the Ohio Historical Society.

DAYTON
Old Court House (1850) Greek Revival; Lincoln once spoke from Court House lawn.
Paul Laurence Dunbar Museum Home of the famous Negro poet.
Newcom Tavern (1796) A log museum.

FAIRPORT HARBOR
Old Lighthouse Now a marine museum.

FREMONT
Spiegel Grove State Park Former estate of President Rutherford B. Hayes, containing the *Hayes House* (not open) and the *Rutherford B. Hayes Library*.

GALLIPOLIS
Our House (1819) A brick tavern in the late Georgian style, now a museum.

GEORGETOWN
Grant Schoolhouse (1804) U. S. Grant attended school in this brick building.

GRANVILLE
Many Colonial and Greek Revival style homes are here. The *Buxton Tavern* has been operating since 1812.

HILLSBORO
Great Serpent Mound is the largest serpent effigy in the world. Nearby are the *Fort Hill Earthworks* (*see* pp. 250-51).

KINSMAN
The *Congregational and Presbyterian Church* (1832) is reminiscent of New England, as is the *Allen House* (1820's), a fine example of the Federal style. The *Darrow Octagon House* is the birthplace of the famous criminal lawyer, Clarence Darrow.

KIRTLAND
Kirtland Temple (1833-36) Unusual structure built by Joseph Smith and his Mormon followers before they fled westward.

LAKEVIEW
Manary Blockhouse Museum A log structure built during the War of 1812.

LANCASTER
The birthplace of General William Tecumseh Sherman and Senator John Sherman is here. Partially restored.

LEBANON
Glendower (c. 1840), restored, is now a museum. Among other fine homes in the area are *Brynhyfryd* (1840's), the *Gothic House* (1840's), *The Pillars* (c. 1850), and the *Thomas Corwin House* (1840's). All are open by request. The *Golden Lamb* (1815) is one of the oldest inns in Ohio still operating. In the Lebanon area are the *Fort Ancient* prehistoric Indian earthworks. *Fort Ancient Museum* has a fine collection of prehistoric relics.

MARIETTA
Marietta was the first permanent settlement in the Northwest Territory under the Ordinance of 1787. Original dwellings were connected in a hollow square known as the Campus Martius. One of these buildings, the *Rufus Putnam House*, has been restored and is enclosed in *Campus Martius Museum*. Another old building of special interest which is now in the museum is the *Ohio Company Land Office* (1788), a small handhewn log house (*see* p. 251).

MENTOR
James A. Garfield House Victorian home where Garfield conducted the first "front

porch" presidential campaign.

MIAMISBURG
Miamisburg Mound The largest prehistoric Indian conical burial mound in Ohio.

MILAN
Thomas A. Edison Birthplace (1841)

MOUNT PLEASANT
Quaker Yearly Meeting House (1814) A large brick building. Being restored.

NEWARK
Two interesting old homes here are the *Buckingham House* in Greek Revival style and the *Davidson House* (1815), a Federal-style home furnished with period pieces which is the museum of Licking County Historical Society. In *Octagon State Park* are ceremonial mounds of the Hopewell Indians. *Mound Builders State Park* contains an eagle effigy mound.

NEW PHILADELPHIA
Schoenbrunn is an accurate reconstruction of the village to which Moravian missionaries led Christian Indians in 1772.

NORTH BEND
The *Tomb of William Henry Harrison*, hero of Tippecanoe and ninth President of the U.S., is here. Nearby is the boyhood

home of Benjamin Harrison, William Henry's grandson, also a President.

NORWALK
Noteworthy are the *Martin House* (1831), the *Fulstow House* (1834), the *Boalt House* (1848), the *Stewart House* (1833), the *Old Baker House* (1830), and the *Vredenburgh-Gardiner House* (1832).

OBERLIN
Oberlin College (1833) The first co-educational college in the world.

OXFORD
McGuffey Memorial Museum On the Miami University campus, this museum contains mementos of William H. McGuffey, author of the famous readers. *William McGuffey House* (1833)

PERRYSBURG
Fort Meigs State Park Earthworks of an early American fort.

PIQUA
Indian Agency House (1814)

POINT PLEASANT
Grant House Museum (1817) Salt-box house where U. S. Grant was born.

SOUTH BASS ISLAND
Perry Memorial at Put-in-Bay Monument

to the War of 1812 victory (*see* pp. 258-59).

SPRINGFIELD
George Rogers Clark State Park Site of a Shawnee village which Clark destroyed. *Hunt Tavern* (1830) Log manor house.

ANTHONY WAYNE PARKWAY
Between Cincinnati and Toledo in western Ohio and eastern Indiana several highways follow the old wilderness trails made by General Anthony Wayne and other commanders during the Northwest Territory Indian campaigns of the 1790's (*see* pp. 254-57).

ZANESVILLE
Some places of interest here are the *Old Stone House* (1808), *Matthews House* (1840), *Guthrie House* (1842), *Nye-Potts House* (1813), and *Headley Inn* (1802).

ZOAR
The most famous attraction of this early religious colony is *Zoar Garden*, which follows the description of the New Jerusalem (Revelations 21-22). *Number One House* (1835) is now a museum. Other notable buildings are the *Versammlunghaus* or Meeting House (1854), the *Bimeler House*, the *Old Hotel*, the *Village Store*, and the *Gardener's House* (*see* pp. 266-67).

WISCONSIN

BELMONT
First Capitol Where territorial legislature held first session in 1836.

BELOIT
Logan Museum On the campus of Beloit College, this fine museum contains artifacts of prehistoric man. There are 22 Indian mounds on the campus.
Rasey House (1850) Cobblestone structure.

BURLINGTON
Strang House At Voree is the home of James Strang a Mormon leader.

CASSVILLE
Stonefield is a former plantation developed by Nelson Dewey, Wisconsin's first governor, and now the state farm and craft museum. The museum is in Dewey's stone horse barn, and the Dewey house and wine-cellar may also be seen. In *Riverside Park* Indian mounds may be visited.

GREEN BAY
Wisconsin's oldest settlement. The oldest surviving house in Wisconsin, the *Tank Cottage*, was built in 1776. The *Fort Howard Surgeon's Quarters and Hospital* (1816) is now a museum. Near here is the site of a French fort. The restored *Cotton House* (1841) is an excellent example of Jeffersonian architecture. Also here are the *Morgan Martin House* (1838); a *Moravian Church* erected in the 1850's; and the *Neville Museum.*

GREENBUSH
Wade House (1851) A well-restored inn.

HAYWARD
Northern Wisconsin Logging Camp and Museum

JANESVILLE
Lincoln-Tallman Homestead (1857) Italian villa-style mansion where Lincoln visited in 1859. An Underground Railroad station.

KAUKAUNA
Grignon House (c. 1850) Partially restored.

LAKE MILLS
Aztalan Mound Park Ceremonial Indian mounds and museum.

LITTLE NORWAY
At Mt. Horeb is this replica of a pioneer Norwegian homestead, restored and furnished in the period. May through Oct.

MADISON
State Historical Museum Includes several period rooms, and material on the history of the upper Mississippi River and the fur trade.

MILTON
Goodrich Log Cabin Once an Underground Railroad station.
Milton House (1844) An early inn with unusual hexagonal three-story lobby.

MILWAUKEE
Kilbourntown House A fine example of Greek Revival style, built by the pioneer architect Benjamin Church.

MINERAL POINT
Gundry Mansion Houses the local *Historical Society Museum.*
Pendarvis House One of three restored Cornish miners' homes, on Shake Rag Street, which were built of solid limestone blocks in the 1830's.

NEENAH
James Doty Cabin (1820) The home of Territorial Governor James Doty, from

1845-61. In City Park, it is now a museum.

NEW GLARUS
Swiss Museum Village Buildings and relics of early community. May-Nov.

PORTAGE
Indian Agency House (1832) Built for John Kinzie, Indian agent, the house has been restored. It is one of the few remaining structures of the kind, and contains huge fireplaces and colonial furniture.
Surgeon's Quarters (1828) The only log building that remains of *Fort Winnebago*, across the canal from the Agency House. The fort was built to protect the Fox-Wisconsin portage. Lieutenant Jefferson Davis was in charge of its construction. Nearby is where Marquette and Joliet portaged to the Wisconsin River in 1673.

PRAIRIE DU CHIEN
The *American Fur Company Warehouse* is one of the early buildings. One of Wisconsin's best stone houses is the *Brisbois House*, built by a trader for the American Fur Company. *Villa Louis* (1843) is the restored mansion of Hercules Dousman, one of John Jacob Astor's agents.

RHINELANDER
Logging Museum Reproduction of a logging camp.

RIPON
Little White School House On the grounds of Ripon College is the building where a meeting was held in 1854 which resulted in the creation of the Republican Party.

WATERTOWN
Octagon House (1850's) An unusual house, with over 50 rooms, now a museum.

273

The Great Plains

Early Life on the Great Plains

Not far from the town of Wall, South Dakota, the broad, dull prairie begins to rise in a long ground swell of bluffs. Before the traveler has gone much farther, these bluffs break up suddenly into a scarred, arid land of fantastic shapes and colors, a maze of sandstone spires, gargoyles, and pinnacles. This is the region the Indians called "mako sica"—the Badlands—which General Custer described as "a part of Hell with the fires burned out."

To see the Badlands National Monument is to see the early history of the earth, for embedded in the accumulated layers of sandstone are fossils dating back to the Age of Reptiles, almost sixty million years ago. In that time much of North America lay under the waters of a huge sea whose shores were flat, swampy jungle. Over the land lumbered giant reptiles—creatures like the brontosaurus, a long-necked vegetarian with a fifteen-ton body and a two-ounce brain; tyrannosaurus rex, the monster with a kangaroo-like body, a huge head, and vicious, grinning jaws; giant crocodiles; and the rhinoceros-like triceratops. Eventually, all these creatures perished, and their bones were covered with layer upon layer of sediment which the flooding streams deposited on the marshy plains. Then, about twenty million years later, in the Oligocene Period, the Badlands region exploded in a series of upheavals at the same time the Rocky Mountains were being formed, and volcanic matter hurled into the air settled like an ashen blanket over the area. This layer covered and preserved the remains of many of the first mammals—mastodons, the tiny three-toed horse, and others—but as the centuries passed the Badlands slowly eroded, its silt washed down gullies into the White River, while spring rains and melting snows cross-sectioned the brittle sandstone to expose the ancient fossils. Some of the best museum collections in America have come from the Badlands area, the Black Hills, and the shale outcroppings near Bismarck, North Dakota, and in this region itself there is a fine paleontological exhibit at the Museum of the School of Mines and Technology in Rapid City, South Dakota.

Although the northern Plains have none of the spectacular ruins of the Southwest, men have lived on the Plains ever since the first Asiatics wandered down from Alaska, about twelve thousand years ago. Coming at the end of the final glacial age, they arrived in time to kill the last animal giants—the mammoths, mastodons, and huge bison. Nomadic Stone Age hunters, these earliest plainsmen lived in caves or tent villages like the one found at Old Signal Butte, near Scotts Bluff, Nebraska. There, on a windswept plateau, they watched for the appearance of deer and buffalo herds, and went after them with their stone-pointed spears.

Not until well into the Christian era did the Indians begin to lead a sedentary, year-round life on the plains. Between A.D. 500 and 1300, groups from the southeast moved into the river valleys, bringing with them pottery and a knowledge of agriculture. Some of these farmers were mound builders, whose strange relics have been found in eastern South Dakota, while others constructed earth lodges of the kind white men imitated hundreds of years later. When Pierre de La Vérendrye claimed the Dakota region for France in 1738, a few of these agricultural settlements still flourished, and he was amazed by one Mandan village, where he found hundreds of acres of tilled fields and a palisaded fort so well constructed that it was practically impregnable. In this village he counted 130 "cabins," in streets so uniform that "often our Frenchmen would lose their way in going about." What he called "cabins" were actually igloo-shaped structures made of earth, measuring from forty to ninety feet in diameter at the base, and supported by heavy cottonwood pillars.

Several good examples of the Mandan lodges may be seen today at Fort Abraham Lincoln State Park in North Dakota, where part of a village site has been restored. This community stood in an unusually well-protected spot, between the Heart River on one side and a deep coulee on the other, with its exposed sides protected by deep moats. Depressions in the earth show that the settlement contained 68 lodges, and the visitor may see four restored homes and a large ceremonial lodge, as well as crude tools and furnishings which have been found here. The Mandans, the Arikaras, and other Plains farmers measured their wealth in terms of how much food they had, and while they were relatively prosperous, by the time the first white adventurers made contact with them, their culture was beginning to lose its vigor, for it was rapidly being replaced by a new and freer way of life.

This new culture, paradoxically, was fostered by the coming of the white man at the same time that it was being hindered by his presence. Whole populations of Indians had been set in motion in the east, and although the tribes closest to the white man had lost their homes, they had acquired firearms, which

In 1832 George Catlin painted the Bull Dance of
the Mandans, a form of buffalo worship which
took place in a clearing between the distinctive
earth-covered lodges. Several examples of Mandan
huts may be seen at Fort Abraham Lincoln State
Park in North Dakota. The picture at right shows
a view of the Badlands, a fantastically eroded
region which General George Custer described
as "a part of Hell with the fires burned out."

enabled them to dislodge the western Indians from
their lands. The Chippewas, for example, had pushed
into Minnesota, driving the Dakotas, or Sioux tribes,
out of the forests into the plains. Here, except for
one great discovery, their way of life would have conformed to that of the Stone Age hunter thousands of
years earlier. This discovery was the horse.

CONTINUED ON PAGE 278

CONTINUED FROM PAGE 277

The Spanish in the Southwest had horses, and although they did everything to prevent Indians from acquiring them, the animals multiplied, ran wild, moved north through California and Texas, and at some stage discovered the magnificent grazing grass on the plains. The Dakotas saw horses for the first time in 1722, and for a time they ate the "mystery dogs," as they were called. Then they learned to ride them, and before long all the great fighting tribes were mounted—Sioux and Blackfeet, Cheyennes, Arapahos and Crows, Kiowas, Comanches, and Piegans. Cornfields were abandoned, and instead of farming, they followed the buffalo. On horseback they could attack the herds directly; with bows and arrows they could kill the animals easily, and relatively safely; and soon the buffalo supplied the Plains Indian's every need. His chief source of food was the meat; his tepees, clothing, and shoes were made from the hides; hoes and axes came from the shoulder blades; thread and bowstring from the sinews; his fuel from the chips. The free, nomadic existence which resulted could last only so long as the great herds of buffalo survived, and by 1880 the white man had killed them off, and with them the whole fabric of Plains Indian life.

GILCREASE INSTITUTE OF AMERICAN HISTORY AND ART, TULSA; ELIOT ELISOFON, COURTESY *Life*

ARNOLD NEWMAN

Horses, captured from herds brought to America by the Spanish, completely revolutionized Plains Indian life and warfare. Alfred Jacob Miller's painting (right) captures a moment of battle between two tribes. Above is a reconstruction of the way Crow Indians lived a hundred years ago.

Jumping-off Places

Jim Baker, famous trapper and scout, lived in the mountains until he died at eighty. He had six wives, all Indians.

In an age when a person can travel across the continent in a matter of hours it is difficult to conceive that, not much more than a century and a half ago, there was only a handful of white men in the vast area beyond the Mississippi River. For a brief interlude of time those who had gone there—the wild, unrestrained breed known as the mountain men—probably achieved the most complete freedom known to recorded history.

Between 1820 and the 1840's, when the beaver was finally trapped out, men like Jed Smith, Jim Bridger, Kit Carson, Thomas Fitzpatrick, and Bill Williams ("Old Solitaire") lived completely on their own in an infinity of open spaces. Taking with them a few of civilization's implements—a rifle, knife, traps, powder, lead, and awl—they disappeared completely from the view of established society to roam the rivers and find the trails which are highways and railroads today, ranging through the trackless unknown from Kansas to California, and from Oregon to the New Mexico deserts. Once a year, in the summer, they traveled to the lusty trappers' rendezvous in the mountains to meet a caravan from St. Louis and exchange their pelts for a brief, glorious binge and some baubles for an Indian woman; but the rest of the time they were content simply to hunt beaver, to go where no other men had been, and to face the constant dangers of the enormous, unbroken wilderness. The Louisiana Purchase in 1803 made this land available for settlement; the expedition of Lewis and Clark opened men's eyes to what it held; and after the first trickle of movement, an unending stream of humanity began surging into the West.

The jumping-off places were back in Missouri, and the first of them was a town which Pierre Laclede had founded as a trading post in the winter of 1763-64, just below the junction of the Missouri and Mississippi Rivers. Located at the foot of a bluff on a bench of land high enough to provide protection from all but the worst spring floods, St. Louis commanded the principal water route to the fur-rich West. In 1817 the first steamboat docked at St. Louis, and within a short time hundreds of boats were stopping there each year, providing access to the town of Independence, where the Oregon and Santa Fe trails began, and to the commerce of the East.

Few of the old St. Louis buildings survived the disastrous fire of 1849 which swept through most of the waterfront area, destroying many of the original houses, stores, and warehouses; but in the Jefferson National Expansion Memorial three early structures are preserved. One is Old Rock House, a two-story limestone building erected by a fur trader in 1818, which became a warehouse for John Jacob Astor's fur company and then a sailmaker's loft where wagon covers, tents and tarpaulins were made for the streams of emigrants. Another is the Old Courthouse, a domed, Greek Revival building begun in 1839. Here Thomas Hart Benton advocated a transcontinental railroad, Henry Clay sold real estate, U. S. Grant freed his only slave, and Dred Scott sued for his freedom.

By 1842 St. Louis had changed from French provincial town to American river city. Colorful, noisy, its levees were crowded with Mexicans, Kentucky woodsmen, Germans, Indians, French, mountain men, and Negro stevedores. Up the Missouri in the rich, black bottomland were plantations worked by slaves. Beyond St. Charles the settlements thinned out into the "land beyond the Sabbath," where squatters eked out a living. Three hundred and sixty miles, or about fifteen days west of St. Louis, a traveler could see, in the early 1840's, signs of the great westward movement. Parties of emigrants, in tents and wagons, camped in open spots along the river, en route to the common rendezvous at Independence.

At that time Independence was the big town on the Missouri frontier, the busiest town in America west of St. Louis. Francis Parkman, arriving there in 1846, found himself "at the farthest outskirts of the great forest that once spread from the western plains to the shore of the Atlantic." Looking westward, he could see only "the green, ocean-like expanse of prairie, stretching swell beyond swell to the horizon." A pioneer woman wrote, "It matters not how far you have come, this is the point to which they all refer to, for the question is never, when did you leave home? but, when did you leave the Missouri River?"

Each spring brought more people to the tent camps outside of town and to Smallwood Noland's inn (accommodations for 400 people, if they did not object to two or more in a bed), and a new town, Westport, grew up to take the overflow. Nearby was an old American Fur Company trading post which also became a town, known as "Kansas." It had a better landing place than Independence, and when the older town was hit by a cholera epidemic in 1849, Kansas became the favorite jumping-off point. Soon it grew so large that it absorbed Westport and became Kansas City—big, booming and, when the Civil War had gone and the railroad had come, ready to handle a fresh army of emigrants.

VIEW OF ST. LOUIS.

This charming view of St. Louis was done about 1840-46, when the town was a gateway to the vast West.

Landmarks of the Trek West

Wagon trains rumbled past Jackson County Courthouse in Independence.

Each spring, from 1842 until the late 1880's, long lines of prairie schooners, horses, cattle, and oxen lumbered out of Missouri's towns on the first lap of a five-month, 2,000-mile westward trek. Each party elected a leader, but the expedition's safety usually depended on the hired guides, many of them ex-mountain men who had turned to this new profession when their beaver empire began to decline. Wilson Price Hunt blazed a trail in 1811, but the route mapped by Robert Stuart in 1812–1813 is the one that came to be known as the Oregon Trail. It began in the grassy swells of Kansas prairie erroneously named the "Great American Desert."

As the parties set out in 1849, spirits were high, the road was easy, and people even enjoyed the novelty of wagon travel. Not far west of Independence, the forests thinned out, and suddenly the emigrants were confronted with a grand sweep of grasslands, running away to the west as far as the eye could see. From here, one stream after another had to be crossed—the Blue River of Missouri, Indian Creek, Bull Creek, the Wakarusa River, Kansas River, and the Big and Little Blue Rivers of Kansas. Where the stream beds were too deep to be forded, there were aggravating waits for a turn at the ferry. Often impatient emigrants calked their wagon beds, stripped off the wheels, and rowed across.

Frequent prairie squalls, with high winds and hail, made the low places soft, and to avoid them the wagons traveled along the swells. Besides, it was safer to stay on high ground in Indian country, for down in the wooded hollows Pawnees would pounce on stragglers. Sometimes during dry spells the Pawnees started grass fires to reduce the animals' ground fodder; often they attacked lone stray wagons; and in the middle of the night they would ride down on a wagon train, whooping and hollering, and frightening off the horses before the emigrants knew what had happened. Because of this, the emigrant companies joined their wagons together at night, forming a hollow circle which served both as fort and corral.

By the time they reached Alcove Springs, near present-day Marysville, Kansas, on the Big Blue River, they began noticing an increasing number of graves along the way. Nearby, the route from St. Joseph joined the Oregon Trail, traffic became heavier, and as the emigrants headed north into sandy, grass-covered hills, they knew they were approaching the valley of the Platte River and the dry, wind-swept "Coast of Nebraska." At the Platte, where nothing but earthworks remain today, was Fort Kearny, one of civilization's few outposts along the trail. From Kearny, the emigrants followed the broad valley to the forks of the Platte, encountering huge buffalo herds which often shook the earth as they roared past. Along the Platte's south branch it was nearly sixty miles to the famous "California" crossing near Brule, Nebraska, where they double-teamed across the quicksand bottom, and then turned north toward the Platte's upper fork. Soon the land broke up into the wooded dell of Ash Hollow, across from present-day Lewellen, Nebraska, and the wagons sloughed through hub-deep sand before heading up the North Platte, where one may still see wagon ruts cut by thousands of wheels.

Through a strange country of fantastically-shaped buttes the trail ran, past Court House and Jail Rocks near Bridgeport; Chimney Rock near Bayard; and Scotts Bluff. From the crest of Mitchell Pass today's visitor will see the Laramie Mountains, far in the distance, which were the emigrants' first view of the Rockies. This was the last of the Great Plains, and from here on the going was infinitely harder.

Near Scotts Bluff, Nebraska, ruts made by thousands of wagons may still be seen. This was one of the natural landmarks on the Oregon Trail.

One of the easiest landmarks to sight was Chimney Rock in Nebraska, visible to pioneers for days before their slow-moving wagons arrived there.

The drawing of Cathedral Rock was done in 1849 by W. H. Tappen, who accompanied the U.S. Mounted Riflemen garrisoning posts along the Oregon Trail.

Stephen F. Austin and Sam Houston, both from Virginia, were rivals in independent Texas.

The first capitol of the Republic of Texas was Byars' smith shop at Washington-on-the-Brazos, where the 1836 declaration of independence was approved.

Independent Texas

When Stephen Austin brought the first few American settlers to Mexican Texas in 1822, he had no intention of making trouble with the country to the south. In the little colony of San Felipe on the Brazos River, he made every effort to be a loyal Mexican citizen, advising his people to do likewise. Looking at the wide, well-watered and unsettled Texas plains, Austin had a vision of expansion and prosperity as big as the country itself. To most Americans, the Plains were the "Great American Desert"—something to get across as quickly as possible—but Austin's followers were the first to see them as something entirely different: a place to settle.

At the same time that Austin was writing friends in the United States, describing Mexico as "the most liberal and munificent government on earth to emigrants," bad blood was developing between the American colonists and their Mexican rulers. The two peoples had little in common—there were differences in religion, language, and customs which were made no less difficult by a Texan attitude of Anglo-Saxon superiority. And the Mexicans, only briefly removed from three centuries of autocratic Spanish rule, resented the American introduction of slavery into Texas—an institution which had unpleasant connotations for them.

During John Quincy Adams' administration the United States made some efforts to buy Texas, and these overtures were pressed with renewed vigor under Andrew Jackson. Time and again, Mexico refused;

The Alamo chapel is all that remains of a larger establishment which 180 Texans defended to the death in 1836.

yet there was always the underlying fear that the U.S. might try to gain by force what it had been unable to purchase, and in the event of such a move, the Mexican government would have few allies among the settlers. By 1830 there were 30,000 Americans in Texas, or nine-tenths of the population. Their log-cabin settlements were scattered across the rich coastal prairies from Nacogdoches on the Louisiana border down to the Guadalupe River, and beyond. The result of Mexico's fears was the law of 1830 which forbade further American immigration into Texas. When this statute failed to curb the movement into the territory, Austin found himself in the middle, on the one hand trying to placate the Mexican government, on the other trying to restrain his followers.

While friction between the two peoples was mounting, General Lopez de Santa Anna staged a successful revolution in Mexico and set up a dictatorship. In September 1835, after a group of Texans seized a Mexican customs station, Santa Anna sent his brother-in-law General Perfecto de Cos with a force of 500 men to San Antonio. By this time Austin realized that negotiation was impossible, and wrote that "War is our only resource." Late in September, armed men began gathering to resist the Mexicans.

After taking the arsenal at Goliad, the Texans laid siege to Cos in San Antonio, and on December 5, 1835, they attacked. House by house they fought their way into the town, and by the night of the eighth, the Mexicans were surrounded in a partially ruined mission known as the Alamo. With all hope gone, Cos raised a white flag in the morning, and by the end of 1835 there were no more Mexicans troops in Texas.

CONTINUED ON PAGE 286

285

CONTINUED FROM PAGE 285

Meantime, the moderate Austin was defeated as governor, and a more radical group of Texans launched an expedition to capture Matamoros on the Rio Grande. At the end of January two columns started south, one moving down the coast, while the other—a group of Americans who were sick of garrison duty at San Antonio—planned to approach Matamoros from inland. This group left behind them less than a hundred men to protect the town, and although the commanding officer wrote to San Felipe, begging for help, few reinforcements arrived. Among those who did come were the legendary Jim Bowie, with nineteen men; Colonel William B. Travis, with 25; and the frontiersman Davy Crockett, who brought twelve Tennesseeans with him.

General Sam Houston, who commanded all the Texas forces, had ordered Bowie and his men to blow up the San Antonio fortifications and retreat eastward, but the idea of retreat was an insult to the men in the town. Meantime, Santa Anna was moving north. On February 23, a lookout spotted the vanguard of the Mexican cavalry, and the 180 Texans holed up in the Alamo. Located east of the San Antonio River, on the outskirts of town, the Alamo had not been used as a mission since 1793, but as a military depot and storehouse. All that is left of the Alamo today is a roofless chapel, but in 1836 there was also a great walled plaza connected to a convent with a large patio, some stone rooms used as a jail, and a corral. The whole establishment sprawled over two and a half acres, and its walls were a quarter of a mile in length. With a maximum of 180 men, the defenders had less than fifteen per cent of the number needed for an adequate defense of the various buildings.

Biding his time, Santa Anna built earthworks on all sides of the old mission, harassed the defenders with light artillery, and put out a cavalry screen to prevent their escape. On February 24 Travis wrote "To the people of Texas and all Americans in the world," saying, "I am determined to sustain myself as long as possible and die like a soldier who never forgets what is due to his own honor and that of his country. VICTORY or DEATH."

No reinforcements came to the Alamo defenders, while Santa Anna had collected 5,000 men. On March 6, he decided to attack. At 4 A.M. four columns, totaling 2,500 men, were sent off to attack the old mission from all sides. Armed with axes, iron bars, and scaling ladders, they moved forward only to be sent reeling back by heavy cannon and rifle fire from the Alamo. As they reformed for another assault, a band across the river played "Degüello," the word and tune that meant "throat-cutting," which, when played in battle, signified that no quarter would be given.

A somewhat fanciful painting depicts the Alamo's fall. In the

In the second attack the Mexicans pressed so close to the walls that the Texan artillery was no longer effective. The Mexicans forced a breach in the north wall, another in the south one, and poured in on the defenders, who fell back to the convent and the roofless church for a desperate last stand. Now the Texans' own cannon were turned on them and, retreating from room to room, those who were left were forced into the chapel, where they were wiped out in a final hand-to-hand combat. When the battle was over, Santa Anna had the corpses of the Texans dragged out onto the open ground in front of the mission and cremated. Not one of the defenders had survived. Yet Santa Anna's victory had cost him dear, for it is estimated that more than 1,600 of his troops were casualties in the one-hour fight.

While the Alamo was still under siege, a group of men had gathered at the town of Washington, on the Brazos, and there, in a little shed, issued a declaration of independence on March 2, 1836. Sam Houston, lately returned from the Indian country, was re-elected commander in chief, and it was his job to create some order out of the chaos resulting from news of the Alamo. "The Raven," as the Cherokees had named him, was a remarkable man—tall and husky, an eloquent speaker who had served two terms in Congress and one as governor of Tennessee—who believed firmly that Texas would be far more useful to the United States than to Mexico.

roofless chapel (left center) the Texans made their last stand.

As he pulled together his disorganized forces in that muddy spring of 1836, his strategy was to move eastward, staying inland where the going was easier, and putting plenty of distance between the Mexicans and the straggling, ill-disciplined men he was trying to shape into an army. Progress through the rain and mud and across swollen rivers was painfully slow, and terrified bands of refugees constantly obstructed the army's "runaway scrape." Houston managed to escape across the Colorado River, just ahead of the Mexicans, and on March 31 he called a halt in a river bottom by the Brazos where he began molding an army.

All the Texan forces to the south had been defeated, and Santa Anna, assuming Houston to be fleeing for the U.S. border, headed for Lynch's Ferry on the San Jacinto River, north of Galveston Bay. Discovering this, Houston quick-marched to the ferry, arriving three hours ahead of the Mexicans. There, along Buffalo Bayou, a stream which emptied into the San Jacinto River, he formed his men in the moss-draped oak woods and waited. In front of them the thick prairie grass extended for nearly a mile of plain over which Santa Anna had to pass to reach the ferry. Early in the afternoon of April 20 the Mexican battle formations came in sight, but in the face of the accurate Texan rifle fire, they retired. Santa Anna selected a position on a low, tree-covered hill and declared a day of rest—he doubted if the Texans had the nerve to attack.

At four-thirty in the afternoon of April 21, the Mexican pickets saw cavalry and infantry moving toward them through the tall prairie grass in perfect battle order. Surprised and confused, and in no mood to fight, they fell in behind a flimsy line of breastworks and opened fire on the Texans, who kept on coming without bothering to shoot back. Soon the Texans broke into a run, and at point-blank range opened fire with a yell: "Remember the Alamo!" Swarming over the breastworks, they swung their rifles like clubs, slaughtering the disorganized Mexicans. Those of Santa Anna's men who retreated down the reverse side of the hill found they were hemmed in by water; those who headed for the bridge at Vince's Creek found that it had been burned by "Deaf" Smith, a Texas scout. Out of a force of 1,300, only forty Mexicans escaped, and Santa Anna, who fled when the shooting started, was found next day crouching in some tall grass, disguised as a cavalryman.

In September of that year Sam Houston triumphed over Stephen Austin to become the first president of the Republic of Texas, and for ten erratic years the new government survived. At last, a majority of the American people came to favor annexation of the area, and on December 29, 1845, President Polk signed the act making Texas a part of the United States.

Today only a few of Texas' earliest buildings remain, like the Eggleston House in Gonzales, and the handsome Fanthorp Stagecoach Inn at Anderson. There is a reproduction of Stephen Austin's log cabin at San Felipe, near an old well built by the first colonists, and one may see, of course, the battlefield of San Jacinto, and the museum in the state park there. In addition to the famous remains of the Alamo, one can get an idea of what San Antonio looked like in 1836 by visiting the restored settlement of La Villita, with its old, high-walled houses of rock and adobe.

Off the beaten track, in Independence, are some fine examples of houses built during the Republic period. The Anson Jones House, home of the last President of Texas, was originally in Independence, but this frame structure with hand-hewn timbers and wide center hall has been moved to Washington-on-the-Brazos State Park.

Two other interesting towns are Fredericksburg and New Braunfels, which German immigrants settled in the 1840's. Fredericksburg's *Vereinskirche*, a combination fort, school, and meeting house, is one of the buildings well worth seeing, as are the stone houses with fancy iron lacework in these towns. In Huntsville, one may see the simple frame house in which Sam Houston spent his last years, and the curious building, patterned after a Mississippi River steamboat, where he died.

The Open Range

From the Canadian border to Mexico there stretches a huge swath of land which rises almost imperceptibly as it fades off to the west. This last American frontier, the Great Plains, is an enormous territory that is still relatively empty, lonely, and alive with a wind which never quite ceases. Into this immensity, whose boundaries were the horizon and the sky, moved the last frontiersman—the cowboy. He was a self-reliant, adaptable man, courageous out of the sheer necessity of his environment; his life conditioned by nature and by animals. From his peculiar and arduous existence arose a special culture, one which was manifested in the cowboy's manner of dress, his speech, his humor, and his songs.

The cowboy originated in southeast Texas, in the *brasada,* or brush country, and he learned his trade from Plains Indians and Mexicans. Somehow the original herds of cattle brought to America by Spaniards survived in the flat, dry *brasada,* and multiplied in almost geometric progression. One estimate puts the number of longhorns in 1830 at 100,000. Twenty years later there were 3,500,000, and when the Civil War took Texans off the ranches to fight for the Confederacy, the tough cattle went wild, breeding in such numbers that they threatened to become pests.

After the war a head of beef in Texas brought only three or four dollars; but in the North the demand was such that a mature steer would fetch ten times that. And so the cattle drives began—to take meat, on the hoof, to market. In 1866, 260,000 head were driven up from Texas, mostly to Sedalia and other railheads in Missouri. Unfortunately the longhorns carried Texas fever, and angry Missouri farmers attacked the cowboys, who soon sought other routes to the North. In the summer of 1867 a cattle dealer named Joseph McCoy bought land in a small Kansas railroad outpost called Abilene, built some stockyards, and sent word of the new market to Texas. By 1869, 350,000 head were driven north to Abilene, following a trail up from Brownsville, San Antonio, Austin, Fort Worth, across the Red River and into Indian Territory (Oklahoma). Known as the Chisholm Trail, after the half-breed trader who marked it out, the route led through lush grass and across the Washita, the Canadian, the Cimarron, and the Salt Fork of the Arkansas.

The dirty, exhausting drives were fraught with danger—there were Indians, rustlers, and hostile homesteaders; rattlesnakes, blizzards, and treacherous

Year's "PICTORIAL HISTORY OF AMERICA"

stream crossings; and the worst hazard of all, stampedes. Yet year after year herds moved north in increasing numbers, and rip-roaring frontier towns sprung up out of nowhere. Eventually the Chisholm Trail was replaced by the Dodge City Trail to the west, and between 1866 and 1885, when the open range came to an end, nearly six million cattle were trailed north. Today there are almost no visible remains of the short-lived heyday of the cattle drives. The Homestead Act of 1862 opened the range to settlers; barbed wire enclosed the open range; and the railroad, which came to the rancher, eventually ended the drives. The terrible winter of 1886-87 nearly destroyed the industry, and the cowboy's way of life changed irrevocably as the Wild West vanished from the Great Plains.

Until 1885, when the open range came to an end, millions of Texas longhorns were driven north to wild towns like Dodge City (above), or Abilene, where cowboys cut loose after a long drive.

A. Y. OWEN

In a few places like Okarche, Oklahoma, ruts made by wagons which used the Chisholm Trail are still visible.

Near Dover, Oklahoma, is a hollowed depression, hundreds of feet wide, worn by the hoofs of longhorns heading north.

Bat Masterson was Wyatt Earp's best-known deputy.

Wyatt Earp served Dodge City as assistant marshal.

Jesse James' wild career lasted from 1866 until 1882.

Deadwood's Calamity Jane was as tough as most men.

Badmen's West

As the railroads pushed into the Great Plains, one town after another mushroomed up in their wake, some of them cow towns like Abilene, Kansas—tough, rowdy places, open around the clock—where cowboys could find entertainment after the long drives. John Wesley Hardin, a Texas killer who claimed to have forty notches on his gun, came to Abilene in the summer of 1871 and observed: "I have seen fast towns, but Abilene beat them all." Swarming with pickpockets, gamblers, and confidence men, Abilene was like a lot of other towns—short on law and civilizing influences. One reason for this was the Civil War. Men who had fought with Quantrill's guerrillas refused to recognize the fact of Appomattox. Violence had become a way of life, and when Union sympathizers and Texas cowboys who were ex-Confederates met head-on in a Kansas cow town, there was bound to be trouble.

Another factor was the Colt revolver. When the first white settlers ventured onto the Plains, they came armed with weapons of the eastern woodlands— the cap-and-ball rifle and the horse pistol, single-shot affairs which were hopelessly inadequate against Indians on horseback. In the time needed to load one of these guns a mounted Indian could ride 300 yards and shoot twenty arrows—and there were no trees to hide behind out here. But Samuel Colt's revolver, which could be fired six times without reloading, was the perfect weapon for a man on horseback. Texans, the first to settle the Plains in large numbers, were also first to discover the six-gun's merits. Texas Rangers used it for Indian fighting as early as 1839, made it famous in the Mexican War, and plainsmen coined a saying that God made some men large and some small, but Colonel Colt made them all equal.

Out of this West came true stories and a thousand legends of good men and bad, and dotting the Plains from Texas to the Dakotas are monuments of a sort from those lawless days. Over in Missouri, in Excelsior Springs, is the birthplace of Frank and Jesse James, who manufactured a Robin Hood legend to cover their careers of crime, and the one-story house where Jesse was shot in the back by a former gang member, Bob Ford, still stands in St. Joseph.

Most Kansas towns survived the collapse of the cattle boom, but there are places like Wallace which are practically ghost communities now. For a brief period in the 1870's Wallace prospered, then suddenly it was nearly deserted except for the plain frame and stone buildings which are relics of its halcyon days.

What is now the National Hotel in Abilene began life as the Old Gulf House. This flat-roofed limestone building was erected in 1871, when the marshal of Abilene was Wild Bill Hickok. So expert a marksman was Hickok that few men dared comment on his Prince Albert coat and checkered trousers, silk-lined cape, and embroidered vest. With shoulder-length hair and handle-bar mustache, Hickok cut quite a figure as marshal; but he was a little too quick on the draw, and after he killed one of his deputies in the smoky confusion of a gun battle, Abilene let him go. The town was tired of violence and gun-toting marshals, and in 1872 the authorities sent word to Texas that the cattle drives could go elsewhere. Yet one town after another competed for the cattle trade. There was Ellsworth, in which one may still see the White House hotel where Buffalo Bill Cody and Hickok stayed. Here Wyatt Earp first gained prominence before moving on to Dodge City, the wildest town of all. Known as "the Gomorrah of the Plains,"

Deadwood, South Dakota, named for a stand of burned timber, looked like this when Bill Hickok arrived in 1876.

A legendary bad man, Sam Bass had only one success.

Buffalo Bill Cody's fame spread with dime novels.

Wild Bill Hickok was noted as a crack marksman.

John Wesley Hardin shot his first man at fifteen.

it had the dubious distinction of originating the terms "Red Light District" and "Boot Hill"—a cemetery for men who died with their boots on.

For those who found life in the Kansas cow towns growing the least bit stale, a new Wild West developed soon enough. In 1874 General George Custer's expedition to the Black Hills discovered gold, and as soon as the news was out the rush began. By Christmas of 1875 close to 10,000 people had gathered in the new town of Custer, but they found very little that glittered. Today's visitor may see maps of the Custer Expedition, as well as a pictorial history of the Black Hills region, at the Custer State Park Museum just east of Custer. The town itself is one of the region's oldest settlements. Nearby is Gordon Stockade, a reconstruction of the original built by one of the first bands of gold-seekers in the area.

If Custer was a disappointment to the thousands of gold-hunters, they got their real chance in 1876, with the fabulous strike at Deadwood. Within a year over 200 stores, thirty hotels, seventy saloons and gambling houses, and a public bath appeared in town, along with literary societies, dancing clubs, and characters like Poker Alice, Lame Johnny, and Fly Speck Billy. The buckskin-clad Calamity Jane, who swaggered into bars and shattered mirrors with gunfire, was here, as was Sam Bass, a Texas cowpoke gone wrong. This was the place where Wild Bill Hickok, grown a little careless, was shot in the back in a poker game. His grave is on "Boot Hill," beside Calamity Jane's.

Deadwood's Adams Memorial Museum, with its relics of the wild years, is an interesting place, and other remnants of this rowdy era are scattered through the Black Hills. One may find them especially in the ghost towns—places like Rockerville, Rochford, or Silver City, which sprang up overnight and died almost as quickly, when the Great Plains ceased to be America's last—and wildest—frontier.

Sod-Hut Frontier

Near Beatrice, Nebraska, the government has erected a national monument to one of the most remarkable events in American history. Here, in 1862, the first claim was filed under the Homestead Act, a law which expressed the basic, eternal demand of the frontiersman for free land. In no sense was this a charitable handout; it was an arrangement whereby the settler repaid the government by opening up and developing the vast, unoccupied areas of the West. Upon payment of a small fee, the settler could claim a quarter-section (160 acres) of unappropriated public land, which would become his property after five years of continuous residence.

The Homestead Act made land available, the railroad made it accessible, and in sixty years more than a million settlers took advantage of it. Yet few periods in our history have been accompanied by more hardship. The typical homesteader, in a stark land which was still the Indian's hunting ground, found almost no wood with which to build a house, so he constructed a rude, temporary dugout, covered with brush, hay, or sod. After he was established, the homesteader built a "soddy," like those which may be seen at Colby, Kansas, and northwest of Morland. The tightly-matted prairie sod was cut into three-foot bricks, then laid up to form walls. Openings were usually covered with buffalo hides, but some settlers were fortunate enough to have real windows, doors, or a board floor. Although the sod "bricks" might last for forty years, they had their share of field mice and fleas, soaked up rain, and in a heavy storm the entire structure might dissolve in mud. Before 1876, when barbed wire was first used for fences, homesteaders planted hedges of the thorny Osage orange, which can still be seen in eastern Kansas, or put up mud fences—so unattractive that they gave rise to the expression "ugly as a mud fence."

Homesteading was an epic struggle—against economic depressions, foreign competition, exorbitant freight and interest rates, cattlemen, Indians, and above all, against nature. There were freezing winters, prolonged droughts, and fierce summer heat; prairie fires, pesky prairie dogs, and ruinous swarms of grasshoppers. And ironically, the size of the homestead grant was partially responsible for the American farmer's first major defeat. Conditions on the Plains were almost totally different from the rest of the country, and not until agriculture became a large-scale commercial enterprise could it be really successful here.

By 1889 the last unappropriated land was in Indian Territory—now Oklahoma. After refusing homesteaders entry for years, the government finally gave in to the pressure of the railroad interests, western congressmen, and hungry land-seekers, and opened the "Oklahoma District" to settlement "at and after the hour of twelve o'clock noon" on April 22, 1889. Long lines of soldiers did their best to keep the excited homesteaders back of the starting line until noon, when a cavalry trumpeter sounded "dinner call" and the run was on. In the next few years more Indian land was opened to white settlement—some of it by

This historic photograph was taken on September 16, 1893, just after the bugle blew the start of the famous land run on the Cherokee Strip. That day an estimated 100,000 land-seekers scrambled for homesteads on the former Indian land tract.

runs, some by lottery—and on September 16, 1893, the biggest tract of all, the Cherokee Outlet, was opened. That day an estimated 100,000 land-seekers lined up for prairie homesteads, and in the memorable scene shown here men on horses and every kind of vehicle lashed their animals forward through the dust, intent on getting somewhere first.

Only a few of the sod huts are left today. By 1900 most of them had been replaced by houses Willa Cather described as "encircled by porches, too narrow for modern notions of comfort, supported by the fussy, fragile pillars of that time, when every honest stick of timber was tortured by the turning-lathe into something hideous." And yet one cannot help feeling that these buildings were a natural response to the environment—an answer to a deep longing for variety in a land which offered very little.

This 1892 photograph of a Nebraska "soddy" shows how the homesteaders laid up "bricks" of prairie sod for shelters.

THE GREAT PLAINS

WRITING ROCK
STATE PARK
LANGDON •
BUFORD •
FORT TOTTEN

NORTH DAKOTA
FORT TOTTEN
COOPERSTOWN •
THEODORE ROOSEVELT
NAT'L MEM. PARK
NEW SALEM • MANDAN
MEDORA • BISMARCK
BLACK BUTTE FORT LINCOLN FORT RANSOM
STATE PARK FORT ABERCROMBIE
STATE PARK
FORT YATES
REVA • STANDING ROCK WHITESTONE
INDIAN RES. BATTLEFIELD
BISON

SOUTH DAKOTA
CENTRAL CITY BLUNT •
• DEADWOOD
SILVER PIERRE
BLACK CITY • RAPID CITY
HILLS • MOUNT RUSHMORE MITCHELL •
CUSTER STATE PARK SCENIC
WIND CAVE NAT'L PARK BADLANDS SIOUX FALLS
WOUNDED KNEE BATTLEFIELD
BATESLAND YANKTON
VERMILLION •
N. Platte FORT ROBINSON
Missouri R.
HORSE CREEK
SCOTTS BLUFF NEBRASKA
R.
ROUBIDOU PASS LEWELLEN
NORTH PLATTE Platte R. OMAHA
GOTHENBURG KEARNY LINCOLN
CULBERTSON HASTINGS NEBRASKA CITY
RED CLOUD BEATRICE
LEBANON MARYSVILLE HIGHLAND
COLBY Kansas R. FORT RILEY TOPEKA LEAVENWORTH
ELLSWORTH ABILENE
HAYS SALINA KANSAS CITY
COUNCIL
CIMARRON GROVE OSAWATOMIE
Arkansas R. CROSSING KANSAS
LARNED LYONS
PAWNEE NEWTON FORT SCOTT
DODGE CITY ROCK WICHITA
MEADE MEDICINE LODGE COFFEYVILLE BAXTER
SPRINGS
KENTON BARTLESVILLE
PONCA CITY PAWHUSKA
ENID CLAREMORE
Canadian R. TULSA TAHLEQUAH
OKLAHOMA STILWELL
OKLAHOMA OKMULGEE SALLISAW
CITY FORT GIBSON
ANADARKO WEWOKA SPIRO
CHICKASHA
LAWTON
TISHOMINGO
Red River
FORT JEFFERSON
WORTH
DALLAS Sabine R.
EL PASO
TEXAS NACOGDOCHES
CHIRENO SAN AUGUSTINE
SAN ANGELO • Brazos R.
ANDERSON HUNTSVILLE
FREDERICKSBURG INDEPENDENCE WASHINGTON
AUSTIN HEMPSTEAD
LANGTRY BRENHAM SAN JACINTO BATTLEFIELD
NEW BRAUNFELS HOUSTON
SAN ANTONIO GONZALES
GALVESTON
Rio Grande GOLIAD
GULF OF MEXICO
RIO GRANDE
CITY

Mississippi River

Mississippi R.

KEY:

🏠 EARLY HOUSE

⟋ PIONEER SITE

🏛 FRONTIER TOWN

🏰 FORT

🐂 CATTLE COUNTRY

✕ HISTORIC INDIAN SITE

◠ INDIAN MOUND

🐚 SPANISH SITE

KANSAS

ABILENE

First of the wild cattle towns which sprang up in Kansas in the late 1860's and 1870's. Two of Abilene's famous frontier peace officers were Tom Smith and Wild Bill Hickok. The old *Gulf House* (now the National Hotel) opened in 1870 when Hickok was marshal. A marker here commemorates the terminus of the *Chisholm Trail*. Also in Abilene are the boyhood home of Dwight D. Eisenhower, and a museum housing a collection of souvenirs from his childhood and military and presidential careers.

BAXTER SPRINGS

Scene of the Baxter Springs Massacre, October 6, 1863, when 87 Union troops were killed by Quantrill's raiders. A number of the victims are buried in the national cemetery near town.

CIMARRON

Cimarron Crossing Park on the Arkansas River marks the area of a famous cutoff on the Santa Fe Trail. Here many caravans took a southern route, crossing a dangerous waterless stretch of prairie to the Cimarron River instead of continuing on the longer route directly west.

COFFEYVILLE

Scene of a raid in 1892 by the notorious Dalton gang. Still to be seen is the so-called *Death Valley*, an alley where the gang was trapped and three members shot down. The *Dalton Defenders Museum* contains mementos of the incident.

COLBY

A typical sod house of the midwestern frontier has been reconstructed and is open to visitors.

COUNCIL GROVE

Council Oak Site of a treaty signed in 1825 by Osage Indians and U.S. commissioners which led to the establishment of the Santa Fe Trail.

Hays Tavern (1857) Although partially modernized, the basic structure is unchanged.

Kaw Mission (1851) For three years a Methodist school for Indians. Later one of the first schools for white children in the territory. The building is preserved and maintained as a state museum.

Post Office Oak Where travelers left letters to be picked up by passing wagon trains.

DODGE CITY

Important shipping point and cattle market on a cattle trail from Texas, it has become known throughout the world as one of the wildest of all the cow towns. The original *Boot Hill*, frontier burial place, is now the site of the City Hall. A reconstructed Boot Hill is nearby. The *Beeson Museum* is dedicated to pioneer days. Nine miles west of Dodge City, off U.S. 50, ruts and tracks of the Santa Fe Trail may still be seen. Four miles southeast is *Fort Dodge*, an important post on

the Indian frontier, 1865-82. Nine buildings remain from the days of military occupancy and are in use by the state soldiers' home.

ELLSWORTH

Once a rowdy cattle town, which succeeded Abilene in 1872 as the terminus of the Texas cattle trail. A reminder of its early days is the *Grand Central Hotel*, now the White House Hotel. Its register includes the names of "Buffalo Bill" Cody and "Wild Bill" Hickok.

FAIRWAY

Shawnee Methodist Mission (1839) Three original brick buildings, used as schoolhouse, chapel, and dormitory, are still standing and are open as a state museum. The mission served temporarily as the second Kansas territorial capitol.

FORT RILEY

Founded in 1853 as Camp Center to protect the Santa Fe Trail, the fort was later headquarters for General Custer's famous Seventh Cavalry. On the fort grounds is a simple limestone building intended as a warehouse but used briefly in 1855 by the first territorial legislature of Kansas, and now maintained as a state museum.

FORT SCOTT

Founded in 1842 to protect the military road between Fort Leavenworth and Fort Gibson, Oklahoma; later a Civil War fortification. Several buildings of the old fort, including a renovated Civil War blockhouse, stand today in *Carroll Plaza*, the original parade ground. A former officers' quarters, *Headquarters House* (c. 1856), is now a historical museum.

GARDEN CITY

South of the city a herd of buffalo may be seen on the *Buffalo Preserve*. When the white man nearly exterminated the herds, the Plains Indians were starved into submission.

HANOVER

One mile northeast is *Hollenberg Ranch Station* (1857) believed to be the only original and unaltered Pony Express station. Now a state museum.

HAYS

South of Hays in *Frontier Historical Park* are the original stone blockhouse and guardhouse of *Fort Hays* (1867), one of the most famous military posts on the frontier. Here "Buffalo Bill" Cody acquired his nickname supplying meat for railroad crews. The blockhouse is now a museum.

HIGHLAND

Two miles northeast is the Iowa, Sac, and Fox mission, established in 1837 by the Presbyterian Church. Part of a later building (1846) still stands, and is operated as a state museum.

IOLA

Five miles north is the boyhood home of Gen. Frederick Funston who won fame by

capturing the Philippine insurgent leader Aguinaldo. The property is preserved and maintained as a state museum.

KANOPOLIS

Site of *Fort Harker*, established in 1867. The old guardhouse is now a museum.

KANSAS CITY

In June, 1804, while exploring the Louisiana Purchase Territory, Lewis and Clark camped at what is now Kaw Point in Kansas City—a neck of land where the Kansas River empties into the Missouri. In the 1840's the area was settled by Wyandot Indians who were moved here from Ohio. Huron Cemetery, their tribal burial ground, may still be seen in the downtown area. White settlers eventually absorbed the Indian community and Kansas City grew to become a major industrial and shipping center (*see* pp. 280-81).

LARNED

Six miles west of town is old *Fort Larned*, one of the most important posts on the Santa Fe Trail and the Indian frontier (1859-78), and one of the best surviving examples of a frontier military post. Several original stone buildings are preserved and are open by permission.

LAWRENCE

Historical markers and monuments serve as reminders of Lawrence's turbulent history during the Territorial years. Founded as a free-state stronghold in 1854, it was the object of frequent attacks by pro-slavery sympathizers, notably in 1856. In a raid of 1863 Quantrill's guerrillas not only burned the city but killed approximately 150 of its citizens.

LEAVENWORTH

Fort Leavenworth Established in 1827 to protect frontier travelers from Indian attacks. Later served as an important starting point for military expeditions. The wagon ruts of a branch of the Oregon and Santa Fe trails are still visible here. Of special interest is the *Fort Leavenworth Museum* which houses a large collection of old wagons and carriages, as well as an assortment of early guns and other frontier relics.

Planters' House (1856) A popular western hotel which was host to many famous men. From its steps Abraham Lincoln made a campaign speech in December, 1859.

LEBANON

Two miles northwest is a monument indicating the geographic center of the U.S.

LECOMPTON

Headquarters for the pro-slavery party in Kansas and capital of the territory as decreed by the "bogus legislature" of 1855. In *Constitution Hall*, a modest frame building, the pro-slavery constitution of 1857 was drafted. It was later repudiated.

LYONS

A large cross west of the city commemorates the martyrdom of Father Juan de

295

Padilla who accompanied Coronado to the land of Quivira (present Kansas) in 1541. Near here is the site of an Indian village believed to have been visited by the Coronado expedition.

MANHATTAN
In *City Park* are an old stagecoach and a pioneer museum in a log cabin.

MARYSVILLE
Five miles southwest of here on the Big Blue River is the site of *Independence Crossing,* where travelers on the Oregon Trail forded the Big Blue River. Seven miles south is *Alcove Springs,* famous emigrant campsite.

MAYETTA
West of here is the 7,040-acre *Pottawatomie Indian Reservation,* largest in Kansas.

MEADE
A barn which is reported to have been a hide-out for the Dalton gang houses a museum of western mementos, including a fine gun collection.

MEDICINE LODGE
Scene of the 1867 peace treaties between the U.S. and five hostile Plains Indian tribes, which opened western Kansas to white settlement and permitted the building of railroads across Indian lands.
Carry A. Nation House Home of the militant prohibitionist.

NEWTON
Center of the largest Mennonite settlement in America. The Mennonites brought hard winter wheat, known as Turkey Red, from Russia in 1874. Well-adapted to the Kansas soil, this grain helped to launch wheat raising on a large scale in Kansas.

OREGON TRAIL
The famous trail, over which thousands of people passed on the way west, went through Kansas, as indicated on the map on pp. 332-33 (*see also* pp. 282-83).

OSAWATOMIE
John Brown Memorial Park Dedicated to the fanatical antislavery leader who came here in 1855 to work with the Free-Staters. In the park is a cabin which he occupied. It served as an *Underground Railroad* station during the Civil War. The area also was the site of the Battle of Osawatomie (1856), during which the town was sacked by pro-slavery sympathizers, Brown participating in its defense.

PAWNEE ROCK STATE PARK
Pawnee Rock was a famous landmark on the Santa Fe Trail. For many years it served as an Indian meeting place and lookout, and was one of the most dangerous points on the central plains.

SALINA
Four miles east of Salina is an ancient Indian burial pit where over 140 skeletons have been uncovered. Necklaces, pottery, and other Indian artifacts are on display.

SCOTT CITY
Twelve miles north of here, in *Scott County State Park,* are the ancient Pueblo Indian

NATIONAL PARK SERVICE

Headquarters House, Fort Scott

ruins of El Quartelejo. It is believed that Indians from the Southwest migrated here about 1650 to escape Spanish oppression. The ruins, excavated in 1898, have since been covered by drifting soil.

TOPEKA
Kansas State Capitol (1866-69)
Kansas State Historical Society Extensive collections of manuscripts and archival materials; largest collection of newspapers in the U.S. except that of the Library of Congress; historical museum containing period rooms and modern displays relating to Kansas history.
Pottawatomie Baptist Mission (1849-59) Two miles west of Topeka, this building was near an important Oregon Trail crossing of the Kansas River and was a stopping place for travelers on the road to Fort Riley. One of the buildings, remodeled, is still in use.

TRADING POST
Four miles northeast of here a park commemorates the scene of the Marais des Cygnes Massacre. In 1858 Missouri-Kansas border difficulties were brought to a head when a group of pro-slavery raiders rounded up eleven Free-State men before a firing squad, killing five. This mass killing inflamed the North.

WABAUNSEE
Beecher Bible and Rifle Church Built in 1862 by members of the abolitionist colony of the same name. The settlement received its title from its sponsor, Henry Ward Beecher, who presented each member with a Bible and a rifle "to defend his faith and his ideas of freedom."

WICHITA
The reconstructed village of *Old Wichita* recalls the town's boom days of the 1870's. Among the original buildings are the first log cabin and hotel, jail, and church.

NEBRASKA

ARBOR LODGE STATE PARK
This park near Nebraska City contains the lovely mansion of J. Sterling Morton, third Secretary of Agriculture, who settled here in 1855. The 52-room house was built over a period of 47 years, and includes period furnishings and a number of objects with historic associations.

BEATRICE
Homestead National Monument A memorial in recognition of the first 160-acre claim made under the Homestead Act of 1862 (*see* pp. 292-93).

CHADRON
Museum of the Fur Trade One of the best collections of early guns and fur trade equipment in America.

CHIMNEY ROCK NATIONAL SITE
A historic landmark along the Oregon Trail which rises 500 feet above the river near Bayard. Near here are *Court House*

and *Jail Rocks,* two other trail landmarks in the North Platte Valley.

FAIRBURY
Site of the *Rock Creek Pony Express Station,* where Wild Bill Hickok was assistant stock tender. In a fracas he killed the owner, but was acquitted.

FORT KEARNY STATE PARK
Site of the famous frontier army post. The fort was abandoned in 1871, after the railroad displaced the wagon train.

FORT ROBINSON
Established in 1874, just before the last great Indian uprisings in the area, it was for five years a scene of much excitement. Many Indian battles had repercussions at the fort. Today the State Historical Society maintains a museum in the headquarters building of the former Army outpost. The parade ground is surrounded by other old Army buildings.

GOTHENBURG
City Park Here is a small log cabin, moved from its original location on the Oregon Trail near Fort McPherson, which served as a fur-trading post, Pony Express station, stage station, and after the coming of the railroad, as a ranch building.

HASTINGS
House of Yesterday Contains a collection of pioneer and historical relics, farm equipment, vehicles, and firearms.

HORSE CREEK
Treaty Monument Commemorates the largest peace council ever held on the Plains. More than 10,000 Indians—Shoshone, Sioux, Cheyenne, Assiniboin, Arapaho, Blackfoot, Crow, Mandan, and others—attended the "Fort Laramie Treaty Council" in September, 1851.

LEWELLEN
Near here is Ash Hollow, a ravine through

which the Oregon Trail descended to the North Platte River. Old ruts are visible at Windlass Hill, where emigrants lowered their wagons by ropes. Across the river is Blue Water Creek, scene of General William S. Harney's massacre of Sioux Indians in 1855.

LINCOLN
William Jennings Bryan House Home of Bryan, 1887 to 1902. Here he addressed crowds who came to congratulate him as the Democratic nominee. Private.
State Historical Society Building Museum of Nebraska archaeology and history.

NORTH PLATTE
Scout's Rest Ranch Former home of Buffalo Bill Cody, where he originated his Wild West show. It is near an old section of the Oregon Trail.

OMAHA
Union Pacific Museum Has objects of interest connected with the development and history of the Union Pacific Railroad. *The Joslyn Museum* houses a fine collection of western art, along with exhibits relating to the early history of the state. Near Omaha is Bellevue, the oldest town in Nebraska, and site of the *Moses Merrill Presbyterian Indian Mission* (1848). In Bellevue the Sarpy County Historical Society maintains a log cabin museum.

Mormon Cemetery. A bronze monument commemorates the 600 Mormon emigrants buried in this vicinity during the winter of 1846-47. Site of the Winter Quarters on the route to Utah.

OREGON TRAIL
The famous trail, over which thousands of people passed on the way west, went through Nebraska, as indicated on the map on pp. 332-33 (*see also* pp. 282-83).

RED CLOUD
Willa Cather Home Childhood home of the famous writer, who came here in 1876 at the age of nine. A lean-to now attached to the garage was her "office."

ROUBIDOUX PASS
Eight miles southwest of Scotts Bluff National Monument, this pass was used for wagon trains before Mitchell Pass could accommodate them. It was named for an early French fur trader in this vicinity.

SCOTTS BLUFF NATIONAL MONUMENT
Celebrated landmark on the Oregon Trail near Gering, Nebraska. Remains of the old trail can be seen along State Highway 86 and in Mitchell Pass. The *Oregon Trail Museum* houses William H. Jackson's watercolors of the trail, and a collection of fossils from western Nebraska. The prominent bluffs on the south side of

William Jennings Bryan House, Lincoln

the North Platte River were named for a fur trader who died here under mysterious circumstances about 1828. A sick man, Hiram Scott was supposedly abandoned by his companions and found by them months later 60 miles from where they had left him. Apparently he had crawled that incredible distance looking for help though sick and starving. *Mitchell Pass* was used after 1851 by emigrants, freighters, Pony Express riders, the Overland Stage, and the first transcontinental telegraph.

NORTH DAKOTA

BISMARCK
Maltese Cross Ranch Cabin Home of Theodore Roosevelt from 1883 to 1885 when he began his ranching career in the North Dakota Badlands. The interior furnishings are copies of those used by T.R. The cabin contains much Rooseveltiana, including books and guns.

BLACK BUTTE
Eagle Pits On the highest point in the state, west of Amidon, are two rock-lined eagle pits, about 4 feet wide and 3 feet deep, where Indians would hide and pluck out the tail feathers of eagles for their war bonnets.

Blockhouse,
Fort Abraham Lincoln State Park

COOPERSTOWN
Opheim Log Cabin (1879) An early homestead which contains handmade furniture used by its first occupants.

FORT ABERCROMBIE STATE PARK
Restored palisades and blockhouses on the site of *Fort Abercrombie* (1858).

FORT ABRAHAM LINCOLN STATE PARK
Fort Lincoln Museum A collection here, near Mandan, tells the story of the Mandan Indians, Fort McKeen, and Fort Lincoln. It was from Fort Lincoln that Custer and his men set out for the last time, before they were massacred at the Battle of the Little Big Horn, in 1876. Three restored blockhouses at *Fort McKeen* look much as they did when built in 1872.
Slant Village Perhaps two centuries before a white man appeared on the Plains, this was the location of a Mandan village (*see* pp. 334-35). Depressions in the earth reveal that the settlement contained 68 lodges, five of which have been reconstructed. The crude tools, furniture, and other articles used by the inhabitants are on display.

FORT BUFORD STATE PARK
This fort was a vital outpost on the Indian frontier. The officer's quarters, where Sitting Bull surrendered in 1881, ruins of the magazine, and the old cemetery remain.

FORT CLARK STATE HISTORIC SITE
Remains of an important Missouri River trading post, built in 1830.

FORT RANSOM
Maintained as a historic site.

FORT RICE STATE HISTORIC SITE
A restored blockhouse 25 miles south of Mandan stands on the site of *Fort Rice*, scene of a peace council with the Sioux in 1868.

FORT YATES
With its log huts and frame buildings, this town in the Standing Rock Indian Reservation retains much of the appearance of frontier days. The *Standing Rock* is regarded as sacred by the older Indians. On the reservation is the lonely grave of Sitting Bull, killed by Indian policemen in the 1890's.

MEDORA
This former cow town, now headquarters of the *Theodore Roosevelt National Memorial Park,* has many visible remains of the cattle industry. Several of the buildings which stood when Theodore Roosevelt ranched nearby in the 1880's may still be seen, notably the *Ferris Store,* the *Rough Rider's Hotel,* and *St. Mary's Church.* Across the river from the town is the *De Mores Château,* a huge frame structure built by a French marquis who tried unsuccessfully to found a cattle empire.

THEODORE ROOSEVELT NATIONAL MEMORIAL PARK
This memorial to Roosevelt's conservation efforts preserves colorful scenes of the Little Missouri River Badlands, where he owned

two ranches. In both the southern unit, with headquarters at Medora, and the northern one, near Watford City, fantastically eroded badland stretches, burning coal veins, and petrified wood may be seen. A third, somewhat isolated section of the park preserves the site of Roosevelt's Elkhorn Ranch, now little more than a few foundation stones.

WHITESTONE HILLS BATTLEFIELD STATE PARK
Near Ellendale a marker commemorates the fierce battle fought here between Sioux and U.S. troops in 1863. A museum contains Indian and pioneer relics.

WRITING ROCK STATE PARK
At the center of the park is a rock covered with Indian hieroglyphics.

OKLAHOMA

ANADARKO
The Indian agency here still serves about 4,500 Indians, who continue to follow their native customs. The *Anadarko City Museum* has a collection of pioneer and Indian relics.

BARTLESVILLE
A replica of the first commercial oil well (April, 1897) stands in Johnstone Park. The *Woolaroc Ranch and Museum,* fourteen miles southwest of Bartlesville is a sandstone building housing a fine collection of Western art and Indian relics.

CHICKASHA
Chisholm Trail Camp Site A favorite spot on the old cattle trail because the Washita River was easily forded here.

CHISHOLM TRAIL
The famous cattle trail is followed today

OKLAHOMA HISTORICAL SOCIETY

Fort Gibson

by Highway 81 from the Red River on the Texas border (near Fleetwood) north through Enid, and on to Caldwell, Kansas. Portions of the trail may still be seen. Its peak was in 1871, when 600,000 head of cattle were moved north across Oklahoma to rail markets in Kansas (*see* pp. 288-89. *also* map, pp. 332-33).

CLAREMORE
Will Rogers Memorial This memorial to the beloved Oklahoma humorist houses four principal galleries—Indian, pioneer, historical, and educational; and a fifth gallery in which mementos of the humorist are displayed. The original twenty-acre hillside site was purchased by Will Rogers for his retirement, and was given to the state by his widow.

ENID
Government Springs Park Most noted stopping place on the Chisholm Trail. Drivers grazed their cattle along Skeleton Creek, two miles to the east, and rested by the springs.

FORT GIBSON
Many old buildings of *Fort Gibson* have been restored, including the log stockade. The fort was established in 1824 to stop the plundering of warlike Osages and other Indians, and served as the chief military center for the entire Indian Territory until 1857. A starting place for many western exploring expeditions, it was occupied during the Civil War by Union troops.

KENTON
Black Mesa A lava-capped plateau where Indians camped. This marked the beginning of the old Penrose Trail into Colorado.
Dinosaur Quarry Burial ground of monsters who lived during the Jurassic Age, over 10 million years ago. The Brontosaurus, which measured 70 feet in length and weighed 36 tons, was found here. The skeletons discovered in the area have been taken to the University of Oklahoma.

LAWTON
Fort Sill Built on the site of the guard house where Geronimo was held prisoner from 1894 until his death in 1909. It is the only one of Oklahoma's early forts still used as a military installation. Among the sites to be seen are the stone stockade, built in 1870, an 1874 chapel, the guardhouse, and the nearby *Apache Indian Cemetery,* where Geronimo is buried.
Wichita Mountains Wildlife Refuge A herd of longhorns may be seen here.

OKLAHOMA CITY
Oil wells One of the richest oil field developments in history began in the Oklahoma City area in 1928. Controversy raged over drilling within city limits. The oil well advocates won, and the approach to the city, with wells visible in its skyline (over 20 are on state-owned land around the capitol) is quite a sight.
State Historical Building Contains interesting Indian and pioneer objects.

OKMULGEE
Creek Indian National Council House A well-proportioned brownstone structure which houses a most interesting museum of Creek history. The building was acquired by the city from the Creeks when the tribal government went out of existence.

PAWHUSKA
Agency Hill Behind the business district are the stone and frame buildings of the Osage Agency, one of them housing the *Osage Tribal Museum.* The *City Hall* was formerly the Osage Council House.

PONCA CITY
Municipal Building This example of Span-ish-Moorish architecture is one of the most beautiful buildings in the state.
Pioneer Woman Statue A monument to the women of pioneer days, probably the most photographed statue in the region.

SALLISAW
Sequoyah Cabin (1829) The one-room cabin enclosed within a stone structure belonged to Sequoyah, the remarkable Indian who invented the Cherokee alphabet. In a nearby museum relics and documents pertaining to his life are displayed. Here Sequoyah tilled his farm, operated a blacksmith shop, and tended his salt kettles.

SANTA FE TRAIL
Traces of the famous route cut across the northwest corner of the Oklahoma panhandle. Near the site of *Fort Nichols,* north of Boise City, three groups of wagon ruts, 10 feet deep and 20 feet wide, are visible (*see* map, pp. 332-33).

SPIRO INDIAN MOUNDS
Best-known archaeological site in the state, at Spiro, where Aztec-type ornaments and artifacts of a pre-Columbian civilization have been discovered.

STILWELL
Bitting Springs Mill (c. 1870) One of the remaining gristmills run by water power.

TAHLEQUAH
County Courthouse (1869) This was the Cherokee capitol building. In 1839 Tahlequah was selected as the permanent capital of the Cherokee nation.
Murrell Mansion (1845) Built soon after the Cherokee removal over the Trail of Tears, this house was center of the surprisingly luxurious life in the Cherokee settlement, Park Hill. The stately frame structure is being restored.
Northeastern State College An outgrowth of the Cherokee Female Seminary, originally established at nearby Park Hill in 1851. The old seminary building is on the campus, and the library and museum contain relics of the Cherokee nation.

TISHOMINGO
Chickasaw Log Capitol A log building which served as the first tribal capitol after the Chickasaws separated from the Choctaws in 1855.

TULSA
Thomas Gilcrease Institute of American History and Art A superb collection of early paintings of the West, as well as maps and manuscripts.

WEWOKA
Seminole Council House (c. 1890) The last council house is now a farm near here.

SOUTH DAKOTA

BADLANDS NATIONAL MONUMENT
Over 100,000 acres of spectacularly eroded and weathered land, where a wealth of fossils and other evidences of prehistoric life have been uncovered. Many fossils from here are on exhibit at the School of Mines in Rapid City.

BISON
Bison Museum Constructed of rammed earth, one outside wall is carved with local cattle brands, and inside are many huge casts of dinosaur tracks found in the vicinity.

BLACK HILLS
A densely wooded, hilly section which was held sacred by the Indians and remained deserted until the discovery of gold in the 1870's. In this area are a number of interesting ghost towns, including Silver City, Rochford, and Rockerville. Deadwood is one of the best examples of an early mining town.

BLUNT
Mentor Graham House Last home of one of Abraham Lincoln's teachers. Being restored by South Dakota Historical Society.

CENTRAL CITY
Many old false-front stores and saloons still stand in this ghost town of a Dakota gold rush, narrow gauge tracks and trestles, and remains of old mills line the nearby hillsides. It is near Deadwood.

CUSTER
Gordon Stockade is a careful reconstruction of the log stockade originally built by the first group of gold prospectors coming into the Black Hills in the winter of 1874-75 against government orders. The enclosure (about 80 feet square) was built on General Custer's old camping grounds on the banks of French Creek for protection against hostile Indians.

CUSTER STATE PARK
The museum near Custer contains a pictorial record of historic events in the Black Hills, with maps of the Custer expedition and early trails. In the park is one of the

SOUTH DAKOTA HISTORICAL SOCIETY

Fort Randall Church, Pickstown

world's largest buffalo herds.

DEADWOOD
One of the rowdiest towns of the Old West is a picturesque mining town set in a gulch containing one main street, the business section. Houses climb the steep sides of the gulch, and overlooking the town is Mt. Moriah, or *Boot Hill Cemetery,* where Wild Bill Hickok, Calamity Jane, and other famous characters are buried. The *Adams Memorial Hall Museum* contains records and relics of the early days, including the first locomotive in the Black Hills which arrived by bull team in 1879.

LEAD
Site of the great *Homestake Gold Mine,* in operation since 1878. Daily tours.

MITCHELL
Arikara Indian Village Site Several acres of concentric rings, 10 to 20 feet in diameter, indicate the location of mud huts which stood here prior to 1700.

MOUNT RUSHMORE NATIONAL MEMORIAL
Gutzon Borglum's famous giant carvings of the faces of Washington, Jefferson, Lincoln, and Theodore Roosevelt are here, near Keystone in the central Black Hills.

PIERRE
Vérendrye Hill and Monument Supposedly the first spot visited by white men in South Dakota. Exploring for a route to India, the Vérendrye brothers stayed here for two weeks in 1743, and buried a lead plate which was discovered by accident in 1913. It is now in the *South Dakota Historical Society Museum.*

PICKSTOWN
Here U.S. 18 crosses the Missouri River over the huge Fort Randall Dam, named for a fort founded in 1856. The ruins of *Fort Randall Church* (1877) are in striking contrast to the great dam.

PINE RIDGE
Pine Ridge Indian Reservation Agency More than 10,000 Oglala Sioux, the largest Indian group in the state, live here in 33 separate communities. Old Indian life and customs persist in some of the remote villages where tribal traditions are maintained.

RAPID CITY
Dinosaur Park Five life-size reptiles modeled in cement stand on a hillside near which their remains have been found. One of the largest collections of Badlands fossils is at the South Dakota State School of Mines and Technology here.
Federal Sioux Indian Museum Interesting collection of Indian relics.

REVA GAP
The *JB Horse Ranch,* in the northwest corner of the state, has existed from the earliest days of white settlement.

SHEEP MOUNTAIN
At the base of the mountain near Scenic,

the State School of Mines and Technology maintains a permanent camp, where students excavate for fossils. This area is a rich source of fossil remains.

SILVER CITY
One of the most interesting Black Hills ghost towns, founded in 1876. Near here is Rochford, another old mining town.

SIOUX FALLS
Pettigrew Museum The former residence of a U.S. senator contains a collection of Indian relics, including a buffalo hide tepee, wampum, tomahawks, and bead work.
Sherman Park Several large Indian mounds are still visible here.

VERMILLION
W. H. Over Museum This museum at the University of South Dakota contains a fine

WATERTOWN CHAMBER OF COMMERCE

Mellette House, Watertown

collection of artifacts from prehistoric Indian villages, Sioux Indian relics, and photographs and objects from the early settlement of the state.

WATERTOWN
Mellette House Home of South Dakota's first governor; now restored as a museum.

WIND CAVE NATIONAL PARK
This is one of the few places where visitors can still glimpse a herd of buffalo, in the game preserve.

WOUNDED KNEE BATTLEFIELD
The Battle of Wounded Knee was the last important conflict between whites and Indians in the United States—the culminating episode of the Sioux religious revival which led to the Ghost Dance War of 1890. The fight occurred on December 29, 1890, when a force of cavalry tried to round up a band of 300 Indians near the present town of Wounded Knee, nine miles east of present-day Pine Ridge. Forty soldiers and 250 Indian men, women, and children were killed.

YANKTON
Walter A. Burleigh House This half-frame, half-chalk home is one of the oldest in the state, and was built in the early 1860's. In the pleasant town are a number of other old houses dating back to Territorial days.

299

TEXAS

ALBANY
Fifteen miles north of town are the ruins of *Fort Griffen,* once a frontier outpost.

ANDERSON
Fanthorp Inn (1834) A mellow Southern Colonial house situated at the former junction of two stagecoach routes. Sam Houston was a frequent visitor, and at the time of the Mexican War Robert E. Lee, Jefferson Davis, and Ulysses S. Grant were here as brother officers.

AUSTIN
Daughters of the Confederacy Museum Contains Confederate relics.
Governor's Mansion Ante-bellum structure open to visitors.
Texas Memorial Museum Historical exhibits are included in its collection.

BANDERA
Frontier Times Museum Contains pioneer relics.

CHIRENO
Old Midway Stagecoach Tavern (early 1840's) First stopping place between the Sabine River and Nacogdoches, located on the Camino Real which extended from Spanish Florida to New Mexico.

DALLAS
John Neely Bryan Cabin The restored log cabin which was built about 1843 by the first citizen of Dallas stands on the courthouse lawn.
Hall of State Here the Dallas Historical Society presents frequent exhibitions.
Hord House (1845) Now recreation center.
Millermore (1855) A Southern Colonial house built by one of Texas' early pioneers. Nearby stands the original Miller home, a log structure. Open on request.

EL PASO
International Museum A collection of Indian, Spanish, and pioneer relics.

FORT DAVIS
Old Fort Davis (1854) Picturesque buildings of a typical frontier outpost.

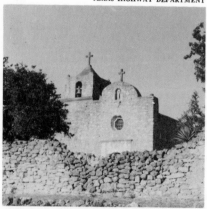

La Bahia, Goliad

FREDERICKSBURG
A town founded by German colonists in 1846 which preserves much of the old atmosphere. Notable buildings are the *Vereinskirche,* an octagonal structure, now a museum, which served as a community center. Also of interest are the *Tatsch House,* old stores, and a *"Sunday House,"* where farm families who lived outside of town were housed on the Sabbath.

GALVESTON
Legends of early visits by Narváez, Cabeza de Vaca, and La Salle center on the island which was named for a Spanish governor of Louisiana. Early in the 1800's pirates made it their base, and Jean Lafitte filled the bay with his ships. A ramshackle house named for him may have been built after a hurricane destroyed his famous Maison Rouge. French gabled houses, Spanish haciendas, and Louisiana bayou-style homes spot the old quarter. The *Williams House* (1838) belongs to the bayou tradition. *The Oaks* (1838) is Greek Revival, and the *Bishop's Castle,* built after the Civil War, is a Victorian extravaganza. *Shady Villa,* a stagecoach inn, stood at the crossroads of a Chisholm Trail branch and the Old Military Road. The *George Ball House* (1857) is an impressive Greek Revival building (open in the spring); and the dignified *Powhatan House* (1847) was an early hotel.

GOLIAD
The Spanish presidio, *La Bahia* (now partly ruined), and the *Mission Espiritu Santo* (restored) were established here about 1749. Texans proclaimed their independence here in 1835 before the official declaration, and Colonel James Fannin and his 350 men were captured by Santa Anna and executed where a monument now stands. The *Boyd House* (1846) and *Peck House* (1842) are open to visitors.

GONZALES
Eggleston House (c. 1840) Built when townspeople returned to their burned village after Santa Anna's defeat. In this town the first battle of the Texas revolution was fought in 1835, and Sam Houston addressed the residents under a huge oak which still stands here.

HEMPSTEAD
Liendo (1853) Greek Revival plantation house with balustered double veranda, in a beautiful setting. Open by appointment.

HOUSTON
Sam Houston Park Contains the *Noble House* (1842) and the *Cherry House,* built in the 1850's. The former has two stories, but no stairs. A ladder was used to reach the upper floor.

HUNTSVILLE
Sam Houston Home In this memorial park are the small white cottage where Houston, his wife, and eight children lived, the General's log-and-plaster law office, the kitchen house, carriage house; and the unusual

Steamboat House, where the "Raven" died in 1863.

INDEPENDENCE
Once the cultural and social center of the young Republic of Texas, Independence (near Brenham) declined with the removal of Baylor College, of which ruins remain. Nearby are the *Hoxie House* (c. 1830), opposite the site of Sam Houston's residence; the *Robertson House* (1845), home of the commander of the famous Civil War Texas Brigade; and the little stone *Baptist Church* where Sam Houston was baptized in 1854. The *Lea House* was the home of Houston's mother-in-law. The one Spanish-style building is the adobe *Toalson House* (1835), once a Mexican jail. The *Seward Plantation,* a mile from Independence, has a hand-hewn cedar house and many outbuildings.

JEFFERSON
During the Jefferson Pilgrimage a number of historic houses are open to visitors in this town, which was an early cotton-shipping port. Among them are the *Old Presbyterian Manse* (1839), the oldest residence in the town; the *Alley-Carlson Home;* *Old Jefferson House* (1860's), which is now an antique shop; *Catalpa Villa* (c. 1852); and the white Colonial *Guarding Oak,* one of the handsomest early Texas homes, built in 1859. The *Excelsior Hotel* is a well-restored structure of heavy timbers and brick; and the *Freeman Plantation House,* built about 1850, and *Blue Bonnet Farm* are other houses which are open during the annual Pilgrimage.

LANGTRY
Jersey Lily Saloon Contains the "hall of justice" presided over by the famous Judge Roy Bean.

NACOGDOCHES
Peter Ellis Bean House (c. 1829) One of many homes of the "Ingenuous Colonel" who served in the Mexican Army and with Lafitte at the Battle of New Orleans. Private.

Sam Houston Home, Huntsville

Old Stone Fort (c. 1780) The original fort, built by Spaniards, has been restored with the old stones. The town was one of the earliest settlements.

Adolphus Sterne House (1830) Home of a Texas patriot. Grounds are open.

NEW BRAUNFELS

House on Seguin Street (late 1840's) Dates from the early German colonists.

RIO GRANDE CITY

Fort Ringgold Grant, Lee, Jackson, and Pershing were stationed here as young officers.

SAN ANGELO

Fort Concho Museum Pioneer relics are housed in one building of the fort.

SAN ANTONIO

The Alamo (Mission San Antonio de Valero, 1744) Once the heart of Spanish and Mexican power in Texas, where the most famous battle of Texan independence was fought in 1836 (see p. 284). A cenotaph in the plaza commemorates the heroes of the fight, and the museum contains relics of Bowie, Crockett, Travis, and other Alamo immortals.

Nat Lewis House Ante-bellum structure of cut stone, with original smokehouse and slave quarters in the rear. Private.

Mission Concepcion (1731) Built of adobe and tufa rock, with square towers and Moorish dome. Fine entrance.

Mission San Francisco de la Espada (1731) Little remains of this once extensive mission, except the façade and hilt-shaped bell tower.

Mission San José (1731-79) Considered the most beautiful of the Texas missions, it still suggests the power and spaciousness of

TEXAS HIGHWAY DEPARTMENT

Mission Señora del Carmen, Ysleta

the Spanish outposts. The mission is enclosed within a six-acre quadrangle whose ramparts formed the outer walls of the dwellings of the mission Indians. Many statues in the elaborately carved façade are intact, and the rose window of the sacristy is a masterpiece. Cloisters, garden, and mission mill are also worth visiting (see p. 311).

Mission San Juan de Capistrano (1731) Like other missions, this one was moved to San Antonio from another site. The main buildings form part of the rampart walls, illustrating its double function as church and fort.

Ruiz House (1745) A reconstructed home which originally stood on the Military Plaza.

San Fernando Cathedral For 200 years the center of the community's religious life.

Spanish Governors' Palace (1749) Where royal governors of the province lived until the end of Spanish rule in 1821. The keystone above the entrance bears the Hapsburg coat of arms, and furnishings and patio garden have been restored.

John Twohig House (1841) Restored house which was the home of an early merchant.

La Villita The oldest settlement in the city, restored with furnishings and patios, composes a "little village" of adobe and rock houses. In the **Cos House** (early 1800's) the Mexican General Cos signed articles of capitulation after his defeat by Texans in 1835.

SAN AUGUSTINE

Blount House (1839) Rambling house built by Colonel S. W. Blount, a signer of the Texas declaration of independence.

SAN FELIPE

Stephen F. Austin State Park A few traces remain of the town where the first American settlement was made in 1822. A replica of the log cabin where Austin lived has been built in the park beside a well dug by colonists in 1824.

SAN JACINTO

East of Houston, stone markers indicate the course of the 1836 battle which decided Texan independence. In the base of the massive **Battle Monument** is a museum.

WASHINGTON-ON-THE-BRAZOS

Anson Jones House (1844) A simple frame house owned by the last president of the Republic of Texas. Nearby is a replica of the building in which the Texas declaration of independence was drafted.

YSLETA

Mission Señora del Carmen The oldest Texas mission, founded 1682.

OVERLEAF: ESTHER HENDERSON, RAPHO-GUILLUMETTE

The Spanish Southwest

Deserted since the thirteenth century, the well-concealed pueblos of Mesa Verde in Colorado remained almost unnoticed until two cowboys happened upon them in 1888.

America's First Dwellings

Nearly every section of the United States bears the mark of prehistoric man, but nowhere is the evidence more spectacular than in the Southwest. Here, 200 years before Columbus' voyage, complex and highly developed societies flourished and then vanished, leaving some of the most fascinating monuments on the North American continent, preserved for centuries by the unique dry climate.

On a snowy December day in 1888 two cowboys named Wetherill and Mason, searching for missing cattle in the wild canyons of southwestern Colorado, rode to the top of a mesa and from a clearing in the junipers and piñon brush suddenly saw a vast cliff ruin nestled in the wall of the canyon opposite them. Above and below the immense ruins, snow fell on the face of the cliff; but the silent city of stone remained untouched by the weather, as it had for centuries. Wetherill and Mason were probably the first men to explore the site in six centuries.

Other men knew of its existence, of course. The Spanish priest and explorer Escalante had seen the ruins and named them Mesa Verde in 1776, but he had not stopped to investigate. The Utes in the region feared these "cities of the dead," and kept their distance. In 1874 a government surveying party led by the photographer W. H. Jackson noted the site of some Mesa Verde ruins, but not until the two cowboys went there was their enormous scope recognized. Since then the 52,000-acre Mesa Verde has been made into a national park where the visitor may see some of the most dramatic and extensive prehistoric ruins ever found.

Ancient men who crossed the 54-mile strait between Siberia and Alaska thousands of years ago eventually worked their way south to Colorado and New Mexico. At Folsom, New Mexico, archaeologists have unearthed chipped dart points near the bones of large bison known to have roamed the region 20,000 years ago. But little is known of the earliest American except that he was a nomadic hunter. About the time of Christ, Indians called Basket Makers settled in the Mesa Verde region, attracted by the fertile land. Their finely woven, decorative baskets of yucca fibre were used for many household purposes, and the Indians lived in caves in which they dug small pits for the storage of corn. The round ceremonial chamber, called kiva, still in evidence in modern pueblos, is an outgrowth of this first primitive reverence for corn.

The next stage in the development of these ancient people is known as the Modified Basket Maker Period, which lasted from A.D. 400 to A.D. 750, an era when the bow and arrow were first used and pottery gradually replaced the basket. At Mesa Verde there are hundreds of pit houses dating back to this period. The next, or Early Pueblo Period, extended from A.D. 750 to A.D. 1100. The pit houses were modified, and became actual stone and adobe houses with vertical walls. Rectangular in shape, and often three or four stories high, they had open courts with circular ceremonial kivas in front. Far View House and Sun Point Pueblo at Mesa Verde are superb examples of the mason's art which was developed at the end of this period.

About 1100 the Pueblo Indians moved into the most advanced stage of their civilization, known as the Great or Classic Pueblo Period, which was to last approximately 200 years. This was the era of huge communal dwellings like Spruce Tree House, Square Tower House, and the remarkable Cliff Palace.

Then, in the year 1276, a terrible 24-year drought began in the San Juan and Colorado River basins. By the start of the fourteenth century, the vast cliff cities had been deserted, never to be inhabited again. Unquestionably many of the Indians perished, while others moved into eastern Arizona, south to Zuñi country, and east to the Rio Grande—areas still occupied by modern Pueblo Indians.

Although Mesa Verde is one of the largest and best-preserved prehistoric pueblos, it is but one of many. Not far from it are Hovenweep and Yucca, also in Colorado, and to the south in New Mexico are extensive remains of two other centers of culture—Aztec and Chaco Canyon. Around Chaco are ruins of eleven great apartment house dwellings, the largest ever uncovered in America, and Aztec has some of the best-preserved ruins in the country. The spectacular Navajo National Park in northeast Arizona includes Betatakin, Keet Seel, and Inscription House, and not far to the east are the sheer red sandstone cliffs of Canyon de Chelly, with its White House ruins. Between Santa Fe and Taos in New Mexico are remains of the last flowering of pueblo culture. The Indians who left the Colorado River basin settled at what is now Bandelier National Monument; but when Coronado visited this latter region in 1550 it was half deserted, and fifty years later the abandonment was complete.

These Indian petroglyphs are at Indian Creek, Utah. Long ago, the White House in Canyon de Chelly (below) was connected to the valley floor by a tower, now destroyed.

The Cities of Gold

For Spaniards the sixteenth century was the time of a vision of gold—a vision that drew men toward the western horizon in a search that brought discoveries, conquest, and deeds of courage almost beyond parallel in the history of mankind. In less than thirty years, Spaniards discovered the Pacific, sailed around the world, conquered huge segments of South America and Mexico, found the great rivers of the Americas, and explored the North American wilderness—all a century before England thought about colonizing the New World. Any story about the fabulous lands to the west could be believed—after all, it was but fifty years since men had doubted the very existence of such a world. There were the stories of Cortés, of Cabeza de Vaca, and, in 1539, those of Father Marcos de Niza, who told of the Seven Cities of Cibola.

This was a land "rich in gold, silver and other wealth," where the people were "very rich, the women even wearing belts of gold." As the conquistadors argued over who should conquer this new land, Hernando de Soto set out toward Florida in 1539, while Francisco Coronado, a thirty-year-old nobleman, left Mexico in 1540. In glittering armor, floating plume, and brilliant cape, he led an army of 1,500 (including Fray Marcos and other missionaries) north across deserts, mountain ranges, and deep forests, finally arriving five months later at Hawikuh, a Zuñi pueblo. This, it seemed, was Fray Marcos' Cibola—a few hovels of clay and stone built upon a high rock. No city of gold, it was an adobe pueblo "all crumpled together," with narrow streets, a filthy watercourse, and barren land all around. Perhaps Fray Marcos tried to explain how, from afar, in the light of the setting sun, he had mistaken it for a city of gold, but for Coronado and his

men it was a bitter disappointment. So often the dream ended thus. A year later Coronado and his army headed east to search for Quivira, a wondrous land of abundance, only to find a drab settlement of Wichita Indians near what is now Lyons, Kansas.

Although the vision of wealth and glory persisted, it was sixty years after Coronado's expedition before a serious effort was made to colonize New Mexico. In 1598 Juan de Oñate, a wealthy grandee equipped with six complete suits of armor, set out with 130 families, 270 single men, the first wheeled vehicles to enter the region, and 7,000 cattle—the ancestors of a vast cattle and sheep empire. After passing through the Jornada del Muerto, they settled in San Gabriel del Yunque, first Spanish capital of New Mexico. But like other conquistadors, Oñate was no sedentary man, and for ten more years he journeyed through the Southwest, forever hoping to find Quivira.

Thirty-five miles east of Zuñi Pueblo in New Mexico a sheer sandstone butte called El Morro, or Inscription Rock, bears over 500 Spanish inscriptions, many left by disillusioned conquistadors. One states: "Passed by here the Adelantado Don Juan de Oñate from the discovery of the sea of the south, the sixteenth of April of 1605." (Oñate was on his way back from learning that the Gulf of California was not overflowing with pearls). Another message here expresses pointedly the spirit of that remarkable era: "Here was the General Don Diego de Vargas, who conquered to our Holy Faith and to the Royal Crown all the New Mexico at his own expense, year of 1692."

From afar, in the light of the setting sun, adobe pueblos like Walpi looked like cities of gold to the Spaniards.

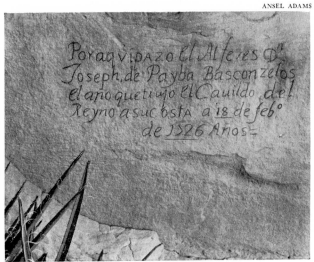

East of Zuñi Pueblo in New Mexico is the towering butte called El Morro, or Inscription Rock, on which more than 500 Spanish writings are carved. The earliest was left there in 1605 by Oñate, returning from the Gulf of California.

The adobe Taos Pueblo has been occupied continuously by the Indians for centuries. Ladders provide the only access to their four- and five-story community houses.

The Three Cultures of Taos

Seventy-five miles north of Santa Fe, in a small, fertile valley east of the Rio Grande gorge, is Taos —symbol of the Indian, Spanish, and American societies that created the Southwest as we know it. Unlike most villages of this area which lie unprotected in the hot, dazzling sun, Taos is sheltered, remote, almost gloomy in the protective shade of the Sangre de Cristo Mountains, which rise sharply behind it.

The Pueblo, often considered the handsomest of all remaining Indian villages, has been continuously occupied for over 200 years. Behind it looms the sacred Taos mountain, with a lake high on its slopes where "the gods still live." The Pueblo itself consists of two terraced community houses four and five stories high, made of a deep gold adobe. Tall ladders provide the only access to upper stories, and other ladders indicate the presence of subterranean kivas, carefully protected from outside intrusion.

In the days when nomads roamed the Southwest, Taos was visited regularly by Plains Indians, and the

Indians of Taos Pueblo—possibly of ancient Kiowan stock—differ from other pueblo tribes. They are taller, handsomer, with sharper features, and the men wear their hair in long braids in Plains Indian fashion. These are people of an independent Indian tribe who have resisted white domination, who have lived next to a non-Indian community without making concessions to the white man's ways. In Taos the Indian leader Popé won his first adherents to the united Pueblo Revolt against the Spanish in 1680; here the Indians rebelled again in 1696; and here they joined the Spanish resistance to American rule in 1847.

In the sixteenth century members of Coronado's expedition decided to settle in Taos, and until the Pueblo Revolt, Spaniards and Indians lived peaceably together. After the Spanish put down the rebellion of 1696 the town grew and prospered as a market center, and long before Americans had seen Taos, traders from all over the West came to its summer fairs. There were French with furs and guns,

Mexicans with silver, Navajos with blankets and pottery, Utes bringing captives to sell as slaves, Comanches offering buffalo robes and booty from their raids.

Sometime around 1730 the Spaniards built at Ranchos de Taos a few miles away the fortress-like adobe Church of Saint Francis of Assisi, whose thick walls and beautifully proportioned apse make it a classic example of strength and dignity. A few years later, mountain men began penetrating the region around Taos, and they found the town the one place west of St. Louis where they could meet civilized women and buy bread, coffee, and sugar. One who stayed to make Taos his home was Kit Carson.

Here one may still see the simple adobe house which was Carson's base for the rest of his life. Carson guided Frémont on two expeditions to the Pacific, led Kearny into California, and conquered the Navajos. He was one of the supreme products of his time and place, and although he died on an expedition to Colorado, it is fitting that he was brought to the simple cemetery in Taos for burial, near the Spaniards and Indians who, like himself, had made this entire section a unique portion of America.

A fortress-like adobe structure built about 1730, the Church of Saint Francis of Assisi combines strength and dignity.

Although the altar is relatively modern, the pictorial reredos of the Taos church probably dates back to its founding.

Spanish Missions

Tumacacori, built in Arizona in 1793

El Santuario of Chimayó, in New Mexico

Santa Barbara, "Queen of the Missions"

W here the sword of Spain went, there went the cross, sometimes following, sometimes leading the way. The armored conquistadors never found their cities of gold, but the men in ragged brown robes with crosses swinging from their waists located the sort of treasure they sought—heathens to be converted for the glory of God. Out of the intense religious fervor burning in Spain came missionary efforts of unmatched magnitude, and all through the Southwest—from Texas to southern California—the landscape is still a space between the missions established there by steadfast, courageous Fathers three centuries ago.

Beginning in 1540, these men endowed the Southwest with some of its handsomest architecture and most interesting historical structures, varying in style from the crudest adobe churches to magnificent baroque cathedrals. Generally speaking, the padres adapted the simple pueblo architecture, adding European touches in the ornamentation. The missions were built of adobe because of the scarcity of wood, and inside the plain façades were brilliantly decorated altars, elaborate carvings, and, because the Indians frequently assisted in the decoration, a conspicuous use of bold, almost pagan symbolism, with strong forms and vivid colors.

Of five missions begun after 1718 near San Antonio, Texas, the most ambitious was San José, which was carefully restored in 1933. Of more than a dozen Arizona missions, only one remains in use today—San Xavier del Bac, which dates from the period of Father Kino, the energetic Jesuit who established 24 missions in the New World. Soaring upward from the sagebrush and cactus-covered valley, San Xavier's luminous white walls create the startling effect shown on pages 302 and 303, like a great, shining mirage in the desert. Forty-three separate missions had been established in New Mexico by 1640, among them the fine examples at Taos, Acoma, and Laguna.

The fourth mission field was in California, along the 500 miles of coast between San Diego and San Francisco, where one can find the largest number of well-preserved Spanish churches. This great chain of missions, begun in 1769 by the remarkable Father Junipero Serra, comprised for half a century the only civilized outposts in that area, and the vineyards, irrigation canals, and farming practices introduced then had a permanent effect on this section of the country. With their red tile roofs, shaded patios, and graceful entrances, the California missions possess a charm seldom equaled elsewhere.

At the rear of San José Mission in San Antonio, Texas, is the arched cloister illustrated above. The beautifully carved figures shown here (above right, and below) are in San Xavier del Bac, the only Arizona mission to survive almost intact.

Of all Texas missions, the most impressive is San José y San Miguel de Aguayo. Completed in 1779, the San Antonio mission is noted for its ornamented façade and beautiful rose window. Allowed to decay after 1794, it was restored in 1933.

The colorful Hopi *kachina* dolls shown in each corner represent divine intermediaries between men and gods, and are used to teach children the difference between the spirits.

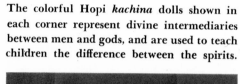

DOLLS, BRACELET, AND BRIDLE: FPG
OTHERS: MUSEUM OF THE AMERICAN INDIAN

At right is an ancient Zuñi pottery jar; at left, an Apache basket; top, an Apache baby carrier; above, an early turquoise bracelet; and on the opposite page, a Hopi shirt.

The Navajos learned silver work in the nineteenth century from itinerant Mexican silversmiths, and became extremely skillful. This bridle is an example of their craftsmanship.

Turquoise, Silver, and Sand

Some of the most interesting aspects of Indian life in the Southwest today are the unusual and beautiful art forms developed by the Indians who live in that area. In the Painted Desert of Arizona, the Hopis live in pueblos little changed since pre-Columbian times, making their distinctive baskets, pottery, textiles, and the brilliant *kachina* dolls shown on the facing page. Hand-carved and beautifully painted, the dolls represent divine spirits who act as intermediaries between man and the gods, and are used to teach the young the differences between the complicated spirit forms. Until recently the Hopis did little work in silver, because it reminded them too clearly of their years of servitude under the Spanish who used silver trinkets to reward or bribe them; but they have overcome this old prejudice and now make exceptionally handsome silver and turquoise jewelry.

Under the influence of the Hopis, the Navajos learned the art of weaving which was to become a hallmark of their culture, and began to practice sand painting, one of the most unusual forms of worship in existence. More than 500 separate sand paintings are known to exist, each one a distinctive ritual through which the Navajos believe that the sick may be healed. Another acquired skill of the Navajos is silversmithing, which they picked up from itinerant Mexicans.

Like most nomadic peoples, the Apaches developed few arts which are comparable to those of more sedentary tribes, but their religion, like those practiced by the Hopis and Navajos, is noteworthy for its elaborate rituals and colorful dances.

J. H. MC GIBBENY, *Arizona Highways*

A form of worship, the elaborate Navajo sand paintings are made to heal patients and are destroyed as rites are completed.

No one knows how long Indians have lived at Ácoma pueblo on top of this sandstone butte, but the village was an ancient one whe

Ácoma: City

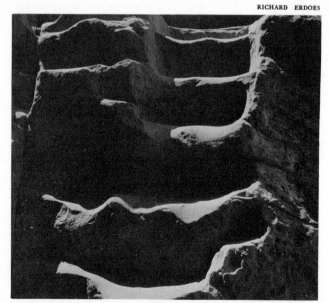

The trails leading up to Ácoma have toe and finger holes cut in the rock centuries ago, worn smooth by moccasined feet.

One of the Southwest's magnificent sights—a scene no visitor is apt to forget—is seventeen miles south of Highway 66 in New Mexico, at the end of a drive across barren, arroyo-cut wasteland. Suddenly one sees, rising out of an immense plain, two enormous buttes whose sheer cliffs tower nearly 400 feet in the air. One is the Enchanted Mesa, the other is Ácoma, city of the sky. No one knows how long Indians lived at Ácoma, but it was already an ancient village when Coronado's men came there in 1540.

From a distance it is difficult to see the 200-odd flat-roofed adobe buildings which seem to merge into the rock itself; and it takes a keen eye to spot the steep trails leading to the pueblo high above. One is the famous "ladder trail," with ancient toe and finger holes cut in the rock and worn smooth and deep by thousands of moccasined feet. In 1540 this was the only access to the pueblo, and it is easy to understand a Spaniard's comment that "no army could possibly be strong enough to capture the village."

Coronado's men saw it in 1540. The only access to the stronghold is by way of steep, narrow trails from the desert floor below.

of the Sky

Yet Ácoma was taken in 1598 by Don Juan de Oñate, whose soldiers found an unguarded pathway up the cliff and slaughtered all but 300 of the 3,000 Ácomas. Not until 1629 was a mission established there, when Fray Juan Ramirez chose to minister to "the most rebellious of all tribes." Alone and unafraid, he walked from Santa Fe to Ácoma, where he was pelted with arrows and stones. On his way up to the summit he is said to have caught and saved the life of a child who fell from the cliff, after which he was welcomed by the Ácomas. Ramirez built the great church of San Esteban Rey which dominates the southern end of the mesa like a huge fortress. Inside it are enormous beams forty feet long, carried on the shoulders of Indians from Mt. Taylor, thirty miles away. The walls are sixty feet high and ten feet thick, of remarkable adobe construction. Today some 1,500 Indians engaged in agriculture and pottery making still occupy the long terraced dwellings of the pueblo and carry on life in the ancient city of the sky.

DAVID E. SCHERMAN, *Life*

The weathered adobe convent at Ácoma is described by author Willa Cather in *Death Comes For The Archbishop.*

Santa Fe's Governors' Palace was the seat of Spanish government for 130 years.

The Santa Fe Trail

All the anguish, the struggle, the blood and toil which Spain had put into its New World empire came to naught in 1821 with the success of a revolution in Mexico. Along with their independence, the Mexicans put an end to the old Spanish commercial restrictions, and in 1822 William Becknell left Franklin, Missouri, on his second successful trading mission to Santa Fe. Within a few years the wagon ruts along Becknell's route deepened and became wide enough to be distinguished as the first great western trail—the Santa Fe.

From Independence, out across the Kansas plains it stretched, past Council Grove, Pawnee Rock, and on to Cimarron Crossing of the Arkansas. There the trail divided—one branch continuing west along the Arkansas River into Colorado to Bent's Fort, then southwest across the mountains to Raton Pass, and Las Vegas. The more dangerous southern branch crossed the hot, dry land between the Arkansas and Cimarron Rivers, into Colorado and Oklahoma, down through the northeast corner of New Mexico, past Wagon Mound to Las Vegas, where the two sections of the trail merged and went on to Taos and Sante Fe. This was Indian country—hunting grounds of the deadly Apaches, Utes, Kiowas, and Comanches, whose raids on wagon trains and isolated ranches went on for five decades.

At the strategic junction of the Santa Fe Trail's two forks, in the heart of the Mora River Valley, stood Fort Union, built in 1851 as the largest and most important garrison in the Southwest. Today it lies in the midst of cattle country, row after row of roofless adobe walls jutting up from the prairie, tall brick chimneys piercing the sky like ghostly sentinels of the past. For in 1891, when the Indian menace had been largely eliminated, Fort Union was abandoned to vandals and the weather, its purpose accomplished. Near the deserted ruins one can still see the ruts of the Santa Fe Trail, irregular furrows worn so wide and deep that a century of dust storms have not obliterated them.

From Fort Union it is about 100 miles by modern road to Santa Fe, where the trail ended in the foothills of the Sangre de Cristo Mountains. Along narrow streets shaded by towering cottonwood trees are many old adobe houses and the mission of San Miguel, built early in the seventeenth century by Spaniards for their Tlascalan Indian servants from Mexico. But the most interesting historical structure in this picturesque town is the Palace of the Governors, the oldest public building in the country.

Ten years before the first English colony was founded in Massachusetts, Don Pedro de Peralta, third Spanish governor of the province of New Mexico, moved the capital from San Gabriel to Santa Fe and began work on the presidio. Completed in 1612, it consisted of a rectangular walled fort measuring about 400 feet by 800 feet, enclosing soldiers' barracks, storerooms, stables, parade ground, and servants' rooms; and in the Palace proper, the residence of the governor and his family, and various governmental offices. For seventy years, the community at Santa Fe survived

316

the difficulties of isolation in an unfriendly land; but when the Pueblo Revolt erupted in 1680, the thousand Spaniards were forced to abandon their capital. The victorious Indians destroyed the church and turned the chapel into a kiva for their own use, sacked the Spanish homes, and for thirteen years remained in the town until they were ousted by the Spaniards. For 128 years the Palace remained the seat of Spanish government. Then in 1821 the Mexican Republic took over, and in 1846 General Stephen Kearny's troops marched into Santa Fe to proclaim it U.S. territory.

Santa Fe, the terminus of the Trail, may have been a "ragamuffin capital," but the bustling community was nevertheless one which travelers from Independence looked forward to with unbounded enthusiasm. And even though the volume of trade over the road was never spectacular, its continuation dispelled many

fears about the "Great American Desert," and did much to hasten settlement of the West. No American traveling the Santa Fe Trail failed to notice the tenuous Mexican hold on the Southwest, and the route thus contributed psychologically to the idea of Manifest Destiny.

Few plots of ground in America have witnessed such a variety of history as the Governors' Palace and the plaza in Santa Fe. Warring Indians, proud conquistadors, Mexicans, mountain men, American hunters, traders, trail drivers, and Civil War soldiers —all have made their mark on this small community. And in spite of alterations, and the twentieth-century influx of artists, anthropologists, tourists, and atomic scientists, the plaza is still the place where old men sit in the sun and chat in Spanish, where Indians from neighboring pueblos come, as they have for three centuries, to sell their wares.

Near the deserted ruins of Fort Union, wagon ruts of the Santa Fe Trail are still visible. Built in 1851 to protect travelers and settlers from attack by Southwest Indian tribes, the fort developed into a thriving settlement before it was finally abandoned in 1891.

Tombstone's City Hall has been used since 1882.

The Lawless Years

Today the town of Lincoln, New Mexico, is a quiet, dusty little community in the heart of stock-raising country. A round stone tower called El Torreón, built as a fortification against Indians by settlers in 1852, stands in the center of town, and the old Lincoln County Courthouse offers a collection of frontier relics. In this sleepy town there is little to indicate that it was the vortex of a bitter, all-out frontier feud which reached such proportions that President Hayes ordered General Lew Wallace to establish law and order, with federal troops if necessary.

In the 1870's Lincoln County covered almost one-fifth of the present state and included four of today's counties. Its 27,000 square miles of rich grazing lands lay in a broad valley between the Rio Grande and Pecos River—a remote territory isolated by surrounding desert, into which thieves, murderers, gamblers, and rustlers naturally drifted. The Lincoln County War, which lasted from 1876 to 1878, resulted from an explosive mixture of homesteaders, squatters, farmers, and cattlemen, all vying for land and water rights, thrown into a hopper with as nasty a group of badmen as it would be possible to assemble anywhere.

The wars themselves achieved widespread and unsavory reputation, but this was pale by comparison with that of an eighteen-year-old punk who was right in the thick of them. He was William H. Bonney, or Billy the Kid, and he was already well-launched on a career of crime when he arrived in Lincoln County.

Billy's reputation as the fastest, deadliest shot in the West was second only to Wild Bill Hickok's, and during his short life he conducted a vicious shooting spree that earned him notoriety as the most sought-after desperado in the Southwest. By the time he was 21 he was dead, but his legend persists to this day—sometimes in a form that makes him out to be a sort of Robin Hood, kind to little children and a friend of the poor. In truth, Billy was a mean thief and professional gambler, a fearless killer who had a remarkable genius for saving his own skin while taking the lives of others.

The same year that Billy the Kid rode into Lincoln, a prospector named Ed Schieffelin ventured into the desolate, dangerous hills of southeastern Arizona and put another community on the map. An army scout had warned him: "All you'll find in those hills, Schieffelin, is your own tombstone." So when the prospector stumbled on one of the richest silver lodes ever discovered in the Southwest, he dubbed the site Tombstone.

When news of his spectacular find spread, a great rush began, and fortune hunters descended in droves to build little communities like Bisbee, Galeyville, Contention City, and Charleston almost overnight. But for lawlessness and local color, none of them equaled Tombstone. Like its name, the town's setting seemed an invitation to badmen. In wild, lonely land gouged with arid gulches and surrounded by forbidding desert, it was still a stronghold of defiant Apaches and a perfect hideout for rustlers and murderers avoiding the law. Within a few years after Schieffelin's strike, it had a population of 7,000. As in other boom towns, its main street was a crazy patchwork of hastily-constructed buildings, and at one time there were 110 places licensed to sell liquor. Its most famous attractions were the Bird Cage burlesque theater and the Crystal Palace gambling casino. It had five newspapers—one of them the *Epitaph,* still operating as the state's oldest continuously published weekly journal.

Boot Hill graveyard, an unfenced, desolate plot, provides evidence of Tombstone's wilder days, with epitaphs like "Margarita Stabbed by Gold Dollar," and "George Johnson, hanged by mistake." Among the town's notable early residents were the famous Wyatt Earp and an Episcopal minister, the Reverend Endicott Peabody, who later became headmaster of Groton School.

In 1886 the mines were flooded, and by 1900 Tombstone was nearly deserted. Today it is a quiet community, pockmarked by abandoned shafts, rows of deserted houses and saloons, and enough of the old landmarks to keep alive the legend of those wild days of the 1880's.

FROM *Wyatt Earp, Frontier Marshal,* BY STUART LAKE; HOUGHTON MIFFLIN CO.

ARIZONA PHOTOGRAPHIC ASSOCIATES, INC.

An epic Tombstone battle was the climax of the Earp-Clanton feud (above) in 1881. At the O.K. Corral three of the Clanton gang were killed and Wyatt Earp's two brothers were wounded, all within sixty seconds. Below is Billy the Kid, to whom legend ascribes one killing for each of his 21 years of life. At right is Tombstone's notorious Boot Hill cemetery.

ED BARTHOLOMEW

The Indians' Last Stand

As the nineteenth century slipped into its final quarter, a war which had been going on for three hundred years approached its inevitable and ugly denouement. This was the desperate struggle in which nearly all the Indians of North America had been engaged since the Spanish landed in Mexico—the fight to preserve their lands against the fateful tide of white settlement. On a Montana hillside the Sioux and Cheyennes put off the final reckoning by destroying George Armstrong Custer and his Seventh Cavalry troop in 1876. In the Northwest, in 1877, Chief Joseph and his Nez Perces were trying to fight their way to Canada and safety; and in the Southwest, the Apaches were making a last, desperate stand.

For seven centuries the mountains and plains of New Mexico and southern Arizona had been Apache hunting grounds. Marvelous horsemen, capable of astounding feats of endurance, the Apaches waged war as a business and a way of life, and only the Comanches exceeded them in ferocity and brutality. During two centuries of Spanish and Mexican rule, Apache raids helped keep the wild deserts and mountains uncivilized and unoccupied, and this section of the country still looks as if there might be Indians lurking behind the rocks or in steep gullies.

In the southeast corner of Arizona, where the Dos Cabezas and Chiricahua mountains meet, is Apache Pass, once the most dangerous spot on the southern stage route to California. At the eastern end of the pass are the crumbled ruins of Fort Bowie, one of the forts erected in the 1860's to protect travelers against attacks led by Mangas Coloradas, Cochise, Victorio, Nana, or Geronimo, whose names brought terror to settlers for fifty years. There is the grotesquely eroded canyon country of Chiricahua National Monument, ancestral home of the Apaches; and Stronghold Canyon, in the Dragoon Mountains, where the remarkable chief Cochise held out for twelve years.

After the deaths of Cochise and of Victorio, who was the most ruthless of all Apache leaders, Chief Nana took up the struggle against the whites, and in 1881, he and forty warriors conducted one of the most spectacularly successful Apache forays. Traveling as much as eighty miles a day over rough country, he led his men 1,200 miles through hostile territory, pursued all the way by American cavalry. Arriving unscathed in Mexico, he had raided everywhere he traveled, fought eight successful battles, killed up to fifty whites, captured 200 horses and mules, and had eluded more than a thousand soldiers and hundreds of civilians. And Nana was seventy years old, and crippled with arthritis!

By 1882 General George Crook was back in Arizona after the Sioux campaigns, and if it had not been for Geronimo, might have subdued the Apaches immediately. Geronimo, whose real name was Goyathlay, or "One Who Yawns," said that he lived for one reason only—to kill whites. After a string of successes, Geronimo was captured by Crook and brought to the reservation; but within weeks, the chief and 32 warriors slipped away to fight again.

For three years Geronimo rode back and forth across the Mexican border, leaving a trail of death and destruction in his wake. In 1886, Crook again captured him, only to lose him once more. After this escape, Crook asked to be relieved, and was replaced by another famous Indian fighter, General Nelson A. Miles. For five months Miles' troopers combed the countryside for the Apache until finally, worn down by the chase, his supplies gone, Geronimo and his band met Miles and agreed to surrender. Near the present town of Apache, in the rugged, mountainous area of Skeleton Canyon, the centuries of Indian fighting ended at last, on September 3, 1886.

For fourteen years Geronimo and his band of Apaches terrorized ranchers and settlers on both sides of the U.S.-Mexican border. He is shown below (center) with his bodyguard before a conference with General Crook in 1886. At right is a vivid moment in an Apache Mountain Spirit Dance.

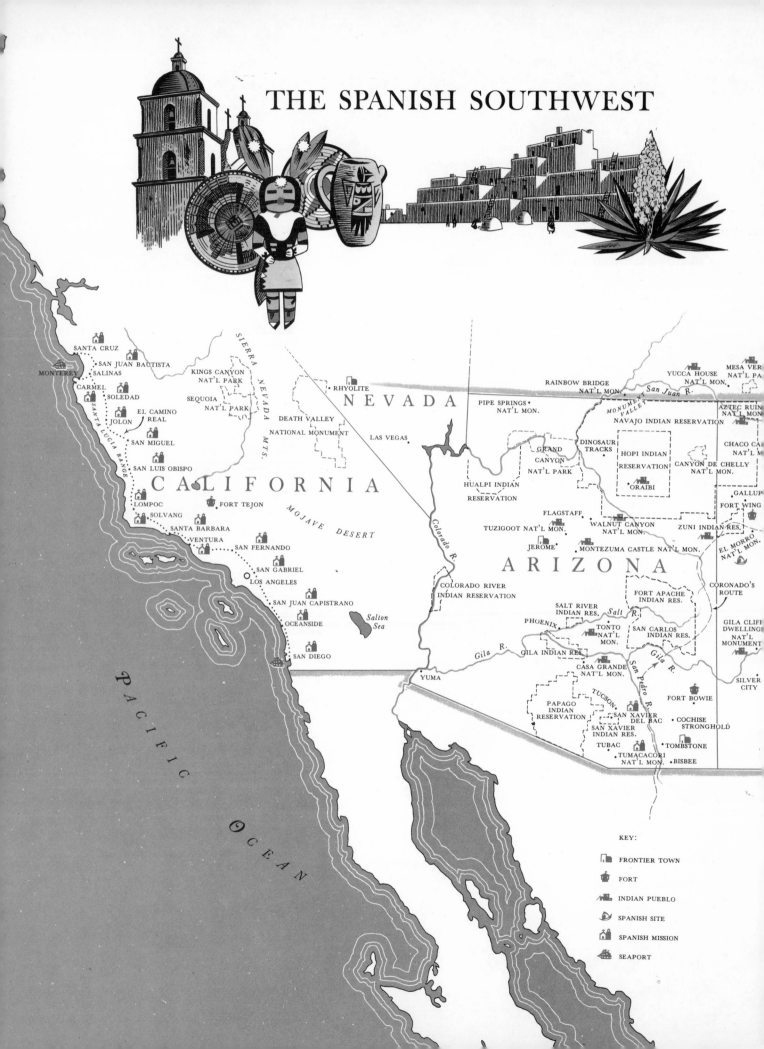

THE SPANISH SOUTHWEST

MONTEREY
SANTA CRUZ
SAN JUAN BAUTISTA
SALINAS
CARMEL
SOLEDAD
JOLON
EL CAMINO REAL
SAN MIGUEL
SAN LUIS OBISPO

SIERRA NEVADA MTS.

KINGS CANYON NAT'L PARK
SEQUOIA NAT'L PARK

RHYOLITE

NEVADA

DEATH VALLEY NATIONAL MONUMENT
LAS VEGAS

RAINBOW BRIDGE NAT'L MON.
San Juan R.

PIPE SPRINGS NAT'L MON.

YUCCA HOUSE NAT'L MON.
MESA VER NAT'L PA

MONUMENT VALLEY

NAVAJO INDIAN RESERVATION

AZTEC RUIN NAT'L MON

DINOSAUR TRACKS
HOPI INDIAN RESERVATION

CHACO CA NAT'L M

GRAND CANYON NAT'L PARK

CANYON DE CHELLY NAT'L MON.

HUALPI INDIAN RESERVATION
ORAIBI

GALLUP

C A L I F O R N I A

MOJAVE DESERT

LOMPOC
FORT TEJON
SOLVANG
SANTA BARBARA
VENTURA
SAN FERNANDO
SAN GABRIEL
LOS ANGELES
SAN JUAN CAPISTRANO
OCEANSIDE

Salton Sea

SAN DIEGO

Colorado R.

COLORADO RIVER INDIAN RESERVATION

FLAGSTAFF

TUZIGOOT NAT'L MON.
JEROME

WALNUT CANYON NAT'L MON.
MONTEZUMA CASTLE NAT'L MON.

A R I Z O N A

ZUNI INDIAN RES.

FORT WING

EL MORRO NAT'L MON.

CORONADO'S ROUTE

FORT APACHE INDIAN RES.
Salt R.

GILA CLIFF DWELLINGS NAT'L MONUMENT

PHOENIX
SALT RIVER INDIAN RES.
TONTO NAT'L MON.
SAN CARLOS INDIAN RES.

Gila R.
GILA INDIAN RES.
CASA GRANDE NAT'L MON.
San Pedro R.
Gila R.

SILVER CITY

YUMA

FORT BOWIE

PAPAGO INDIAN RESERVATION
TUCSON
SAN XAVIER DEL BAC
SAN XAVIER INDIAN RES.
TUBAC
TUMACACORI NAT'L MON.

COCHISE STRONGHOLD
TOMBSTONE
BISBEE

P A C I F I C   O C E A N

SANTA LUCIA RANGE

KEY:

🏠 FRONTIER TOWN

⛪ FORT

🏘 INDIAN PUEBLO

🐚 SPANISH SITE

⛪ SPANISH MISSION

⛵ SEAPORT

ARIZONA

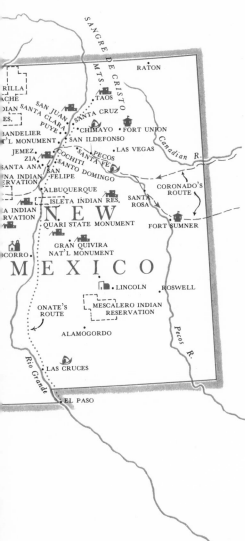

APACHE

Nearby in *Skeleton Canyon*, close to the Mexican border, Geronimo surrendered in 1886 to U.S. Army officers (*see* pp. 320-21).

APACHE INDIAN RESERVATIONS

On *Fort Apache* and *San Carlos Indian Reservations* in east-central Arizona live the Apaches, once the most warlike of all Arizona Indians. Following their bitter struggle against the encroachment of white settlers, they were settled here and have since developed a successful cattle-raising industry. *Fort Apache* (1870), formerly an important garrison during the period of Apache warfare, is now a government Indian school. Near here is the partially excavated *Kinishba Ruin,* remains of a 14th-century Indian pueblo.

APACHE PASS

A narrow pass in the southeast corner of the state, where the Dos Cabezas and Chiricahua mountains meet, was probably the most dangerous point on the southern overland route to California. Here in July, 1862, a fierce battle took place between Union infantry and Apaches led by Cochise and Mangas Coloradas. At the eastern end of the pass are crumbled ruins of *Fort Bowie,* built in 1862 to protect travelers.

BISBEE

A tough copper camp of the 1870's and 1880's, located in a mountain area which still produces large quantities of valuable ores.

CANYON DE CHELLY
NATIONAL MONUMENT

A spectacularly scenic region in the Navajo Reservation, where three great canyons with sheer walls rise to a height of 1,000 feet. In this ancient Indian dwelling place are many prehistoric cliff ruins. *Mummy Cave* dates in part from A.D. 348 and is one of the best-preserved Basket Maker sites ever uncovered. The large ruins of *White House,* occupied from about 1060 to 1300, rest on a ledge in a canyon wall (*see* p. 305). Navajos still inhabit the canyon which has been their home and stronghold for over 200 years.

CASA GRANDE NATIONAL
MONUMENT

Southwest of Coolidge is the site of an ancient Hohokam and Salado Indian walled village dominated by a four-story earthen tower which still stands. Occupied from before 1300 to about 1450, the ruins indicate a highly developed culture of Indians who irrigated and farmed the surrounding desert.

CHIRICAHUA NATIONAL
MONUMENT

Wild mountain-canyon country in southeastern Arizona noted for its grotesque, eroded rock pinnacles. This was the ancestral home and last stronghold of a major band of Apaches.

COCHISE MEMORIAL PARK

Stronghold Canyon in the Dragoon Mountains of southern Arizona remained from 1860 to 1872 the hideout of Cochise. During this period the remarkable Apache chief and his warriors conducted a series of destructive raids against white settlements in the Southwest.

COLORADO RIVER RESERVATION

Along the Colorado River, with headquarters at Parker, live the Mojave Indians and the Chemehuevis, southern Paiutes.

CORONADO TRAIL

Between Clifton and Springerville is the route Coronado is thought to have taken in 1540 when he led his men north from Mexico (*see* map, p. 322). They probably followed the San Pedro River to the Gila, then headed across the present-day Apache Indian reservations to the Zuñi country in western New Mexico.

DINOSAUR CANYON

In the *Painted Desert,* 10 miles north of Cameron, are over 300 dinosaur tracks estimated to be between 60 and 200 million years old.

FLAGSTAFF

Scene of the annual July Pow-Wow in which Southwest Indians representing 20 tribal nations participate in ceremonial dances and athletic contests. The *Museum of Northern Arizona* houses a collection of material on the natural sciences of the region, prehistoric Indians, and contemporary Indian arts.

GLOBE

A mining town with a winding, uneven main street once lined with saloons and dance halls. Settled in 1876 as a result of a silver strike.

GRAND CANYON NATIONAL
MONUMENT AND PARK

One of the world's greatest natural wonders, where the Colorado River has cut a tortuous 217-mile-long gorge, from 4 to 18 miles wide and over a mile deep. The brilliant and varying colors of the steep, eroded canyon walls provide views of unsurpassed beauty and grandeur. The first white men to visit the canyon were Coronado's men, who stopped here in 1540.

HOPI INDIAN RESERVATION

Living in rocky mesa and desert country, surrounded by the lands of their former enemies the Navajos, the Hopis are the only Pueblo Indians in Arizona today. They reside in twelve villages where the ancient pattern of their life has varied little, and where they conduct year-round religious ceremonies which are the focal point of their lives. The Hopis are known for the rich tradition of their mythology and folklore, and for their weaving, pottery, and jewelry making. A famous Hopi ceremony is the Snake Dance held each August in the villages. On a precipitous cliff is *Walpi,* most picturesque of the Hopi towns and little changed since it was built in 1680 (*see* p. 306). The oldest and once the largest of the villages is *Oraibi,* a near-deserted cluster of stone houses, two to four stories high, built on a mesa top. It is known to have been continuously occupied since A.D. 1150.

HUALPAI INDIAN RESERVATION
In the region west and southwest of the Grand Canyon live the Hualpai Indians, a declining tribe which clings to its ancient customs.

JEROME
A ghost town on the side of Mingus Mountain, with frame houses propped up on stilts. Over 85 miles of tunnels run under the town site. Jerome was a roaring mining camp of the 1890's and early 1900's, and produced over $600,000,000 worth of copper, silver, and gold before its reserves were exhausted. Deserted stores, hotels, saloons, and the *Mine Museum* maintained by the Jerome Historical Society may be seen.

MONTEZUMA CASTLE NATIONAL MONUMENT
Southeast of Cottonwood is a well-preserved ruin built in the recess of a high. vertical cliff. The community dwelling, inaccessible except by ladders, was occupied from about 1250 until the early 1400's. Nearby are other pueblo ruins and ancient irrigation ditches.

MONUMENT VALLEY
In a remote portion of the Navajo Reservation, this beautiful valley is dominated by red sandstone buttes and pinnacles which rise spectacularly from the desert floor. Here Chief Hoskinini led his people in 1863-64 to escape Kit Carson's Navajo round-up. Today isolated groups of Navajos live in the valley.

NAVAJO INDIAN RESERVATION
Largest Indian reservation in the United States. It occupies 25,000 square miles of badly eroded, semidesert country in Arizona, western New Mexico, southern Colorado, and Utah, with headquarters at Window Rock, Arizona. The Navajos have a rich folklore which is revealed in their religious sand paintings, myths, and ceremonial dances. Today thousands of Navajo hogans are scattered throughout the lonely reaches of the reservation.

NAVAJO NATIONAL MONUMENT
In Navajo Reservation are three important cliff-dwelling sites dating from the early 13th century. *Keet Seel,* the largest cliff ruin in Arizona, is an impressive community house dramatically situated in a large cave in a canyon wall. *Betatakin,* built on the steep sloping floor of a high cave, contains over 150 rooms, many with their original roofs still intact. *Inscription House,* located on a wall near Navajo Canyon, contains 50 rooms. A weathered inscription is thought to be of Spanish origin, dating from the 1660's.

NOGALES
An international border town with a pronounced Mexican flavor. Scene of lively

The Epitaph *Building, Tombstone*

border skirmishes from 1897 to 1918, involving Pancho Villa and others.

PAPAGO INDIAN RESERVATION
Over 7,000 Papago Indians live in the vast desert region west of Tucson. Their native rituals reflect the influence of Catholic missionaries who began their work with Father Kino in 1692.

PASCUA
North of Tucson is a Yaqui Indian village of mud-chinked huts. The Yaquis fled to Arizona early in the 1900's from Sonora during an uprising and have remained here since. During Holy Week they conduct colorful ceremonial dances. The Yaquis have also settled in Guadalupe Village near Phoenix.

PHOENIX
Founded in the 1860's, this community was an important supply point for the northern Arizona territory. The *Heard Museum* contains a large collection of early Indian and Spanish relics and contemporary Indian artifacts. In the *Arizona Museum* are Indian exhibits and material from the state's pioneer days. In *Hieroglyphic Canyon* south of Phoenix are ancient Indian wall drawings and inscriptions of uncertain origin. *Pueblo Grande Prehistoric Monument* contains an ancient Hohokam dwelling site noted for its extensive irrigation canals, parts of which still remain.

PIMA INDIAN RESERVATION
A tribe of farmers and stock raisers who have lost most of their ancient Papago culture. Some of their lands southeast of Phoenix have been irrigated for 14 centuries.

PIPE SPRING NATIONAL MONUMENT
Southwest of Fredonia in the Kaibab Indian Reservation is a well-preserved Mormon fort. Built in 1869 to protect Mormon cattle interests from Indians, it is virtually unchanged. The main structure consists of two red sandstone buildings connected by an enclosed courtyard. The monument is dedicated to pioneers who settled this region.

PRESCOTT
First temporary capital of Arizona Terri-

tory (1864). *Pioneer Square,* surrounded by a stockade, contains a group of buildings dating from the town's early years. The *Governor's House* (1864) is a substantial log structure where some of the first sessions of the legislature were held. The *Sharlot Hall Museum* and the original Governor's Home contain a large collection of early Arizona documents. The *Log Cabin* is a reconstruction of a typical pioneer ranch house complete with furnishings. *Fort Misery,* a two-room log cabin, is a reproduction of the first house in Prescott, built in 1863-64. The *Smoki Museum* contains a collection of Indian art objects and a library of Indian history.

QUARTZSITE
Near this former stagecoach station in western Arizona are the ruins of *Fort Tyson,* built in 1856 to protect travelers from the Mojaves. In the Quartzsite cemetery is the grave of Hadji Ali, a Syrian camel driver known as Hi Jolly. The Syrian came to the United States with a camel corps which the Army hoped to use for desert transportation. The experiment failed chiefly because the Americans—and their horses—could not learn to like the camels.

SAN XAVIER DEL BAC MISSION
Nine miles south of Tucson, this magnificent Spanish Renaissance-style church is the sole intact survivor of the Arizona mission chain (*see* pp. 302-3). Built by Franciscans between 1783 and 1803 near the site of a mission founded prior to 1700 by the Jesuit priest, Father Kino. The white stuccoed brick structure has a richly carved central facade. The lovely baroque interior contains interesting native art work and other fine religious objects (*see* p. 311).

TOMBSTONE
One of the most notorious of all mining towns. Tombstone boomed during the 1880's, and was the scene of the famous Earp-Clanton feud. Depletion of the mines, fire, and floods reduced Tombstone to ghost-town status before 1900. Two well-preserved landmarks of the town's lawless years are the *Bird Cage Theater* (1881), famous gambling house and vaudeville theater; and the *Crystal Palace Bar and Saloon,* once noted for its luxurious furnishings. *Schieffelin Hall* (1881), formerly the local opera house, is now the community museum. *Boot Hill* contains the graves of some of the town's unruly citizens (*see* p. 319). The *Tombstone* Epitaph *Building* houses the famous local weekly.

TONTO NATIONAL MONUMENT
On the Apache Trail southeast of Roosevelt are two well-preserved prehistoric dwellings built into the side of a steep canyon wall. These rock and adobe houses were occupied in the 14th century by the Pueblo Indians.

TUBAC
A small cluster of adobe houses in the lower Santa Cruz valley marks the site of a Spanish presidio established in 1752. It was later a stop on the emigrant route to the west. Prior to the Civil War, it was a min-

ing town, and briefly Arizona's principal community; it was deserted in the 1860's because of Apache raids.

TUCSON

The oldest town in Arizona began as a walled presidio established in 1776 to protect Spanish settlers from the Indians. Later Tucson became an important trade center and stopping point on the Butterfield Stage route. The *Arizona State Museum* houses an important collection of Southwest archaeological and ethnological material. The *Arizona Pioneer Historical Society Museum* contains period rooms and other exhibits pertaining to the state's frontier days. Twelve miles south is *Old Tucson,* a reconstruction of the way Tucson probably looked in the 1860's.

TUMACACORI NATIONAL MONUMENT

Eighteen miles north of Nogales in the Santa Cruz valley are partially preserved remains of *Tumacacori,* one of the Sonora mission chain founded in the 1690's by Father Kino (*see* p. 310). The present church, a lovely baroque structure, dates from about 1800 when it was a busy center of Franciscan mission activity. The adjoining museum contains exhibits of Southwest mission life.

TUZIGOOT NATIONAL MONUMENT

An impressive hilltop ruin, across the Verde River from Clarkdale, it is the site of a fortified Pueblo community of the 12th

Montezuma Castle National Monument

to 14th century. Over 110 terraced rooms are clustered around the summit. A museum exhibits artifacts.

WALNUT CANYON NATIONAL MONUMENT

Southwest of Flagstaff in shallow caves of a steep canyon wall are over 300 small cliff dwellings inhabited between A.D. 1000 and 1200. The Indians who lived here engaged in farming, hunting, and pottery-making.

WUPATKI NATIONAL MONUMENT

About 45 miles northeast of Flagstaff, on a series of sandstone bluffs overlooking the Painted Desert, are more than 800 prehistoric home sites. The largest ruin is a three-story stone structure of over 100 rooms. Indians came to Wupatki during the 12th century after a volcanic eruption had produced an exceptionally fertile soil.

YUMA

An important ferry crossing for emigrants traveling to the California gold fields. *Old Territorial Prison* (1876) is a weathered fortress with thick adobe walls, now used as a museum for frontier relics. The *Fort Yuma Indian Reservation* lies across the Colorado River in California.

CALIFORNIA

(Southern section: for northern California listings, see page 363.)

BAKERSFIELD

Thirty-eight miles south of here is *Fort Tejon,* which served from 1854 to 1864 as U.S. Army outpost and stage stop. The adobe walls are fairly well preserved.

BODIE

One of the best-preserved ghost towns of the Mono mining region despite the ravages of time and fire. Its weathered buildings typify a trans-Sierra boom town of the 1860's and 1870's.

BISHOP

In the Chalfant Valley, once a Pah-Ute Indian stronghold, is an interesting series of prehistoric carvings of animals, birds, and human figures.

CARMEL

In this picturesque art colony overlooking Carmel Bay is *Mission San Carlos Borromeo.* Founded at Monterey by Father Junipero Serra in 1770, it was moved to its present site the following year. The mission was Serra's home until his death in 1784.

EL CENTRO

At Carrizon and Vallecito, north of Highway 80, are two restored stagecoach stations which served the transcontinental Butterfield Overland Mail.

ESCONDIDO

East of here is *San Pasqual Battlefield,* site of a battle in the American conquest of California. General Kearny lost the battle to the Californians under General Andrés Pico.

GLENDALE

Casa Adobe de San Rafael (1870's) Built on land (now a park) that was once part of the 36,000-acre Rancho San Rafael. This was one of the first Spanish land grants in California (1784).

INGLEWOOD

Freeman Adobe House Built in the early 1800's and furnished with period pieces.

JOLON

San Antonio de Padua A handsome reconstruction of the Spanish mission founded by Father Junipero Serra in 1771 is near Jolon. In the early 1800's it had extensive vineyards and orchards, and herds of cattle, sheep, and horses.

KING'S HIGHWAY

Known to the Spanish as *El Camino Real,* this route extends approximately 600 miles along California's coastal region from San Diego to Sonoma. Along its course are 21 Franciscan missions founded between 1769 and 1823, a missionary project started under Father Serra.

LOMPOC

Mission La Purisima Concepción A faithful restoration of the original, founded in 1787, is four miles from here. One of the handsomest of the restored missions, it includes a re-creation of the old water system and a beautiful mission garden.

LOS ANGELES

Around the downtown *Plaza,* once the site of the early Spanish community, are several old houses and a historic church. The

Plaza Church (Nuestra Señora la Reina de Los Angeles), oldest in the city, was dedicated in 1822 but has been rebuilt and restored since. *Olvera Street,* lined with shops, is restored in the manner of an old Mexican street. *Avila Adobe* (1818-24), the oldest house in Los Angeles, is now preserved as a museum. The *Old Pico House* was built in 1869 as a hotel by Pio Pico, last Mexican governor. The *Southwest Museum* contains exhibits pertaining to the American Indians.

MONTEREY

In 1775 Monterey became the first Spanish capital of California, and remained the political, military, and social center throughout much of the period of Spanish and Mexican rule. The *Old Custom House,* a long, galleried building of stone and adobe, is the oldest public building on the Coast. Its oldest part dates from 1827. During the American conquest the United States flag was first officially raised over the Custom House on July 7, 1846. *Colton Hall* (1847-49), a handsome columned structure, was built by the Reverend Walter Colton, first American mayor of Monterey and co-publisher of California's first newspaper. Its upper floor, where the first constitution of California was written in 1849, is now a museum. The *Old Whaling Station* (1855) was built for Portuguese whalers. The garden walks are paved with whale vertebrae. The *Royal Presidio Chapel,* second in the California chain of missions, was founded in 1770 by Father Serra. When the mission was moved to Carmel in 1771, it became the presidio chapel. Rebuilt in 1795, it has been in continuous use ever since. The Monterey *Presidio* is built on the site of the fort founded in 1770 by Captain Gáspar de Portolá. On the grounds are statues of Father Serra and Commodore Sloat, who was in charge of the U.S. forces who took Monterey. The *First Theater,* a long adobe building, was built in 1846-47 as a boarding house and saloon. The building is a state monument and contains exhibits of early California history. *Casa Del Oro* (Boston Store) was a general merchandise store in the 1850's. A restoration is being undertaken to show what trade was like during Monterey's early years. The *Stevenson House* (1830's) is a white-plastered adobe house where Robert Louis Stevenson lived briefly in 1879. It has been restored as a home of the Mexican era. The *Larkin House* (1834) was built by Thomas Oliver Larkin who served in the 1840's as the only American consul to California. This galleried residence, one of the handsomest, best-preserved early homes in the area, is now a state historical monument.

OCEANSIDE

Mission San Luis Rey de Francia Founded in 1798, this composite Spanish-Moorish-Mexican-style mission east of Oceanside was once one of the largest and richest of the Franciscan chain. Handsomely restored, it is now used as a Franciscan seminary.

PALA

Asistencia de San Antonio de Pala In this small trading center for the Pala Indian Reservation, the chapel was founded in 1816 as a branch establishment of Mission San Luis Rey. Considerably restored, it is interesting for its large number of Indian communicants, its colorful Indian decorations, and its unique separate campanile.

POMONA

Palomares Adobe (late 1830's) A low California ranch house, restored. Typical of its period.

REDLANDS

San Bernardino Asistencia (1830-34) A reproduction of an outpost of San Gabriel Mission that served as a chapel for Indians and Mexicans. The original was sold in 1852 to a colony of Mormons who used it for a tithing house. Later it was razed.

SAN DIEGO

Cabrillo National Monument, overlooking the bay, marks the 1542 landing of the Portuguese sailor Juan Rodriguez Cabrillo, the first white man to make contact with this part of the world. In 1769 a Spanish presidio and fort were established here, in the first Spanish settlement in California. *Old Town Plaza,* the original center of town, retains some of its old Spanish flavor. *Casa de Estudillo* (c. 1825) is a handsome Spanish-style residence built around a charming patio. It is now a museum, carefully preserved as a distinguished period home. *Casa de Bandini* (1820's), a spacious adobe building with broad overhanging balconies, was remodeled in 1869 and has

served as a hotel ever since. The *Adobe Chapel,* consecrated in 1858, has been restored. On Presidio Hill overlooking Old Town are outlines of the old presidio established in 1769, which was in ruins by 1835. The *Junipero Serra Museum* contains collections of the local Pioneer and Historical Society. *San Diego de Alcalá* was the first of the Franciscan missions and the beginning of El Camino Real. Founded on the site of San Diego in 1769, in 1774 it was moved to its present location six miles north. Only the facade and base of the belfry remain of the original adobe structure. The restored mission is maintained as a museum.

SAN FERNANDO

San Fernando Rey de España (1797) One of the most prosperous of the missions. The church and cloister, a picturesque structure noted for its long arcade with 19 semi-circular arches, have been carefully restored. Mission relics are on display.

SAN GABRIEL

San Gabriel Arcangel Spanish mission founded under Father Serra in 1771. The present structure, dating from the early 1800's, is a handsome stone building noted for its row of slender buttresses and for its fine collection of early native church art.

SAN JUAN BAUTISTA

San Juan Bautista State Monument Several old buildings built around a picturesque plaza have been preserved to maintain a feeling of the period prior to the American occupation. *The San Juan Bautista Mission,* founded in 1797 and one of the largest in the chain, is now being restored. Parts of the original wall, early Indian decorations, and tile floor remain. *Castro House* (1825) is a handsome galleried adobe house built by José Castro, prominent during Mexican rule, and twice acting governor. *The Plaza Hotel* (1792) was a residence until 1856 when it was remodeled and made into a hotel. *Zanetta House* was a private residence and the center of entertainment in the 1870's and 1880's.

SAN JUAN CAPISTRANO

Mission San Juan Capistrano (1776) One of the most elaborate mission structures, nearly destroyed in the earthquake of 1812. Remaining are the picturesque church ruins grouped around a charming garden. The site is famous for the Capistrano swal-

Colton Hall, Monterey

lows who return at the same time each year to nest in the ruins. An adjoining museum contains early church relics.

SAN LUIS OBISPO

San Luis Obispo de Tolosa (1772) Restored mission which serves today as a parish church. The museum exhibits relics from the old mission. This was the first of the churches to use tile roofs in order to prevent the Indians from setting fire to the reed thatching originally used. Tile roofs were soon adopted by all the missions.

SAN MARINO

Huntington Library and Art Gallery One of the world's great collections of rare books and early American manuscripts. There is also a gallery of fine paintings and rare period furnishings. The gardens are famous.

SAN MIGUEL

San Miguel Arcangel (1797) Probably the least spoiled of the Spanish missions. It is noted for its original Indian paintings and decorations, handsome beamed ceiling, choir gallery, and old pulpit. There is an adjoining museum of Indian and mission relics.

SANTA BARBARA

In this charming town which dates from the founding of a Spanish presidio here in 1782, are many Spanish Provincial buildings. *Casa de la Guerra,* a long adobe residence built in the 1820's by Don José de la Guerra, commandant of the presidio, is preserved as a prosperous home of early Santa Barbara. *Covarrubias Adobe,* a large adobe residence built about 1817, is considered one of the finest existing examples of early domestic California architecture. It is handsomely restored and furnished with period pieces. Isabel Larkin, first child born in California of American parents, was born in *Carillo Adobe* (1830's). *El Cuartel* (1780's) is one of the oldest adobes in Santa Barbara. *Santa Barbara Mission* (1786) is a handsome, well-preserved structure known as "The Queen of the Missions" (*see* p. 310). A rich and powerful establishment in its early days, it is the only mission which has remained continuously active since its founding.

SOLVANG

Mission Santa Ynez Founded in 1804 and restored, it is one of the most attractive of the missions. A museum adjoins it.

VENTURA

Mission San Buenaventura. The last mission founded by Father Serra (1782). The buildings, destroyed by fire and earthquake, have been restored, and remains of the old aqueduct system are still visible. The museum contains a display of early church relics.

Pioneer Museum Contains exhibits of early California history.

WHITTIER

Pio Pico State Historical Monument Home of the last Mexican governor in California. The old adobe house built around a courtyard has been restored.

NEVADA

(Southern section: for northern Nevada listings, see page 366.)

BEATTY

Near Death Valley is this town of timbered buildings and wooden awnings, a former supply base for mining camps. The center of mining activity was at nearby Rhyolite. *The O'Brien House* Has a collection of ore specimens gathered all over the world.

LAS VEGAS

The "meadows" is the Spanish name of this site on the Old Spanish Trail. Spaniards, then Mexicans, then American explorers refreshed themselves at the springs here. Frémont visited the site in 1844, and the first American settlement was made in 1855 by thirty men sent by Brigham Young to build a fort to protect emigrants. Only the orchards and vineyards remain from the Mormon mission, which ceased functioning in 1857. Nearby *Hoover Dam* is a point of interest, and to the northeast is the colorful *Valley of Fire,* where Indian petroglyphs are carved on the rocks. Under gypsum deposits there, fossilized bones of the giant sloth, along with primitive javelins and dart shafts, have been found. More recent Indians built a pueblo at Overton, called Lost City, which has been submerged under Lake Mead. A reconstruction of the interesting village found there has been built at a museum near Overton.

RHYOLITE

A town near Beatty and Death Valley, which boomed in 1905, lasted for three years, and then was deserted. Many substantial buildings, erected in the hope of a prolonged future, were torn down or left to disintegrate; and even the railroad tracks were torn up. The ruins of one rather elaborate depot remain, with the *Bottle House,* built of quart beer bottles, which has Victorian jigsaw frills on the eaves.

NEW MEXICO

ABO STATE MONUMENT

Twelve miles southwest of Mountainair are well-preserved red sandstone ruins of a Franciscan mission established in 1629 for Piro Indians. The mission was abandoned about 1670.

ÁCOMA

About 13 miles south of Highway 66, west of Laguna, this ancient Indian village is situated on top of a steep mesa (*see* pp. 314-15). This sky city is noted for its massive adobe church, *San Esteban Rey* (begun 1629, additions after 1680) which is one of the finest examples of pueblo mission architecture in the Southwest. Huge carved ceiling beams, old wall paintings, and a richly carved reredos decorate the otherwise plain interior.

ALAMOGORDO

The *Mescalero Apache Reservation,* northeast of Alamogordo, is occupied by a group of Apaches who are known for their colorful Mountain Spirit Dance (*see* p. 321). Near Three Rivers, north of Alamogordo, is an exceptionally large collection of ancient Indian pictographs.

ALBUQUERQUE

In *Old Town,* simple adobe dwellings and the old church of *San Felipe de Neri* convey the atmosphere of the early Spanish settlement. The church, built when the town was founded in 1706, has remained basically unchanged except for a remodeled facade. It has thick adobe walls, a spiral staircase built around a tree trunk, and hand-carved ecclesiastical objects.

AZTEC RUINS NATIONAL MONUMENT

Near Aztec are remarkable ruins of a Pueblo Indian village built early in the 12th century. The largest dwelling, a three-story structure, contained about 500 rooms, some still intact. Of special interest is the restored *Great Kiva,* an enormous ceremonial chamber enclosed by a ring of small surface rooms. A museum adjoins the ruins.

BANDELIER NATIONAL MONUMENT

On Pajarito Plateau, 45 miles northwest of Santa Fe, are numerous impressive ruins representing a late flowering of Pueblo culture. An Indian civilization thrived here from the late 13th century until the region was abandoned about 300 years later. The most accessible of the many ruin sites are in Frijoles Canyon which contains hundreds of cave homes cut out of the canyon walls and a large circular communal dwelling built on the floor of the valley.

CHACO CANYON NATIONAL MONUMENT

Twelve impressive prehistoric apartment house ruins and many smaller sites, 64 miles north of Highway 66 from Thoreau. The largest ruin is *Pueblo Bonito,* a huge D-shaped apartment which housed over 1,200 people in its 800 rooms and contained 32 kivas. Once thickly populated, the Chaco Canyon region was abandoned late in the 12th century.

CHIMAYÓ

A picturesque rural Spanish-American community settled late in the 17th century, famous for its lovely chapel, *El Santuario* (*see* p. 310). Built for a Spanish colonial family in 1816, the church contains exceptionally fine examples of native folk art which developed in remote villages of the province.

CIMARRON

Cimarron was a rough frontier town frequented by outlaws and popular with travelers on the nearby Santa Fe Trail. Several buildings help preserve an atmosphere of its lively 19th-century past. The *Lucien B. Maxwell House* (c. 1864), now in ruins, once housed a gambling hall, billiard room, and dance hall. The *St. James Hotel* (1870-80), currently a tavern, was the scene of 26 killings. Also of interest are an old gristmill; the *Agency Warehouse* (1848), the old *County Jail and Courthouse* (1854), *Swink's Gambling Hall* (now a garage), and *Cimarron Cemetery.*

COCHITI PUEBLO

Thirty miles southwest of Santa Fe is a pre-Columbian Indian village of one-story adobe houses built around a plaza. The Cochitis make handsome pottery and fine drums.

CORONADO STATE MONUMENT

Kuaua, a partially restored pueblo ruin 17 miles north of Albuquerque, is in the region where Coronado wintered, 1540-42. Exceptionally interesting mural decorations have been uncovered on the walls of a subterranean kiva.

CORONADO'S ROUTE

In 1540 Francisco Vasquez de Coronado, a Spanish nobleman, led an army north from Mexico in search of the fabled golden Cities of Cibola. Entering present New Mexico near the Indian villages of Zuñi (*see* map, p. 322), he continued into northern New Mexico and eastward into the Great Plains as far as central Kansas. For two winters he stayed at the Tiguex pueblos. In April, 1542 Coronado returned to Mexico, ill, discredited, and disillusioned, in spite of having made one of the most remarkable early explorations of the North American continent.

EL MORRO NATIONAL MONUMENT

Inscription Rock 35 miles east of the Zuñi pueblo is a sheer sandstone butte with inscriptions left by prehistoric Indians, Spanish conquerors and missionaries, and American pioneers (*see* p. 307). The oldest Spanish inscription dates from 1605 when General Don Juan de Oñate left a record of his trip to the Gulf of California. Ancient pueblo ruins rest on the summit of the huge rock.

ENCHANTED MESA

Three miles northeast of Ácoma is this sandstone butte, a striking landmark on the desert plain. According to Ácoma Indian tradition this was the home of their ances-

327

tors until a severe storm destroyed the only path to the top.

FORT SUMNER
Old Fort Sumner Crumbled adobe walls mark the site of the frontier fort where 7,000 Navajos were held in captivity from 1864 to 1868 following their roundup by Kit Carson and his regiment. The fort later became Lucien B. Maxwell's home, where Billy the Kid was shot in 1881 while visiting Maxwell's son. Billy the Kid is buried in the fort cemetery.

FORT UNION NATIONAL MONUMENT
Northeast of Las Vegas are the brick and adobe ruins of old **Fort Union**, one of the most important landmarks on the **Santa Fe Trail** (see pp. 316-17). Ruins of the soldiers' quarters, storehouses, and a well-preserved military prison remain. Ruts of the well-worn trail are visible nearby.

GALLUP
A trading center on the edge of Indian country where the colorful Inter-Tribal Indian Ceremonial is held each August.

MUSEUM OF NEW MEXICO

Quarai Mission, near Mountainair

GILA CLIFF DWELLINGS NATIONAL MONUMENT
North of Silver City in the remote wilderness of the Mogollón Mountains a series of small cliff dwellings are tucked into the recesses of caves. Many of these ancient Indian homes are two-storied and contain at least a dozen rooms.

GLORIETA PASS
A narrow pass in Apache Canyon, 15 miles southeast of Santa Fe, was the scene of a decisive engagement in March, 1862 when Union forces turned back Confederates on their way to take Fort Union.

GRAN QUIVIRA NATIONAL MONUMENT
Twenty-four miles south of Mountainair are early pueblo ruins and the remains of two missions built by the Spanish about 1627 and 1659. Of interest are the well-constructed Piro Indian irrigation ditches.

ISLETA
A surviving Indian village of the old Tiguex Province known to Coronado. *Mis-*

sion San Antonio de Isleta (1621-30), partially destroyed during the pueblo revolt of 1680, was restored after the Spanish reconquest.

JÉMEZ PUEBLO
Thirty miles northwest of Bernalillo is this Pueblo village, built between 1696 and 1700. The Jémez Indians were active in the revolt against the Spanish. They are noted today for their embroidered ceremonial costumes and colorful Corn and Buffalo dances held in August and November.

JÉMEZ STATE MONUMENT
Thirteen miles north of Jémez Pueblo are ruins of a large pueblo and the *San Diego de Jémez Mission* (1617), formerly one of the most important Franciscan posts. This mission was abandoned in 1622.

JICARILLA APACHE RESERVATION
West of Chama is one of two Apache reservations in the state.

LAGUNA PUEBLO
Off Highway 66, west of Albuquerque, is this Indian community built in 1697. The Lagunas are farmers, herders, and railroad workers. Their *Mission* (1699) is noted for its Indian murals with their combination of pagan and Christian symbols.

LAS TRAMPAS
On a winding mountain road between Santa Fe and Taos are several Spanish-American communities where the native ways of 17th-century Spanish New Mexico prevail. The small adobe-walled village of Las Trampas is the center of the Penitentes, an ancient flagellant sect. In the sacristy of **Las Trampas Church** (1760) is the small wooden Death Cart used in the Penitente Holy Week processions. Other isolated villages are Truchas and Córdova, another Penitente community.

LINCOLN
In this center of the Lincoln County Cattle War (1876-78) is a restored stone tower, built by early settlers, which served as a watch tower and refuge from attacking Indians. *Old Lincoln County Courthouse* (1874) was founded as a general store; later it became the courthouse and jail from which Billy the Kid made his famous escape in 1881. The building, much restored and now a state monument, houses a historical museum.

NAMBÉ PUEBLO
A small Pueblo village, about 16 miles north of Santa Fe.

OLD MESILLA
A quiet Spanish-American community, south of Las Cruces, with central plaza surrounded by simple adobe houses. Settled in 1853 when it was still part of Mexico. In 1858 it became a stopping point on the Overland Mail Route. The adobe building where Billy the Kid was tried houses a museum with relics of the town's early years. Old homes in the area are opened during Mesilla's annual May pilgrimage.

OÑATE'S ROUTE
Juan de Oñate, Spanish grandee, left Mex-

ico in January, 1598, with a small army and group of colonists to establish the first colony in New Mexico. The party followed the Rio Grande north, past many pueblo villages, to the settlement of San Juan where the first capital was founded (see map, p. 322). Oñate explored the region west to the mouth of the Colorado and east into Kansas and Texas.

PAAKO STATE MONUMENT
Partially excavated ruins of an ancient Indian pueblo, 22 miles northeast of Albuquerque. The village was inhabited as late as 1629.

PECOS STATE MONUMENT
Southeast of Santa Fe near Pecos are ruins of a large, well-fortified Indian village visited by Coronado in 1541. Remains of a large thick-walled mission and adjacent monastery established in 1617 are visible. Pecos was finally abandoned in 1838.

PUYE RUINS
Remains of a once thriving prehistoric Tewa community, 12 miles west of Española. In the early 16th century the town consisted of a series of cliff dwellings and a four-storied community house containing about 1,200 rooms. Specimens from the ruins are found in the Puyé Room at the Palace of the Governors in Santa Fe.

PICURIS PUEBLO
Home of a once hostile Pueblo tribe, and a hotbed of revolt against Spanish rule in the late 17th century. The *Mission of San Lorenzo* was rebuilt after the Spanish reconquest in 1692. The interior is decorated with interesting Indian art work. The village is about 20 miles south of Taos.

QUARAI STATE MONUMENT
The largest remaining Franciscan mission ruins are here, 8 miles north of Mountainair. Thick walls of the church and adjoining convent, built in 1629, rise to a height of nearly 40 feet. The area apparently was abandoned late in the 17th century.

SANDÍA PUEBLO
South of Bernalillo, low adobe buildings surround the plaza of an Indian village, remnant of the once populous Tiguex province of Coronado's time. The 17th-century Franciscan mission is in ruins.

SAN FELIPE PUEBLO
Northeast of Bernalillo is the *Mission of San Felipe* (c. 1720), one of the finest surviving examples of early Franciscan architecture. The facade is adorned with twin belfries connected by a latticed gallery railing. The pueblo is also known for its Spring Corn Dance held on May 1.

SAN ILDEFONSO PUEBLO
An Indian community 24 miles northwest of Santa Fe, located at the foot of the sacred Black Mesa. Famous for its black and red pottery, especially that made by Julian and Maria Martinez. In the center of one of the plazas is an impressive ceremonial kiva. San Ildefonso's interesting dances include the Eagle and Hunting dances, held in January, and the fall Harvest Dance.

SAN JUAN PUEBLO

A Tewa Indian farming community 28 miles northwest of Santa Fe on the east bank of the Rio Grande. Across the river are ruins of *Yunque-Yunque* where in 1598 Oñate founded the first capital of New Mexico. Named San Gabriel, it was abandoned within ten years for Santa Fe.

SANTA ANA PUEBLO

In this near-deserted village northwest of Bernalillo is the *Mission of Santa Ana,* one of the oldest and most primitive Franciscan churches.

SANTA CLARA PUEBLO

On the west bank of the Rio Grande near Española is this sprawling Indian community.

SANTA CRUZ

In a lovely little valley north of Santa Fe is one of the state's oldest and most interesting Spanish-American villages. Simple adobe homes, small gardens, orchards, and the fine old church on the plaza date from early days. The *Church of Santa Cruz* (1733), one of the largest in New Mexico, contains a wealth of old Spanish and Mexican art and a collection of rare church documents.

SANTA FE

Founded in 1610 as a Spanish colonial capital, the town is the oldest seat of government in the United States. Occupied by Pueblo Indians after their 1680 revolt, it was also an important Spanish and Mexican provincial city until the American occupation in 1846, when it became territorial capital, trading center, and terminus for the Santa Fe Trail. Its Spanish atmosphere and customs, adobe buildings, narrow streets, and tree-shaded patios make it unlike any other city in America. The *Palace of the Governors* (1610-12) is a long adobe building used by Spanish captains-general until 1821 (*see* p. 316), and occupied by Mexican governors until 1846, when it became the residence of American territorial governors (until 1907). Although much restored, it remains a fine example of Spanish-Indian architecture, and houses the *Museum of New Mexico,* whose *Laboratory of Anthropology* has an outstanding collection of post-Spanish Indian pottery, baskets, textiles, and jewelry. The museum's *Art Gallery* is an architectural composite of six ancient Franciscan missions built around a patio. On view are relics from ancient pueblos and historical material from the Spanish, Mexican, and early American periods. The *Plaza* was a market place for Spanish and Mexican farmers and pueblo Indians; here the wagon trains ended their long journey over the Santa Fe Trail. *The Cathedral of Saint Francis of Assisi* (1869) is a Romanesque-style structure built by Archbishop Lamy on the site of two early Spanish churches, and *Church of Our Lady of Guadalupe* is a mission-type building established sometime after 1777, and restored in 1880 and 1918. Another early church is *Santo Rosario.* The *Mission of San Miguel* was built about 1636 for Indian slaves of Spanish officials, and rebuilt in 1710. Much restored today, it contains ancient religious paintings. *Cristo Rey Church* is a modern pueblo mission-style church featuring a famous stone reredos (1761) which is a fine example of early native art. The *Museum of Navajo Ceremonial Art* is a modern structure, built like a Navajo ceremonial hogan, which contains the finest reproductions of Navajo sand paintings in the world. *Sena Plaza* is a restoration of the old Sena home (c. 1840), built around a patio.

SANTA FE TRAIL

This great trade and colonization route of the early West started at Independence, Missouri, and continued across Kansas and New Mexico to Santa Fe (*see* pp. 316-17).

SANTO DOMINGO PUEBLO

One of the least changed and most interesting Rio Grande pueblos, inhabited by a conservative and well-integrated tribe. Known for its dances, particularly the Green Corn Ceremonial held on August 4. The present mission (1886) contains records dating back to the original Franciscan church built in 1605.

SOCORRO

An old Spanish-American town which boomed in the 1870's and 1880's with discovery of nearby silver mines. The *Church of San Miguel,* a fine example of Spanish mission style, dates from the early 17th century. One of the original walls from the first Franciscan mission of 1598 remains.

TAOS

The community of Taos (*see* pp. 308-9) consists of three villages. Don Fernando de Taos is an old Spanish settlement once frequented by mountain men and fur traders. It is now a picturesque town and art colony. The *Kit Carson House* is a plain adobe structure where the famous scout lived from 1858 to 1866. Other typical Spanish Colonial residences include the *Trujillo House* (1856); the *Montañer House* which belonged to Padre Antonio José Martinez; and the residence of Governor Charles Bent, who was scalped during the insurrection of 1847. Kit Carson and Padre Martinez are buried in the local cemetery. In the Spanish community Ranchos de Taos, four miles south, is the *Church of Saint Francis of Assisi* (c. 1732), one of the most beautiful in the Southwest (*see* p. 309). Distinguished by boldly projecting buttresses and its unadorned, well-proportioned apse, it contains valuable old art objects and a notable decorated reredos. Two miles north of Taos is the ancient Pueblo de Taos, where two terraced Indian community houses have been continuously occupied for hundreds of years (*see* p. 308). This picturesque pueblo is famous for its well-preserved ancient customs and colorful ceremonial dances. Nearby are ruins of the old Spanish mission of *San Gerónimo de Taos,* built in 1706 and destroyed in 1847 during the final Mexican and Indian resistance to American rule.

TESUQUE

About 10 miles north of Santa Fe is this ancient Indian farming community, a picturesque adobe village built around a plaza.

ZIA PUEBLO

A declining Keres Indian village located on a black lava mesa northwest of Bernalillo. The *Zia Mission Church* (1692), flanked by massive adobe buttresses, was re-established after the Pueblo uprising.

ZUNI INDIAN RESERVATION

Forty miles south of Gallup is Zuñi, one of the largest modern pueblos. The older sections, compactly built around small plazas, are terraced up to three stories. The Zuñi farmers and sheepherders are noted for their turquoise and silver jewelry and for their Shalako, a sacred dance held late in November. Also on the reservation are ruins of the villages known to Coronado's men as "The Seven Cities of Cibola."

329

The Farthest Frontier

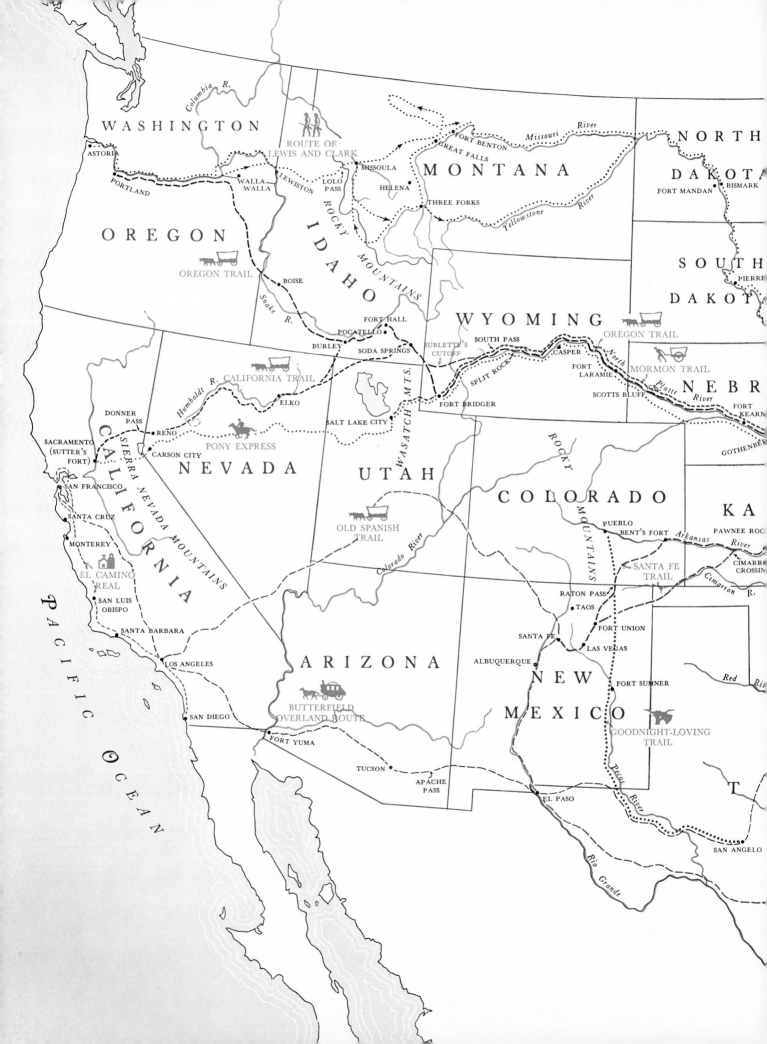

WASHINGTON

Columbia R.

ASTORIA

PORTLAND

OREGON

WALLA
WALLA

LEWISTON

ROUTE OF
LEWIS AND CLARK

LOLO
PASS

MISSOULA

ROCKY

IDAHO

MOUNTAINS

BOISE

Snake R.

OREGON TRAIL

FORT HALL

POCATELLO

BURLEY

SODA SPRINGS

SUBLETTE'S
CUTOFF

Humboldt R. CALIFORNIA TRAIL

ELKO

WASATCH MTS.

SALT LAKE CITY

DONNER
PASS

RENO

CARSON CITY

PONY EXPRESS

NEVADA

UTAH

SACRAMENTO
(SUTTER'S
FORT)

SIERRA NEVADA MOUNTAINS

CALIFORNIA

SAN FRANCISCO

SANTA CRUZ

MONTEREY

EL CAMINO
REAL

SAN LUIS
OBISPO

SANTA BARBARA

OLD SPANISH
TRAIL

Colorado River

LOS ANGELES

ARIZONA

PACIFIC

SAN DIEGO

BUTTERFIELD
OVERLAND ROUTE

FORT YUMA

TUCSON

APACHE
PASS

OCEAN

MONTANA

FORT BENTON

GREAT FALLS

Missouri   River

NORTH

DAKOTA

FORT MANDAN

BISMARK

HELENA

THREE FORKS

Yellowstone   River

SOUTH

DAKOTA

PIERRE

WYOMING

SOUTH PASS

OREGON TRAIL

CASPER

SPLIT ROCK

FORT
LARAMIE

MORMON TRAIL

NEBR

FORT BRIDGER

SCOTTS BLUFF

North

Platte   River

FORT
KEARN

GOTHENBE

ROCKY

MOUNTAINS

COLORADO

KA

PUEBLO

BENT'S FORT

Arkansas

PAWNEE ROC

River

SANTA FE
TRAIL

CIMARR

CROSSING

RATON PASS

TAOS

Cimarron   R.

FORT UNION

SANTA FE

LAS VEGAS

ALBUQUERQUE

NEW

MEXICO

FORT SUMNER

GOODNIGHT-LOVING
TRAIL

Red   Riv

Pecos   River

EL PASO

Rio   Grande

SAN ANGELO

T

THE GREAT TRAILS

ROUTE OF LEWIS AND CLARK

IOWA

MORMON TRAIL

COUNCIL BLUFFS

NAUVOO

OREGON TRAIL

ILLINOIS

PONY EXPRESS

ST. JOSEPH

ABILENE

KANSAS CITY

INDEPENDENCE

ST. LOUIS

SANTA FE TRAIL

TIPTON

MISSOURI

SPRINGFIELD

BUTTERFIELD OVERLAND ROUTE

ENID

FAYETTEVILLE

OKLAHOMA

FORT SMITH

ARKANSAS

CHISHOLM TRAIL

BELKNAP

LOUISIANA

OLD SPANISH TRAIL

NEW ORLEANS

AUSTIN

HOUSTON

SAN ANTONIO

GULF OF MEXICO

At first the Great Plains and the Rocky Mountains were places through which men on their way to a promised land hurried as quickly as possible. For a long time there were no real trails through this country like the Indian and buffalo paths found by eastern settlers. The eyes of America had been opened to the wonders of the West by Lewis and Clark in 1806, yet few men followed precisely the explorers' route.

In 1824 Jedediah Smith led a party through South Pass, the only feasible wagon route across the "Great Shining Mountains," and this pass became the primary objective of the thousands who followed over the Mormon, the Oregon, and the California Trails. These three routes were one until South Pass had been breached. Then the Mormon Trail headed toward Fort Bridger and across the Wasatch; the California Trail went toward Soda Springs, then along the Humboldt into the desert; and the Oregon Trail swung northwest from Fort Hall, and down the Snake River to its junction with the Columbia.

The first great southwestern route, the Santa Fe Trail, began at Independence, crossed the Kansas plains, skirted the Arkansas and Cimarron Rivers, and moved on to Bent's Fort and the Spanish settlements. Starting in the 1820's, these were the highways men traveled to the West, and Americans who head that way today will find that they are highways yet. In time, other trails served men in this vast land, and this map shows most of the important ones.

In spite of the thousands upon thousands of people who have come to live in this area in a century and a quarter, what we have called the Farthest Frontier is still the best place to see a part of America as it was when men first saw it. In this land of the Great Shining Mountains, of forbidding deserts, cascading waterfalls, deep canyons, and magnificent coastline, you can still see some of nature's most wondrous creations, and the limitless space that brought men here in the first place.

William Clark

Meriwether Lewis

333

The Journey of Lewis and Clark

FROM *Two Captains West,*
BY ALBERT AND JANE SALISBURY, SUPERIOR PUBLISHING CO., SEATTLE

On May 14, 1804, William Clark wrote, "I set out . . . in the presence of the neighbouring inhabitents and proceeded under a jentle brease up the Missourie." The photograph below shows the point, ten miles above St. Louis, where the Big Muddy joins the Mississippi. Above is a rebuilt Mandan lodge near Mandan, North Dakota, on the site of a village Lewis and Clark visited. The statue of Sacajawea (left) is in Bismarck.

MARIE HANSEN WESLEY, *Life*

Thirty years after Lewis and Clark visited the Dakotas, Charles Bodmer depicted the interior of a Mandan chief's hut. In his journal Clark describes these lodges as being in a stockade with "the houses round and verry large, containing several families, as also their horses . . ."

Long before the purchase of the Louisiana Territory from France in 1803, men's thoughts had turned toward the land mass spreading west and north from the Mississippi River to the Pacific Ocean—a huge unexplored area about which they knew almost nothing. For twenty years Thomas Jefferson had urged exploration of the territory, but little had come of it beyond the few ships which touched the coastline north of California. To American eyes the most important voyage was that of Captain Robert Gray, who in 1792 discovered the mouth of the Columbia River, gave the stream its name, and thereby provided America with its most tangible claim to the region.

After he became President, Jefferson did not wait long to ask Congress for the sum of $2,500 to finance a journey of discovery. As leader of the expedition he had already settled on his private secretary, 29-year-old Meriwether Lewis, a Virginia neighbor who knew something of the western country from a hitch in the Army. To share his command, Lewis chose a boyhood friend and army superior, William Clark, a

33-year-old Virginian whose older brother was George Rogers Clark, the frontier hero. The two leaders' personalities were almost totally different: Lewis was brooding, melancholy, a man who sought solitude even on their expedition, thousands of miles from civilization; while Clark, or "Red Head" as the Indians called him, was nearly always frank and cheerful; yet in the history of joint commands there are few examples of such mutual confidence, comradeship, or lack of envy. The rest of the party was made up of nine young Kentuckians, fourteen U.S. Army regulars, two Frenchmen, Clark's Negro servant York, and Lewis' Newfoundland dog.

On May 14, 1804, the expedition left the mouth of Wood River, on the Illinois bank of the Mississippi across from the Missouri's mouth, and set forth on what was surely the most thrilling travel drama in U.S. history. It is a journey which Americans may still retrace, because the territory covered by the expedition has changed so little in a century and a half. There is an excitement—a sense of achievement—in

TEXT CONTINUED ON PAGE 338

335

When Lewis and Clark reached the Missouri Canyon near the Judith River in Montana late in May, 1805, they found themselves

BRADLEY SMITH, COURTESY *Time*

in a region never before explored by white men. Standing on these eroded hills, they saw the Rocky Mountains for the first time.

FROM *Two Captains West,*
BY ALBERT AND JANE SALISBURY, SUPERIOR PUBLISHING CO., SEATTLE

Lewis likened the White Cliffs (above) to vast ruins with "parapets well stocked with statuary." Below is the Indian trail over Lemhi Pass in the Bitterroots which the party followed down the western slope of the Continental Divide.

TEXT CONTINUED FROM PAGE 335

sighting the landmarks they named, following the very trails Lewis and Clark took over wild, rugged stretches unaltered by five subsequent generations.

At first they traveled by boat up the Missouri, making about ten miles a day before their first important stop, some twenty miles north of the future Omaha, where they held their first powwow with Indians. The name they gave this site is perpetuated in Council Bluffs, the Iowa city south of their meeting place. On August 20 Sergeant Floyd died—the only casualty of the two-year expedition—and was buried on a high hill about a mile below the mouth of Floyd's River, near Sioux City.

A week later they killed their first buffalo, and

soon afterward sighted an antelope and some prairie dogs, the first known to science. Late in October, 165 days from their start at the Mississippi River, they reached the Mandan villages, thirty miles north of present-day Bismarck, North Dakota, on the north bank of the Missouri. Only two of the old villages that occupied this location remained when Lewis and Clark settled down for the winter. Here they hired a whisky-guzzling French-Canadian halfbreed named Toussaint Charbonneau, who had lived among the Mandans for twenty years and who, as part of his bargain with the two captains, threw in his wife Sakakawea, or Sacajawea, "The Bird Woman," who could row, carry, and stand the beatings Charbonneau gave her. As it turned out, it was the courageous Sacajawea, rather than her unreliable husband, who was of inestimable help to the expedition.

With the coming of spring, the party left the Mandan villages and headed up the Missouri. Crossing country that was loaded with game, they saw herds of buffalo, deer, antelope, moose, elk, and bighorn sheep, not to mention birds of every description. It was Lewis' opinion that two hunters, in this region, could supply a regiment; but they restrained themselves and shot only what they needed for food. Then, on April 26, 1805, they arrived at the mouth of the *Roche Jaune*—the Yellowstone. Although most of the territory traversed by Lewis and Clark was unknown to white men, the Yellowstone had been visited and named by the French explorer, La Vérendrye, fifty years earlier.

On the last day of May Lewis recorded his impression of the White Cliffs, east of Fort Benton, Montana: ". . . a white soft sandstone bluff which rises to about half the height of the hills," which the river had worn down "into a thousand grotesque figures." On June 13 Lewis, tramping on ahead of the boats, came on the Great Falls of the Missouri, which he thought "the grandest sight I ever beheld."

Still following the Missouri, they now headed almost due south until they reached the river's three forks, which they named for Jefferson, Madison, and Gallatin. They went up the Jefferson, largest of the three, to its source in the Continental Divide, and then struck out through the lofty Bitterroot Range which marks the boundary of Montana and Idaho, the roughest and most difficult part of the trip. Often hungry, the party ate nothing but berries for a time, but were providentially assisted by Sacajawea's tribe. The daughter of a Shoshone chief, she had been cap-

TEXT CONTINUED ON PAGE 340

The Bitterroots were covered with snow by mid-September, and the expedition nearly starved here on the Lolo trail.

While portaging Celilo Falls at this spot on the Columbia, Lewis and Clark caught sight of snow-covered Mount Hood.

TEXT CONTINUED FROM PAGE 338

tured by Hidatsa Indians and sold to Charbonneau; and at this time of dire need, among the barren defiles of the Rockies, the expedition was saved by the near-miraculous appearance of the very tribe from which she had been stolen. Her brother Cameahwait was chief, and he gave Lewis and Clark the horses and supplies they needed to cross the Continental Divide.

Once beyond the Bitterroots, they headed down the Clearwater River to its junction with the Lewis or Snake River, then went on to the Columbia. After building new canoes, the party passed through The Dalles of the Columbia on October 24, shot the Long Narrows the next day, and on November 2 slipped through the Cascades. Five days later, on November 7, 1805, they saw for the first time the "object of all our labors, the reward of all anxieties"—the crashing surf of the Pacific Ocean. It was more than eighteen months since the 32 gaunt men had seen civilization, back in St. Louis.

They were astonished to find that the Northwest Indians had been in touch with other white men (along the Columbia they had seen white men's articles, and near the Pacific one Indian astonished them by saying "son of a pitch").

Five miles from Astoria, Oregon, is the careful reconstruction of Fort Clatsop, where they spent the winter of 1805–6; in Seaside, Oregon, is a cobblestone cairn where Lewis and Clark boiled sea water to make salt; and at the foot of the town's main street, a plaque that marks the end of the trail.

This was not, by any stretch of the imagination, the end of the trail for Lewis and Clark. To begin with, there was the first American Christmas in the Northwest, spent at Fort Clatsop, which was a meager affair. "After brackfast," Clark wrote, "we divided our Tobacco which amounted to 12 carrots one half of which we gave to the men of the party who used tobacco, and to those who doe not use it we make a present of a handkerchief . . . our Dinner concisted of pore Elk, so much Spoiled that we eate it thro' mear necessity." The "Musquetors" (fleas) contributed by the Clatsop Indians on their daily visits were "so troublesom," Clark added, that "I have slept but little for 2 night past."

Then there were those thousands of miles to retrace, days and nights of hardship and discomfort, pain and danger. When they finally returned to St. Louis on September 23, 1806, they had been gone for two years, four months, and nine days. They had added immeasurably to scientific and geographic knowledge; they had strengthened the U.S. claim to the whole bountiful area; but above all they had blazed the trail and opened the eyes of all Americans to the rich and wonderful lands which were there, almost for the taking.

Thomas Jefferson, who had finally seen his dream come true, submitted a report to Congress on December 2, 1806: "The Expedition of Messrs. Lewis and Clarke, for exploring the river Missouri, and the best communication from that to the Pacific Ocean, has had all the success which could have been expected, they have traced the Missouri nearly to its source, descended the Columbia to the Pacific Ocean, ascertained with accuracy the geography of that interesting communication across our continent, learned the character of the country, of its commerce and inhabitants: and it is but justice to say that Messrs. Lewis and Clarke and their brave companions have by this arduous service deserved well of their country."

The location at which Lewis and Clark reached the Columbia's mouth in November, 1805, looks much the same today.

340

In 1837 Alfred Jacob Miller painted Fort Laramie, showing the colorfully dressed Indians who came to trade there. Above are the ruins of the enlisted men's barracks.

The Way West

In 1849 something like fifty thousand Americans, all of them in a hurry, traveled across the continent by overland routes. That year the procession of caravans on the Oregon Trail was so continuous that the lead wagon of one train frequently was not more than a few hundred yards behind the tail wagon of the group ahead. It was a spring of constant rain—of deep mud, of wet food, blankets, and clothing, of head colds, and of cholera. Perhaps five thousand Forty Niners died of cholera before they reached the high plains, while many more succumbed to the physical strain of the trip itself. A few foolhardy ones, eager to get to California, set off alone with their possessions on their backs, only to go insane in the desert, slit their throats, or end up begging for food along the trail; but most of the travelers were wise enough to stick to the wagon trains.

After they left Mitchell Pass, Nebraska, the route was fairly easy along the upward grade to the way station at Fort Laramie. The ruins of the old fort still guard the fertile, level plain where wagon trains provisioned at exorbitant prices a century ago, but from here on the trail is marked almost entirely by natural landmarks. At the Upper Crossing of the North Platte, alkali salts swirled up to burn the skin, causing ugly sores to form around the mouth and across the knuckles. Here the trail bent to the south again, passing through sagebrush plains dappled with shim-

342

mering lakes, then on to the Sweetwater River, near Split Rock, Wyoming, and to Independence Rock which lies on the plain like a sleeping Gulliver, tempting emigrants to pause and inscribe their names.

From here the land rises steadily up to South Pass, the unobtrusive gateway through the Rockies, where men suddenly felt unaccountably fatigued, short of breath, and quick to anger. When they arrived at Pacific Springs, the more observant ones noticed that the water flowed west—they had passed the Continental Divide. Now there was a choice of routes: the southern hook past Fort Bridger or the Sublette Cutoff. The trouble with the latter was that it led across

In Samuel Colman's painting, prairie schooners heading west along the Oregon Trail ford a shallow desert stream.

desert, over two ridges of the Wind River Range, and several difficult streams. Even though it was 53 miles longer, most people chose the Fort Bridger route, where there was plenty of water, and some meager provisions at Jim Bridger's ramshackle establishment.

Not far from Soda Springs, Idaho, the more impatient gold seekers branched off to the south, taking the Hudspeth Cutoff through the desert to the Raft River; but the majority went on to Fort Hall. Out in the middle of a bug-ridden flat, and swarming with dirty Shoshoni who came to trade, beg, or steal, Fort Hall was a disappointment—but it was the last way station. Beyond lay the hot, semi-arid bottoms of the Snake River, and a fork in the trail. The northern branch, hardly traveled in 1849, wound on to Oregon. The other took the desert plunge to California.

In the High Sierras, snow piles deep in Donner Pass, named for the party from Illinois which was stranded here during the winter of 1846-47. They were far behind schedule when they were trapped by an early storm.

End of the Trail

No one traveling through the states of Washington or Oregon today can fail to see what drew people to this supremely beautiful section of the country. Parts of it, especially along the Oregon coast, are as wild and untouched as when Lewis and Clark first saw the Pacific; and in the lush Willamette and Columbia valleys one may see the fruits of a thousand pioneer dreams.

Scattered through the two states are a few remains of their earliest days, like the Jackson House in Chehalis, Washington, whose owner used to welcome immigrants from the East. In Vancouver are some of the oldest buildings, dating from the time when Fort Vancouver, the Hudson's Bay Company base, was under the rule of Dr. John McLoughlin, and was the only civilized spot in the Northwest. From 1825 to 1845 Dr. McLoughlin ruled a vast empire which extended from the Rockies to the Pacific, from Alaska to California; and although his first allegiance was to the Hudson's Bay Company, it was he who sent supplies to starving American immigrants, provided passage for them in company boats, and protected them

from hostile Indians. Many of the first settlers owed their survival in the Oregon country to his generous assistance; but as friction increased between the U.S. and Great Britain over claims to this territory, McLoughlin's friendship to the Americans was resented by his employers. In 1845 he resigned and went to Oregon City, Oregon, where he built the square, clapboarded mansion which has been restored and moved to the park bearing his name.

Among Dr. McLoughlin's visitors in the fall of 1836 were Dr. Marcus Whitman and his wife Narcissa, who had come to the Oregon country to establish an Indian mission. Waiilatpu, or "Place of Rye Grass," where they founded the mission, is about six miles west of the present Walla Walla, Washington, and the little community where the Whitmans taught the nomadic Indians agricultural and industrial pursuits became one of the landmarks of the Oregon Trail. As the years passed, there were signs of restiveness among the Cayuse Indians, and in November, 1847, they attacked the mission, massacring the Whitmans and twelve others. The settlement that had begun

344

with such high hopes was destroyed completely, and today the visitor will see only the ruined foundations of the mission buildings, and a few Indian artifacts uncovered by excavations at the site.

It is easy to forget that there was not always a pot of gold at the end of the rainbow, and that for each group that reached the promised land there were some who fell by the wayside, never to glimpse it. Every trail to the West was marked by little mounds of earth containing the bones of the hopeful who had passed that way; and there are memories of dark disasters that still strike terror to the heart.

One of these stories began in Illinois, where the well-to-do Donner brothers read Lansford W. Hastings' exaggerated *The Emigrants' Guide to Oregon and California,* and organized an overland party. Hastings' book glibly advised travelers to reduce time and distance to California by leaving the regular trail at Fort Bridger, and taking a cutoff "southwest to the Salt Lake; and thence continuing down to the Bay of San Francisco." What it did not say was that this led across Utah's Wasatch Range—almost an impossible route for wagons to negotiate—over the terrible Salt Lake Desert, the Nevada desert, and the High Sierras. Against the advice of experienced trailsmen, the Donners took the cutoff at Fort Bridger, and pushed on toward disaster.

After a harrowing trip across the fiery desert, the party was rife with dissension and ill feeling. By the time the Donners reached the Truckee River at the foot of the Sierras it was late October, they were far behind schedule, and as they prepared to climb the 2,000-foot granite ridge of the Sierra the first winter storm came whistling out of the north. Before long the mountains were buried under snow, stalling them completely, and by December the emigrants were reduced to eating twigs and bark. After four men died and one went insane, a party of fifteen of the strongest started for help. Thirty-two days later seven of them arrived at an Indian village, more dead than alive, to tell of having been forced to eat the bodies of companions who died along the way. The first of several relief parties reached Donner Lake on February 18, 1847, where those who had stayed behind had suffered unimaginably. Of the 89 men, women, and children who set out from Fort Bridger, only 45 had survived the awful winter.

Anyone who takes U.S. 40, the winding route that leads up the all but perpendicular wall of lonely Donner Pass, may pause for a moment to imagine what it was like there, not much more than a hundred years ago, when the exhausted pioneers, struggling against the deep drifting snow, started up the cliffs that lay between them and the end of the trail.

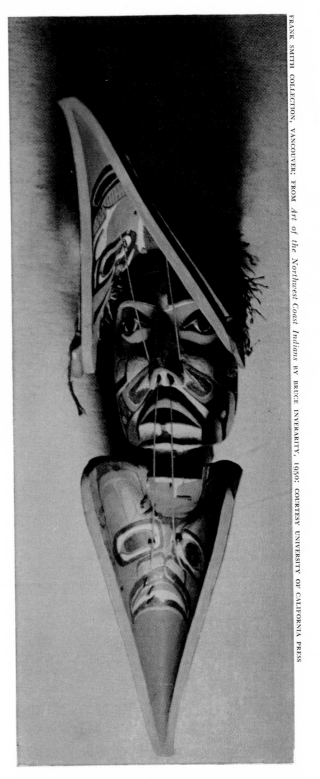

Indians of the Northwest achieved a remarkably high level of civilization, largely because of the bountiful natural resources around them. The Kwakiutl mask shown here is an example of the Northwest Indians' superb craftsmanship. Four feet in height, the wooden mask represents a human head when fully open. When the visor is pulled down, it becomes a raven.

345

Salt Lake City was laid out on a grandiose scale and, against formidable obstacles, blossomed into a desert metropolis. This early picture shows the multi-gabled house (right) of Brigham Young's wives.

Much of the Mormons' success was the result of Brigham Young's leadership.

This Is the Place

The vision sprang to life in 1827, on a hill near Palmyra, New York, where Joseph Smith said he had found the golden tablets, inscribed with sacred writing. Three years later, Smith and the members of the church he founded felt the hostility and distrust of their neighbors, and in 1831 began a trek which was to continue for sixteen years, transporting Smith's vision to the other side of the continent. It was a journey marked by persecution, bloodshed, hatred, and hardship without parallel in American history, and Joseph Smith was only one of many who died along the way.

In 1831 the handful of Mormons were in Kirtland, Ohio, where one of their temples still stands. Until 1838 the neighbors left them in peace, and then they were forced to move on, this time to Independence and Far West, Missouri. Soon the mobs were at their heels again, the governor announced they must be driven from the state, and they headed east to Commerce, Illinois, renamed Nauvoo. By 1844 they had built a prosperous city of 15,000 on the Mississippi's

Begun in 1853, the Salt Lake Temple was built of granite hauled twenty miles by ox-teams. A figure of the Angel Moroni is on top of the tower. In the background the impressive Utah Capitol may be seen.

banks. That year trouble struck again. Joseph Smith and his brother Hyrum were taken to jail in Carthage, and killed by a mob. Once more the faithful had to decide whether they should stand or flee.

One leader, James Jesse Strang, took a group north to Voree, Wisconsin, and then on to Beaver Island, Michigan, where he became "king" of one of the strangest colonies in American history.

Most of the people, however, decided to follow the 43-year-old Brigham Young, who had decided that the only place they could find repose was in an isolated, unwanted spot far beyond civilization. From John C. Frémont's account of his 1842 expedition, Young knew that such a place existed beside the Great Salt Lake.

Late in 1845 the Mormons began preparations for their migration, and early in February of the following year the first band set out across the Mississippi to Iowa, where they established Camp of Israel, the first of many way stations along the route. Not as a mass migration, but party by party they left, and by June of 1846 Nauvoo was deserted. Brigham Young and a group of pioneers went ahead, establishing way stations like Garden Grove and Mount Pisgah in Iowa. By the time the last covered wagon and handcart had left Nauvoo, Young was at the Missouri, where he laid

out Winter Quarters. That winter food and fuel were scarce and 600 died of a plague, but on April 9, 1847, Young and his pioneer band set off once again.

Beyond South Pass they met Jim Bridger, who directed them across the Wasatch Mountains, and the red-walled cliffs of Echo Canyon. Finally, as Emigration Canyon broadened, they caught sight of the land Brigham Young had promised them. "This is the place," he said; but the brethren could see little to gladden their hearts. It was "a broad and barren plain hemmed in by mountains, blistering in the burning rays of the midsummer sun. No waving fields, no swaying forests, no verdant meadows . . . but on all sides a seemingly interminable waste of sagebrush."

In spite of the overwhelming natural difficulties, in spite of frosts, insects, and drought that killed their crops, in spite of public distrust, government opposition, and attacks by other settlers, they succeeded in carrying through Brigham Young's plan for a Zion in the West. Today, when one visits Salt Lake City's great Mormon Temple, the Tabernacle, the Beehive House, and Brigham Young Museum or any of the quiet old Mormon villages like Toquerville, he can only marvel at the courage which brought life to a desert and substance to a vision.

347

The Gold Rush

John A. Sutter was a man with grandiose dreams, but in the light of what happened, it is ironic that the discovery of gold did not seem to be one of them. A Swiss adventurer who came to Mexican California in 1839, Sutter had wangled a huge land grant in the lower Sacramento Valley which he christened New Helvetia. At the junction of the Sacramento and American rivers, Sutter built an adobe-walled fort, enclosing a whole village of homes, stores, and warehouses. His fort, which has been restored in Sacramento, was an important trading post for the American settlers coming overland to California, and Sutter said of himself, "I was everything—patriarch, priest, father, and judge."

Sutter hired a carpenter named James Marshall to supervise construction of a sawmill forty miles above the fort in a mountain valley the Indians called Coloma, or "beautiful vale," and on January 24, 1848, after the men had done some blasting in the stream, Marshall noticed some yellow particles glittering in the bedrock. He collected them and that night announced to his crew, "Boys, I think I've found a gold mine." No one believed him, but next day the yellow flakes turned up again, and Marshall gathered three ounces of the dust and rode off to the fort. There he and Sutter tested it and, convinced it was gold, did their best to squelch the news. They succeeded fairly well until the middle of May, when a Mormon named Sam Brannan appeared in San Francisco, brandishing a quinine bottle full of gold dust and yelling, "Gold, gold, gold from the American River!" Something about Brannan's antics fused the town into action and before anyone quite knew what had happened, everyone seemed to be off for the river.

San Francisco became a ghost town. By June three-fourths of its population of 800 had departed, business was almost non-existent, and sailorless ships rotted in the bay. As prospectors ranged over the western slopes of the Sierra they seemed to find gold everywhere. What they had come upon was a long, narrow strip of gold-bearing quartz, a mile wide and 120 miles long—the "Mother Lode." By the end of the year, eight or ten thousand men were working the Sierra diggings—one taking out $40,000 in seven weeks, but the majority collecting an ounce a day, or about twenty dollars' worth.

While gold brought riches to a few, it spelled ruin for Marshall and Sutter. As his employees deserted him for the gold fields, Sutter's commercial enterprises collapsed, squatters usurped his land, and he lost his fort through bankruptcy. Miners swarmed over Marshall's claims and appropriated them, and in 1885 Marshall died broke and forgotten, within sight of his discovery. Today a lonely stone shaft on the bank of the American River near Coloma marks the site of Sutter's Mill, and close by is the cabin where Marshall spent many sad, protesting years.

Back East, the initial reaction to the gold discoveries was one of disbelief until President Polk devoted an enthusiastic paragraph of his message to Congress to "the abundance of gold in that territory." This was in December, 1848, and the President's words were dramatized shortly thereafter by the arrival in Washington of an army officer, bearing a tea caddy containing 230 ounces of pure gold. The sensation was

This contemporary etching was an Easterner's acid comment on the attempt of some Forty-Niners to be self-sufficient.

immediate and complete, and from all over the United States—indeed, from all over the world—men pulled up stakes and headed for California. By ship, by wagon train, enduring every conceivable hardship, they came by the thousands to a land where riches lay on the ground, waiting to be picked.

In 1849 the majority of miners worked alone or in small partnerships, using the most rudimentary tools —picks, shovels, and pans. They were too busy seeking their fortunes to worry about cleanliness, and a mining camp like Humbug Creek, Flapjack Canyon, or Gouge Eye was no more than a dusty street, lined with saloons, gambling parlors, and discarded trash, surrounded by the lean-tos or tents of the miners. Some men lived in barrels, and all were beset with fleas, lice, and the various diseases of filth and exposure. Flour sold for $400 a barrel, sugar for $4 a pound, whisky for $20 a quart, but the men objected most to the absence of women.

CONTINUED ON PAGE 350

Decaying, lonely buildings are all that remain of once-booming Melones. The town had a population of 5,000 at the height of the Gold Rush, but less than a hundred live there today. Below, specimens of gold nuggets are shown.

EDMUND B. GERARD, *Life*

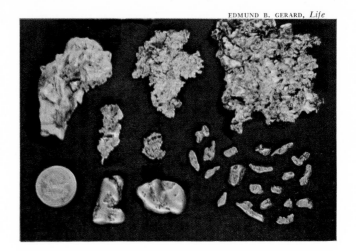

HANSEL MIETH, *Life*

A rough stone shaft on the bank of the American River marks the site of Sutter's Mill, where James Marshall spied flakes of gold one January morning in 1848. Although gold had been found before in California—six years earlier Mexicans had worked claims in Placerita Canyon near Los Angeles —Marshall's chance discovery was the one that provoked the famous 1849 Gold Rush.

CONTINUED FROM PAGE 349

By the end of 1852, with as many as 100,000 miners in the diggings, the individual had a hard time making it pay. Gold was no longer within easy reach and soon large companies backed by eastern capital moved in, transforming the gold hunt from an enormous, squalid stag party into an efficient industry. The prospectors began drifting away to seek Eldorados elsewhere—in Colorado, the Klondike, or the Black Hills.

Driving along California State Highway 49, the traveler will see the permanent marks made by the Gold Rush on the Mother Lode country. Some of them are not pretty, like the man-made badlands which have resulted from the hydraulic workings, or the hanging trees where the quick "justice" of miners' courts was executed. But there are many charming old mining villages with their narrow, winding streets to delight the visitor. Off the main road, a few abandoned shanties of the "pick and pan" men are left, but the buildings which have weathered the years best are those which were built to last, like stores and the iron-shuttered Wells Fargo offices. There are towns like Downieville, with its board sidewalks and dirt streets, its Costa Store, and a pioneer museum, housed in an 1852 building. Sonora is another place which is fairly typical of the Mother Lode region.

Placerville is a pretty town that boomed during the 1850's, and El Dorado has a few ruins of the Gold Rush days. There is Mokelumne Hill, Murphys, Angels Camp, and Melones, which was called Slumgullion when Mark Twain and Bret Harte lived there. Best preserved of all these old towns, however, is Columbia, which is now a state historic site. When Columbia was the "gem of the southern mines," 15,000 people lived here—now the population is 200. The Wells Fargo office is a museum, as is the Stage Driver's Retreat, a bar which has a piano brought around the Horn. In the town's firehouse are two 1850 fire engines, and the Pioneer Saloon once contained a bar, gambling parlor, and dance hall.

Downieville, a quiet California town, rests on gravel once so rich that 60 square feet yielded $12,000. Many buildings are remnants of boom days.

Part of the Gold Hill district in Colorado, where a strike occurred in 1859, is visible below from an abandoned cabin.

Men once prospected with pitchforks in Cripple Creek, Colorado (above), and called it the "$300,000,000 cow pasture."

Ghost Towns

No one who caught the gold fever ever quite recovered. By the middle of the 1850's, most of the large placer finds in California began to give out, and when the big crusher mills moved in the individual prospector began to seek out more fertile fields. With not much more than a grub stake, a washing pan, and a burro or mule, he roamed from the Pacific to the Rockies, from the Gila north to British Columbia.

There was gold in the eastern Sierras, in Nevada—but not enough water to work the placers. So in 1859 some miners dug a reservoir to hold the runoff of mountain snows at the head of Six Mile Canyon, uncovering, in the process, a vein of bluish rock flecked with gold. At first the "black stuff" was thrown away as worthless; then someone took the trouble to have it assayed and discovered that it held nearly $5,000 worth of silver and $1,600 of gold to the ton. This was the Comstock Lode, and the leading camp in these parts was Virginia City, named for a drunk called "Old Virginny." Today the town has about 1,000 people and a past which is very much in evidence—along A and B streets, the old residential district of unpainted Gothic houses; Piper's Opera House, where Edwin Booth, Maude Adams, and Lily Langtry once appeared; and on C Street, the Crystal Bar, Delta Saloon, and the Bucket of Blood. The *Territorial Enterprise,* again operating, was the first newspaper in Nevada, where Mark Twain served his apprenticeship.

In the spring of 1859 an estimated 100,000 gold-seekers were streaming westward toward Colorado, the words "Pike's Peak or Bust" printed on their packs and on their wagons. There followed, in the next few decades, some of the most spectacular strikes ever made—each creating out of nothing the towns which dot the Colorado landscape today. The list is a long one, and there is no end to the interesting places to see. There is Central City, once known as "the richest square mile on earth," with its famous Opera House and the Teller House, to which President Grant, on his visit in 1873, walked from the stagecoach on a path of silver bricks. Nearby is Nevadaville, a genuine ghost town; and there is Silver Cliff, once the third largest town in the state, but now almost deserted. Leadville, where Horace Tabor struck it rich, is still a mining town; but here you may see the old Wyman Saloon, the former Tabor Grand Opera House on Harrison Avenue, Tabor's Grand Hotel, his house, and the Matchless Mine, where his widow "Baby Doe," forlornly hoping to recoup a lost fortune, froze to death.

All around the Cripple Creek district, behind Pike's Peak, there are abandoned houses and mine workings. Victor was the site of the great Gold Coin Mine, discovered during excavation of a hotel basement. Cripple Creek itself, once known as "the $300,000,000 cow pasture," is a shade of its former self; and towns like Elkton and Gillett are practically deserted.

Another great nineteenth-century bonanza took place in Montana, in Alder Gulch, and the town most representative of that place and era is another Virginia City, also very much worth seeing. Along Wallace Street, the main thoroughfare, are the Fairweather Inn, Rank's Drugstore, an assay office, and the Wells Fargo office, all dating from the days of the big strike in the 1860's.

Virginia City, Nevada, named for a drunk called "Old Virginny,"
was the leading camp of the fabulous Comstock Lode, found in 1859.

Past Split Rock in the Sweetwater Valley, a Pony Express rider is pursued by Indians. The most dangerous part of the Missouri-to-California route was in Utah and Nevada, but the couriers' horses were so fast that few of them were ever caught.

Passing of the Pony Express

Only one mail bag carried by the short-lived Pony Express failed to be delivered; but in 1861 the service was discontinued after completion of the transcontinental telegraph line. At first the Indians were superstitious of the so-called "talking wires." Later, realizing the significance of the lines, they cut the wires and attacked many of the isolated telegraph stations along the route.

"Away across the dead level of the Prairie a black speck appears against the sky. . . . In a second or two it becomes a horse and rider . . . soon the flutter of hoofs comes faintly to the ear. In another instant, a whoop and a hurrah from the upper deck of our coach, a wave of the rider's hand, but no reply, and man and horse burst past our excited faces, and go swinging away like the belated fragments of a storm."

In *Roughing It* Mark Twain described the thrill of seeing a Pony Express rider one summer day in 1861. It was a sight no one could forget. During its short lifetime—it was discontinued after a year and a half of service—the Pony Express was the object of almost universal respect and admiration. Until it was introduced, twenty days to a month was considered fast delivery for mail from Missouri to California. The Pony Express cut at least ten days off that time.

On April 3, 1860, the freight and passenger hauling firm of Russell, Majors & Waddell, operating out of St. Joseph, Missouri, and Nebraska City, inaugurated its innovation in mail-carrying. In effect, it was a kind of horse-telegraph, like the one Genghis Khan had employed to bind his empire together. The road began in St. Joseph, where the original stables still stand, and ran west to Sacramento, following in general the Oregon Trail to Fort Bridger, then turning southwest. Before sections of the route were replaced by telegraph, there were 190 stations, 420 horses, 400 station men, and 80 riders. The stations were set up at ten-mile intervals, and although few of them remain today, one can see an example of them at Hanover, Kansas, where the Hollenberg Station is the only original and unaltered one left. At Fairbury, Nebraska, is the site of the Rock Creek Station where Wild Bill Hickok was an agent. Nearby, incidentally, is the George Winslow grave, one of the few marked graves on the Oregon Trail. The town park at Gothenburg, Nebraska, has a log fur-trading house that was once a Pony Express station, and at Fort Bridger, Wyoming, one may see some remaining stables.

The typical rider was a young man in his early twenties, light, tough, and inured to the saddle. In Mark Twain's words, "he rode a splendid horse that was born for a racer and fed and lodged like a gentleman"—usually a small, fast California mustang. The rider's daily stint was 75 or 100 miles, and he made two round trips a week. He was expected to average nine miles an hour, and was allowed only two minutes for changing horses. Arriving at a relay station, he received a gulp of water and a bite of bread while the *mochila,* a square leather pad with mail pouches fitted at each corner, was slung over the saddle of a fresh horse. If he arrived to find his replacement sick or injured, he had to keep going. One man, "Pony Bob"

These stables at Fort Bridger, Wyoming, are among the last remaining examples of nearly 200 Pony Express stations.

Haslam, once rode through 380 miles of hostile Indian territory in 45 hours, stopping only nine hours to rest.

The station agents' lives were hardly easier. Alone, often surrounded by hostile Indians, they usually lived in shacks, tents, or adobe hovels. One station in the Utah desert was described as a "hole, four feet deep, roofed over with split cedar trunks and with a rough adobe chimney." The most dangerous section of the route was in Utah and Nevada, where the Paiutes were on a rampage of destruction and murder in the early 1860's. Here a number of stations were burned, and agents killed. Because their horses were so fast, few riders were ever killed, but the trips were no less harrowing on that account.

Only the most important mail was carried by the Pony Express. It was always an expensive venture, and unfortunately its returns were never enough to keep it out of the red. To make matters worse, the Pony Express received no financial aid from the government (ironically, the insignia worn by postmen today depicts a Pony Express rider), since the subsidy for transcontinental mail belonged to the Butterfield Overland Mail firm. When Russell, Majors & Waddell had lost an estimated $200,000 in the Pony Express venture they went bankrupt, and received no recompense from the government despite the fact that news of Southern secession, carried by Pony Express, had helped to nip an uprising of California Confederates, and kept the Far West in the Union.

Beyond any financial failure, however, construction of a transcontinental telegraph brought the end of the Pony Express. Neither romantic nor spectacular, the "talking wires," as the Indians called them, were joined from east to west at Salt Lake City in October, 1861. From that moment on, there was no more need for a cross-country horse-telegraph.

The full story of Custer's last stand at the Battle of the Little Big Horn may never be known. Overwhelmed by a furious Indian assault, his small cavalry force had no hope of escape, and not a single man survived.

Custer's Last Stand

Driving along Montana Route 8, from Lame Deer to Crow Agency, the traveler may pause for a moment high in the Wolf Mountains to look westward, toward the valley of the Little Big Horn, just as Colonel George Armstrong Custer's scouts did near here on the morning of June 25, 1876. The Sioux and Cheyennes were known to be gathering in this area, and Custer was under the command of General Terry in a three-way pincer movement in which the forces of General Terry, General Crook, and Colonel Gibbon were to converge upon the enemy. Custer split off from Terry with a small band along Rosebud Creek.

This three-way attack was all very well on paper, but it did not take into account the rough, untracked country, the deep, swift streams, or the mountain ranges which would have to be crossed before it could be made to work. At the Battle of Rosebud Creek on

June 17, Crook was repulsed by a large force of Indians; but neither Custer nor Gibbon was aware of this. All they knew was that a sizable enemy force was gathering somewhere near the headquarters of Rosebud Creek and the Little Big Horn—but exactly where, they were not certain.

Marching south, Custer saw traces of a large band of moving Indians, and without bothering to ask for reinforcements he set off in pursuit. By June 24 the trail was hot, and it seemed probable that the Indians were camped only a short distance to the west, on the other side of the Wolf Mountains.

Shortly after sunrise on June 25, Custer's scouts could see, perhaps fifteen miles away, an ominous blue haze spreading out over the land, the collective smoke of many campfires. Although Custer did not realize it, this was the largest Indian mobilization in

U.S. history, and when his favorite scout Bloody Knife warned him that the odds were too great, Custer replied, "Oh, I guess we'll get through them in one day." About nine o'clock he ordered his dead-tired men forward. Down in the foothills, he inexplicably divided his small force into four parts: Captain Fred Benteen to the southwest to scout for Indians; two detachments commanded by Major Marcus Reno and Custer to the northwest in the direction of the Indian camp; and the pack train to the rear.

Sitting Bull was a power behind the Indian uprising. The 1865 photograph of Custer was taken by Brady.

A little after two, riding through a wide valley where the grass was heat-burned to a dark brown color, Custer and Reno saw their first Indians, some Sioux who rode up close and then dashed away, yelling derisively. Custer sent Reno and his troopers off in pursuit, and across the river they came face to face with a superior force of Sioux, who drove them back with heavy losses.

Meantime, Custer continued northwest, riding along the brown, ravine-gutted bluffs. He had sent a message to Benteen, asking for reinforcements, but Benteen had joined Reno, to help him stave off complete disaster. While Custer waited, he lost whatever time advantage he might have had, and once the Indians repulsed Reno, they hurried to attack Custer's force. With a sudden fury, they must have come at him from all sides, jumping him from the ravines and gullies that crisscross these bare hills. Knowledge of what happened after that comes only from the Indians who were there—because not one of Custer's 265 men survived. From the position of the bodies it was possible to surmise that the main Indian attack came from the rear, and that Custer's troopers resisted in an orderly enough manner at first, only to be routed by the 2,500 vengeful Indians.

The battle ranged along an L-shaped ridge, and because the Indians had segmented Custer's force, it was impossible for him to organize a concerted stand. The place where he might have made it—on the summit of this ridge—was overwhelmed by the mounted Indians, so Custer's cavalry had to fight it out on the slope under the brow of the hill, and on foot.

The fiercely contested battle lasted but a short time, and must have been over by the middle of the afternoon. In spite of its brevity, and the fact that it was a relatively unimportant incident in American history, few battles before or since have held quite the same fascination for writers or the public.

Anyone who visits the sage-covered ridge and the little cemetery in the heart of the Crow Reservation will have to contend with a variety of legends and facts relating to the battle itself. And anyone who wishes to philosophize about the lightning pace of American history may pause a moment to think that this happened not quite seventy years before the Atomic Age began.

A group of Sioux Indians leaves Sitting Bull's solitary grave in North Dakota's Standing Rock Reservation.

Many of Custer's men lie buried where they made their last stand on a high bluff above the Little Big Horn.

357

In Joseph Becker's painting, Chinese gandy dancers wave at a Central Pacific train passing through snow sheds in the Sierras. These sheds were built in places where avalanche danger was great.

Spanning the Continent

The discovery of gold in California gave wings to men's imaginations. In 1830 intelligent men were insisting that it would take anywhere from 500 to 2,000 years to settle and develop the country. What happened in 1848 changed the timetable forever, and 21 years later Americans had a railroad all the way across the continent, with settlements springing up along its path. The Civil War and the necessity of binding West to East were decisive factors in bringing it about, but the prospect of riches kept the issue in the public eye for many years.

In California, a man named Theodore Dehone Judah, popularly known as Crazy Judah, had engineered a railroad from Sacramento to the gold fields and by 1855 he was publicly urging a road across the Sierras to the East. Judah was backed by four Sacramento merchants: Collis P. Huntington, Mark Hop-kins, Leland Stanford, and Charles P. Crocker. In return for financing Judah's survey over the Sierra Nevada, these men later became officers of the Central Pacific Railroad, and later still, four of the wealthiest men in America.

In July, 1862, President Lincoln signed the Enabling Act, which created the Union Pacific Railroad and authorized construction of a "continuous railroad and telegraph line" starting west from Council Bluffs, Iowa. It provided land grants of 12,000 acres to the mile in alternate sections along the line, and bond issues to help finance construction. Upon the same terms, the Central Pacific Railroad was authorized to start building eastward from the Coast.

Hundreds of workmen—many of them Irishmen fresh from the Union Army—began the backbreaking job of grading and laying track west from Council

358

Bluffs. The route, even at that time, was an historic one—a natural thoroughfare along the rivers which had been followed by buffalo, Indians, fur traders, explorers, Mormons, gold hunters, the Overland stagecoaches, and the Pony Express. First there was the problem of supply—providing the 6,250,000 ties and 50,000 tons of rails and fittings, bridges, and other installations. Until completion of the Chicago & Northwestern Railroad as far as Council Bluffs in 1867, the only means of transporting supplies to the workers on the Union Pacific end of the line was by boat up the Missouri River, or by team. Along the way, gamblers, ex-convicts, and con-men plagued the workers as they moved across the plains and mountains, and always there were Indians, harassing the workmen at every opportunity, seeking to halt this permanent intrusion into their lands. By the end of 1866, 300 miles of track had been laid; the following year saw 240 miles added, and the railroad reached its highest point near Cheyenne, Wyoming. In 1868, 425 miles were covered, and the road was within 125 miles of its proposed meeting with the Central Pacific.

On the western section, the first year's work produced only 18 miles of track, from Sacramento to Roseville. The Central Pacific, like the Union Pacific, had a welter of investment difficulties, and because of the continuing search for gold, there was a shortage of laborers. Finally Crocker, superintending construction, introduced Chinese workers, or Crocker's Pets, as they were called. Many of them were imported from China specifically for this job, and eventually thousands of Chinese pushed the rails through the deep snow and solid granite walls of the Sierra Nevada, using picks, shovels, and wheelbarrows for the enormous task.

By June of 1868 the Central Pacific had reached the California-Utah line, and the race for completion began in earnest, each company seeking the land grants and bonds that came with every completed mile. Finally, the government set the meeting place at Promontory Point, six miles west of Ogden, Utah, and on May 10, 1869, the great day arrived. Shortly after dawn, two cheering groups of workmen met, and later that morning the official parties arrived to see the last section of track laid and to drive the golden spike tying East and West together for all time. Later the road was rerouted across Great Salt Lake, and today only a monument marks the meeting of the rails near Promontory. The golden spike is in a vault in the Wells Fargo Bank and Union Trust Company in San Francisco. But the meaning of that May day in 1869 will not be lost on anyone who has seen the shining steel rails, stretching to the horizon across the plains and deserts and mountains of the West.

Irish laborers of the Union Pacific joined forces with Central Pacific Chinese as the last mile was blasted out.

Like many railbeds through western mountains, the Animas Canyon passage in Colorado was blasted from sheer cliffs.

When the golden spike was driven at Promontory Point, two engines met, one from the East and the other from the West.

359

Soon after gold was discovered, San Francisco was practically a ghost town, and sailing ships which had brought the Forty-Niners to the coast rotted in the harbor, deserted by their gold-crazy crews. These daguerreotypes were made about 1850.

Golden Gate

At 5:16 on the morning of April 18, 1906, "the deeps of the earth . . . began to rumble and vibrate." The great San Andreas fault on the Pacific Coast had settled violently, and in San Francisco all hell broke loose. For three days fire raged unchecked through the city, destroying four square miles of buildings, taking over 600 lives, and leaving "a mass of smoldering ruins" in its wake.

Across the continent, a San Franciscan named Will Irwin read the dispatches and sat down to write his classic story of "The City That Was." Before the earthquake, this had been a world center of trade and finance, "the gayest, lightest hearted, most pleasure loving city of the western continent." But the old San Francisco was dead, Irwin concluded, and "if it rises out of the ashes it must be a modern city, much like other cities and without its old atmosphere."

A modern San Francisco did rise phoenix-like from the ashes, but it was never to be like any other place. Instead, it is one which many Americans consider the best their country has to offer, a city of atmosphere and spectacular beauty where one can still catch glimpses of a past as colorful as its present.

There is the Mission Dolores, founded in 1776, and the old Presidio, once a Spanish garrison. There is Portsmouth Square, the Plaza of Mexican days, where Captain John Montgomery hoisted the American flag in 1846. Four years after that event San Francisco was the gateway to the gold fields, and the buildings around Portsmouth Square the heart of a lusty, topsy-turvy town. Fort Gunnybags, on Sacramento Street, was headquarters for Vigilance Committees created to preserve law and order; and what is now the city's financial district was the water front, where scores of ships lay rotting, unable to sail because all hands had run off to the gold fields. Some of the hulks were drawn up on shore, to be converted into stores and homes, and one of them, the Ship Building on Montgomery Street, survived until recently.

In 1860 Pony Express riders came into town after the 10½-day trip from Missouri; and in 1875 the Palace, first great luxury hotel of the West, went up on Market Street where its successor now stands. This was the place that moved Emperor Dom Pedro II to say: "Nothing makes me ashamed of Brazil so much as the Palace Hotel." And on Market Street is Lotta's Fountain, presented to the city by Lotta Crabtree, toast of the golden age.

There is Nob Hill, where financial and industrial giants built their palaces; remnants of the Barbary Coast, once the wickedest section of a wicked city; Chinatown, the largest Chinese settlement outside Asia; and the redoubtable cable cars which have climbed the city's hills since 1873.

Of downtown San Francisco, little but the Montgomery Block survived the fire; but what has been added, like the Bay Bridge and the beautiful Golden Gate Bridge, sum up the magic, the beauty, and the future of a city known as the "Baghdad of the West."

The magnificent Golden Gate Bridge spans the entrance to San Francisco Bay. At its southern terminal is the Presidio.

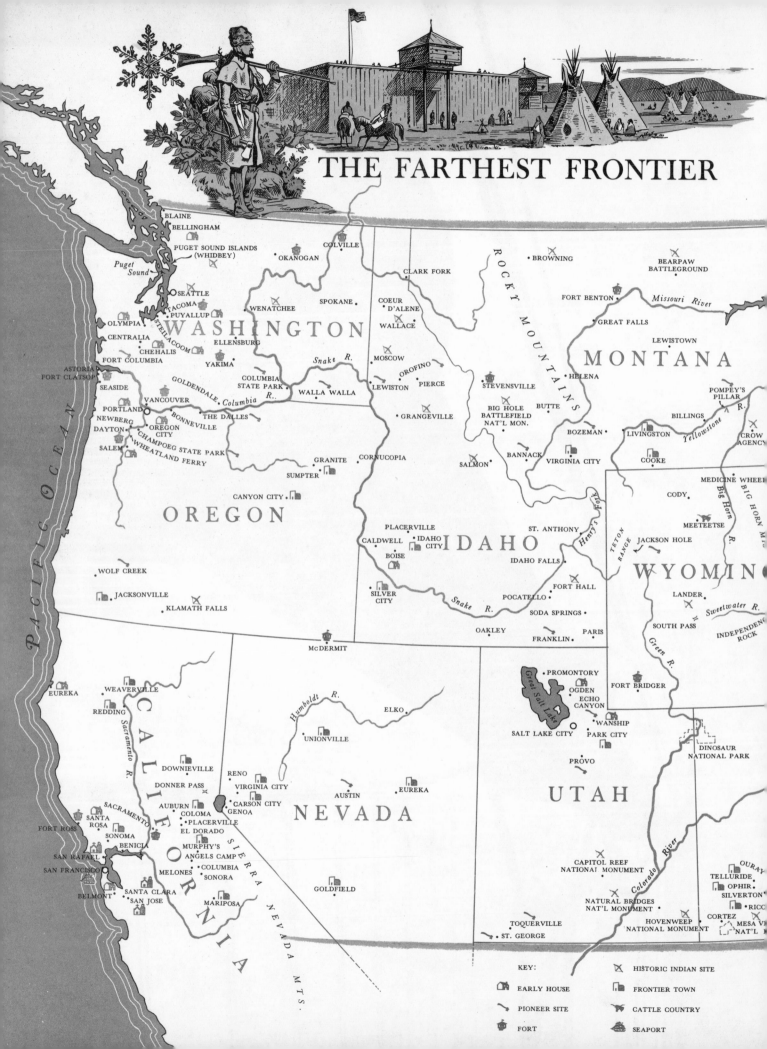

THE FARTHEST FRONTIER

BLAINE
BELLINGHAM
PUGET SOUND ISLANDS (WHIDBEY)
COLVILLE
OKANOGAN
BROWNING
BEARPAW BATTLEGROUND
Puget Sound
SEATTLE
TACOMA
PUYALLUP
WENATCHEE
SPOKANE
CLARK FORK
COEUR D'ALENE
WALLACE
FORT BENTON
Missouri River
GREAT FALLS
LEWISTOWN
MONTANA
OLYMPIA
WASHINGTON
CENTRALIA
STEILACOOM
CHEHALIS
ELLENSBURG
YAKIMA
Snake R.
MOSCOW
LEWISTON
PIERCE
OROFINO
HELENA
STEVENSVILLE
POMPEY'S PILLAR
ASTORIA
FORT CLATSOP
SEASIDE
GOLDENDALE
COLUMBIA STATE PARK
WALLA WALLA
Columbia R.
BIG HOLE BATTLEFIELD NAT'L MON.
BUTTE
BILLINGS
VANCOUVER
PORTLAND
NEWBERG
DAYTON
OREGON CITY
CHAMPOEG STATE PARK
THE DALLES
BONNEVILLE
GRANGEVILLE
SALMON
BANNACK
VIRGINIA CITY
BOZEMAN
LIVINGSTON
COOKE
Yellowstone
CROW AGENCY
SALEM
WHEATLAND FERRY
GRANITE
CORNUCOPIA
MEDICINE WHEEL
CODY
SUMPTER
CANYON CITY
OREGON
MEETEETSE
Big Horn
BIG HORN MTS
PLACERVILLE
CALDWELL
IDAHO CITY
BOISE
IDAHO
ST. ANTHONY
IDAHO FALLS
Henry's Fork
TETON RANGE
JACKSON HOLE
WYOMING
WOLF CREEK
SILVER CITY
FORT HALL
POCATELLO
Snake R.
SODA SPRINGS
LANDER
Sweetwater R.
JACKSONVILLE
KLAMATH FALLS
OAKLEY
FRANKLIN
PARIS
SOUTH PASS
INDEPENDENCE ROCK
McDERMIT
Green R.
PROMONTORY
Great Salt Lake
OGDEN
ECHO CANYON
FORT BRIDGER
EUREKA
WEAVERVILLE
REDDING
Humboldt R.
ELKO
SALT LAKE CITY
WANSHIP
PARK CITY
DINOSAUR NATIONAL PARK
Sacramento R.
UNIONVILLE
PROVO
DOWNIEVILLE
DONNER PASS
RENO
VIRGINIA CITY
AUSTIN
EUREKA
UTAH
CALIFORNIA
SACRAMENTO
AUBURN
COLOMA
CARSON CITY
GENOA
NEVADA
SANTA ROSA
SONOMA
FORT ROSS
PLACERVILLE
EL DORADO
MURPHY'S
ANGELS CAMP
BENICIA
SAN RAFAEL
SAN FRANCISCO
MELONES
COLUMBIA
SONORA
CAPITOL REEF NATIONAL MONUMENT
Colorado River
OURAY
TELLURIDE
OPHIR
SILVERTON
BELMONT
SANTA CLARA
SAN JOSE
MARIPOSA
GOLDFIELD
NATURAL BRIDGES NAT'L MONUMENT
HOVENWEEP NATIONAL MONUMENT
CORTEZ
RICO
MESA NAT'L
SIERRA NEVADA MTS.
TOQUERVILLE
ST. GEORGE

PACIFIC OCEAN

ROCKY MOUNTAINS

KEY:
EARLY HOUSE
PIONEER SITE
FORT
HISTORIC INDIAN SITE
FRONTIER TOWN
CATTLE COUNTRY
SEAPORT

CALIFORNIA

(Northern section: for southern California listings, see page 325.)

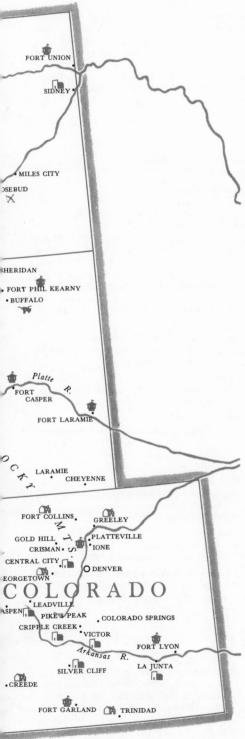

ANGELS CAMP

A picturesque gold camp with a few old buildings, which claims to be the scene of Mark Twain's "The Celebrated Jumping Frog of Calaveras County."

BENICIA

A well-preserved old town which includes California's first *Capitol* (1853).

COLOMA

Site of James W. Marshall's famous discovery of gold. A stone monument stands on the location of *Sutter's Mill,* and a cabin where Marshall lived (1848-68) has been restored in a state park nearby.

COLUMBIA HISTORICAL STATE PARK

Probably the best-preserved ghost town of the Mother Lode region, with a *Wells Fargo Office,* now a museum, the *Stage Driver's Retreat, Masonic Lodge Building, Fallon Theater,* and *Hotel Columbia.* A brick schoolhouse which opened in 1862 is being refitted.

DOWNIEVILLE

Among the interesting survivals of the Gold Rush (*see* p. 351) are the *Costa Store* (1852) and the *Pioneer Museum,* housed in a building erected in 1852 of skillfully laid schist slabs.

DUTCH FLAT

Dutch Flat Hotel One of the stopping places on a main trans-Sierra stage route in the 1850's and 1860's.

EUREKA

Carson House Striking example of California's early Victorian architecture.

FORT ROSS STATE HISTORICAL MONUMENT

Once the principal Russian outpost in California, which provisioned fur-trading posts in Alaska. In 1841 the Russians sold Fort Ross to John Sutter, who transported most of what he bought to New Helvetia, in present Sacramento. Among the buildings restored are a crude Greek Orthodox chapel, the Russian commandant's house, and two blockhouses.

FREMONT

San José de Guadelupe Mission (1797) 15 miles north of the city; restored.

HORNITOS

Established by Mexicans expelled from a nearby mining camp in the Gold Rush, this town retains a Mexican flavor, and has a *Wells Fargo Office* built in 1851.

MARIPOSA

Courthouse (1854) A handsome white frame building, the oldest courthouse in the state.

MELONES

On Jackass Hill is a replica of the cabin occupied by Mark Twain. The town (*see* p. 349) was once called Slumgullion. This was the locale of many Bret Harte stories.

MURPHYS

Mitchler Hotel (1855) This building remains in its original condition.

NEVADA CITY

In this old Mother Lode town are the *Assay Office* (1853), in continuous use since its construction; the old firehouse; and the *National Hotel.*

REDDING

Old Shasta State Historic Monument An interesting ghost town, well preserved.

SACRAMENTO

Governor's Mansion (1870's) An ornate Victorian dwelling.

Pony Express Museum (1860) An office and relay station of the Pony Express.

Leland Stanford House (1860's) A 38-room mansion.

Sutter's Fort State Historical Monument Founded in 1839 by John Sutter (*see* pp. 348-51), the original buildings have been reconstructed as a museum of early California. The low adobe structures were originally surrounded by a thick wall, 18 feet high. The *State Indian Museum* outside Sutter's Fort houses articles pertaining to the life and crafts of California Indians.

SAN FRANCISCO

Although much of the city was destroyed by the earthquake and fire of 1906, a number of the early buildings survive. One of the oldest buildings is *Mission Dolores,* founded in 1776. Interior walls were painted by the Indians with vegetable colors which are still bright today. A famed landmark is *Nob Hill,* where the mansions of Comstock millionaires and the Big Four of railroad fame, called "Nabobs," were located before the earthquake and fire. The only residence in the area to escape complete destruction in 1906 was that of James L. Flood, now the *Pacific Union Club.* The *Palace Hotel* was erected in 1909 on the site of its predecessor, the first great luxury hotel of the West. In *Portsmouth Square,* "birthplace of San Francisco," Captain John B. Montgomery raised the American flag in 1846. In the early 1850's this area, the village of Yerba Buena, was the site of saloons, theatres, and gambling houses. *Montgomery Block* is one of the few downtown office buildings not destroyed by the fire. On Market Street is *Lotta's Fountain,* presented to the city by Lotta Crabtree, who dodged gold nuggets, coins, and watches hurled onto the stage by ardent admirers. On *Telegraph Hill* a giant semaphore signaled the arrival of ships through the Golden Gate in the clipper ship era. The *Presidio,* once the home of the Spanish garrison, is another historic area, now a U.S. military reservation. In the *Wells Fargo Bank* is a museum containing a stagecoach shipped around the Horn in the 1850's; the Golden Spike from Promontory, Utah; and the huge scales from the Wells Fargo office at the gold-rush town of Columbia, which are said to have weighed 55 of the

87 million dollars in gold mined in the Mother Lode.

SAN RAFAEL
Mission San Rafael (1817) Twentieth in the mission chain; restored.

SANTA CLARA
Santa Clara de Asis Replica of a Franciscan mission (1777), on the campus of the University of Santa Clara.

SANTA CRUZ
Santa Cruz Mission A one-half scale replica of the original founded in 1791 and destroyed by earthquake.

SANTA ROSA
Luther Burbank House Where Burbank lived and worked for 50 years; now owned by Santa Rosa Junior College. The gardens are open daily.

SONOMA
Established as a frontier post in the 1830's. Besides *Sonoma Mission* (1823) on the plaza, the visitor should see the *Blue Wing Inn* (1840's), the *Sonoma Barracks* (c. 1836), the *Vallejo Home State Historical Monument* (c. 1851), and the old *Hotel El Dorado*. One mile northeast of Sonoma is *Buena Vista Rancho,* which belonged to the Hungarian nobleman, Count Ágoston Haraszthy, who planted the experimental vineyards from which California's vast grape industry developed. The oldest stone wine cellars in the state are on the grounds. The winery is in operation and may be visited.

TRUCKEE
Near here are Donner Lake and *Donner State Historic Monument,* site of the tragedy of the ill-fated Donner Party in the winter of 1846-47 (*see* pp. 344-45).

TULELAKE
Lava Beds National Monument The jagged lava formations here were the scene of the bitter Modoc War (1872-73), the last Indian uprising in California and southern Oregon. Defenses built by soldiers and Indians still stand.

WEAVERVILLE
One of the least changed of the California gold towns. Some of the old buildings have graceful circular stairways leading up from the sidewalk. The *Joss House,* a Chinese temple which served the 2,000 Chinese building a railroad along the Trinity River, is a state historical monument.

COLORADO

ASPEN
Hotel Jerome Opened in 1889, this three-story brick building contains some of the original furnishings.
Old Opera House Restored.

CENTRAL CITY
Gilpin County Mining and Historical Museum Pioneer relics and active gold mine.
Opera House A stone building with four-foot walls, completed in 1878; restored.
Teller House The last word in frontier hotels when it was completed in 1872. President Grant walked from his stagecoach to the door over a path of silver bricks in 1873.

COLORADO SPRINGS
Pioneer Museum Contains historical and archaeological collections.
Territorial Capitol A log cabin where the first legislature met.

CRIPPLE CREEK
This old mining town (*see* p. 352) once had a population of 20,000. Most of the buildings are old unpainted structures. The *Cripple Creek District Museum* preserves the history of the gold camp, and the *Imperial Hotel* (1896) is worth visiting. This district had eleven camps, among them Cripple Creek, Victor, Goldfield, Gillett, Altman, and Independence.

DENVER
Chappell House (late 1800's) Belongs to the Denver Art Association and is used for lectures and exhibits.
State Museum Has fine Indian and pioneer collections, rare manuscripts, and photographs.

Tabor Grand Opera House (1881) The pride of Denver in its day; now a movie theater.

FORT COLLINS
Antoine Janis Cabin (1855) The first settler's dwelling on the Cache la Poudre River. Moved to Lincoln Park from its original site near Laporte.

FORT GARLAND
Old Fort Garland State Historical Monument Part of the fort, built in 1858 and abandoned in 1883, has been meticulously restored. The commandant's quarters have been re-created as they were when Colonel Kit Carson was in charge (1866-67).

FORT VASQUEZ
A reconstruction of a Platte Valley fur-trading post, built about 1836.

GEORGETOWN
Hamill House Restored home of mine operator. Now a museum.
Hotel de Paris One of the best-known hotels west of the Mississippi in the 1880's and 1890's. Ornate inner décor.
Old Firehouse A tall wooden tower still houses outmoded fire-fighting equipment.

GOLD HILL
Miners' Hotel (1872) A 25-room log building; many original furnishings.

GREELEY
Meeker Museum (1871) This building was the home of Nathan C. Meeker, founder of a colony here.

LA JUNTA
Fort Bent Museum Exhibits fossils and remains of the early frontier days in the Arkansas Valley.

LEADVILLE
Healy House (1880's) Restored and maintained as an example of one of the better homes of frontier days.
Elks Opera House Formerly the Tabor Grand Opera House, built by Leadville's most fabulous character, who struck it rich and died penniless. Now a museum.
Tabor House (1878) A small red clapboard house, once home of H. A. W. Tabor.
Hotel Vendôme (1885) Once Tabor Grand Hotel.

MESA VERDE NATIONAL PARK
One of the country's outstanding prehistoric Indian ruins (*see* p. 304).

OURAY
Beaumont Hotel (1886) Ornate white brick structure in an old mining town.

PLATTEVILLE
Fort Vasquez This fort has been reconstructed on the site of the original post destroyed by Indians in 1842.

SILVERTON
Courthouse Gold-domed building indicating the town's former prosperity as center of the San Juan mining district.
Imperial Hotel Houses a pioneer museum.

TRINIDAD
Kit Carson Museum An adobe structure dating from early settlement days.

VIRGINIA DALE STAGE STATION
Near the Wyoming border on U.S. 287, it is in a fine state of preservation.

IDAHO

BOISE
In this state capital is *Julia Davis Park,* with its new *State Historical Museum.* The *Pioneer Village* contains the *Coston Cabin* (1863) moved from its original site near Boise, where it had been built of driftwood held together with pegs; and the *Pearce Cabin,* built the same year. *Christ's Church* (1866), the *Halladay Stage Station,* the *O'Farrell Cabin* (1863), and the old *U.S. Assay Office* (1872), are reminders of pioneer days, and the *De Lamar House* (1890) is an elaborate dwelling built by a silver king. *Urquides Little Village* is where Jesús Urquides, a frontiersman from San Francisco, established in 1863 a freighting station to cart supplies to the mining towns in the region. The 30 one-room cabins he

put up for his wranglers and packers are still standing. In Boise are the buildings of *Fort Boise,* established by the U.S. Army in 1863. Forty miles distant is the site of the Hudson's Bay Company's Fort Boise.

CALDWELL
Site of Fort Boise During the rivalry between American and British fur companies, the Hudson's Bay Company built Fort Boise in 1834 to compete with the more famous Fort Hall (near Pocatello), built by the American Nathaniel Wyeth.
Site of the Walters Ferry Near the bridge on State 45 was the Snake River crossing used for nearly 60 years by travelers and freight traffic. The ferrymaster's adobe house remains on the bank.

FORT HALL
Fort Hall Indian Reservation is near the site of the important trading post and port of call for emigrant trains.

FORT HENRY
Site of the fort built in 1810 near St. Anthony, the first on the Snake River.

FRANKLIN
The first permanent white settlement in Idaho. *Franklin Pioneer Hall* contains relics of the old days.

LEWISTON
Heart of the Nez Perce country, at the junction of the Snake and Clearwater rivers. Nearby is historic Spalding, where in 1836 the Reverend Henry Spalding built a school and church, ran a gristmill, and operated a printing press. The area is a state memorial park and contains the graves of Spalding and his wife. The so-called Spalding log cabin probably belongs to a later era, but the house museum has some fine Indian exhibits.

MASSACRE ROCKS
About 35 miles west of Pocatello on U.S. 30 is the site of an 1862 Indian attack on a wagon train. Three miles farther along the trail is *Emigrant Rock,* where the autographs of many emigrants remain.

MOSCOW
Site of Fort Russell
De Smet Mission of the Sacred Heart A few miles from Moscow is the site of a mission founded in 1842 by Father De Smet. Most of the buildings have been destroyed by fire, but a group of shacks are still used by Indians who come in from the countryside for Sunday services.

OAKLEY
From the town a dirt road leads to the *Silent City of Rocks,* an area of 25 square miles of grotesque formations. Through it ran the California Trail, and here the Lander Cutoff ended. The granite walls bear thousands of names and dates left by west-bound settlers.

OROFINO
Two miles from here Lewis and Clark established their *Canoe Camp Site* on the Clearwater River in 1805. Here they cached their extra gear and made canoes for the trip to the Pacific.

PEND OREILLE NATIONAL FOREST
Site of Thompson Trading Post This was the earliest white post in the Northwest within the boundaries of the U.S.

PIERCE
Site of Idaho's first gold strike, 1860. The *Shoshone County Courthouse* (1862) is now a recreation center.

POCATELLO
The city stands on a part of the *Fort Hall Indian Reservation.* In *Idaho State College* there is a historical museum with interesting exhibits, and above *Ross Park* are petroglyphs carved by the Indians.

SALMON
Nearby, in Lemhi Valley, is a monument to Sacajawea, the Indian woman who helped Lewis and Clark on their expedition. Mormons colonized the Lemhi Valley in 1855. An adobe wall of *Fort Lemhi* still stands, south of Salmon.

SILVER CITY
A ghost town which was once known internationally as a fabulously rich gold- and silver-mining center. A church, a Masonic hall, a deserted county courthouse, a hotel, saloons, and other buildings remain. Other ghost towns in the Owyhee region are Ruby City, Dewey, and DeLamar.

SODA SPRINGS
The mineral waters here attracted emigrants for many years. Here the oldest California trail branched from the Oregon Trail to follow the Bear River to the Great Salt Lake. *Camp Connor,* a military post, was established in 1863.

WALLACE
Center of the Coeur d'Alene mining district and scene of the mining wars of 1892-99. About 20 miles from here is the *Cataldo Mission,* established in 1848 by Father Ravalli.

WHITE BIRD BATTLEGROUND
Near Grangeville is the canyon where a U.S. Army force was defeated by Nez Perces in 1877. Long friendly to the whites, the tribe had suffered much at their hands, and after this battle, the non-treaty bands began their tragic expedition to Canada.

MONTANA

BANNACK
First capital of Montana Territory, which came into existence following the discovery of gold in Grasshopper Creek in 1862. It was soon eclipsed by Virginia City. The first jail and hotel in Montana are here.

BEARPAW BATTLEGROUND
Site of one of the last conflicts between Indians and whites, a four-day battle between U.S. troops under General Nelson Miles and a band of Nez Perce Indians whom Chief Joseph had led from Idaho with the hope of escaping to Canada.

BIG HOLE BATTLEFIELD
NATIONAL MONUMENT
On the Idaho border is another site of a battle between U.S. troops and Chief Joseph and the Nez Perces.

BILLINGS
Begun in 1882 when the Northern Pacific entered the valley. In *Boot Hill Cemetery* are the graves of badmen and Indian skirmishers. The *Parmly Billings Memorial Library* has a museum of pioneer relics.

BOZEMAN
In 1864 Jim Bridger and John M. Bozeman

MONTANA HIGHWAY COMMISSION

St. Mary's Mission, Stevensville

guided the first emigrants here to settle the town. Bozeman blazed a trail from northern Colorado to Virginia City, Montana. The *City Hall* was originally the Opera House (1890).

BROWNING
Headquarters for the Blackfoot Indian Agency, which administers a reservation with 5,000 Indians. The *Museum of Plains Indians* here has an important collection. Open June through September.

CROW AGENCY
Created in 1868, the *Crow Indian Reservation* is interesting to visitors in the summer, when the Crows put up tepees in the old way, and stage sun dances.

CUSTER BATTLEFIELD
NATIONAL CEMETERY
Irregularly placed markers on the hillside mark the spots where Custer and his men fell on June 25, 1876 (*see* pp. 356-57).

FORT BENTON
At the head of navigation on the Missouri River, this town was once an important outpost. Ruins of the old trading post and blockhouse of the American Fur Company are here. The *Grand Union Hotel,* an ornate three-story hostelry, is still standing.

HELENA
Main Street of the state capital runs along Last Chance Gulch, where gold was found

in 1864. A log cabin (1865) is the sole survivor of an early fire, but the "golden era" of the 1870's and 1880's is reflected in the rococo houses on Dearborn Avenue, and by log and brick buildings in the *Old Business District.*

LIVINGSTON

The Bucket of Blood is a visible relic of the days when Calamity Jane, Madame Bulldog, and Tex Rickard, with his fellow gamblers Kid Brown and Soapy Smith, were habitués of the town.

MILES CITY
Range Riders Museum

ROSEBUD
Site of the battle between General Crook and the Sioux on June 17, 1876.

SIDNEY
Near the North Dakota border on State 16 several buildings of a stage station on the old Fort Union Trail remain.

STEVENSVILLE
St. Mary's Mission (1867) There is a mu-

seum in the rear of the church.

VIRGINIA CITY
Like its famous sister in Nevada, this former roaring gold camp has been restored as a tourist attraction. Twenty structures of the 1860's have been rebuilt: an assay office, blacksmith shop, dressmaker's establishment, saloon, general store, hotel, and Wells Fargo office are among them. The *Thompson-Hickman Memorial Museum* has many relics of the past.

NEVADA

(Northern section: for southern Nevada listings, see page 327.)

AUSTIN
Many old buildings remain from the boom days when Austin was the center of a mining area. The *International Hotel* of boom days is still in use; three churches and the old *Lander County Courthouse* are survivals of the 1860's. West of Austin is the ghost town of Belmont, with the old *Nye County Courthouse* among remnants of other buildings.

CARSON CITY
This pleasant town is the smallest state capital in the U.S. Gold-seekers came to the area in the 1850's, and in another decade the fabulous Comstock Lode was found nearby, and the town boomed. In 1872 its stone *Capitol* was built. In 1878 the great *Opera House* was opened by the Reverend Henry Ward Beecher. Of interest are the *Old Mint,* now a museum; the *Abe Curry, H. M. Yerrington,* and *Ormsby* houses (none of them open to the public); the *Warren Engine Company Firehouse;* and the old *Post Office and Federal Building.* The *Matt Rinkle House* is one of the few old Nevada houses still in its original state, and still in the builder's family; it is now a museum. Two miles east of Carson City, on the grounds of the state penitentiary, the fossilized skeletons of many prehistoric animals were found, along with footprints of the giant sloth and the bones of mastodons. Not far away is a partial reconstruction of *Fort Churchill,* now a state park.

ELKO
This community was freighting station for the boom camps of Eureka and Hamilton. Many Victorian structures remain. Following U.S. 40 westward along what was the Humboldt Road are *Emigrant Pass,* a narrow divide which was a landmark for

wagon trains, and *Gravelly Ford,* a river crossing often mentioned in early diaries. Southeast of Elko, near the *Humboldt National Forest,* is *Camp Ruby,* once a stage station of the Overland Mail Company, a change station for the Pony Express, and a relay station for the telegraph.

EUREKA
A town where the first big U.S. lead and silver deposits were found. By 1870 it had 125 saloons and 25 gambling places. The *Colonnade Hotel, Jackson House,* and the *Opera House* still stand, as do two early churches and the *Eureka County Courthouse.*

FORT McDERMIT
On the north central border of Nevada, on U.S. 95, is the partly restored fort. Farther south is the *Awakening Mining District* in the Slumbering Hills. In the surrounding rough country are other old forts, fossil beds of Eocene creatures, deserted mines, and *Massacre Lakes,* the dry sinks where forty settlers were killed by Indians in 1850.

GENOA
Fifteen miles south of Carson City is the oldest permanent white settlement in Nevada, made about 1851. The old fort and stockade, now a state park, has a museum with relics of the first days as a Mormon station. Open May through October.

GOLDFIELD
South of Tonopah, this ghost town has 52 city blocks, now covered with sagebrush.

HAMILTON
A deserted mining town, east of Austin, where 10,000 people lived in the 1860's.

LAS VEGAS
The ghost towns of Eldorado, Rhyolite,

and Beatty lie to the west, where a corner of Death Valley extends over the state line.

RENO
Nevada State Historical Society Museum
Has a rich collection of objects, pictures, and books illuminating Nevada's early days.

UNIONVILLE
Only a few houses remain of this old mining camp. It is near Winnemucca, the first trading station on the Humboldt Trail.

VIRGINIA CITY
No spot in Nevada has a more colorful past than this town in the heart of the Comstock Lode region, which in the 1870's was an elegant, sophisticated center (*see* pp. 352-53). Since its chief attraction to visitors is its old-time atmosphere, many of the early buildings have been tenderly, and shrewdly, preserved. Probably nowhere else can the traveler get such a complete picture of a boom town. The visitor can see *Piper's Opera House,* where Edwin Booth performed; the *Storey County Courthouse,* with the records of many American fortunes; *St. Mary's in the Mountains* (1877), a beautiful church with a bell of Comstock silver; and *Odd Fellows Hall,* the National Theater of bonanza days. The *Crystal Bar,* with fabulous glass chandeliers, is another spot which visitors enjoy. Old mining offices, saloons like the *Bucket of Blood,* faded stores, and a few fine or not-so-fine old houses fill out the illusion of a once-fabulous city. One house, called *The Castle* is well preserved and worth a visit. The most famous house, the *Bowers Mansion,* is outside of town. It was built by one of the first Comstock millionaires, Sandy Bowers, who could neither read nor write.

OREGON

ASTORIA
First American settlement on the Pacific coast. Named for John Jacob Astor, who sent expeditions here to break the British monopoly of the beaver trade.

CANYON CITY
Founded in 1862 with the discovery of gold on Whiskey Flat, nearby, this is almost a

ghost town. A fire destroyed most of the landmarks, but a few old buildings and a cemetery set aside for badmen remain. The restored *Joaquin Miller Cabin,* home of the poet and his family, is here, as are some of the apple trees he planted in the 1860's. The *Grant County Museum* is here. One mile distant is John Day, a town at

the confluence of Canyon Creek and John Day River, named for a member of Astor's overland expedition of 1811-12, commanded by Wilson Price Hunt. During the gold rush of 1862-64 the Pony Express came through here.

CHAMPOEG STATE PARK
A small museum of pioneer and Indian

relics is on the site of the first settlement in the Willamette Valley, south of Portland, formerly the location of Fort Wallace, an outpost of Astoria. The *Robert Newell House* has been reconstructed.

THE DALLES
The name of the Columbia River narrows came from French-Canadian *voyageurs* who thought the basalt walls of the narrows resembled the flagstones (*dalles*) of their native streets. Lewis and Clark passed through The Dalles on October 24, 1805, and *Fort Lee* was built here in 1847-78 during the Cayuse Indian war. Later it was a military post to protect emigrants who put their wagons on rafts to float down the Columbia. The *Wasco County Historical Society Museum* has Indian and pioneer relics in the *Surgeon's Quarters* of Fort Dalles; and *Pioneer Cemetery* contains many graves of the first comers.

DAYTON
Fort Yamhill Blockhouse (1856) Built by troops under Lt. Phil Sheridan during the Indian campaigns.

FORT CLATSOP
The fort built by Lewis and Clark, where they spent the winter of 1805-6, has been completely reconstructed under auspices of the Oregon Historical Society.

GRIFFIN'S GULCH
Along Griffin Creek the first Oregon gold strike was made on October 23, 1861, and there are a number of crumbling ghost towns in this area.

JACKSONVILLE
Described as "queen of the ghost cities," this was the center of a region where a lucky man could wash a cup of gold in a day. The *Methodist Church* was built in 1854 with one night's take at the gaming tables. Still to be seen are the *J. A. Brunner Building* (1855), where fortunes in gold were weighed, and where miners sometimes took refuge from hostile Indians; the *United States Hotel;* and the *Old Barn*, used for relay horses of the California-Oregon Stage Line. The *Old Courthouse* is now a county museum; and the *Beekman (Wells Fargo) Bank* is owned by the Oregon Historical Society.

KLAMATH FALLS
Upper Klamath Lake Where Captain John C. Frémont and an exploration party were ambushed in 1846.
Klamath Indian Reservation Over 1,500

OREGON HISTORICAL SOCIETY
McLoughlin House, Oregon City

Klamath, Modoc, and Yahooskin Snake Indians still live here in a region which was the scene of bloody struggles between whites and Modoc Indians.

NEWBERG
Herbert Hoover House The boyhood home of the President has been restored in this early Quaker settlement.

OREGON CITY
First provisional and territorial capital, and the first incorporated town west of the Missouri River, Oregon City was part of the earliest beginnings of American settlement in the Northwest. The site was claimed in 1829 by Dr. John McLoughlin, chief factor of the Hudson's Bay Company at Fort Vancouver. When this area became U.S. territory in 1846, McLoughlin moved from Fort Vancouver to Oregon City, became an American citizen, and in 1846 built the square clapboarded mansion which now stands in the park named for him. Next to it is the *Barclay House,* constructed the same year. Barclay was surgeon at Fort Vancouver and a close friend of McLoughlin's. Like the *Cochran House* (1852) on Washington Street, the Barclay House is a Cape Cod type. The *Masonic Lodge* here is the oldest one west of the Missouri, and its charter was brought across the Plains by ox team. The *Clackamas County Courthouse* has the original plat of San Francisco, filed in 1850 when Oregon City was the only seat of American government on the Pacific coast.

PORTLAND
The city at the confluence of the Willamette and Columbia rivers was incorporated in 1851, and soon became important as a river port, the best in the area for sea-

going vessels. Among the older buildings are the *Old Post Office* (1875), which contains the courtroom in which many land-fraud cases were tried. *Erickson's* (still standing), once the most famous saloon in the Northwest, had a mahogany bar 674 feet long, where seafaring men, loggers, and other rough characters congregated. The *Oregon Historical Society Collections* on Market Street include a fine library of volumes on the Northwest; the tiny Mission Press, first printing press west of the Rockies; Indian collections; and the sea chest carried by Captain Robert Gray on the *Columbia* when he discovered the river named for his ship. The *Forestry Building* is a logging museum.

SALEM
Once the territorial capital, and capital of the state since 1856, this city on the Willamette River was founded by Methodist missionary Jason Lee, sent from New England as "Missionary to the Flatheads." Lee began a school for white children arriving in emigrant trains in the 1840's, and the school was later chartered as *Willamette University,* one of the oldest colleges in the Northwest. The *Jason Lee Cemetery* is where the founder, his family, and many pioneers are buried. The *Marion Hotel* (1870), is the oldest Northwest hotel still operating.

SEASIDE
End of the Trail Monument Commemorates the end of the Lewis and Clark journey.
Salt Cairn Brine-crusted rocks on which Lewis and Clark boiled sea water for salt are protected by a railing. The explorers also boiled whale blubber here.

SNAKE RIVER
Site of Olds Ferry Before the ferry was established here at Farewell Bend in 1862, pioneers following the Oregon Trail crossed as best they could, saying farewell to their water supply.

WHEATLAND FERRY
Site of Jason Lee Mission On the east bank of the Willamette River is where Methodist missionary Jason Lee and his companions established a small mission in 1834.

WOLF CREEK
Tavern (1857) On the old Oregon-California stage road, this two-story frame building has been an inn since stagecoach days, and is little changed.

UTAH

CAPITOL REEF NATIONAL MONUMENT
In southern Utah ancient Basket Maker and then Pueblo Indians built cliff dwellings and made beautiful pottery, textiles, and objects of bone and stone. To visit them the National Park Service should be consulted. Capitol Reef, on State 24 near Fruita, has many cliff houses, petroglyphs, and pictographs. Some of the excavated

objects are in two private museums in nearby Torrey; open to visitors.

ECHO CANYON
East of Ogden, near the Wyoming border, are the ruins of Mormon breastworks built during the "Utah War" of 1857, when the U.S. Government sent troops to enforce federal jurisdiction of the territory.

GRAND GULCH
Near Blanding, in the *Natural Bridges Na-*

tional Monument, is a plateau where visitors may see cliff dwellings of Basket Maker and Pueblo Indians. The Gulch is a vast box canyon with several hundred dwellings.

HENRY'S FORK
Weathered log buildings here may date back to the days when the region was being explored for beaver. Here in 1825 General William H. Ashley held the first mountain rendezvous with the beaver hunters.

HOVENWEEP NATIONAL MONUMENT

On U.S. 160 near Blanding is a remarkable ancient Indian city which spreads over four canyons, with towers, huge communal dwellings, and underground kivas. Some of the walls are over twenty feet high.

JENSEN

Dinosaur National Monument A primitive region in northwestern Colorado and northeastern Utah which was an early haunt of fur trappers. At Jensen, U.S. 40 leads to one of the richest deposits of prehistoric fossils ever discovered.

OGDEN

The site of Ogden was the rendezvous of mountain men—Bill Sublette, Jed Smith, Jim Bridger, and Thomas Fitzpatrick—in the 1820's. They were hopeful that the Great Salt Lake was an arm of the Pacific, and Jed Smith and Jim Clyman explored it in bullboats. After the fur trade declined, Miles Goodyear arrived as Utah's first white settler. The cabin he built in 1844, of cottonwood logs, is still intact. Many Victorian houses remain from the 1880's. Some were "polygamous houses" with several divisions and separate entrances for multiple families. In *City Hall Park* there is a monument to Jedediah Smith; the *Old Mill* (1849), now a dance hall; and the *Broom Hotel* (1882), once the finest between Omaha and San Francisco. The Browning brothers, John, Matt, and Jonathan, who invented automatic pistols, shotguns, and rifles, lived in a house which is still standing. The *Charles Penrose House* (1860's), *Robert Chapman House* (1855), and *Francis Brown House* (1870) are noteworthy.

PROMONTORY

Golden Spike National Historic Site Marks the spot where the Central Pacific's *Jupiter* and the Union Pacific's *No. 119* rubbed

Gardo House, Salt Lake City

noses on May 10, 1869, linking East and West with the first transcontinental railroad (*see* p. 359).

ST. GEORGE

This interesting town was the site of the "Dixie Mission" launched by Brigham Young in 1861, when he sent 300 colonists here to raise cotton. The tall white stucco *Temple* (1877) is the first built in Utah (closed to non-Mormons). The *Tabernacle* (open on application) was built in 1871, and has a slender steeple reminiscent of New England meetinghouses. The *Washington County Courthouse* (1869), *Brigham Young Winter Home* (1869), and the *Angus Cannon* (1863), *Erastus Snow* (1875), and *Jed Gates* (1863) houses are among the oldest. The Gates House is the "polygamous" type. Santa Clara, about five miles west, has the little house of rough stone (1870) where lived Jacob Hamblin, missionary to the Indians.

SALT LAKE CITY

Located near the unusual natural wonder, the Great Salt Lake, this city is the center of Mormonism. Its most imposing edifices are the *Capitol*, the *Tabernacle*, and the *Temple*, which nobody can overlook. There is the *Brigham Young Monument* on Main Street, which includes the figures of the friendly Indian chief Washakie and of Jim Bridger, who was largely responsible for Young's decision to settle near the lake. *Pioneer Square* (the Old Fort) was the heart of the earliest city. Of great interest are Brigham Young's *Lion House* (1856), with its twenty gables (now a museum of his personal effects); and *Beehive House* (1855), a two-story adobe building with Young's office and living quarters. Between the Lion and Beehive houses is a small adobe building which the leader also used as an office. The *Brigham Young Cemetery* has the graves of the leader, three of his wives, and several of his children. In Temple Square is the oldest house in the city, a log cabin built by Osmyn Deuel in 1847. *This is the Place Monument*, near Hogle Gardens Zoo, is on the spot where Young, coming out of Emigration Canyon, caught his first sight of the great lake, and remembering Jim Bridger's description, said: "This is the right place, drive on." In Pioneer Square is the Gothic *Empey House* (c. 1855), built by Brigham Young for his wife Ann Eliza, the only wife who sued him for divorce. The *Gardo House*, or "Amelia's Palace," was the home of another wife. The University's *Archaeological Museum* has a collection of Utah's Indian artifacts.

WANSHIP

On U.S. 189, east of Salt Lake City, this small town was an important station on the Overland Trail. It has many original houses dating from the 1860's, and the *Overland Stage Station* (1862) near the town is one of the few remaining.

WASHINGTON

BELLINGHAM

Captain George Pickett House (c. 1856) Home of the famous Confederate officer while he was stationed in Washington in connection with the International Boundary dispute. Now a museum, open by appointment.

BLAINE

Peace Arch On the Canadian border, this arch symbolizes the friendship between the U.S. and Canada.

BONNEVILLE

Lewis and Clark camped at Little Beacon Rock, near the spectacular Big Beacon, in 1805 and 1806.

CENTRALIA

Borst Blockhouse (1855) Built for defense against the Indians.

CHEHALIS

Claquato Church (1858) One of the oldest in Washington, 3 miles west of Chehalis.

John R. Jackson House (1845) A small log house, 11 miles south of present Chehalis, where the Jacksons welcomed immigrants. Later courthouse and church.

COLUMBIA STATE PARK

Site of Lewis and Clark's first camp in the present state of Washington. There is an Indian museum.

COLVILLE

Site of the Hudson's Bay Company Fort Colville (1826). Near the town is the U.S. *Fort Colville* (1859) and the restored *St. Paul's Mission*.

ELLENSBURG

Ginkgo Petrified Forest State Park Examples of prehistoric trees and a fine museum, 25 miles east of town.

FORT COLUMBIA

The fort on the north bank of the Columbia River, near Chinook, overlooks the spot where Captain Robert Gray landed in 1792,

after he discovered the Columbia River. There is a state museum on the site.

GOLDENDALE

Maryhill Museum A fine western museum.

OKANOGAN

Old Astor's Fort (1811) Site of the Pacific Fur Company's base.

PUGET SOUND ISLANDS

In this state park area, the islands of Whidbey and Fidalgo have many interesting old buildings. On the Swinomish Indian Reservation on Fidalgo is a tribal *Long House*, scene of an Indian festival in late January. The *Alexander Blockhouse* (1855), restored, is now a museum of Indian racing craft. Two other interesting structures are the *Thomas J. Dow House* (1855) and the *Captain Thomas Coupe House* (1853). In the neighborhood is the *John Kineth House* (1855) built, curiously enough, of lumber brought around the Horn. The *David Blockhouse* was built in 1855; nearby is a replica of the Crockett Blockhouse.

SEATTLE

Suquamish Old-Man House Across the Sound from Seattle, the home of Chief Seattle, one of the most unusual communal houses in the Puget Sound area. The house may have been 900 feet long, of varying widths, and curved slightly to conform to the outline of the shore. Chief Seattle was the head of six tribes, and a true friend of white settlers.

Washington State Museum On the campus of the University of Washington, it has a fine Northwest Indian collection.

SPOKANE

Spokane House Site of earliest post of the North West Fur Company in Washington has been excavated.

Spokane Public Museum Contains many relics of the Northwest.

TACOMA

Fort Nisqually (1843) Successor to the first Hudson's Bay Company fort (1833); restored in *Point Defiance Park.* There are two original buildings, the *Old Granary* and the *Factor's House* (now a museum).

St. Peter's Church (1874) Recently restored.

State Historical Society Museum An outstanding collection of Northwest material.

VANCOUVER

Fort Vancouver The Hudson's Bay Company base from 1824 to 1846, under the direction of Dr. John McLoughlin. In 1848 the fort was made part of the U.S. defense system, and in 1852 Lieutenant U. S. Grant was assigned here as quartermaster.

Covington House (1840-45) Oldest house in the state.

WALLA WALLA

Whitman National Monument Site of the mission founded by Marcus and Narcissa Whitman in 1836. Ruins of the main house, blacksmith shop, gristmill, and other buildings have been excavated (*see* pp. 344-45). There is a small museum.

WENATCHEE

Indian Rock Pictures Along the walls of the Columbia River.

YAKIMA

Some original buildings of *Fort Simcoe* (1856) remain, and others have been restored. Points of interest in the area include the *Indian Painted Rocks,* a geologic formation, and *Yakima Indian Reservation.*

WYOMING

Schoolhouse, Fort Bridger

BUFFALO

Main Street False-front buildings recall the cattle wars of the 1880's when this town was the "rustlers' capital" and Cheyenne the "cowmens' capital."

CHEYENNE

Frontier Park Scene of the annual Frontier Days celebration, it contains the cabin of an early scout, Jim Baker (*see* p. 280), moved from its original site. The old trail to Fort Laramie is indicated by a marker.

State Historical Museum Has many relics of the early West, including Indian handicrafts and pioneer homes.

Union Pacific Station An early stagecoach is on display here.

CODY

William Cody House Supposedly "Buffalo Bill's" birthplace, moved here from Iowa.

Cody Museum Contains personal effects of the Wild West figure.

Irma Hotel Has Remington paintings, and a bar Cody brought from Europe.

FORT BRIDGER

In the southwestern corner of Wyoming, on U.S.30S, is the tree-shaded site of an important post built by Jim Bridger as a supply station for emigrant trains. It was open in time for the Great Migration of 1843, and from then on thousands of emigrants stopped here. One of the 1847 visitors was Brigham Young, who later created a rival post, Fort Supply, nearby. Fort Bridger was used by the U.S. Army as a base for many years. The site is now a state park. The second school in the state; the Pony Express stables; one of the barracks, now a museum; and part of the stone wall built by the Mormons are among the early buildings sheltered under tall cottonwoods and willows.

FORT CASPAR

A reconstruction of a fort built in 1863 on the Oregon Trail midway between Fort Laramie and Independence Rock. In 1865, when Indians tried to stop migrations on the Oregon Trail, there was a battle here.

FORT LARAMIE

No spot was more important in Wyoming history than this natural oasis of deep grass and clear water (*see* p. 342). The original log stockade, built in 1834 by William L. Sublette and Robert Campbell, was for years a mecca for fur trappers and Indians. Its location was strategic: at the crossroads of an ancient north-south Indian trail and the east-west natural passage across the mountains which became the Oregon Trail, and also at the junction of the North Platte and Laramie rivers. In 1849 it became a military post, was abandoned in 1890, and is now a national monument, with many buildings restored. The adobe *Sutler's Store,* a general store and post office, and *Old Bedlam,* the officers' club, were both begun in 1849 and are the oldest buildings in the state. The remains of several other historic buildings and a museum occupy the grounds.

FORT PHIL KEARNEY

Reproduction of a post built on the Bozeman Trail east of the Big Horn Mountains, when gold was discovered in Montana. The fort saw plenty of trouble in 1865-66, when Chief Red Cloud united several tribes to drive out the military. Abandoned in 1868.

INDEPENDENCE ROCK

Most famous landmark on the Oregon Trail, with inscriptions carved by hundreds of emigrants. It lies north of the Sweetwater River, and may be reached on State 220. Near here was a military post, Sweetwater Station, to protect travelers on the Oregon Trail and to guard the transcontinental telegraph line. About ten miles east of Independence Rock are the graves of Cattle Kate Maxwell and Jim Averill, hanged in 1889 for rustling cattle.

LANDER

Wind River Cemetery Near the town, on the Wind River Indian Reservation, are the probable graves of Sacajawea and her nephew Bazil. In Lander are several old pioneer cabins.

LARAMIE

University of Wyoming Library Has an interesting collection of Western Americana. Nearby is the site of Fort Sanders.

MEDICINE WHEEL

On State 14, near the Big Horn National Forest, is a mysterious Indian structure. A gigantic wheel of limestone slabs about three feet high, it seems to have had astronomical significance.

SOUTH PASS

Here emigrant trains crossed the Continental Divide, and at Pacific Springs just beyond the pass, the travelers drank for the first time from a westward-flowing stream. The first Fourth of July celebration on the far side of the Divide was held by Dr. Marcus Whitman and the Reverend Samuel Parker in 1836. With a Bible in one hand and an American flag in the other, Dr. Whitman knelt and claimed the West as "the home of American mothers and the Church of Christ." A *Whitman-Spalding Monument* marks the spot. Deep ruts in the earth at South Pass were made by thousands of wagons bound to Oregon and California. Nearby, South Pass City was the scene of a gold rush in the 1860's.

Acknowledgments

The editors have been most fortunate in the co-operation and suggestions they have received from hundreds of authorities on national and local historic sites. Their gratitude is extended to all the individuals and organizations listed on this page, to the photographers and artists whose work appears in the book, and to all others whose advice and guidance have made this volume possible.

American Association for State & Local History: Albert B. Corey, S. K. Stevens; *National Trust for Historic Preservation:* Richard Howland, Helen Bullock; *Society for the Preservation of New England Antiquities:* Bertram K. Little; *U.S. Department of the Interior, National Park Service:* Herbert E. Kahler, Howard W. Baker, Harthon L. Bill, Elbert Cox, William C. Everhart, John A. Hussey, Herbert Maier, Merrill J. Mattes, Lawrence Merriam, Hugh Miller, Erik K. Reed, Charlie R. Steen, Dan Tobin.

ALABAMA: Senator Lister Hill; Representatives Frank W. Boykir George Grant; *Department of Archives and History:* Peter A. Brannon

ARIZONA: Senator Barry Goldwater; *Department of Library and Archives:* the late Dr. Mulford Winsor, Alice B. Good

ARKANSAS: Senator J. W. Fulbright; Representative Brooks Hays; *Publicity and Parks Commission:* Sam B. Kirby; *Industrial Development Commission:* William R. Ewald, Jr.; *History Commission:* Ted R. Worley

CALIFORNIA: Representatives John J. Allen, Jr., Charles S. Gubser, Patrick J. Hillings, John E. Moss, Jr., Bob Wilson; *State Library:* Allan R. Ottley; *Department of Natural Resources:* Aubrey Neasham; *San Francisco Chamber of Commerce:* Robert N. Blum; *Historical Society:* Allen L. Chickering

COLORADO: Senator Gordon Allott; *Historical Society:* Agnes Wright Spring, Maurice Frink

CONNECTICUT: Senator Prescott Bush; *Development Commission:* Don Parry; *Historical Society:* Thompson R. Harlow; *State Library:* James Brewster; *Marine Historical Association:* Alma Eshenfelder

DELAWARE: Senator J. Allen Frear, Jr.; Representative Harris B. McDowell, Jr.; *Public Archives Commission:* Leon deValinger, Jr.; *Historical Society:* Marie E. Windell; *Eleutherian Mills-Hagley Foundation:* Joseph P. Monigle, Bettina Sargeant; *The Henry Francis du Pont Winterthur Museum:* Dorothy W. Greer

FLORIDA: Senators Spessard L. Holland, George Smathers; Representatives Charles E. Bennett, Bob Sikes; *Florida Development Commission:* Lamar Bledsoe; *University of Florida:* Julien C. Yonge; *Historical Association of Southern Florida:* Thomas W. Hagan

GEORGIA: Representatives Iris Faircloth Blitch, Prince H. Preston; *Department of Archives and History:* Mary G. Bryan; *Georgia Historical Society:* Lilla M. Hawes

IDAHO: Senator Henry Dworshak; Representative Gracie Pfost; *Department of Commerce and Development:* A. B. Jonasson; *Historical Society:* Gertrude McDevitt, Merle W. Wells

ILLINOIS: Senator Paul H. Douglas; Representatives Marguerite Stitt Church, Sid Simpson; *Department of Conservation:* Richard S. Hagen; *Department of Finance:* Carl G. Hodges; *Historical Society:* Margaret A. Flint, Harry E. Pratt

INDIANA: Representatives E. Ross Adair, John V. Beamer; *Historical Bureau:* Helen C. Gray

IOWA: Representatives James I. Dolliver, H. R. Gross, Charles B. Hoeven, Fred Schwengel, Henry O. Talle; *Development Commission:* Clare Kessell; *Historical Society:* William J. Petersen

KANSAS: Representative William H. Avery; *Historical Society:* Nyle H. Miller; *Chamber of Commerce:* Leon Decker

KENTUCKY: The late Senator Alben W. Barkley; Representative Frank Chelf; *Historical Society:* Bayless E. Hardin

LOUISIANA: Senator Allen J. Ellender; *Historical Society:* E. A. Parsons; *Department of Commerce and Industry:* L. Gibbs Adams; *State University:* V. L. Bedsole, Marcelle F. Schertz

MAINE: *Department of Development:* Everett F. Greaton; *Historical Society:* Marian B. Rowe; *State Library:* Margaret A. Whalen

MARYLAND: Senator John Marshall Butler; Representative James P. S. Devereux; *Department of Information:* Earle R. Poorbaugh; *Historical Society:* James W. Foster

MASSACHUSETTS: Representative Laurence Curtis; *Historical Society:* Stephen T. Riley, Warren G. Wheeler; *Lexington Historical Society:* Grace L. Merriam; *Old Deerfield Historical Society:* Henry N. Flynt; *Peabody Museum:* Marion V. Brewington; *Pilgrim Society:* Warren P. Strong

MICHIGAN: Senator Charles E. Potter; Representatives George A. Dondero, Gerald R. Ford, Don Hayworth, August E. Johansen, John Lesinski, Ruth Thompson; *Historical Commission:* Philip P. Mason; *State Tourist Council:* Katherine E. O'Shea; *Detroit Historical Commission:* Henry D. Brown

MINNESOTA: Senator Hubert H. Humphrey; *Historical Society:* Russell W. Fridley

MISSISSIPPI: Senator John Stennis; *Department of Archives and History:* Charlotte Capers; *Agricultural and Industrial Board:* Ned O'Brien

MISSOURI: Senators Stuart Symington, Thomas C. Hennings, Jr.; Representatives Clarence Cannon, Frank M. Karsten; *Historical Society:* Charles van Ravenswaay, Floyd C. Shoemaker; *Division of Resources:* Gerald R. Massie

MONTANA: *Historical Society:* Virginia Walton

NEBRASKA: *Historical Society:* W. D. Aeschbacher, James C. Olson

NEVADA: Senator George W. Malone; *Historical Society:* Clara S. Beatty; *State Library:* Joseph F. Shubert; *Department of Economic Development:* Peter T. Kelley

NEW HAMPSHIRE: *Planning and Development Commission:* Edward Androvette; *Historical Society:* Charlotte D. Conover; *Portsmouth Public Library:* Dorothy M. Vaughan

NEW JERSEY: Senator Clifford P. Case; Representatives James C. Auchincloss, Peter Frelinghuysen, Jr., Charles A. Wolverton; *Department of Conservation:* Arlene R. Sayre; *Historical Society:* Alexander J. Wall, Jr., Howard W. Wiseman

NEW MEXICO: Senator Clinton P. Anderson; *State Tourist Bureau:* Joseph A. Bursey; *Museum of New Mexico:* Gertrude Hill

NEW YORK: Senator Irving M. Ives; Representatives Sterling Cole, Steven B. Derounian, John H. Ray, John J. Rooney, Katherine St. George, Dean P. Taylor, William R. Williams; *Department of Commerce:* Francis P. Kimball; *University of the State of New York:* Albert B. Corey; *Wells College:* John Hunter Detmold; *Staten Island Historical Society:* Loring McMillen; *Museum of the American Indian:* Frederick J. Dockstader; *Museum of the City of New York; New-York Historical Society; New York Public Library; New York State Historical Association*

NORTH CAROLINA: Senators Sam J. Ervin, Jr., W. Kerr Scott; Representatives Graham A. Barden, Thurmond Chatham, Charles B. Deane, Carl T. Durham; *Department of Archives and History:* Christopher Crittenden; *Department of Conservation and Development:* Miriam Rabb

NORTH DAKOTA: *Historical Society:* Russell Reid

OHIO: Senator George H. Bender; Representatives William M. McCulloch, William E. Hess; *Department of Natural Resources:* V. W. Flickinger; *Development and Publicity Commission:* Paul Sherlock; *Historical Society:* Erwin C. Zepp, James H. Rodabaugh; *Western Reserve Historical Society*

OKLAHOMA: Senator Robert Kerr; Representatives Page Belcher, Ed Edmondson; *Planning and Resources Board:* Jeff Griffin; *Historical Society:* Muriel H. Wright

OREGON: Senator Richard L. Neuberger; *State Highway Department:* Eric Bergman

PENNSYLVANIA: Senator Edward Martin; Representatives Robert J. Corbett, Paul B. Dague, Herman P. Eberharter, Carroll D. Kearns, Augustine B. Kelley; *Historical and Museum Commission:* S. K. Stevens

RHODE ISLAND: *Historical Society:* Clifford P. Monahon; *Development Council:* Leonard J. Panaggio; *Department of Education:* Edward F. Wilcox

SOUTH CAROLINA: Senator Strom Thurmond; Representative William J. B. Dorn; *State Development Board:* George M. McNabb; *University of South Carolina Press:* Louise Jones DuBose

SOUTH DAKOTA: Representative Harold O. Lovre

TENNESSEE: Senator Albert Gore; Representatives Howard H. Baker, Ross Bass, Joe L. Evins, J. Percy Priest, Carroll Reece; *State Library and Archives:* Dan M. Robison

TEXAS: Senator Lyndon B. Johnson; Representatives W. R. Poage, J. T. Rutherford, Olin E. Teague; *Highway Department:* Jack Stearns; *Austin State Parks:* Marvin Steck; *Panhandle-Plains Historical Museum:* C. Boone McClure; *Dallas Historical Society:* Virginia L. Gambrell; *Historical Association:* H. Bailey Carroll

UTAH: Senator Arthur V. Watkins; *Historical Society:* A. R. Mortensen, John James, Jr.; *Pioneer Memorial Foundation:* Virgil V. Peterson

VERMONT: Senator George D. Aiken; *Historic Sites Commission:* Vrest Orton; *Vermont Life Magazine:* Walter Hard, Jr.; *Historical Society:* Richard G. Wood

VIRGINIA: Senator A. Willis Robertson; Representatives Edward J. Robeson, Jr., W. Pat Jennings; *Division of Public Relations:* J. Stuart White; *350th Anniversary Commission:* Parke Rouse, Jr.; *State Library:* W. Edwin Hemphill; *Historical Society:* John Melville Jennings; *Virginia Travel Council:* Robert F. Nelson; *Kenmore Association:* Robert P. L. Frick; *Colonial National Historical Park:* Charles E. Hatch

WASHINGTON: Representative Thor C. Tollefson; *Historical Society:* Chapin D. Foster; *State Advertising Commission:* C. E. Johns

WEST VIRGINIA: Representatives Cleveland M. Bailey, M. G. Burnside, Robert H. Mollohan, Harley O. Staggers; *Industrial and Publicity Commission:* Andrew V. Ruckman; *Wesleyan College:* James L. Hupp

WISCONSIN: *Historical Society:* Raymond S. Sivesind, Paul Vanderbilt; *Conservation Department:* J. H. H. Alexander

WYOMING: Senator Frank A. Barrett; *Archives and Historical Department:* Reta Ridings

For co-operation and assistance in locating and obtaining many photographs used in this book, the editors are indebted to *Holiday* (Louis F. V. Mercier); *The Ladies' Home Journal* (Richard Pratt); *Life* (Dorothy L. Smith); and *Time* (Michael J. Phillips)

Index